The Parenting Bible

Best Wishes,

Robin Goldstein

The Parenting Bible

Robin Goldstein, Ph.D., with Janet Gallant

SOURCEBOOKS, INC.
NAPERVILLE, ILLINOIS

Published by Sourcebooks, Inc.
P.O. Box 4410, Naperville, Illinois 60567-4410
(630) 961-3900
FAX: (630) 961-2168
www.sourcebooks.com

Library of Congress Cataloging-in-Publication Data
    Goldstein, Robin.
    The parenting bible: the answers to parents' most common questions / by Robin Goldstein.
            p. cm.
    Includes index.
    ISBN 1-57071-907-1 (alk. paper)
    1. Child rearing. 2. Parenting. I. Title.

HQ769.G6655 2002
649'.1—dc21

                                                                2001057582

                Printed and bound in the United States of America
                    VHG   10   9   8   7   6   5   4   3   2   1

With love to my husband Miles, my children Ari and Anna,
and my parents Cynthia and Rez.

TABLE OF CONTENTS

ACKNOWLEDGMENTS

This mission—helping parents gain a better understanding of their children—could not have been realized without the help and encouragement of family, friends, and colleagues. Thanks so much to Nina Graybill for her guidance in directing me to Sourcebooks; Deb Werksman, my editor, for all her assistance and for taking this project on; Andy Gallant for his support and technical know-how; Janet Gallant for her unfailing help, her incredible way with words, and our friendship which I so greatly value; my husband Miles for all his love and support, and for encouraging me to go ahead with this project; and my children, Ari and Anna, who continue to teach me the deepest meaning of love and the importance of trusting and respecting children.

INTRODUCTION

"Should I pick my baby up when he cries?"

"Do I always have to be consistent?"

"Why won't my child cooperate in the morning?"

"How can I teach my child to be more responsible?"

"Are all thirteen-year-olds so embarrassed by their parents?"

Raising children is a vitally important job that can be difficult, demanding, and exciting all at the same time. Inevitably, you'll have mixed emotions as your child grows. You'll feel joy as he becomes more independent, but you'll also feel some doubt. Often, your questions will range from the mundane (clean-up, time on the phone, arguments over hairstyles) to the complex (teaching right from wrong, sibling rivalry, dealing with divorce), to the truly frightening (gun violence, drugs, and alcohol).

The Parenting Bible answers the questions parents have asked me most frequently in my twenty years in practice advising parents and educators on childhood development. It fills the "support gap" created as traditional sources of advice and information—the nearby family, the at-home neighbors—have disappeared. Here, you'll find workable solutions to problems as well as insights into children's thinking, based on the work of renowned child development researcher Jean Piaget.

You'll also find a great deal of reassurance. As you learn about typical experiences and the predictable stages of development (as defined by psychosocial theorist Erik Erikson), you'll find that most of your child's behavior is perfectly normal. All toddlers are strong-willed, all seven-year-olds need frequent reminders, all early adolescents are moody. You'll be able to form realistic expectations. In turn, you'll eliminate many of the conflicts that come from anticipating, for example, that your three-year-old will act as a four- or five-year-old would, or that your twelve-year-old will show mature judgment with peers.

This book encourages you to spend time with your child, listening to him, setting limits, and taking an interest in him. He will benefit in every way and at every stage from your love and active involvement. Even if some or most of his care is provided by others, parenting, of course, is truly your responsibility. Therefore, the answers in *The Parenting Bible* are addressed to you, the parent, although the advice applies to all the caregivers, teachers, and other adults involved in your child's life.

The questions and answers are arranged first by kids' age groups: Part I—The First Five Years; Part II—The Six- to Nine-Year-Old; and Part III—The Ten- to Thirteen-Year-Old. Within age groups, questions are arranged by major issues. Each question and answer is self-contained, so you can begin reading anywhere. Since many of the topics complement each other, you'll gain a fuller understanding if you read everything in a particular section.

You also can follow a topic through the three age groups. For instance, sibling relationships appear in Part I as "How can I help my children get along with each other?"; in Part II as "What should I do about sibling rivalry?"; and in Part III as "Why is my daughter jealous of her siblings?" The answers are age-appropriate but will be helpful regardless of how old your child is. Likewise, some issues, such as adjusting to a blended family, appear only once but are clearly useful at any developmental stage.

The questions and answers alternate genders so that an article about "he" is usually followed by an article about "she." However, the answers for the most part apply to either gender. Similarly, the answers generally speak of parents dealing with one child, but the advice is applicable to families with any number of children.

Getting specific answers to your child-rearing questions is important because you want to do the best you can for your child. Your day-to-day actions and attitudes can guide his character and behavior in positive ways. The challenging job of parenting requires love, sacrifice, time, and attention, and you deserve all the help and encouragement you can get. *The Parenting Bible* acknowledges your natural frustrations and uncertainty and gives you reassurance and answers to make parenting easier, more successful, and more enjoyable.

The
Parenting
Bible

Part One

The First Five Years

"Is my child too dependent on me?"

"Why is my baby so fussy?"

"What can I do if my child has a temper tantrum in the grocery store?"

"Why do I have to repeat the rules over and over again?"

"Is my child ready for kindergarten?"

Parenting during the first five years is certainly rewarding and enjoyable, but also physically and emotionally demanding. It requires a great deal of effort to consistently meet your infant's needs so she learns to trust. Later your two-year-old will assert her independence and growing autonomy by trying things for herself. Your three-, four-, and five-year-old will strive to be creatively and actively involved in her environment. The sense of accomplishment and confidence you encourage at these ages will help determine your child's success during the elementary years and beyond.

Children under the age of five or six view the world differently than older children and adults do. They are by nature egocentric and aren't thinking yet about other people's needs or points of view. That's normal development. Because of this, they benefit from constant supervision and clear limits that are repeated often.

Raising your young child takes patience and understanding. At times you may wonder, "Is she the only eighteen-month-old not sleeping through the night?" "Do other parents struggle so much over sharing?" "Are other children such picky eaters?" Take comfort knowing you're not alone. Most families with young children go through similar conflicts and experiences. The more you understand about your child's developmental patterns, the easier it will be for you to be patient and understanding with her.

DEPENDENCY

Is my child too dependent on me?

Many new parents are surprised at how much time, attention, and effort childcare involves. When they discover that their baby is naturally demanding and dependent, they sometimes worry about "giving in" to all his needs. If they pick him up when he cries, offer a bottle or breast on demand, or keep him near through the day, will he soon become too dependent? In our society, independence is viewed as a positive trait, and many parents are concerned if their babies seem too attached to people or objects. Yet, when parents fully understand their child's dependency needs, they can see there's no need to worry about their baby's lack of self-sufficiency.

Infants and young children are almost totally dependent on adults; this is a natural and necessary condition of early childhood. It's normal for babies to want the constant comfort of being cared for, held, fed, changed, loved, and played with, and there's nothing harmful about giving to a young child. A child whose needs are met and who has a strong attachment to his parents develops a foundation of trust that will allow him to gradually become independent.

Some adults feel that it's never too soon to start teaching a child to become independent: "He's going to have to learn sometime that he can't always have his way." "He has to find out what life is really like." And some people also believe that giving in to a child's needs in infancy will make it that much harder to get him to give up his dependencies later on.

Parents who are uneasy about how dependent their young child is may, in an attempt to foster independence, make conscious decisions not to meet all of his needs. They may hesitate to pick him up when he cries, or hold back on cuddling or frequent nursing. They may feel guilty and full of self-doubt whenever they do give more than they think they should.

However, if your baby learns to trust your care and support, he'll turn into a toddler who explores his surroundings with confidence. And as he grows, his natural drive for independence will begin to show. The ten-month-old will want to feed himself, the two-year-old will cry out, "I'll do it myself," the three-year-old will feel good going off on his tricycle, and the five-year-old will happily spend time with his friends.

Your young child will always have a strong need to be cared for, of course, but as he gets older, he'll become more and more independent, and you'll spend less time giving. Although there will be times when he temporarily becomes more dependent—when he enters preschool, when the family moves, when a sibling is born—if his early dependency needs have been met, he'll move into the world with a greater sense of trust and confidence.

Should I pick my baby up when she cries?

Crying is a baby's way of communicating. Particularly in the early months, a child cries when she's hungry, cold, wet, tired, or wants to be held and played with. Between six and nine months, she may cry—particularly at night—because she doesn't understand that her parents exist unless she sees them. She knows the world as either pleasurable or uncomfortable; when her needs are met she feels good, and when they aren't she feels bad and cries.

Many parents wonder how they should respond when their child cries. If they pick her up each time, will her demands increase? Is there a chance she'll become spoiled? Parents who wish to follow their instincts and respond to their child's tears often are confused by people who say, "Don't pick her up, you'll spoil her," "Let her cry, it's good for her lungs," or, "You can't always be there for her."

The truth is that picking up a crying baby won't spoil her. Rather, it will help her develop a sense of security that will actually make her less likely to cry in the long run. Babies whose cries bring a helpful response begin to anticipate that whenever they cry, someone will respond. This cause-and-effect connection gives a child a secure and comfortable feeling and also teaches her to trust her parents. Learning to trust is a critical part of early development. If her parents don't respond to her cries, or respond erratically and unpredictably, she'll quickly sense that there's little she can do to affect her environment. In such a situation, she'll learn to mistrust those around her.

Of course, there's a wide range of parental behavior between the extremes of total responsiveness and unresponsiveness. No matter how hard parents try to calm and comfort their child, there'll be times when she remains frustrated. But if they're consistently caring during the early months, she'll start life with a sense of trust.

Comforting a crying child is very important, but it also can be difficult, especially if she cries often or during a busy moment. If you find that your baby needs a lot of comforting during the day, you may want to try a cloth infant carrier that will let you hold her close while leaving your hands free. The contact and constant movement can be very soothing to a child.

If your baby does a lot of crying at night, you may feel frustrated and unsure about how to respond. Your natural instinct may be to pick her up, but you also may be tired and you may be getting negative advice. Your pediatrician might advise you to let your child "cry it out at night," particularly once she turns three months old. Many people advocate ignoring a child's cries in the hope that she'll learn to sleep through the night. One theory says that if parents refuse to comfort or feed their child during the night, she'll stop crying after twenty minutes to an hour and go back to sleep. After many days or weeks of this routine, she'll no longer wake up at night.

Although the prospect of an evening of uninterrupted sleep may certainly be attractive to you, when you comfort your baby, you let her know that she can depend on you, that she's worthwhile, and that you care about meeting her needs. Holding and soothing her, you give her a sense of security and a basis for developing trust in her world.

Is my baby "good"?

Is a "good" baby one who sleeps a lot and doesn't cry much? Most people say "yes," and their answer is understandable. "Good" and "bad" are judgmental terms people often use to describe the behavior and temperament of a baby. A "good" baby is a quiet one, and a "bad" baby is fussy.

Parents often believe that their child is a reflection on them. They want a contented baby who's easy to care for and who gives them a feeling of success. And many parents feel bad if their baby cries or has colic. Yet, the fussing baby is not "bad" and the quiet one is not "good." All babies are different. Labeling and judging them for their behavior is inappropriate because they're only expressing their needs in the best way they can. When they cry and fuss, they're telling their parents that something's wrong. They're tired, hurt, uncomfortable, hungry, wet, scared, or needing to be held.

Labeling babies begins very early. One new mother was told by a maternity nurse that her hungry infant had been crying in the nursery. "What a bad baby you have!" Out in public, a well-meaning person will approach a mother and infant and say, "What a good baby. Is he always like this?" Such a question can put the mother in a bind. Although she may answer "yes," she may also remember that the previous week he cried all during a shopping trip.

One of the hardest times to deal with a crying infant is at night, when a wakeful baby may truly seem "bad." If you've been giving to your child all day, you may feel drained and resentful when you have to give again at night. You may grit your teeth when awakened at 3 A.M. and feel overwhelmed. But if you can think of your baby as expressing needs rather than being "bad," you may feel more accepting.

Once you understand that his crying is a kind of communication, you may find yourself responding differently, trying to understand why he cries or why he doesn't sleep as much as you think he should, or as you would like. And you may also feel less harassed when he fusses in public. It's easier to be comfortable with him when you no longer feel pressured to have a "good" baby.

How long will my baby be anxious around strangers?

A baby, until the age of six months or so, usually is content to be held by relatives and family friends. She may even smile and play when her parents place her in someone else's arms. But between seven and nine months, she'll begin to resist people other than her parents, and may cry and reach for her parents when someone else tries to hold her. During this stage, she may even feel anxious about her grandparents and familiar baby-sitters.

Such reactions, which are a normal part of a baby's development, result from her growing awareness of the world. She recognizes her parents as special and different and views them with pleasure. Because she has good feelings about them, she wants to be with them and isn't as comfortable or trusting with other people.

Also, at this age she believes that something exists only as long as she can see it. When her parents walk out of sight, she feels anxious and cries. When she's back in their arms, she feels pleasure.

This developmental stage can be difficult for parents because it sometimes causes embarrassment and makes it hard to accept help with childcare. A relative or friend, offering to care for the baby, may feel rejected by the child's anxious cries. Some adults blame the parents, saying, "You've spoiled her by holding her so much!" Or they may try to persuade the baby to come, saying, "I won't hurt you. You have to get used to other people."

When your baby enters this developmental stage, remember that anxiety about strangers and separation is normal. It isn't necessary to force her to go to other people—she'll soon do that willingly. Just try to meet her needs and have others talk to her and play with her while you hold her. You can explain to people that, while you understand their feelings of frustration and rejection, you know that your child is acting as most children her age do.

During this stage, many babies have trouble separating from their parents at day care or when a baby-sitter comes. Explain the situation to your caregiver and let her know that your baby may need extra holding and comforting. If your child cries as you go, you also may find it hard to separate. Have your caregiver try to distract her. Call shortly after leaving if you'd like to reassure yourself that all is going well.

At times you might be tempted to leave while your baby is distracted and unaware that you're going. While this eliminates the initial rush of tears, she may react with surprise and fear when she discovers you've left. It's always better to say a quick good-bye.

You'll know that your child's fear of strangers and separation is lessening when you see her reach for someone other than you, and when you see her go happily to someone who's reaching for her. As this stage passes, she'll once again feel more comfortable and content with others.

Is it OK if my child is attached to a blanket or other objects?

A child clutching a blanket is a familiar sight. Between the ages of six and nine months, many young children become attached to a security object such as a blanket or stuffed animal. The attachment may last until the child is five or older. This is a natural part of development, although not all children pick out a special object, and some choose several soft items to hold on to. A child with a strong attachment may wake up clutching his blanket and hold it as his parents pick him up. He may put the blanket against his face and carry it around with him as he gets older.

To a young child, a blanket or other soft object is a source of comfort. As he moves away from infancy and his close union with his mother, he nurtures and cares for his special object, receiving warmth and comfort in return. He may use his blanket most often during times of transition throughout the day—when he goes to sleep, wakes up, feels tired or hurt, goes for a car trip, visits the doctor, or goes to day care—and during major changes in his life or routine. Such changes can include the birth of a sibling, the beginning of day care or nursery school, or a parent's absence. Children who are left to cry themselves to sleep or whose dependency needs are not consistently met may become particularly dependent on an object for comfort.

The child's attachment to his special object may go through different stages. At times he'll have an intense need for his blanket and will let his parents know that he wants it, even if he can't yet tell them in words. At other times, during calm periods and as he gets older, he may have less need for the special object.

One child had a strong attachment to a stuffed animal she'd been given when she was a few months old and took the toy everywhere. When she turned four, her attachment began to lessen. First she threw the animal out of her bed, although she quickly retrieved it. Then she began moving it, night by night, into less favorable positions on the bed. Eventually she simply put it away on a shelf.

If your child is attached to a special object, you may find it hard to trust that he'll ever give it up. You may wonder if you should remove it or wean him away from it, but such actions are unnecessary. As time goes on, his desire for the object will diminish and he'll give it up on his own. However, you may not see this happen until he's five, since many four- and five-year-olds keep their objects with them at night as a source of comfort. Interestingly, when parents recognize how strong and long-lasting their child's attachment is, they sometimes begin to feel protective of the object themselves.

Should I give my child a pacifier?

A baby feels calm when her natural sucking instinct is satisfied. Some babies suck their thumbs, some nurse frequently, some suck on fingers or a blanket, and many use pacifiers. When parents first offer a pacifier to their child, they see how tranquil she becomes and how convenient the pacifier is to use. It's an easy, concrete, accessible way to soothe a crying baby. Parents can offer it in the car, leave it in the crib so their child can suck as she falls asleep, or, as she gets older, leave it near her toys so she can use it whenever she wants.

There's nothing wrong with a pacifier, and a child who uses one is not harmed. Yet, despite growing acceptance, some people believe pacifiers symbolize dependency and immaturity, especially when used by a child past infancy. A parent can easily feel under attack when told, "That thing looks awful hanging out of her mouth," or, "She's much too old to use a pacifier."

Parents look to their pediatricians for advice and support on all aspects of child rearing, including pacifier use, but there are pediatricians who oppose pacifiers. One mother never let her child take her pacifier along on doctor visits because the pediatrician disapproved. It was easier for this mother to hide what she did rather than face ridicule or a challenge to her parenting beliefs.

Aside from dealing with outside criticism, many parents have their own doubts. When and how will the child ever give up such a comforting and satisfying object?

Children do give it up. Gradually, and in spite of the strong attachment you may now observe, your child will limit her use of the pacifier to times when she's tired or feeling stress. By age two, she may wean herself completely from it, or at least let you know, by rejecting it at times or accepting it less often, that she's ready to stop using it.

However, if you decide to take your child's pacifier away before she shows a willingness to give it up on her own, do so gradually over several weeks. Be prepared for the possibility that she'll begin sucking her thumb, blanket, or other object. Offer substitutes such as a glass of juice, extra holding and cuddling, gentle patting on the back, or a new source of comfort such as a stuffed animal or pillow.

My child sucks his thumb. Should I stop him?

People's reactions vary when they see a child sucking his thumb. Some feel strongly that it's good for him to fulfill his own needs this way, while others feel just as strongly that it's not. Because of the differing opinions offered on the subject, parents are sometimes unsure about what to do.

Babies begin sucking their thumbs for the same reasons they use pacifiers and frequent nursing or bottle drinking—to satisfy their sucking needs. The thumb is always there and so the child is always in control, which is not the case with the pacifier, breast, or bottle. And a baby who sucks his thumb may be less dependent on his parents to calm and soothe him since, with his thumb, he's able at times to comfort himself.

It's not unusual for a child to suck his thumb for years—sometimes until he is five, six, or even older. During the preschool years, sucking gradually decreases, and by the time he's of school age, he's usually sucking his thumb only at night before bed or during an anxious time, such as the birth of a sibling or a move to a new house. Some children, however, may occasionally suck their thumbs during the day when they first enter elementary school.

There are pediatricians who advocate thumb-sucking and even encourage new parents to help their baby get started on the habit. These doctors reason that thumb-sucking is a natural and easy way for a child to satisfy himself. Other doctors say that a child who's given the breast or bottle on demand will already have his sucking needs met and will not need or desire a thumb. Finally, there are pediatricians who are against thumb-sucking, believing it's an unnecessary habit that may harm the child's teeth.

Just as pediatricians offer various opinions, parents, too, have different feelings about thumb-sucking. Many are unconcerned but do feel bothered by negative comments they hear from others. Friends, relatives, and even strangers will criticize a child for thumb-sucking and try to pressure his parents to stop him. For many families, this is the only problem connected with the habit.

In other families, thumb-sucking is looked on with ambivalence. Parents worry about their child's teeth, about how long he'll continue, about how he'll finally give it up, and about whether they should try to make him stop. And there are parents who don't want their child to suck his thumb at all, and worry about how to stop him right away.

What are parents' choices? If they notice this habit during their child's early months, they can try to feed more frequently, which may satisfy sucking needs. Otherwise, they can accept thumb-sucking as a natural habit and try to make the best of it even if they don't like it, or they can try to force the child to stop. This latter course can have negative consequences for the child, and it is usually unsuccessful because a thumb, unlike a pacifier, can't be taken away. If the parents pull a child's thumb out of his mouth, he'll cry and then most likely will suck his thumb again as soon as he can. As he gets older, if they paint his thumb with one of the foul-tasting commercial products sold to discourage thumb-sucking, he'll feel helpless and may whine, show increased aggression, or become obstinate.

Since sucking provides comfort, the more pressure parents put on their child to stop, the more attached and dependent on his thumb he may become. Fearing ridicule and feeling vulnerable, he may depend more and more on himself and his thumb for comfort. This is not an attempt to rebel or get back at his parents, although they may see increased thumb-sucking as a sign of stubbornness or "badness." He has a strong desire to please his parents, but he also has a strong desire to suck his thumb in order to make himself feel better. One four-year-old who knew her parents disapproved of her thumb-sucking hid under a table to suck her thumb. Parents who want their child to stop this habit should try decreasing the pressure they put on him. This, in turn, may eliminate some of his need to soothe himself.

Another drawback to struggling over thumb-sucking is the bad self-image a child can eventually develop when he senses that his parents don't like what he's doing. Parents who try to make their child feel bad about his habit ("I don't like that!") may end up having him feel bad about himself. Some parents can remember back to their own child-hood embarrassment and pain over the issue.

The best thing you can do if your child sucks his thumb is accept the situation and be patient. Try not to discourage him from thumb-sucking, at least through his preschool years when his need may be strongest. Usually by age five or six he'll stop because his friends have stopped, he no longer has the need, or he's self-conscious about doing it in public. Certainly, by these ages you and he can come up with a plan and perhaps incentives for stopping, and you can firmly let him know you want him to give up the habit.

Now she needs me, now she doesn't. What's going on?

Parents are puzzled when their toddler shifts from being dependent to being independent and back again. Why, for example, would she suddenly dart away from her mother and then just as suddenly come running back to check that she's still there?

Such on and off behavior comes from the child's mixed feelings about her place in the world. When she first learns to walk, she develops a sense of independence and joy. She's delighted with her new-found skill and control, feeling that the world is at her command. Soon after exercising her new independence, however (sometime between seventeen months and two years), her perceptions of her place in the world change and she feels quite small and vulnerable. It's her joy in exploration combined with her feelings of inadequacy that lead her to run off and run back.

Typical of a child at this stage is an eighteen-month-old girl waiting in line with her mother at the post office. She wiggles away and goes to look at a chain hanging across a doorway. As soon as she reaches the chain she says, "Mommy, Mommy," and runs to get picked up. After a few seconds, she gets back down, runs and touches the chain, and then runs back to her mother. She repeats this cycle as long as she and her mother wait in line.

This developmental phase of emotional dependence-independence, which is a normal part of growth, can last until the child is two and one-half to three years old. Different children show different degrees of dependence. Some aren't comfortable exploring their surroundings on their own and may cling to their parents. Most children need more reassurance when they're out of their secure and comfortable homes.

During this stage, your child may be especially sensitive to your responses and easily upset when you disapprove of her behavior, just as she's pleased when you approve. Over time, as she gains more experience, a change will occur and she'll be able to play, explore, and move about without coming to you for repeated reassurance. Until then, try to accept her behavior, smile and wave when she goes off a bit on her own, and give her the emotional support she needs to feel secure about her world.

Why does my child like to be where I am?

When they're at home, young children want to be near their parents. While the intensity of need varies with age and personality, children, especially between the ages of fifteen months and three years, are usually most content playing and exploring when their parents are close by.

Young children like to be with their parents much of the time, day and night. Often, parents find that their child has an easier time falling asleep if they stay with him, patting his back or keeping him company. In the uneasy moments before sleep, he gains comfort when they are near.

His desire to be with his parents is normal, and the attention he receives from them is essential for his development. As he comes to understand that they are there even when he can't see them, and that every time they go away they come back, he begins to feel secure and trusting. Gradually, based on these feelings of trust, he'll develop the ability and desire to separate from his parents.

Waiting for that separation to occur, however, can be frustrating for parents who would like more time to themselves. They don't often have a chance to be alone at home, especially when they're followed by a young child who won't let them out of his sight. And at times, a child who stays close by his parents can be an embarrassment in public or when other adults are visiting.

A baby will indicate his need for closeness by reaching out to be picked up. When he can crawl, he'll follow his parents' voices and crawl to be near them. Later as a toddler, he'll often carry his toys from room to room to be with his parents. And although at three or four years old he may spend time at school, day care, or a neighbor's house, he'll still prefer to be near his parents when he's home. Children, like adults, want company—especially the company of their own families.

When your child wants to be with you, try to be understanding and accommodate him when possible, knowing that this stage of development is normal. When you need time for yourself at home, try distracting him with an interesting puzzle, book, or box of toys that he hasn't seen for a while. You also can invite one of his playmates for a visit. When your preschooler has friends over, he may play happily without having you nearby; if the children are old enough to play safely without close supervision, you can have some time to yourself.

If you're having adult guests over, try to anticipate your child's need for attention. Suggest he draw pictures for the visitors to take home. Place some interesting toys next to your seat so he can play nearby without having to involve you. Such diversions work, but it's unrealistic to expect him to leave you entirely alone. If you exclude him, he may become demanding, silly, or whiney. But if you partially include him, focusing attention on him at least some of the time, you should be able to talk to your guests without too much interruption.

As he reaches the early elementary years, he'll spend more and more time playing with friends or occupying himself in his room, and less time with you. One mother, whose seven-year-old always stayed close to her when he was a preschooler, was surprised to find herself greatly wishing he'd spend more time with her now.

Do all children say, "Only Mommy do it"?

Between the ages of twenty months and three years, some children won't let their fathers help them. When a father tries to comfort his child during the night, get her dressed, get her some juice, or even fasten her seat belt, she resists: "No! Only Mommy do it." Young children are often strongly attached to their mothers, and during this brief developmental phase they seem to reject their fathers.

This stage can be very frustrating. A father who wants to take an active role in caring for his child may find it hard to understand her resistance and rejection. At times he may feel like giving up and telling his wife, "You take care of her. Why should I even try?" His feelings may be hurt and he may show signs of resentment towards his child.

The mother's role, too, is difficult during this stage. It's hard for her to see her husband rejected and hard to try and persuade her child to allow him to help. There's also more pressure on the mother to take over the work of childcare. This means she's always the one to get up at night, give comfort, and get the child ready in the morning.

One mother no sooner got into bed after feeding her two-month-old baby, when her three-year-old daughter called out for water. The tired mother asked her husband to respond, but their daughter refused his help: "Not you. I want water from Mommy." To avoid a middle-of-the-night struggle, the mother got up, but the encounter was unpleasant for both parents.

Some parents try reasoning with their child ("Mommy's tired") or forcing her to accept the father's help. They say firmly, "If you want a drink, you'll have to let Daddy get it." Sometimes such statements work, but sometimes tears and tantrums follow. It may be easier to give in, at least during the night, and have the mother get the drink so the family can go quickly back to sleep rather than deal with a struggle.

If the father's unable to help his child because she rejects him, he can still help his wife by taking over additional household responsibilities or caring for the couple's other children. And both parents should try not to let the father's feelings of rejection interfere with their basic relationship with their child. In the course of development, the stage of "only Mommy do it" is rather short.

Why does my child want me with him at birthday parties?

When a birthday invitation arrives in the mail, children are excited. They ask, "Can I go? When is it?" and talk eagerly about presents, cake, and goodie bags. But when the first excitement is over, a child may ask his parents another question: "Will you stay with me at the party?"

For some children, attending a party is difficult. Between the ages of two and three and one-half, a child may only want to go to a birthday party if his parents come along, and he may cling and ask them not to leave once he's arrived. This can happen even when the birthday child is a close friend and the birthday home is familiar.

Children who are shy are likely to have a harder time separating than children who are outgoing and self confident. A child who's quiet in groups may prefer to observe at parties rather than to participate and may only feel comfortable doing this when his parents are with him. He also may want them around because he feels temporarily overwhelmed by the excitement, the number of people at the party, the sight of strange children, or the unusual appearance of a friend's house decorated for a birthday. If the party is in a restaurant or other unfamiliar place, he may feel even more unsure.

Some children feel insecure at parties because their friends' fathers are there. Many two- and three-year-olds aren't comfortable with other children's fathers. In some cases, children have not been around men as much as around women, and they may find fathers a bit scary because of their deep voices, big size, or beards. Occasionally, a child becomes afraid of a father because of the man's profession. "He's a policeman and can put you in jail," one four-year-old told his three-year-old brother.

Whatever the reason for a child's reluctance to attend a party alone, his parents may experience frustration because of the situation. They may wonder why he needs to be with them when other children the same age seem willing to stay at parties by themselves. And parents may worry about his ability to interact with other children, or his lack of independence.

In addition, parents can become angry, especially if they have other plans for the hours of the party, or if they don't generally like to stay and participate at birthday parties. A parent may tell a child, "If you don't stay at the party by yourself you'll have to come home right now!" Such a message can leave the child feeling unaccepted, angry, and "bad" over something that he's already having difficulty working through. And an angry parental outburst can make the parent feel bad later.

If parents can recall their own childhood experiences at parties, they may feel more tolerant and accepting about their child's anxieties. Most of us have mixed memories. We may have been happy about the cake and ice cream and games, but we also remember some disappointments and feelings of shyness and embarrassment.

If your child is anxious about attending a party, you can look for ways to make him feel more comfortable. For example, see if a close friend or neighbor is invited to the same party so the two children can go together. Being with a friend may ease the pressure your child feels and make separating from you easier.

If you take him to the party and he wants you to remain, try staying for a few minutes to see if he begins to feel at ease. The parent giving the party can help by getting your child involved with another guest or with a toy or game. And sometimes just showing your child the cake and goodie bags will be enough to make him feel comfortable. If he decides he can stay alone, let him know that you're leaving and tell him you'll be back when the party's over.

If, however, he wants to have you stay with him for the entire party, you may need to make spontaneous plans to do so. Tell the host that your child will feel more comfortable with you there. Most parents will be understanding, especially if you offer to help out. And keep in mind that although this situation may seem difficult, your child will become more independent with time. By the age of four or five, he'll probably go more confidently to parties without you and enjoy participating and playing on his own.

Why does my child act differently when she's away from me?

When parents hear how well-behaved their child is with a relative, teacher, friend, or caretaker, their response is often, "That's not how she acts when she's with me." And conversely, when parents hear that their usually energetic child seemed withdrawn while spending time away from home, they wonder, "Why does she act differently when she's away?"

A child's behavior does change, depending on whom she's with and where she is. Parents see this when they pick her up from school, day care, or a friend's house. As soon as they arrive, she may start acting negatively—whining, making demands, and clinging. When a parent asks if she's acted this way all along, the usual answer is, "No, she was fine until you arrived." Parents may be partly relieved to hear their child enjoyed herself, but also partly upset by her actions.

Most often, a child's behavior changes when her parents arrive because she's more comfortable when they're around. Once she sees them, she can express the feelings she may have been keeping to herself. Perhaps the day was frustrating because she couldn't play with a favorite toy or because a teacher put pressure on her. Or perhaps she was angry at her parents for leaving her with a caregiver. The day's frustrations all come out when her parents come to pick her up.

It's natural for a child to feel less comfortable expressing her needs and feelings when she's away from home. Adults, too, are more reserved when at work or in the company of others. Therefore, it's not surprising that a child who seems content all day will let off steam when she's with her parents.

Sometimes parents experience the opposite situation with their child. She seems happy and playful when they arrive and is reluctant to go home. The parents assume that she's had a wonderful time, but often she has actually spent the day acting withdrawn and uninvolved. Such behavior, typical of two-year-olds, occurs because she's more comfortable playing and exploring when her parents are around. Therefore, she doesn't really begin to enjoy herself until it's time to leave.

If your child seems fussy after a day away from you, or starts complaining when it's time to go home, be sure to question the teacher, friend, or caregiver. Ask about your child's interest and activity level, and try to get a true picture of her day. When communication is good between you and your child's caregivers, you'll be better able to anticipate and understand her behavior.

If you know that her mood will change when she sees you, you can plan ahead. If she's whining, try to distract her. "When we get home, I'm going to get the play dough out." And if you know she'll want to start playing when you're ready to pick her up from school or day care, plan to arrive a little early or stay a little longer. That way, she'll have time to explore comfortably and then leave in a pleasant way.

SLEEPING

When will my baby sleep through the night?

"Does your baby sleep through the night yet?" That's a familiar question for new parents and one they dread answering if their child is still waking up. Many people believe that a baby should be sleeping through the night by the time he's three months old, and if he isn't, his parents may naturally feel frustrated and worried. Losing sleep is one of the hardest adjustments new parents have to make.

Actually, it's rare for an infant consistently to sleep through the night. Some babies do sleep through when they're three weeks old, but many are still waking up at ten months and others are two or three years old before they sleep all night. The frequency of waking varies from child to child and depends on many circumstances.

An infant may wake up at night to be fed, changed, or held. A slightly older child may turn himself over during the night, waking up in the process. If a baby has new teeth coming in, he may be uncomfortable and wake up to be comforted. And if he is developmentally at the stage when he believes people exist only if he can see them, he may wake up to see his parents and be reassured. Parents often consider this last type of wakefulness to be manipulative because the child stops crying as soon as they come in his room. But he does not intend to manipulate—he just wants to see his parents and be close to them.

Basically, a baby wakes up because he needs to be loved, comforted, fed, or helped. He doesn't understand that his parents prefer to meet his needs during the day and sleep during the night. He wants them whenever he needs them—day or night.

A wakeful baby can be difficult and frustrating for parents. If they get up at night to respond to their child, they lose sleep and suffer all the physical and emotional consequences of being tired. They also face the criticism of others who say, "The only way your baby is going to learn to sleep is if you let him cry it out." Such comments are unfortunate because parents who do get up at night with their children need support and encouragement. Many parents eventually become secretive about getting up because they don't want to be ridiculed by friends and relatives.

Sometimes parents of a wakeful child become resentful, envying other parents whose children sleep all night, and wondering what's wrong with their own child. "Does everyone else have an easier baby?" Parents may blame themselves for their situation, believing that they caused their child's wakefulness by being too attentive to his cries: "If only we had let him cry it out earlier, maybe we'd all be sleeping now."

There's really no need for doubt and self-blame. Parents who go to their child at night give him a sense of security and show that they care about his needs. When a child is left to cry it out at night (which is what many childcare advisors advocate), he learns only that he has no options, that his needs will not be consistently met, and that his only choice is to give up. It's important to go to a baby who wakes up crying.

Parents of a wakeful child need to know that they are not alone. Many babies wake up during the night. One mother who was frequently up with her child in the middle of the night took comfort looking out at the house next door. There she saw a brightly lit window indicating that her neighbors were awake with their own infant. This mother felt relieved knowing that other people were going through the same thing she was. Once parents understand this—that they are not alone—they can alter their expectations about normal sleeping patterns and begin to feel better about their child's behavior.

If you are the parent of a wakeful child, you will want to help him get back to sleep as quickly as possible. First, try to meet his needs by changing him, feeding him, or making him more comfortable. If he's still wakeful, try soothing him with rocking or singing. Sometimes mechanical, repetitive sounds are calming. On a "loop" tape you can record the hum of a hair dryer, humidifier, air conditioner, fan, even a vacuum cleaner, and play it when your baby needs to be comforted. There are special tapes, CDs, and toys that play the sounds of heartbeats; you might try one of these. You can try staying with your child in his room, rubbing his back until he falls asleep. Or you might want to bring him back to bed with you so he can nurse or just calm down while you rest. Having him sleep with you may be less exhausting and frustrating than getting up several times to comfort and feed him.

If you're not getting enough sleep, try napping during the day or early evening, or going to bed early at night. And recognize that, exhausting as this part of childcare can be, wakefulness will decrease as your child gets older. Eventually, you will get a full night's sleep again.

What should I do if my child won't fall asleep alone?

Many parents have problems getting their child to sleep at night. When it's time for bed, she may want to be fed, held, walked, sung to, talked to, read to, or comforted. She would like her parents to spend time with her as she falls asleep, but they would rather put her quickly and peacefully to bed and then get on with their own activities.

Parents wonder why their child won't fall asleep alone when they hear, or imagine, that other people's children go to sleep easily. It's true that some quickly fall asleep and that others are content to lie down with a bottle, pacifier, blanket, or stuffed animal. But most young children have a genuine need for their parents to be with them at night.

Bedtime can be a lonely, frightening time for young children, who naturally feel safer and more comfortable if their parents stay with them. Even three-, four-, and five-year-olds prefer not to be alone at night. One child said, "I can fall asleep better if you stay in my room," and another asked her parents, "Why do you want me to go to sleep? Don't you want to be with me?" A child finds it hard to understand her parents' need to be alone—she obviously has no such need herself.

The intensity of a child's bedtime need for her parents can be judged by the struggles that occur when they leave her in her room. A baby might spend a long time crying while an older child might get up or call out for water, another kiss, a trip to the bathroom, and anything else that would bring her parents close again. Elaborate bedtime rituals can take forty minutes or longer and often leave parents angry and frustrated. It's not unusual for a parent to sing "Rock-a-Bye Baby" through clenched teeth.

But what happens if, instead of spending forty minutes trying to get the child to fall asleep alone, parents spend ten to twenty minutes keeping her company—feeding her or rubbing her back or lying next to her? She will feel content and secure and fall asleep peacefully without a bedtime struggle.

Once parents see how strong their child's need and desire for closeness is, they may choose to stay with her at bedtime. In this situation, as in many others, parents will have to lower their expectations. They'll have less free time than they'd like. But they'll also eliminate many nighttime problems associated with a child's loneliness, fear, and insecurity, and they'll end their child's day in a calm and relaxed way.

If you decide to stay with your child until she falls asleep, you may find that few people you discuss the situation with will give you support and encouragement. Many parents do stay with their children, but few talk about it because they fear criticism. In a parent discussion group, one mother blurted out that her child would not fall asleep unless she was nursed. She expected to hear criticism, but instead saw other mothers at the meeting nod their heads. Their children behaved the same way.

The time you spend helping your child fall asleep should be restful for both of you. You can use the time to relax, think, enjoy your child's closeness, or read. At times you will probably nap or even fall asleep for the night. You may want to adjust your schedule to accommodate this by getting up earlier in the morning.

You may be afraid that if you stay with your child at bedtime, she'll become manipulative or unwilling ever to fall asleep alone. It's true that she will get used to having you with her, but as she gets older, her need for your company will lessen. And when you think she's ready, you can let her know that you expect her to fall asleep alone most of the time, perhaps with the help of soothing music, a night light, or another comforting device. At that point, she'll know that she can count on you, and that when she really needs you, you will come.

My child wants to sleep in our bed. Is this all right?

A young child often needs his parents during the night. As an infant, he may wake up crying for them, and as a toddler he may call out for them or get out of bed to find them. Some parents meet their child's nighttime needs by going to his room and comforting him there. But other parents find it easier at times to let their child sleep in bed with them. These parents believe that they and their child sleep better when they're all together.

The thought of a child sleeping with his parents shocks some people who've been conditioned by "experts" to believe the experience is harmful. Many parents who let their child sleep with them at night are reluctant to discuss the issue because they think their situation is unique. Actually, many parents have their children sleep in bed with them at some point, and they find the experience easy, enjoyable, and beneficial.

Children end up in their parents' beds for a variety of reasons. Parents might bring a wakeful infant to bed so they can tend to him without having to get up during the night. Or they might want him near so they can be sure he's safe, and so he can feel emotionally secure. Parents of a toddler may find their child climbing into bed with them on his own during the night. While some toddlers sleep easily in their rooms, others are too frightened or lonely to stay by themselves and try desperately to sleep with their parents. A child who's determined to be with them will climb out of his crib or bed and go to their room. One child told his parents, "I think of scary things in my bed, but when I get into your bed they go away." If they won't let him into their bed, he might try to sleep on the floor next to their bed or in the hallway outside their door.

Parents who do choose to let their child sleep with them still may express concerns. They wonder if they're being too responsive to their infant or toddler, or if he will become too dependent on them. It's true that he may develop a habit of sleeping in his parents' bed, but he won't be harmed by this. Rather, he'll benefit from the reassurance and sense of security he receives from such closeness.

When parents start letting their child sleep with them, they may wonder if they will ever again have a bed to themselves. Parents of a nine-month-old can feel overwhelmed by the thought that their child may be in bed with them for a few years, although actually, children's sleeping patterns and needs are hard to predict and parents' expectations change as children develop. The amount of time a child will spend in his parents' bed varies between families and within families over time. Some parents have their infant with them for the first six months to a year. Others let their child fall asleep in their bed and then move him to his own room each night; he may spend the whole night there or wake up and come back to his parents' room. Some children spend part of every night with their parents, while others come to their parents' bed only occasionally.

Ultimately, the parents' goal is to have their child sleep on his own, and as he becomes less dependent on their reassurance, he'll be ready to spend nights in his own bed. At that point, his parents can help him get used to sleeping in his room by offering a night light, music, or back rub.

Parents wonder how their sexual relations will be affected by the presence of a child in bed. Since sexual relations should always be private from children, parents should not become intimate when their child is in bed with them. They can either be together in another room in the house or carry their sleeping child back to his own room. To assure privacy, they should close and lock the bedroom door when they're having sexual relations. And if the child does surprise them during an intimate moment, they should try not to overreact to the intrusion. The chances are good that the sleepy child has not observed his parents very closely. Although they might feel that the child who sleeps with them interferes with sexual spontaneity, they should remember that a child who wakes up crying in his own room also interrupts his parents' intimacy.

Aside from effects on sexual relations, there's another aspect to having a child in bed that parents are sometimes concerned about—the quality of sleep. While many parents are happy to avoid getting up with their children at night, others find that having a child in bed is not very restful. An infant makes many sounds as he sleeps, and a toddler may toss and turn, waking his parents. Some pediatricians recommend that parents buy themselves a queen or king size bed so they can accommodate their child. Another possibility is for parents to place a mattress or crib in their room so the child can sleep nearby.

Most parents who let their child sleep in bed with them are pleased with the result. Parents who are away from their child all day enjoy the chance to be close to him at night, to give a middle-of-the-night hug and say, "I love you," and to wake up next to him in the morning. They often report that he doesn't have nightmares and has fewer problems falling asleep when he's in bed with them. And families tend to get more sleep when parents don't have to wake up and go to a child in another room.

If you're concerned about having your child in your bed, remember that there are different ways to meet his needs. If you're comfortable going to your child's room, that's a good choice for you. And if you prefer bringing your child back to your own room, that also is fine. Whichever way you choose to respond, the important thing is to give him the security that comes with attention and care.

Isn't it reasonable to want my child to play in her crib when she wakes up?

Parents always value the times when their child wakes up and plays contentedly in her crib. An infant may be entertained by looking at or randomly batting a mobile, and a baby who can sit up may be happy with toys left for her. The cheerful sounds of a child playing in her crib are delightful to parents—and so are the extra bits of free time that come when she entertains herself.

The length of time a child will spend playing alone varies, depending on her age and needs. Some children will play happily as long as they hear their parents nearby, while others will stop playing and want to be picked up right away. Many babies won't play at all and will want to be taken out of the crib as soon as they're awake. It's not unusual for babies to go through different phases: a child who's been happy to play in her crib may suddenly stop wanting to spend time there. And often, a baby who shows anxiety about being separated from her parents during the day will not want to play alone in her crib.

If your child doesn't play when she wakes up, you probably feel frustrated, especially if she's an early riser. In order to get a little more sleep, you might try bringing her back to bed with you when she first wakes up. Even if she doesn't fall asleep again, she may lie quietly with you for a while. You can also put some toys on your bed or on the floor nearby and encourage her to play quietly while you rest.

If she does play in her crib, be sure the toys you leave are safe and appropriate. And since she does a lot of moving and turning while she sleeps, be sure the objects in her crib won't harm her or wake her up if she bumps them. You might also want to switch toys in the crib every few weeks so she'll have some new things to play with. And occasionally try putting her in her crib to play after a bath or meal—you might have a little extra time to yourself if she's content to stay there for a while.

What about naptime?

Since parents spend a lot of time giving to their child and putting off their own needs, they look forward to the free time they have when their child naps. While parents are adjusting to their newborn, they often use free time to catch up on sleep. But gradually they feel the need to be "productive" during their child's naptime and may plan to do something during that period every day.

Each child has his own patterns of napping which change as he grows. During the first months of infancy, he may spend most of the day sleeping and then, for the next six months to a year, nap several hours at a time in the morning and again in the afternoon. Over the next year, he will most likely drop one of these naps and then gradually give up napping altogether. Of course, there are many children who stop napping at eighteen months old, and others who never take predictable naps, even in infancy. Some parents are flexible about naps and let their children follow their own natural sleep patterns, while other parents are advocates of strict scheduling.

A child's napping pattern may depend on the amount of sleep he gets at night. A child who sleeps nine or ten hours at night will probably need an afternoon nap, while a child who sleeps twelve hours may not need to sleep again during the day. By the time he's two or two and one-half years old, his napping might interfere with his nighttime sleeping so that if he naps for several hours he may be filled with energy late at night. This is fine if his parents' schedules permit late morning sleeping, or if they like to spend the evening hours with him. But if they want him to go to bed earlier, they should try and keep him from napping or at least from napping so long. Some parents are especially reluctant to let their child nap in the car, since a few minutes of sleeping in a car seat can take the place of a much longer nap at home.

Keeping a child from napping, however, can sometimes cause problems. Some children are very irritable when they don't sleep during the day, and their parents might decide that eliminating the nap is not worth the struggle. The child might go to bed earlier if he doesn't nap, but if he's unhappy all afternoon and evening, the family hasn't gained much. Similarly, many children are tired and irritable if their nap is cut short, although some are able to wake up after a short nap feeling rested and ready to play.

Children in day care often nap as they would at home. Infants sleep when they need to, and older children, who are usually up early in the mornings, generally nap for a couple of hours. These naps keep them from being sleepy during the early evening hours and allow parents extra time with them at night.

Many babies only fall asleep for their nap after being fed. Some older children who don't want to separate from their parents or their play may need to be rocked or patted to sleep.

If your child doesn't nap regularly, you may naturally feel frustrated at the lack of time for yourself. But you shouldn't try to force him to nap, since there will be negative consequences. He may spend long periods crying and you'll probably become angry at him and at yourself for forcing the issue. Instead, look for alternatives to napping. If you're home, you can hire a baby-sitter to play with him several afternoons a week so you can have time alone, or you can try waking your child up earlier in the morning so he'll go to sleep earlier at night. As he reaches preschool age, you might try having him stay in his room for a short quiet period of reading and playing.

When should my child sleep in a bed?

Moving from a crib to a bed is a big change for a toddler. She'll leave the security of a small, closed-in space for the freedom of a larger space. And after spending a few years in a confining crib, she'll be able to control her movements in and out of bed.

Parents often wonder what it will be like when their child has her own bed. Will she fall out at night? Will she get out of bed frequently? Will she play and entertain herself in bed as she did in the crib? Will she feel comfortable and secure? They sometimes have mixed feelings about the transition from crib to bed. It's exciting to watch a child grow, but it's also easy to feel sentimental as she gets older.

One of the questions parents frequently ask is, "When will my child be old enough to sleep in a bed?" Some children move to a bed when they're as young as twenty months—usually because a new sibling needs the crib. But if the crib isn't needed, parents should probably wait until their child is two and one-half or three years old before making the switch. By that time, she may be ready for the move and excited by the idea of having her own bed.

The transition from crib to bed shouldn't come when a child is going through major changes such as her mother's return to work or the beginning of day care or nursery school. At these times, she will probably need the security of her familiar crib. If the change to a bed is planned in anticipation of a new baby, the parents should not wait until the baby is born to make the switch, but rather give their child at least three or four months to get used to sleeping in a bed.

Before you move your child out of the crib, prepare her for the change. If you're buying a new bed or sheets, you might want to take her shopping with you. Spend some time talking to her about her move from the crib, but be careful about telling her that she's getting a bed because she's "big now." Toddlers feel a desire and pressure to be older and sometimes the suggestion that they should act "big" adds stress to a situation. Your child may feel you want her to do something she's not yet ready for.

Once you have the bed, try putting it right next to her crib so she can make a gradual switch from one to the other. She can begin by taking naps in the bed, then slowly start spending nights there. If she was used to having toys in her crib, put some on her bed. After a few weeks, when she no longer needs her crib, take it down, letting her help. Or, if you're going to use the crib for a new baby, let your child help move it to the other room.

If you're concerned about your child's safety in a bed, you can buy a safety bar that will keep her from falling out. You also can put the box spring and mattress on the floor rather than on a frame so she can climb in and out of bed easily without getting hurt—and she can even jump on her bed safely this way.

During the time of transition, notice how she feels about the change. If she's having a difficult time giving up her crib, slow down. Even if you planned to use the crib for a new baby, you can postpone the change by putting the newborn in a cradle or portable crib for several months. And when you do give the crib to the baby, don't be surprised if your older child still shows an interest in playing or sleeping in it. Children occasionally like to pretend they're babies and go back to familiar objects and places. As long as your child doesn't feel pressure to give up her crib before she's ready, her transition to a bed should be smooth.

When will my child stop needing diapers at night?

There's a wide age range for toilet training, but by three or three and one-half years old, most children learn to use the toilet during the day. However, learning to stay dry at night sometimes takes another six months, and many children occasionally wet at night until they're four or five years old. Nighttime control generally comes later than day control because a child must go for many hours without using a toilet before he's physiologically ready, and because a sleeping child can't consciously decide to go to the bathroom.

A child will stay dry at night when he's ready. He may tell his parents that he wants to stop wearing diapers, or his parents may decide that he's ready because he has been consistently dry for many days.

Sometimes a child who's dry at night will find it hard to give his diapers up, but if his parents let him know that diapers are available at night if he needs them, he will probably switch to underpants without a problem. Parents should not be alarmed if their child asks to go back to wearing a nighttime diaper. Such a request is usually just a temporary desire to re-experience something familiar.

Some parents choose to help their child stay dry at night by waking him up to use the bathroom, especially if he's had a lot to drink before bed. Other parents encourage their child to be a "big boy," although such urging misses the point. He will be dry when he's mature enough and his body is ready. Pressuring him to act older will not help, and neither will shaming him or trying to make him feel guilty about wetting.

Even if a child has been dry for weeks or months, accidents are inevitable. If your child wets his bed, keep in mind that he's not doing it to frustrate or harass you. Either he's not quite ready to give up diapers or, if the accidents are occasional, he's sleeping too deeply to get himself to the bathroom. It is also possible that your child is reacting to the temporary stress of a move, a new baby in the family, or the start of school.

Whether your child has been having accidents or has not yet been dry enough to give up diapers or pull-ups, you probably feel impatient and frustrated. You may feel that he's been in diapers long enough, or that you don't want to wash and change sheets frequently. These feelings are understandable, but once you realize that he'll be dry as soon as he's able, you can adjust your expectations and relax.

EATING

Should I schedule my child's feedings or feed on demand?

Infants do not have the ability to control or postpone their needs. If they're hungry or need to be comforted, they desire immediate gratification. When parents respond to their infant's cries, providing food and comfort, the baby begins to trust her world and to feel some small ability to affect what happens to her. If her cries for food are ignored, she has no way to satisfy herself.

Feeding an infant on demand, which means whenever the baby begins to fuss, is one way parents can meet their child's needs. Demand-fed babies and their parents are usually calmer and more content than families with babies who are fed on a schedule. This is because an infant fed on demand does less crying for food and comfort, and her parents spend less time distracting her since she doesn't have to be held off until a scheduled feeding. A demand-fed baby also may be easier to put to sleep since she can be soothed with nursing or a bottle when she seems tired. There's no chance of overfeeding a demand-fed child; an infant will not drink more than she wants or needs.

Parents who do not choose to feed their baby on demand, but rather on a schedule, often find themselves trying to comfort or put off their crying child. She might want to be fed, but the parents feel that it's too soon, that the baby should wait three or four hours because she has "just been fed." While it's true that some babies can wait four hours between feedings, it is equally true that some babies need feeding much more frequently.

If a baby fed on a schedule is hungry before feeding time, her parents will have try to soothe her. And if they are not able to calm her down, they may be likely to leave her fussing or crying for long periods of time. Since it's often hard for parents to listen to her cry, this can be a difficult situation, and one that probably takes as much time and energy as the extra feedings given to a demand-fed child.

New parents often decide to feed their child on a schedule because of advice from friends, relatives, and the pediatrician. In the face of such advice, they find it difficult to trust their instincts and begin demand feeding. They also worry that demand feeding means giving in to their child and letting her have too much control. Yet, an infant, because she's helpless, needs to feel she has some control, some ability to make other people respond. When her needs are met, she learns to trust that her parents will take care of her.

The decision to demand-feed or feed on a schedule is often influenced by the way the child is fed—by breast or bottle. Although either method can be adapted to scheduled or demand feeding, it's more likely that a breast-fed baby will be demand-fed, if only because of the ease of feeding. A mother can easily offer her breast at any time, while the parents of a bottle-fed infant must first prepare and warm bottles.

A bottle-fed infant is more likely to be fed on a schedule because her parents can easily see how much milk she's drinking, and thus can decide when they think she's had enough. Parents of a breast-fed baby, on the other hand, don't know how much their child is drinking. When she cries soon after nursing, her mother is likely to offer the breast again because the child might not have had enough milk at the last feeding.

You can be successful breast-feeding or bottle-feeding, but using either method, you will satisfy your child best if you feed her on demand. If you feel you must follow a schedule, be flexible enough to offer a feeding when she truly seems to need it. When comforting doesn't work between scheduled feedings, your child's cries probably mean she's hungry or so tired she needs to soothe herself to sleep after feeding. At such times, you should ignore the clock, follow your instincts, and meet your child's needs.

When should I wean?

It's hard for parents to follow their young child's lead, especially when it comes to weaning. A child will nurse or use a bottle only as long as he needs to, but most parents don't trust that he will stop on his own. Instead, they try to hurry him by taking away the bottle, breast, or pacifier before he's ready.

There's a lot of pressure on parents to wean their child. The pressure can be strong when the child reaches one year old, and increases as he grows. Friends and relatives ask, "What's he doing with a bottle? Can't he drink from a cup yet?" The pediatrician may say, "He doesn't need to nurse or use a bottle anymore." One mother reluctantly weaned her twenty-one-month-old son after such a statement from his doctor, although the child still enjoyed the bottle. Even passersby may comment, "He's too big for a bottle." Negative remarks are directed not just at the child, but at the parents. "What's wrong with you? Why are you still nursing?" "Why don't you take his bottle away?"

Parents feel especially self-conscious when judged by other parents. If the parents of a two and one-half-year-old believe theirs is the only child on the playground who still drinks from a bottle, they will wonder how it looks to other people and what other parents are thinking. They'll doubt their own judgment and wonder what they've done wrong or what's wrong with their child: "Do I baby him too much? Do we give in to him?" These parents would feel better if they knew that many children are just not ready to be weaned at an early age. Parents can avoid feeling embarrassed in public by distracting their young child and telling him that he'll have to wait before he can nurse or have his bottle.

If the bottle, breast, or pacifier is taken away from him too soon, he'll probably look for other ways to satisfy his sucking needs. He might become irritable or start sucking his blanket. One mother, who threw out her fifteen-month-old's bottles on the advice of her pediatrician, said, "My son seems OK but he started sucking his thumb." Some breast-fed babies who are weaned at twelve to eighteen months may not yet be ready to give up sucking. If they are only offered a training cup, they may suck the top of the cup just as they would suck on a nipple.

Many children who drink frequently and successfully from a cup still nurse (usually under the age of two) or use a bottle. Between ages two and three, a child may want to suck when he's tired, feeling stress from a fall or hurt feelings, spending time with a caregiver, or just relaxing with a favorite blanket or stuffed animal. He also may want a bottle whenever he sees another child with one. And during times of transition, such as a move or the arrival of a new baby, a child's sucking needs may increase.

If he's allowed to nurse, drink from a bottle, or use his pacifier when he wants, his needs gradually will decrease. Then either on his own or with your help, he will wean himself. This often happens by the time the child is eighteen months to two and one-half, although many older children will still relax before sleep with a bottle.

If parents feel they must hurry the weaning process, they should do so carefully. They should be sure that weaning will not interfere with another stage of development such as learning to use the toilet, beginning day care or nursery school, or adjusting to a new sibling. The process should be stretched over several weeks so the child is not forced abruptly to give up something important.

As your child gives up the bottle or breast, you may have ambivalent feelings. If you nursed, you may feel good about "having your body to yourself" again, or you may be glad to stop fussing with bottles. But you also may feel sad to give up the warm, close feeling you had as you held your child and offered him milk or watched him lie contentedly with his bottle. You also may miss the free time you had when he drank quietly by himself. Whatever your feelings—impatience or reluctance—in time your child will be weaned. If you can wait until he is ready to wean himself, the process will be simpler and more natural.

My child puts everything in her mouth. What can I do?

During infancy, a child's mouth is her main source of pleasure and satisfaction. She enjoys sucking at the breast or bottle, drinking warm milk, and sucking on her fingers or thumb. Starting at about six months, she also gets oral enjoyment and relief from teething by sucking and biting on objects around her.

Babies don't just put things in their mouths for pleasure or comfort, though—they also use their mouths for exploration. They learn about objects by tasting them, feeling their texture, and experimenting with them. Until a child is about two years old, many things that she plays with will eventually go into her mouth. She'll pick up things from the floor, chew on her stroller safety strap, and even try to put her parents' keys in her mouth.

Because she can't tell what's safe or unsafe, parents have to be very watchful. If your child is at this oral stage, you must pick up pieces of fuzz, crumbs, and small toys so she will not accidentally choke on them. You also have to be sure that the objects she puts in her mouth are clean.

This developmental phase may seem long and tiresome to you, but if you start pulling safe objects out of your child's mouth, or telling her that "only food should go in your mouth," you will be depriving her of pleasure and a chance to explore. Try instead to realize and accept the fact that she has to put objects in her mouth because that's a major way she learns about her environment.

Do other children drop food from the high chair?

Young children, especially between the ages of ten and eighteen months, tend to make a mess when they eat. As they sit in their high chairs, they mash food, spread it around, and drop it on the floor—sometimes pea by pea, occasionally a bowlful at a time.

Parents wonder why their child acts this way. Is he doing it to bother, defy, or manipulate them? Usually not. He might throw his food down because he's finished eating and doesn't want any more, or because he doesn't like the food he's been given. He might also just be tired and ready to get down from the high chair. Often, a child makes a mess because he's playing with his food, experimenting with the textures and spreading the food around to see what happens. A young child is interested in his meal not just for its taste but for its color and feel, and he doesn't mind getting messy in his explorations.

When a child methodically drops bits of food onto the floor, he may be testing his own power over objects and his ability to make things happen. Children repeat this process because they seem to have a strong inner need to perform the same actions over and over. As a child drops his food, he feels delighted that he can control each piece, deciding where it will land and watching it fall.

This phase, in which your child likes to drop things (toys as well as food), can be irritating. If he's at this developmental stage, you will find that he won't listen when you tell him to stop. This happens because your young, egocentric child cannot consider your wishes and his at the same time. He ends up considering just his own desires and drops food even when you tell him not to. If you can view this impersonally or even playfully, without thinking that he's trying to provoke you, you'll have an easier time dealing with him.

To ease the clean up, you can spread newspaper or a piece of vinyl under your child's high chair so you don't have to wipe the floor. And you can try putting less food on his tray. That way he will still have a little to experiment with while you will have less to clean up.

When should my child use a spoon and fork?

Soon after a child begins sitting in a high chair, she will probably want to try feeding herself. At first, she'll use her hands to pick up food, getting some in her hair, on her clothes, and on the floor. Eventually, she'll become a bit neater and start eating with utensils, although she'll still use her hands.

Some parents are so bothered by messy eating that they try to stop their child from feeding herself. They think that meals will be faster and more efficient if they do the feeding, and they're probably right. Yet there are other considerations. A child can become so frustrated when she isn't allowed to touch her food or feed herself that she might push away what her parents offer and even refuse to eat. All children at some point have a desire to feed themselves, and they're usually more cooperative at the table when their parents let them try.

When your child is ready to start feeding herself, you can minimize messiness by putting only a small amount of food on the tray (although some tolerant parents let their child plunge into a whole bowlful). When your child is ten to fourteen months old, you may see signs that she's ready to try a utensil. She might reach for the spoon you're using or imitate your actions as you eat your meals or feed her.

Her first utensil should be a spoon, since it's safer to use than a fork. You can continue to feed her with your spoon while letting her dip her own spoon into the bowls of food. By the time she's eighteen months old, she may be ready to use a child-sized fork, as long as you watch to see she doesn't harm herself.

Don't be concerned about the way your child holds her utensils; if she seems comfortable and is able to get some food into her mouth, there's no need to worry. If she seems uncomfortable, you can show her how to hold a spoon or fork correctly, but don't get into a struggle if she refuses to follow your example. Eventually she'll learn by imitating you.

If she doesn't want to use a utensil even though she's old enough, and prefers eating with her hands, try to accept the situation. She may be more successful eating that way, or may just prefer to touch her food directly. Since eating should be a relaxed and enjoyable experience, it's not wise to try forcing your child to use a spoon and fork. Just have utensils available so she can try them out when she's ready. By the time she's two and one-half to three years old, she'll be using utensils much of the time.

Should my child at least taste new foods?

Parents want mealtime to be pleasant, enjoyable, and healthy, and they want their children to eat a variety of foods. But often the ways in which they try to accomplish these goals are self-defeating.

Parents may put new food in front of a child and say, "Just taste it." They hope, of course, that he'll enjoy the food and therefore ask for more. They also hope that after trying one taste, he'll get used to experimenting with new foods. However, what often happens is that he refuses the taste and a power struggle develops.

Parents sometimes try threats or various types of persuasion. "You won't get dessert unless you taste this." Using dessert as an incentive focuses too much attention on sweets and often causes a child to expect dessert as a reward. Parents also say, "But it's good for you," "It will make you big and strong," and, "Some poor children don't have any food to eat." But children tend to ignore such statements, which are based in part on falsehoods. There is no instant strength from food, and eating a meal won't help another child who has to go without.

Although parents may succeed in having their child taste something new, there can certainly be negative consequences. First, he seldom, if ever, asks for more of the originally rejected food. And if the family is eating in public, his refusal to eat more than one bite can lead to embarrassment. One young child, forced to taste apple pie at a friend's party, declared loudly, "I hate this dessert!" Once a child decides he doesn't want what's offered, he'll seldom reverse his decision. Another negative effect of forcing children to taste food is the risk of establishing a life-long pattern of aversion. Many adults continue to avoid food they remember being forced to eat when they were young.

Basically, struggles over food are not so much about eating as they are about power. Parents try to make children taste something while children try to resist the pressure. They feel powerless when they're not able to say, "I don't want it." And when they do try a bite of something they don't want, they eat only because they feel they have no choice, or they want to please their parents, or they want dessert.

When a child resists food, he's usually not being stubborn. It may be hard for him to tolerate a taste he finds unpleasant. Often, he decides that he likes or doesn't like something based on its looks and consistency. Therefore, he may know at first sight that he doesn't want to try something new. Occasionally, he may refuse food because he's afraid that once he tries a bite, he'll have to keep on trying more and more new foods.

Yet, despite all the negative effects and emotions involved in forcing a taste, parents get into mealtime struggles for a positive reason: they want their children willingly to eat nutritious foods. And there are ways to accomplish this without resorting to arguments. You can talk to your pediatrician or a nutritionist about alternatives for a healthy diet and consult books with advice and recipes for meals with a range of tastes. Try providing healthy snacks that children generally enjoy, such as homemade frozen juice bars, carrots, raisins, sunflowers seeds, or fresh fruit, and model for your child the kind of healthy eating habits you want him to adopt.

At mealtime, provide healthful food and leave him free to choose what he wants to eat. You'll find that when there's no coercion or arguing, meals are more relaxed and he's more willing to try new foods. As your child gets older, his tastes will change, and he'll eat different types and amounts of food. For pleasant and healthy eating, the best thing to do is offer a variety of good food without putting on the pressure.

INDEPENDENCE

Is it OK for my child to spend time in a playpen?

In theory, a playpen that's used according to safety recommendations is a help to parents and provides a secure place for a baby to play. The problem is that most babies spend less time in playpens than their parents would like, or won't stay in a playpen at all.

Most children aren't content for long in a confined area. They want to explore their surroundings and move around, and they want to be with their parents. Although babies' temperaments and activity levels vary, all young children have strong needs that aren't met in a playpen. Some babies may play quietly there for twenty minutes, others for only a few minutes. Then they want to get out and explore or be held. One mother of a nine-month-old was determined to have her child spend a certain amount of time in the playpen each day, but he was unhappy there and became fussy and irritable. After several weeks, the mother stopped using the playpen and found that he was happier and more pleasant. So often children's needs don't match parents' needs.

When parents buy a playpen, they usually think their child will play contentedly in it for long periods. They look forward to putting the playpen outside on nice days and taking it to the beach where they'll shade their child with an umbrella and let her play. When they discover she doesn't want to spend time in the playpen, they often feel frustrated and angry, wondering why she isn't happy to stay there with all her toys.

If you want to encourage your child to spend some time in her playpen, try placing it near you so she can watch you and you can talk or play peek-a-boo with her. Give her a play object such as a toy telephone, pot, or bowl that's similar to an object you're using. Then she can occupy herself imitating you. You also can try changing the toys in the playpen frequently so she will have something different to play with. But be careful not to clutter the playpen with too many toys.

If you see that your child is becoming frustrated, pick her up and let her explore. A playpen should not be the main place where she's allowed to play. She should have a safe, childproofed space where she can move around freely. Take some of the toys and put them in the room where you are so she can play near you. And if she wants to be held, try using a baby carrier so you can keep her close and still accomplish something for yourself.

The playpen has its use as a safe place to put your child for short periods, but she will never want to spend as much time there as you'd like. As long as your expectations are realistic, you probably won't feel too frustrated when she lets you know she wants to get out.

Why won't my child hold still during diaper changes?

A father walked out of his son's bedroom shaking his head. "I don't believe it. He only weighs twenty pounds and I still can't get him to hold still for a diaper change." Getting a baby diapered and dressed requires a surprising amount of skill and patience, even though the job is a short one. Young children, who are usually in constant motion, squirm and resist being held down. They're excited about their world, their interests change constantly, and they want to move and explore. Because they have a hard time putting off any of their urges, even for a moment, they don't like to lie still.

Distraction can sometimes make your diapering job a little easier. Try putting some toys or interesting playthings nearby and keep handing them to your child. This might occupy him during a quick change. You also can try singing to him or making interesting noises, but most of the time you'll have to restrain him a bit until you get him changed and dressed. You'll naturally feel frustrated as he resists and struggles, but just remember that he has a strong drive to assert himself and explore and that's why he won't hold still.

How should I handle crawling?

Crawling is an important stage in development, and parents watch with delight as their child becomes mobile. Although some babies start crawling before they are six months old, most begin between six and nine months, and some never crawl, going from sitting to walking without the middle step. Because children develop at their own pace, each child will begin to crawl when she's ready. But if a child has not begun by the time she's nine months old, you may want to talk to a pediatrician about her motor development.

Some parents wonder if they can motivate their baby to crawl by putting attractive toys just out of her reach. Rather than help, this may only frustrate her if she's not able to start moving. There's really no need to encourage crawling because children have an innate desire to get to many different objects and explore their surroundings. As soon as she's developmentally ready and able to extend herself, she'll start crawling.

When your child first begins to move, you may see her "belly crawl" across the floor. She'll move backwards or forwards, pulling with alternating arms while her belly stays flat on the floor. Later, she'll get up on all fours, rocking a little. Eventually, she'll move slowly on all fours, mastering the movement until she becomes a proficient crawler.

At that point (if not earlier), since your child will be able to reach many potentially dangerous objects, you will have to babyproof your home, an often time-consuming and frustrating task. You should put plants, small toys, and fragile items out of reach, but you should not stifle your child's natural curiosity about the objects she sees. As long as harmful items are out of the way, let her crawl to the curtains, touch the table leg, or reach for a toy. That's how she learns about her world. Of course, during this stage you'll need to keep your floors clear of fuzz, small objects, and crumbs that could end up in your child's mouth.

You will naturally be concerned about stairs once your child is mobile. The best way to be sure she's safe is to use gates at the top and bottom of the stairway. If you have carpeting on the steps and bottom landing, you may want to attach your gate a few steps up so your child can crawl up and down the short distance safely. However, if your landing is not carpeted, you will want to attach the gate to the bottom step to minimize harmful falls. She will quickly learn to climb the stairs and will enjoy going up, but most children don't come down steps safely until they're one and one-half to two years old. That's why it's so important to close the top gate each time you pass through. Once you've made your child's environment safe, you can relax and let her enjoy crawling.

When will my child start walking?

A child will begin to walk as soon as he's developmentally ready. For some children that means at nine months; for others, eighteen months. The age at which a healthy child walks has no effect on or connection with his intelligence, yet parents often feel pressure if their child is a late walker. Friends and relatives may ask, "Are you sure he's all right? Why isn't he walking yet?" or say, "My daughter was walking when she was ten months old and your child's already seventeen months," or, "Maybe your son needs to be around other children so he can learn by watching them." Such comments cause parents needless anxiety because there's nothing wrong with a developmentally healthy child who doesn't walk until he's fifteen to eighteen months old.

There's no need to try and teach a child to walk. Although it might be fun for you to hold your child's hands and let him walk along, such an exercise will not help him walk alone any faster. Try to be patient and wait until he's ready for this stage of development.

He'll prepare for independent walking by first learning to pull himself up to a standing position while holding onto furniture. Once he's mastered this skill (which might take days, weeks, or even months), he'll begin to take steps while holding onto furniture or onto his parent's hand. Eventually, he'll let go and take some steps alone. A child who starts walking is usually so delighted with himself that he hardly notices his frequent falls.

As he begins to stand and walk, his perspective will change. Before, he looked at everything from ground level, but once he's upright, he'll see more. People, objects, and even his own body will look different. He'll be able to reach more things and to roam farther and faster, and that means his parents will have to continue childproofing his environment.

You'll find that one of the most delightful aspects of this developmental stage is your child's ability to go for walks with you. As soon as he's steady on his feet, take him for a leisurely stroll outside. Walk at his pace, sometimes letting him choose the direction, and see how many wonderful discoveries he makes. He'll want to stop and examine pebbles, grass, worms, and flowers, and if you bring a collecting bag along, he can take some treasures home.

The more your child walks, the less he'll want to use his stroller, which can cause problems when you're in a hurry or when you're going far. If you're in a crowded shopping center and want to encourage him to stay in his stroller, try distracting him with food or a toy. If this doesn't work, try to find an uncrowded spot where he can walk for a little while without bumping into people. Often, he'll want to push the stroller himself, and in a crowd this can cause quite a fuss. If you let him push for a little while, he may be more agreeable when you place him back in his stroller. Although his slowness and desire to practice his new skill may temporarily frustrate you, you'll enjoy his excitement and independence. And you may be surprised to see that once he masters walking, he'll be just as likely to run as to walk.

How different is the view from my child's level?

Toddlers scramble out of their strollers, climb on anything handy, and insist on being picked up because they want to see better and reach farther. When a child stands on the floor, he can't look out of most windows. Beds and toilets seem very high and big, and doorknobs and light switches are unreachable.

In public places, almost nothing is placed at a child's eye level. One mother walked into a health clinic and introduced her three-year-old son to the receptionist, who was sitting behind a high counter. The boy couldn't see anyone to say hello to and just stared at the wall in front of him until the woman peeked over to look at him.

When a child goes to a public bathroom, the toilets, sinks, towels, and dryers are all out of reach. Most water fountains are too high for him to use, and most of the interesting features of stores and restaurants—cash registers, cafeteria counters, bakery bins—are out of sight. When he has to sit in a stroller, his view is even more limited.

To see what your child sees, get down to his level and look around. You won't see your own kitchen sink or the tops of your tables. In a store, you won't be able to look at what people are doing behind counters or see most of the interesting merchandise. You'll notice that at nursery schools and day care centers everything is at eye level, and all the tables, chairs, and shelves are easy for children to reach.

Once you see how unsatisfying your child's view can be, you'll understand why he wants to climb and be carried. Pick him up often so he can see what is happening around him, let him sit on store counters (while you carefully supervise), and provide safe stools or pillows at home so he can climb a little and see more of his world.

What should I do about falls and accidents?

Young children spend so much time running, climbing, and jumping that minor injuries are inevitable. Sometimes a child is so absorbed in play that she ignores her scrapes and goes right back to her game, perhaps after yelling, "You bumped me, you stupid chair." At other times, especially when she's tired, she may cry for a long time after a fall.

A child's reaction to an injury often depends on who's around her. Since she feels most comfortable expressing her feelings to her parents, she might cry or complain more about a fall when they're with her. Many parents have seen their child fall, get up looking unhurt, and then start crying as soon as she sees them. A child cries like this because she wants to be comforted. If her parents are not close by, she may comfort herself or seek help from another child or adult. Adults react the same way to their own injuries: when an adult bumps into something at home where he's comfortable, he'll express his pain, but if he hurts himself away from home, he's likely to hide his discomfort.

The way a child reacts to a fall also depends on her age. A very young child is much more likely than a four- or five-year-old to cry after a minor injury. One five-year-old told her friend, "Just don't think about your cut and it won't hurt anymore."

Many children want Band-Aids for every scrape and bruise. Band-Aids seem magical to a young child because she believes that once small cuts are covered up, they're gone. Parents can make Band-Aids easily accessible and should let their child wear one whenever she thinks she needs it, even if she just wants to cover an old scab she's rediscovered—the comfort is worth the small expense.

Just as children react in different ways to injuries, so do parents. Some minimize their child's pain and say, "You're OK. Stop crying." Others offer to rub or kiss the sore spot. Certainly children need comfort when they're upset after a fall, and they need to know their parents understand: "Yes, I know it really hurts when you scrape your knee." But children get hurt so frequently that it can be hard for parents constantly to comfort and reassure. Yet, some young children seem to need attention for each new cut, bump, or bruise.

Parents should try not to overreact to their child's injuries. Some parents, who usually realize they're overreacting but have trouble controlling their impulses, rush to their child after a fall, anxiously asking, "Are you all right?" When a child sees her parents looking so concerned, she may start to cry simply because she thinks something must be wrong. If parents continually overreact, she may eventually feel that she's incapable of making herself feel better, and that she should seek help for even minor accidents.

Some parents are very uncomfortable seeing their son cry after a fall. They may tell him, "You're a big boy, you can handle it. It's only a little cut." Even now, there are parents who think it's all right for girls, but not for boys, to cry. Parents should remember that young children of both sexes sometimes need comfort and sometimes need to handle minor injuries on their own.

When you watch your child playing, you probably warn her about dangerous situations: "Don't climb up there or you'll fall!" If she climbs and falls anyway, you may have a hard time being sympathetic. It's tempting to say, "I told you you'd get hurt if you played like that," but if your child is in need of comfort, she will feel rejected by such a statement and not understand the safety message you intend. In such a situation, you should pay attention to her pain while also telling her that what she did was unsafe.

On rare occasions, your child's injury may be serious enough for a trip to the doctor or the hospital. A serious accident is always frightening for parents and children, especially if there's a great deal of rush and concern. If your child needs special treatment, reassure her: "I know your arm hurts and I'm going to see what we can do to make you feel better. That's why we're going to the hospital."

Try to remain calm and explain (or ask the doctors or nurses to explain) the medical procedures to your child. Let her know if she will be put on a stretcher or in a papoose, and if a particular procedure will be painful. You and she may not be able to avoid pain and unpleasantness in this situation, but you can be there to help her and go with her to the treatment room if permitted.

It's always hard to see your child in pain after a serious accident, and you might feel better if you bring someone along to help and comfort you—a friend, neighbor, or relative. As one mother said after her daughter received stitches, "I hear about this happening to other children, but it's very different when it happens to your own."

What can I do about climbing?

After a child has been walking for a month or so, she'll probably start climbing on chairs, beds, couches, counters, and anything else she can reach. She climbs because she has a strong urge to touch and explore things around her. When she sees her parents doing seemingly magical things like talking on the phone, washing dishes, turning on the lights, or opening doors, she wants to get closer and imitate them. And in order to do that—to reach the phone or the desktop—she has to climb.

The climbing stage can be difficult for parents because they have to keep their child safe, and that can mean almost constant supervision. If they leave her alone for even a few moments, they may hear the sound of a chair scraping along as she prepares for her next climb. They often stop her from climbing because they fear for her safety, or because furniture might be damaged, or simply because they don't want her to climb just then. But her urge to climb is strong and she may get angry and frustrated when she's held back. Then her parents will either have to deal with her behavior or try to distract her.

A child who climbs during the day may climb out of her crib at night or at naptime, either to be with her parents or to explore the room. Parents often are surprised the first time this happens. One mother put her child in the crib for a nap, then went to take a shower. As she was lathering her hair, she heard a noise in the bathroom and looked out to see her daughter standing there.

It's almost impossible to force your child to stay in her crib, but you can take precautions to make her climbing safer. If she is consistently climbing out of her crib, clear the nearby area and be sure there are no toys or pieces of furniture for her to trip or fall on. Close the stairway gates whenever she's in her crib, and use a night light in the hall so she can see if she climbs out during the night. If you feel she's ready, you might want to put the crib away and have her sleep in a bed.

To keep her safe and satisfied during the day, try at times to make climbing easy for her. You might give her a small stepstool to carry around or get a small piece of indoor climbing equipment, such as a slide, for her to play on safely. You also can place a chair near a window so she can look out, take cushions off your couch so she can climb on them, or even put a mattress on the floor so she can climb, jump, and explore in safety.

How much childproofing should I do?

Childproofing the home is important because young children explore indiscriminately. If an object is within reach, a child under three will touch it without considering his own safety or the value of the object. Because young children have such a strong natural compulsion to touch, see, and explore, their parents have to protect them and make their environment safe. But parents also have to balance their child-proofing with an understanding of their child's need to explore.

Most parents know to put plugs in electrical sockets, to put locks on cabinets containing dangerous substances, to keep plants and sharp items out of reach, and to put away valuables. But beyond that, they wonder how much accommodating they should do. Some parents feel they should teach their child the meaning of "no" by leaving out objects that he's not allowed to handle: "Sooner or later, he's going to have to learn not to touch everything." Other parents leave out forbidden objects or refuse to let their child touch accessible items in order to train him to behave well in other people's homes. One mother who wouldn't let her son play behind the living room curtains, said, "I don't care about my own curtains but I'm afraid he'll play with the curtains at his friend's house." Such fears prevent many parents from allowing their child to explore his own house. Yet, children can be allowed to touch and play with things at home and taught not to do the same thing at other people's homes.

Parents who leave out knickknacks and declare many items and appliances untouchable find themselves in constant conflict with their child, who simply does not have the impulse control to resist touching. One common battleground is the kitchen. Frustrated parents who don't understand the developmental urge to explore sometimes try to limit their child's access to the dishwasher, trash can, and refrigerator by tying up doors and lids. Yet, such denial may only make him more frantic to experiment with the interesting appliances he sees his parents use. He may run to the kitchen every time he hears the refrigerator open, or he may struggle to climb on the dishwasher door to get at the silverware. He just wants to touch, but parents often expect too much from a child under three and then feel drained by having to say "no" all day.

It's certainly true that a child needs limits, but he will inevitably learn his limitations because there are dangerous and valuable objects that can't be put away: a fireplace, lamps, a TV, a stereo. There is no need to intentionally leave out other forbidden things, just as there is no need to automatically declare all appliances off-limits. The dishwasher, for instance, won't need to be tied up if parents keep some spoons and plastic dishes and cups within their child's reach inside and let him occasionally practice taking them out and putting them back. Likewise, if parents put some healthy snacks on the bottom shelf of the refrigerator, their child will probably feel satisfied to help himself to those without feeling a need to touch everything else in the refrigerator. If parents are firm about not letting their child handle a few items, but otherwise allow him freedom to touch, both he and they will not be overly frustrated during this developmental stage. The more freedom he has, the more likely he'll be to listen when they tell him not to touch.

Once you have fully childproofed your home, you'll feel comfortable leaving your child alone in one room for a brief time while you work or answer the phone in another room. If you have limited the number of objects he may not touch, you won't feel tense when he explores. However, expect to keep reminding him of his limits; his urge to touch is so strong that he may not be able to stop himself.

If you want to keep your child from handling things at someone else's house, try telling him ahead of time, "I know you play with the cushions here, but when we're at Grandma's you can't do that." You might find that your child is more cautious when he's away from home and that he does less exploring in other people's homes than you expected.

Whenever you visit, you may have to do some temporary child-proofing, especially if your host has no young children. Ask if you can temporarily move fragile items. Most people will understand, particularly if you offer to put the objects back in place before you leave.

Childproofing is basically a way of accommodating the normal developmental needs of a child under three. Young children want to touch and try everything, so if you prepare for this stage, you will have an easier time getting through it. And, although it may seem to you that the touching phase will never end, you'll see a gradual decrease in your child's need to explore everything in sight. By the time he's three and one-half, he'll gain more understanding about objects, safety, and impulse control, and have less need to touch. You will then be able to put back on your tables and shelves many of the objects you had to keep out of reach.

In stores, my child wants to touch everything. What can I do?

Everyone likes to touch interesting and attractive objects. Adults in stores are drawn to gadgets they can manipulate and products they can pick up and feel. Children also want to handle what they see in stores, but many store owners and parents are too impatient or fearful to let children touch.

Touching is one of the main ways a child learns about things around her, especially in new surroundings. She explores with her hands and often can only "see" something by feeling it. One three-year-old told her mother, who was holding an interesting object right in front of her daughter's eyes, "I can't see that far." The child was really saying that she wanted to touch.

When children shop with their parents, struggles often develop as parents pick up, handle, and buy items, and children want to do the same. And because most stores try to display their products in the most attractive and appealing ways possible, the temptations for a child to touch are great. Parents usually keep their children from handling merchandise because they're worried about items getting broken. While it's true that young children don't understand the consequences of breaking things, it's also true that most children, if properly supervised, won't hurt items in a store. Parents can hold fragile objects for close-up viewing or gentle touching, and can allow their children, within limits, to pick up interesting merchandise.

Sometimes a child will feel satisfied in a store if she is just given enough time to examine an object. Parents are often in too much of a hurry while shopping to wait while she looks at boxes of paint brushes or piles of scarves. But many struggles can be avoided if parents slow down a bit and allow an extra few minutes for her interests.

Some stores make shopping easier by providing toys and play areas for children. If possible, try to patronize such stores and let the owners know that you value their service. Always support their efforts by watching your child while she's in the play area and by straightening up some of the toys before you leave the store. If children are left unsupervised and store employees have to take complete responsibility for clean up, owners may discontinue the service.

Although play areas are very helpful, most of the stores you shop in will not have them and will show little tolerance for children. Since that's the case, carry small toys from home when you shop with your child, or have her bring a backpack with her choice of a few small items. Such playthings may distract her from some, but not all, of the attractive merchandise around her. When parents, store owners, and employees recognize and become more patient with children's needs to see, touch, and explore, shopping will become easier for everyone.

"I want to do it myself!" How long will this last?

Children want to try doing many things for themselves. An eighteen-month-old wants to push buttons, put a key in the keyhole, walk down the steps, and get his own vitamin. A two-year-old wants to take the wrapper off his candy and fasten his seat belt, while a three-year-old wants to work the computer and pour his own juice. Sometimes children are successful at the tasks they choose for themselves, and at other times they struggle in frustration because they lack skills and dexterity. Still, the drive to do for themselves is very strong.

Parents who respect their child's desire to do things for himself help him develop a strong sense of autonomy. Since his self-image is partly determined by the way his parents respond to his desire for independence, he'll feel good about himself when he's allowed to tackle jobs on his own. On the other hand, if his parents discourage him too often, he'll begin to doubt his own abilities.

In general, parents should let their child at least start a task he's interested in. If he's unsuccessful, they can offer guidance, and if he's unable to follow their suggestions they can then offer to do the job for him. Parents often jump in too soon because they find it difficult to watch their child struggle with a task. They naturally want to help, but often he doesn't want help. If they find it too hard to stay uninvolved, they should occupy themselves with something else while he works.

Sometimes parents will not be able to let their child do a task for himself. One family, for example, was about to go home after seeing a circus when their two-year-old insisted on tying his own shoe. As they tried to help him and hurry him along, he became angry and frustrated, and nearby families stopped to watch the struggle. The parents finally solved the problem by telling their son he could carry his shoe out and tie it himself in the car, but often such conflicts are not easily resolved.

Despite the best intentions, parents may find themselves in an embarrassing situation, carrying away a screaming, angry child who wants to stay put until he's finished a task. Such times are difficult for parents, who feel judged by others and frustrated by their child's actions. Yet, he doesn't understand his parents' feelings, and often will focus only on his own needs unless he's distracted.

Sometimes parents don't want him to do a job for himself because they don't want to deal with the mess that will result, or because they're in a hurry. But when they say, "Let me do that for you," they may be in for arguments, struggles, or temper tantrums.

To minimize such resistance, warn your child ahead of time if there won't be time for him to dress himself or do some other task. "We're in a hurry today, so I'm going to help you." Try to distract him: "Why don't you look at this book while I put your shoes on?" "Let me tell you a story while I get your breakfast ready."

If a task your child wants to try is too difficult or messy, break it into steps and let him try a small part of the job. If he can't yet brush his teeth, let him hold the toothbrush while you put the toothpaste on, and let him hold your hand as you brush. He will feel pleased to participate, and in time, step by step, he'll take over the job for himself.

Being patient with children at this stage is difficult because patience, distraction, and preparation don't necessarily work—your child will angrily demand to do something for himself when you don't want him to or when he is incapable of doing the job. Still, the more he is allowed to try on his own, the less likely he is to argue when you have to take over a task. And as you see how pleased he is with his accomplishments and how good he feels about his abilities, you will understand why it is important to let him do many things for himself.

My daughter wants to dress herself. How do I handle this?

One of the first tasks most children try is getting dressed on their own. They feel proud and excited when they dress themselves, and they look to their parents for approval.

There's no need to try convincing or teaching a young child to dress herself because most children express an interest in the activity on their own. First, a child will learn to take off her shoes, socks, and pants, since children are able to take their clothes off before they can put them on. By age three, she may want to do most of her own dressing (excluding snaps and buttons), although her clothes will often be inside out or backwards. By the time she's four or five, she'll be able to dress completely with little help.

When your child begins dressing herself, she may be frustrated by zippers, snaps, buttons, and shirts with small neck openings. Even though she can't master these, she may insist on trying—a situation that often leads to anger and tantrums. You might want to avoid difficult clothes and buy pull-on pants and tops until she's ready to use fasteners.

As she learns to dress herself, she may want to practice her new skills by changing her clothes several times a day, creating great piles of clothing to clean up or launder. She also may want to choose her own clothes, sometimes picking the same easy-to-put-on outfit over and over, or choosing clothes that don't fit well, don't match, or are inappropriate for the weather or the occasion. As long as you're staying inside, there's no need to make an issue out of how she looks. But at times when you want her to look nice, you may end up struggling over her choices.

You can eliminate some of the problem by laying out two outfits and letting her choose one to wear, or by putting in her drawers only those clothes that fit and are suitable for the season. Another possibility is to fill one drawer with a few sets of clothes that mix and match, letting her choose what to wear from these preselected outfits. These suggestions require time and energy, but the effort might be worth it if she's determined to pick out her own clothes each day.

When you're rushed, you may end up struggling with your child if she's determined to dress herself. If you leave the house every morning, you may be able to avoid arguments by setting the alarm clock fifteen minutes early to give her time to dress. At other times, let her know that you are going to help with dressing because you're rushed. If she has generally been allowed to dress herself, she may not resist your efforts. But if she does, try offering a distraction such as, "Let's get dressed quickly so we can get some crackers."

A surprising development may occur once your child has learned to dress herself efficiently: she may not want to do it anymore. She may say, "I can't," or "I don't want to," or, "You get me dressed." Frequently, when a child has mastered a skill such as dressing, she loses interest and it becomes a chore rather than a challenge. You may feel that if you give in and dress her, you're being manipulated. You may even try to force her to dress herself, although when children are forced, they often slow down and procrastinate. You have to decide whether this is an issue worth struggling over.

Compromise and flexibility seem most effective. If your child is tired, uninterested, or simply wants to be taken care of for a while, it's all right to dress her yourself. At other times you may want to help her get dressed: "You do the shirt and I'll put on your pants." And when you want her to consistently dress herself, usually by the time she is five, let her know: "Before you come down for breakfast, I want you to get dressed."

It's best to avoid power struggles over getting dressed. In child development, steps forward are often followed by steps backward. Enjoy your child's pride when she's able to dress herself, and trust that by age five or six she will take on the job permanently.

When will my child be ready to use the toilet?

The transition from diapers to toilet use is an important one in a child's development. If parents are patient and non-pressuring as their child learns to use the toilet, the family will get through this stage easily.

But if they try to force toilet-training, this stage may cause a lot of anger and unhappiness.

Parents often initiate early toilet-training because they feel a great deal of pressure. Nursery schools and day care centers want children to be trained, and friends and relatives offer criticism: "You were trained at two! What's wrong with your child?" "You really should start toilet-training him." There's often competition among parents to see who has the youngest toilet-trained child, as though toilet-training were a race. Many people mistakenly feel that the faster a child develops (and the sooner he's toilet-trained), the smarter or better he is.

Aside from starting toilet-training in response to pressure, many parents start because they don't believe their child will acquire the skill on his own. Although they have seen their child learn to crawl, walk, and talk, they find it hard to trust that he'll also use the toilet when he's ready.

Children can train themselves, but the ages at which they're able to do so vary since in this, as in all areas of development, some children are ready sooner than others. Between two and three, most gain enough bladder and bowel control to be able to use the toilet on their own, although some don't use the toilet until they are three and one-half. Emotional factors such as the birth of a sibling, a move, or a mother going back to work can delay a child's readiness.

Often, children show an interest in the toilet at eighteen months, but parents should not take this as a sign that a child is ready for toilet training. At this age, a child's body is not mature enough and any toilet use will be controlled by his parents. He's just temporarily interested in flushing the toilet, tearing toilet paper, and imitating the other members of his family. Some children under two are afraid of the toilet. It's large, and they fear they'll fall in or be flushed down and disappear. A small potty seat is less frightening, but many children won't use one, insisting on the same toilet the rest of the family uses.

If parents initiate toilet-training before their child is ready, the whole family may suffer. Parents use up a great deal of energy putting him on the toilet every twenty minutes, constantly praising or scolding him, doing the extra laundry and cleanup that results from frequent accidents, and working out reward systems using candy or stars to motivate their child. It's particularly difficult for parents to handle the resistance of a two-year-old who reacts negatively to any parental pressure or suggestions. At that age, a child strives for autonomy and wants to assert himself and take charge of all aspects of his life: "I can do it myself!" Certainly there are some children who are easily trained by their parents, and other children who quickly learn to use the toilet because they temporarily fear losing their parents' love and acceptance. But most are not successfully trained if their parents start too soon.

Often, all of the efforts backfire, and the child becomes strongly opposed to using the toilet. This situation can develop because he has been over-praised for toilet use. Once he sees how important the issue is to his parents and how happy they are when he goes to the bathroom, he may realize on some level how unhappy he can make them by not going. This may become his weapon in power struggles.

Toilet-training efforts also can backfire because he has been pressed too hard to be "a big boy." Sometimes he feels so anxious about disappointing his parents that he won't even try using the toilet for fear of failure. Finally, a child who doesn't like to be pushed and controlled might try to exert his own power by rejecting his parents' suggestions. Rather than use the toilet, he might become constipated or else urinate or have a bowel movement as soon as he's taken off the toilet, soiling the floor or his pants. If parents feel they must initiate toilet-training, they should hold off until he's three and make sure training doesn't interfere with other developmental changes.

The best approach is simply to wait until the child is ready to start on his own. Children have an innate drive to grow and develop, a strong desire to imitate and please their parents, and determination to do things for themselves. All of these urges will come together if he's not pressured to use the toilet before he's physically and emotionally ready. It takes a great deal of patience and confidence in your child to wait. But eventually he will let you know that he wants to use the toilet. Offer support and help: "Would you like me to turn on the light? Can I help you with your pants?" You can give simple acknowledgment of what he's done, or you might want to reflect back to him his own pleasure and pride.

Once he's initiated toilet use, he'll quickly give up diapers. However, even past four years old, he'll occasionally have accidents because of stress or he'll forget to get to a bathroom on time because he will be too busy playing. As long as you haven't excessively praised him or shamed him for his previous toilet use and accidents, he won't feel too bad when he wets.

Your attitudes towards toilet-training determine, in large part, how successful this phase of your child's development will be. If you anticipate struggles, you'll probably have them. But if you're relaxed and willing to let your child set the pace, you and he will have an easier time.

SETTING LIMITS

How do I handle discipline and punishment?

Parents often feel they spend a great part of each day disciplining their young children: "Don't use the toy that way—you might hurt someone," "No hitting," "Leave the dog alone," "You have to come in now," "That's too loud." Setting limits for young children can be difficult, complex, and time-consuming, but it's essential. Parents have to teach their child acceptable behavior while controlling or changing unacceptable behavior until she's old enough to exert some self-control and understand why rules are important. In order to handle this task effectively, parents need information about their child's egocentric development plus realistic expectations, empathy, patience, love, and respect for their child.

Disciplining young children is an extremely important part of parenting, yet there are parents who don't set adequate limits. Some feel overwhelmed by their child's behavior and may not know where to start. Other parents just don't think about the importance of setting limits or leave the job to neighbors, friends, relatives, and most commonly, teachers. Probably the major reason parents fail to discipline their child is because they fear her anger and the loss of her love. Rather than face rejection, they ignore unacceptable behavior, give in, or rationalize, "Kids will be kids." But setting consistent limits is one of the major responsibilities of parenting and is not a job that should be ignored or put off.

Many parents doubt their ability: "Am I too strict or too lenient? Do I expect too much?" Parents are embarrassed by their child's misbehavior in public and wonder what they've done wrong or why she seems worse than others. Since a child's behavior is often a reflection on her parents, they feel vulnerable and judged by others when their child acts inappropriately; such feelings are normal. Yet, parents should realize that misbehavior is a basic part of childhood. A child learns what is correct by trying all sorts of behavior, "good" and "bad," until she finds out what is and isn't acceptable.

Parents should base their expectations and methods of disciplining on their child's age and ability to understand. A child under two needs constant watching and reminding, while a four- or five-year-old is developing enough self-control and understanding to have some sense of right and wrong. Methods that work with older children, such as telling a child to spend "time out," or spelling out the consequences of her misbehavior, are ineffective with younger children who do not understand or have trouble remembering the rules.

Children three and younger have such strong developmental needs to explore, touch, and do things for themselves that they have difficulty sticking to limits. Because their immediate needs are so great and because they focus so completely on the here and now, they usually don't realize they're doing something wrong, even if they've been told many times. When reprimanded, children this age often will look surprised and hurt.

In order to set limits, parents (or caregivers) have to stay fairly close by, offer frequent reminders, get involved with the child, and always be aware of what she's doing. When children are not supervised, they lose sight of acceptable and unacceptable behavior. If a child is playing inappropriately, her parents have to be right there, gently but firmly correcting her: "No, you can't play that way—it's too dangerous." If talking doesn't work, parents should remove her from the situation and then involve her in something else. "I'm not going to let you climb over that chair because you might fall, but you can play here on the cushions." Sometimes offering an alternative works because children can be easily distracted by interesting objects and activities. Connecting a restriction to an activity also works because a young child can understand the relationship: "If you want to ride your bike, you have to stay in front of the house," "If you want to play outside, you have to keep your jacket on."

Children three and under often reject limits and say "no," not only because they want to continue their activities, but because they are asserting their independence and learning what they can do. And sometimes parents set limits unnecessarily because they underestimate what a young child can do. A three-year-old who wanted to hold a screwdriver was told, "No, it's too sharp." But when she protested, her father decided to let her try as long as she sat at a table next to him so he could supervise. She was happy, and her father realized that he could relax some of the limitations he'd set.

Usually, though, parents know how they want their child to act. When she misbehaves, parents may feel angry and momentarily withdraw their love and attention. Since a young child wants parental approval, she feels hurt when she's criticized for doing something wrong. She can't separate her action from herself and feels that she's being rejected for who she is, not for what she has done. The removal of parental acceptance often motivates a two- or three-year-old to change her behavior and to run to her parents for a hug after she's been disciplined.

A four- or five-year-old may not react this way. After being disciplined, her hurt feelings and embarrassment might turn to anger and resistance, and she may test her own power and her parents' limits. Yet, she too wants to be loved and accepted, and finds parental approval a strong motivator.

Verbal limit-setting and distraction work with four- and five-year-olds, but since they have a better understanding of consequences than younger children do, they also respond to other methods of disciplining. When a four- or five-year-old becomes angry and aggressive, her parents can try to distract her. If she doesn't calm down, they should firmly say, "Your behavior is unacceptable. If you keep acting this way you'll spend time in your room." If parents have to follow through on this, they can tell their child she can come out of her room as soon as she is in control of herself.

It's better, in such a situation, to let her determine the amount of time she'll spend in her room. When parents set a limit, but not a time limit, the cooling off period lasts only as long as is necessary for her to calm down. If instead parents dictate a waiting period of twenty minutes or half an hour, she may calm down and then forget why she was sent to her room as she involves herself with her toys and books. Even fifteen minutes of isolation is a long time unless the choice to stay away is the child's. The point of taking time out is not to spend time away from the family, but to change unacceptable behavior. However, if the child abuses the right to set her own time-out period or if her behavior remains unchanged, her parents should set a time limit themselves.

Many times, parents punish four- and five-year olds by taking away toys or privileges. This can be most effective when there's a connection between the misbehavior and what's taken away. For instance, if a child uses her bike in a dangerous way, an appropriate consequence would be to have her give up the bike temporarily. A child who continually throws sand would lose the privilege of playing in the sandbox for an afternoon. Before taking something away, parents should warn their child about what will happen if she continues to misbehave. The object or privilege should not be removed for an excessively long time or she'll concentrate only on the unfairness of the situation, not on her misbehavior. The point of this punishment is to help her see a connection between, for instance, abusing the bike and losing the bike. Often the warning that there will be consequences is enough to deter a child from misbehaving again.

However, it's not always possible to find a connection. If a child hits her brother, what should her parents take away? Parents sometimes remove something unrelated, such as a toy, privilege, or dessert. Although it's unwise to make dessert a focus of power, many parents find that their child changes her behavior when threatened with the loss of sweets for a meal. She does this not because she understands her parents' point but because she wants to avoid the punishment.

When taking something away, or using any other form of discipline, parents should be sure the consequences come soon after the misbehavior. This gives the child a chance to connect her actions with their consequences, and it ensures that parents will follow through. Often, when parents tell a child in the morning that she'll be punished in the evening, she knows that they may forget or change their minds.

One mother, eating lunch in a fast food restaurant with her five-year-old, said, "If you keep misbehaving you're going to bed at 7:00 tonight." When the child continued acting up the mother said, "All right. Now you're going to bed at 6:30." The punishment seemed so far away and so drastic to the child that she felt helpless and continued misbehaving. Instead of making a distant threat, the mother could have tried distracting her daughter or telling her she would have to move to the next table, or warning her they'd have to leave the restaurant. Then the child could have made the connection between her behavior and the consequences.

A disciplining method that some parents find successful with three- to five-year-olds is counting: "By the time I count to five, I want you indoors," or, "I'll count to ten while you get ready for your bath." This usually offers a limit, a warning, and a bit of time, although if the technique is overused it becomes ineffective.

An important element of disciplining a child of any age is the tone of voice parents use. When they sound firm and sure of themselves, children often respond well, but when parents are unsure about what limits to impose, their children get mixed messages. The most effective tone is respectful but firm. Parents should begin setting a limit by speaking in a quiet, polite, firm voice. If that doesn't work, they can assert themselves more forcefully and speak in an authoritative voice. But yelling at a child is not as effective as firmly stating a limit (although it's often difficult to keep from yelling). It's sometimes helpful to stand close to a child, quietly repeating a warning or prohibition.

When disciplining a child, parents should always consider their own anger. Sometimes, when bothered by personal problems, parents may overreact to their child's behavior. They should let their four- or five-year-old know when they are in a bad mood and at some point apologize if they've been unreasonably mad. When they feel out of control and unable to deal with their anger, they should spend some time in a separate room away from their child until they calm down.

Parents should not be too forceful and harsh when disciplining their child. If the child always loses, or is always given negative feedback and doesn't feel accepted, what incentive does she have to behave well? Parents who are too hard on their child only encourage her anger and aggression while causing her to feel bad about herself.

It may be helpful for parents to remember their own feelings as children. Were they disciplined harshly? Do they want their child to know the same anger and frustration they once experienced? Parents who felt unfairly disciplined often say they won't treat their child the same way, but in moments of anger, it takes a great deal of patience to deal with misbehavior in appropriate ways.

Remember that children learn not just from your words, but from your actions. If you treat your child with kindness and respect and show that you value her, she'll model her behavior after yours. When children feel good, they usually behave nicely and have an easier time accepting the limits you impose. And when children are treated courteously, they learn what courteous behavior is. It's as important to praise and encourage your child when you're pleased with her as it is to set limits when you're unhappy.

It takes time and patience to help children learn self-discipline. Distinguishing right from wrong is a gradual process, and children these ages don't yet have the necessary reasoning skills. If you have tried everything you can and your child still acts inappropriately at an age when she should have learned a fair amount of control, see if something is disturbing your family relationship. The birth of a baby, a move, family illness, or divorce can cause behavior problems. Perhaps you're spending too much time away from your child. If discipline problems caused by such circumstances persist, consider seeking professional advice on how to help your child.

What should I do about temper tantrums?

"I want this now!" shouts a two-year-old, pulling candy off a grocery shelf.

"Not today," says his mother.

"Yes, I want candy!"

When his mother again refuses, the child responds with a full-fledged temper tantrum: screaming, crying, thrashing, and kicking. Tantrums like this are hard to watch, they are embarrassing, and they can make parents feel helpless.

Why do children have tantrums? At times, the child is simply overtired or hungry. Most often, however, the answers are rooted in developmental characteristics. Children have very little self-control; they live in the here and now and act on their immediate desires. When parents respond to a child's wishes by saying "no," he reacts negatively, sometimes sensing rejection. Young children lack the ability to think logically and follow adult reasoning. A child will probably not understand why his parents deny one of his wishes, even though their explanations may make perfect sense to them. Another reason for temper tantrums, particularly with pre-verbal toddlers, is the young child's inability to express his needs and wants fully. When his parents can't understand him, he becomes easily frustrated.

If you're concerned about temper tantrums, there are a number of approaches you can try, including prevention. Since you know your child's wants, you can guess which situations are likely to cause tantrums and plan ahead for these times. For example, when you anticipate a struggle at the candy counter or when shopping at a mall, carry a few small toys, some juice, or crackers with you. If the situation becomes tense, use these to distract your child. You also can set limits for your three- or four-year-old before you leave the house: "We're only looking today," or, "Remember, I'm only buying you one thing." Try to be sure he understands the limits, but remember it's hard for him to "only look" and not buy.

There's another technique that may prevent a tantrum: compromise. You can tell your child, "I won't buy candy, but I will buy you a pretzel." This and the other prevention methods sometimes work well, but at times he may have a temper tantrum in spite of your efforts. If this happens, you'll have to decide how to respond. Most likely your reaction will vary with the situation, depending on where you are and whom you're with. But your choices will be the same—you can meet your child's demand, distract him, or let him have the tantrum.

You may choose to meet his demand because you realize that it's not so unreasonable after all. Perhaps you were being too rigid when you first rejected his request. Or perhaps you feel that saying "no" is not worth the struggle or tantrum.

If you don't give in to your child, you may try distracting him. Remind him about a recent pleasurable experience, point out something interesting, or talk about something good that will happen soon.

You may be surprised at how effective distraction can be in defusing a conflict.

Finally, you may choose to let the tantrum run its course. Although coping can be hard, if you wait calmly, your child will soon quiet down. Just be sure he's safe during his tantrum and unable to harm himself or others or cause any damage.

Tantrums are difficult for you and your young child. But as he grows older he'll gain more understanding and you'll find it easier to set limits. Once he outgrows that urgent need to have everything *now*, there will be far fewer tantrums to struggle with.

Does spanking really help?

Parents may spank their child in anger or frustration or when they don't know how else to get their point across. Some parents believe that spanking is the only way to teach children to listen and behave well. Yet, spanking is not necessary; there are other, more effective ways to get children to change their behavior.

In our society, spanking is still a widely accepted method of discipline. Although many parents defend spanking by saying, "I was spanked and I turned out OK," or, "It's the only way to get the message across," others feel guilty, defensive, and embarrassed about hitting their children: "I know I shouldn't have spanked him, but..." They often wince when seeing a child spanked in public and wonder, "Is that what I do to my child?" Some parents feel guilty after spanking and want to follow up with a hug or an apology to assure themselves they haven't lost their child's love. Still other parents say that, though they spank, they really don't believe spanking changes their child's negative behavior. Even those parents who strongly believe in the effectiveness of spanking say it usually only temporarily stops inappropriate behavior.

There are problems with spanking. One is that a child will imitate what her parents do. If they hit her in order to change her behavior, why shouldn't she also hit when someone does something she doesn't like? Can they fairly tell her not to hit when they discipline her by spanking?

Spanking can be a particular problem with a child under two and one-half, who often doesn't understand ahead of time that an action is wrong. She may touch a glass vase because she thinks it's beautiful. If she's suddenly spanked, she won't easily see that she has done something inappropriate, but rather will focus on the pain and shock of the spanking. It's very difficult for a child this age to make a connection between her own behavior and a spanking, yet one of the goals of discipline is to have children make those connections.

Spanking a child who is over three or four may actually hinder discipline. Parents hope their child will eventually develop self-discipline and a sense of right and wrong. As she grows older, she should begin to feel bad about her unacceptable behavior, and her gradual emerging sense of guilt should start to keep her from misbehaving as frequently. But when she is spanked for her wrongdoings, she doesn't learn to monitor her own behavior. She may learn instead that as long as she doesn't get caught, she can misbehave. And if she does get caught, any guilt feelings she has will be relieved by the spanking, since she has "paid the consequences." Eventually, she will learn that if she can tolerate the spanking, she no longer has to feel bad about her negative actions or try to alter her behavior. Even when parents explain to the child why they have spanked her and how they want her to change, she may be too angry or humiliated at the time of the spanking to listen and learn.

Discipline works best when parents set firm limits verbally and then follow through by removing their child from the scene of her misbehavior, taking away an object or privilege she's abused, or having her spend time alone until she can change her behavior. When punishment is relevant to the inappropriate behavior—when the child who throws a block has to stop playing with the blocks—she can make the connection between her actions and its consequences. Until children develop self-control, they are motivated best by the desire for parental approval and the fear of losing privileges and toys.

Even a child under two can make a connection when she's given a firm "no" and removed from a dangerous situation. Parents often feel that they must spank their young child to teach her critical safety rules such as not to play in the street. But firm and consistent warnings, frequent reminders, and most importantly, close supervision are effective in keeping children out of danger.

Sometimes parents say, "When I tell my child to stop, she ignores me, but when I spank her, she does what I want." One mother who was browsing in a department store with her three-year-old became angry when he tried to investigate the dressing rooms. She repeatedly warned him not to go near them and then spanked him for not listening. He cried, turned around in circles several times, and looked defeated. The situation is a familiar one, yet the mother had other options that would have left her and her child feeling happier. Since young children have a hard time listening to limits when they have an intense need to explore, the mother could have acknowledged her child's interest and even taken a moment to look into the dressing room with him. This might have made it easier for him to do what she wanted. Or she could have gently but firmly told him there was no time to explore that day. She also could have tried to distract him or to carry him away from the area of the dressing room.

Because children's behavior can be so frustrating, parents sometimes find themselves on the verge of "losing it" and may feel ready to hit or spank their child. At such times, it's important to remember that young children have only a limited ability to integrate rules.

Disciplining children is a complex, gradual task. Your young child needs to be reminded of the limits over and over, and you will have to be patient as she slowly learns self-discipline. If you spank her, she will feel defenseless, humiliated, and angry, and may not understand the connection between what she did and what you are doing to her. It takes a lot of self-control not to spank and to trust that she can still learn appropriate behavior. If, instead of spanking your child, you set firm limits and follow through in relevant ways, she will be able to listen to you without feeling vulnerable and defeated.

Must I always be consistent?

Parents often wonder how important it is to be consistent when setting limits. Should they stick with a rule in order to help their child learn what's expected of him? Does consistency teach the child that he can't always have his way? Will bending the rules harm him or cause parents to lose control?

When parents are consistent, they provide their child with a sense of what is and isn't acceptable behavior. And in some areas, such as vital safety rules, consistency is essential. Yet, if parents tried to unfailingly enforce every rule they set, they'd spend all of their time saying, "No, don't do that," and, "No, you can't have that." Virtually every parent makes exceptions to the rules, depending on circumstance and personality. Some parents are quite flexible, others generally inflexible. Yet, they all find themselves at some point saying, "No, not today," then changing that to, "Maybe," and finally saying, "OK."

One father took his daughter to a convenience store. The girl said, "I want a Coke," but her father replied, "I'm only going in this store for milk and eggs." The girl said, "But I want one Coke for me." The father said, "I'm not buying you a Coke, but I'll give you a drink when we get home." Minutes later the father and daughter walked out of the store. The father held his bag of eggs and milk and his daughter walked out with a Coke—with a straw in it.

Parents often fear that when they give in, their child will expect the same response the next time a similar situation arises. But as long as parents are generally firm about discipline, they can make exceptions and still stay in control. When they show some flexibility, they let their child know that his desires are important, and that life is not too rigid. He learns that sometimes people get what they want, and sometimes they don't, and he learns what compromise feels like. And he has the experience of occasionally winning a struggle with his parents.

You probably find that time, place, and mood influence your decision to stick to a rule or give in. Sometimes you feel tolerant, and other times you're impatient and tired. In public, you don't want to be embarrassed by your child's behavior. You may be especially likely to give in when you need to distract him because you're working or you are on the phone.

One mother would not generally let her son mix spices and water together in a bowl as he had done with great enjoyment at a friend's house. But he learned a way around the prohibition. Whenever his mother took a business call, he would start getting spices off the shelf, usually with his mother's reluctant help. She needed to keep him quiet when she was on the phone, and gave in.

If you're concerned about consistency, consider your overall relationship with your child. If you generally give the message that he is loved, cared for, and accepted, and that you have basic, firm expectations about how he should behave, you don't have to worry about incidental exceptions you make. Being reasonably consistent is good enough. After all, you can't enforce a set of rules at all times. Flexibility is an important part of life, and give and take is an important part of parenting.

Can too much praise backfire?

To many people, praise seems like a wonderful tool to use with children. Praise helps them feel good about themselves and motivates them to do what pleases their parents. Yet too much praise, even when delivered with the best of intentions, can have a negative impact.

A young child has strong inner drives to accomplish things for herself and to succeed at many tasks. She's excited about learning, motivated to try new things, and eager to imitate adults. Parents can tell how proud their child is when she says, "Look, I got my shirt on by myself," or, "I know how to count to ten." Her reward for these achievements is her own sense of accomplishment.

When parents offer moderate praise for these achievements and reflect their child's own excitement ("I can see how happy you are.") the child knows that her parents are pleased. But when parents offer excessive praise ("Great job!" "I'm so proud of you!"), especially for everyday aspects of life such as toilet use or eating, the child may begin to expect such praise for everything she does. Eventually she may try to achieve not for internal satisfaction, but for the reward of praise, and her feelings of accomplishment may become of secondary importance. She may think, "I'll tie my shoe because Mom will think it's great."

A child who is praised for every achievement may begin to distrust the praise and her own abilities. Is everything she does really that good? Or is anything she does really good at all? She may become dependent on praise and may not believe she has done something worthwhile unless she hears lavish compliments. Excessive praise can put pressure on her, too. When she's praised so heavily for doing well, she may feel she has to continue achieving or she will lose the praise and attention. Many parents will understand these negative effects if they consider how dependent they, as adults, are on external praise and rewards.

It is fine to praise your child, and you certainly want to let her know that you feel good about her. But give praise in moderation and try to encourage her to feel good about her own abilities. Focus on her desire to do things for herself, and praise her by speaking more about her feelings than your own: "You really felt good about climbing that jungle gym, didn't you?" By responding that way, you recognize her pride in her success. You also can praise her effectively in nonverbal ways. A hug, a smile, a look of approval all communicate your good feelings about her.

Should I say, "You're a big boy now"?

Parents often can be heard telling their young child to act more mature: "You're a big boy now, so you should use the toilet," or, "You're too big to make such a mess." Parents use "big boy" as a discipline tool and as a way to change their child's behavior, either by appealing to his desire to do what older children do or by shaming him with a comparison to younger children.

The problem with urging him to be a "big boy" is that the child, who already wants to act older and more capable, feels pressure from his parents to change and do things he may not be able to do. When he can't act like a "big boy," he may feel bad about parts of himself that he usually can't control and about not being able to please his parents. In a public restroom, a mother changed her son's diaper while telling him, "You're a big boy now. You're too old for diapers." He looked ashamed. Yet, if he had been ready to use the toilet, he would have given up diapers on his own. Exhortations to be "bigger" won't help him—they'll only make him feel bad about himself.

In a similar situation, a woman took her grandson to a toy store and asked him to pick something out. When he chose a stuffed animals, she said, "Oh, no. Not that. You're too big to want that." When adults say such things, they tell a child that his feelings and desires are unacceptable, and that he should be acting differently.

If you think your child is not as "big" as he should be, try to understand why. He might use baby talk or play with a younger child's toys because of a new sibling or the start of nursery school. And since each child develops at his own pace, your child may just not be ready for the behavior changes you'd like to see. By temperament, he may be a child who cries more than other children or who needs more closeness and security. Also, children struggle as they grow, and for every step forward, there's usually a short step backward to earlier behavior.

All children have a strong drive to be independent and imitate older people. If you accept your child as he is and wait patiently without pressuring him, you will see him begin to act "bigger" on his own.

Why does my child bite?

During infancy, children find satisfaction in sucking and biting. Until about eighteen months of age, they bite and chew on toys, household objects, and other things they find in their explorations.

Sometimes a baby will bite other people, especially when her gums are sore from teething. Although such a bite can be painful, parents should remember that she is not intentionally trying to hurt. Occasionally, a very young child may bite her mother during nursing. Mothers may be so alarmed at this that they wonder if they should start weaning, but such a drastic step isn't necessary. If the mother takes the breast away from her biting child and says "no" firmly, the child will learn quickly.

An infant's innocent biting is very different from the deliberate, frustrated biting of a two-year-old. Sometimes a toddler's anger cannot be expressed through words, and she impulsively bites. Parents of toddlers who bite don't often feel understanding and accepting about the problem—and rightly so. When a child bites, parents should set firm limits, saying, "I don't want you biting anyone," "I know you're really angry, but you can't bite," "You'll have to find another way to let me know you're angry," or simply, "I won't let you bite." Letting her know immediately and firmly that biting is unacceptable is important.

If talking doesn't solve the problem, parents of a biting toddler or preschooler should move off a distance from their child, letting her know with a quiet but firm tone that they're angry with her and don't want to be near her when she bites. Parents also can sit her on a step or in her room for a short while. Since children often change their behavior in order to please their parents, some children will stop biting so they can feel accepted again.

Occasionally you may be tempted to cure your child's biting habit by biting her back to "show her what it feels like." But biting a child back is wrong. First, you give a mixed message: you tell her not to bite, but then do it yourself. Second, she can't put herself in another person's place and doesn't understand that the pain she feels from a bite is the same pain that she inflicts. You can teach appropriate behavior best by setting limits, being a good model for your child, and reminding her how to act in socially acceptable ways.

If she continually bites, she's probably troubled by something deeper than momentary frustration. In such a case, admonitions and firm limits usually won't work. Since biting is a sign of anger, frustration, and aggression, try to discover the cause of her behavior. Perhaps there is stress in the family or not enough attention for her at home. If you can't find the cause of continued biting, seek advice from your pediatrician or mental health professional who can explore possible areas of tension in the family.

Is it OK to bribe children?

"If you...then you can..." It's a familiar pattern heard when parents try to persuade their child to do something: "If you come with me now, we'll stop at the park." "If you put your toys away, you can stay up fifteen minutes later tonight." There are always family struggles about the routines and necessities of life: bedtime, bathtime, shopping, leaving a friend's house, getting dressed, getting ready for school or day care. When logic fails (as it will) and a young child refuses to do what his parents wish, they often resort to bribing.

In theory, most parents are opposed to bribes. They want their children to cooperate and learn to tolerate frustration, and they don't want their children to expect rewards for good behavior. But it takes years for a child to learn self-control and to understand that certain things have to be done, even when people don't want to do them. Until he can motivate himself to do necessary tasks, bribery has its uses, and parents will find that an occasional bribe is a strong motivator. But they should be careful not to overuse bribes, or children will look for constant rewards.

One mother could not get her son to leave his friend's house, even though it was time for dinner. Finally she said, "If you come home now, you can paint with watercolors after dinner." After hearing this, the boy agreed to leave. Another mother wanted to have her child come and play indoors, but he resisted. However, when she said, "Let's go in and I'll play a game with you, and then we'll have a cookie," the child came in. Incentives such as these can distract or redirect a child, and often eliminate struggles.

Bribes also can be used to avoid embarrassment. When parents are out in public, they may offer a bribe rather than face a tantrum. When parents go shopping with their child, they may give him a cookie or toy to gain his cooperation and make the shopping trip go smoothly.

You may be worried that once you offer a bribe in a situation your child will expect one whenever a similar situation comes up. But this is rarely a problem, since children can accept compromise and a degree of inconsistency. If you bribed your child to go grocery shopping with you last week, but don't want to offer a bribe this week, let him know ahead of time: "Last time I bought you gum, but today I'm not buying a treat." When you get to the store, remind him of your warning, if necessary, and try to distract him: "I like to bring you to the store so you can help pick out food for dinner." If you're firm and allow occasional rewards and compromises, he usually will cooperate.

Sometimes, a way to eliminate the need for frequent bribes is to give your child plenty of warning when you want him to switch activities or go along with you cooperatively. If he's engrossed in play, tell him, "We need to go to the post office this afternoon." Then remind him ten minutes before you're ready to leave so he can bring his game to a pleasant, slow close. That way, he won't have to abruptly stop what he's doing in order to do what you want. And the chances are good that he'll come along peacefully, without needing a bribe.

Should I make my child clean up?

Trying to clean up after young children is an endless task. They pull toys out of closets, drawers, and shelves, and when they're done playing with one thing, they drop it on the floor and get out something new. They also take pots and pans out of cabinets, unroll toilet paper, and leave clothes and shoes lying around. In just a short time, a young child can create a mess.

Some of this can be explained. Young children's interests shift quickly from one object to another, so even a brief play period may result in a big pile of toys. And because they like to play wherever their parents are, they carry (and leave) toys all over the house. Taking toys out is fun, but picking them up is not.

That job usually is left for parents, and the daily process of putting things away can be both demanding and unrewarding. Many parents want or expect help from their children, but until children reach early elementary age, parents get little relief. That's because young children don't think about cleaning up in the same way that adults do. Children are truly unaware of the tasks they leave for their parents.

All parents must decide whether to constantly clean up after their children or let the cleaning go at times so the family can accomplish other things. Of course some adults care more about neatness than others. And some parents fear letting things get too messy because of unexpected visitors or the prospect of large-scale cleanups. Parents who work outside the home may feel a particular desire for a neat house because their cleanup time is so limited.

Although everyone would like help in maintaining a clean home, parents who pressure their young children to clean up actually may stifle the exploration and play that are a necessary part of childhood. For example, a child who always is expected to put her blocks away eventually may lose interest in using the blocks or may decide it's easier to simply watch TV. Also, those parents who feel compelled to establish early patterns of cleaning up may find the process frustrating and time-consuming. They usually have to stand over their young children and coach them through the entire chore. The effort expended in such supervising is often greater than the effort of cleaning up without the help.

Although straightening up after young children remains an adult task, there are ways you can involve your child. Your two and one-half- or three-year-old can put a few toys back in place, particularly if you do the job with her or if you hand her the toys and tell her where they go. Your four- or five-year-old can take a more active role in straightening up, although she will still be most successful when you're close by helping.

Your child may be willing to cooperate in cleanups if you give her some warning: "In five minutes it will be time to put the toys away." If your child seems overwhelmed, help her focus by giving specific instructions: "Jesse, you're in charge of putting the puzzles and books away." Sometimes she will go along with you if you offer concrete choices: "You can either put the trucks back on the shelf or put the toy soldiers in this basket." And when several children are playing together you can ask, "Who's going to put the crayons away? Who will clean up the train set?"

If your child spends time in day care, strike a balance between your child's desire to play freely when she's home and your desire to keep cleanup to a minimum. Most evenings let her play with her toys, and some evenings structure her play so she takes out only a few things such as dolls or a game to use in a specific place.

If your children resist putting their toys away, there are many other household jobs they may actually enjoy doing. These include dusting, washing windows, vacuuming, putting utensils away, or polishing silver. As they get older, they will take on more responsibility for putting their things away. In the meantime, your young children may occasionally surprise you with an unexpected cleanup, done just to help you out and make you happy.

CHILDREN'S THINKING

What does my child think about nature?

A young child's thoughts about the world are not based on logic and fact. When a child under five is asked about the sun, he may explain that a man lit a match and threw it up in the sky, and that's how the sun got there. Young children often believe that humans created the oceans, trees, space, mountains, and other natural phenomena. A child will ask, "Why did they make that mountain so high? Why did they put Switzerland so far away?" After a snowstorm, one child said, "I guess the people ran out of snowflakes."

Young children assume that inanimate objects have the same motives, intentions, and feelings a child has. One boy looked in his bucket after a downpour and said, "Guess what the rain did. It gave me water. Wasn't that nice?" Another child, trying his bike for the first time in several months, declared, "Look, my bike got smaller!" Sometimes a child will blame an object for a mishap: "That chair bumped into me!" And when a child misses a ball during a game of catch, he may not feel bad about his own abilities: "That ball started flying crooked."

To a young child, many objects are alive—a pencil because it writes, a cloud because it moves. Picture books and fairy tales entrance him because they mirror his world by presenting talking objects and animals and trees that walk and sing.

To find out what your child thinks about nature and the objects around him, listen to his explanations of events and ask, "How do you think the stars got there? Why do you think worms crawl?" When he asks you a question, ask for his thoughts before you answer. You'll be delighted with his responses and fascinated by the insights you get into his thinking. Keep asking and noticing the changing answers he gives as he grows older.

You may be tempted to correct him when he gives you answers that are clearly not factual. Sometimes it's best to just accept what he says, although at other times you'll want to offer as much information as you think he can understand. But don't be surprised if he listens and then sticks to his own thoughts and beliefs. This is natural behavior for children under five or six years old, who generally prefer their own ideas about the world.

My child asks questions and talks all the time. Is this normal?

Young children are natural learners and great observers of the here and now. They constantly try to gather information about what goes on around them, and that means they ask many questions and talk a lot: "Who's that?" "Why is she doing that?" "Where is that truck going?" Since a child believes that adults know everything, she assumes that her parents will have the answer to each question. She also assumes that everything has a purpose that can be discovered just by asking: "Why is that man so tall?"

Sometimes she uses questions to relieve her anxieties. She may ask, "Why is that dog barking?" because she's afraid of the animal. At other times, she might ask a stream of questions or talk on and on just to be sociable and stay in constant contact with her parents.

Many times, as soon as parents have answered their child's question, she asks the same question again, or follows their explanation with an immediate, "Why?" This can be annoying because parents feel they're constantly replying to their child. At times it's hard to know what she wants, since she's often not satisfied by the explanations she receives. If parents question her before they offer a complex answer, they may gain some insight into her real needs: "What do you think that word means?" "Tell me why you think that man was running?"

Sometimes she repeatedly asks "why" and rejects an answer because she doesn't understand it. She may have difficulty absorbing facts that aren't familiar or that don't relate directly to her experience. That's why parents should answer questions on a level that's appropriate for their child. And they should expect to hear the same questions over and over because it takes time and repetition before she masters complex information.

A child may occasionally ask a question that's difficult to answer. One four-year-old from a family with three children asked her friend's mother, "Why do you only have two kids?" The mother, concerned that the child might be upset by an honest answer (two was all she wanted), put the question back to the child, "Why do you think I only have two children?" She replied, "Because you wanted to," and was satisfied.

A problem often arises when young children ask socially embarrassing questions. You may be in a store with your child when she points to someone and loudly asks, "Why is he so fat?" She has no understanding of the man's feelings and asks only because she's spontaneous and curious. Yet, you'll naturally feel ashamed and sorry. The best you can do at such moments is give her a brief, quiet answer ("That's just the way he looks."), and then try to distract her or promise to discuss the situation later in private.

When your child's constant questions and general chatter bother you, remember that you don't have to be ready to respond at all times. You can acknowledge her talk by nodding or saying, "I'm listening," or even, "Um hmm." She will know you're aware of her words and, often, that will be enough to make her happy.

Does my child know what's real and what's not?

Young children often believe that whatever they hear and see is real. Until a child is between five and seven years old, his experience is limited and his ability to reason is not fully developed; therefore he can't truly be logical. It may not make sense to an adult, but to a young child, clowns are real, everything on TV is true, everything other children say is true, and a disguise changes a person. The young child's inability to distinguish make-believe from reality explains his fear of monsters, masks, and costumed figures.

When a young child watches television, he thinks he's watching real life. One four-year-old saw a Superman program followed by a televised demonstration intended to prove that Superman really didn't fly. A man lay down on a table and showed how camera tricks simulate flying. After the demonstration, the child's mother asked if he still thought Superman could fly. "Yes," he answered, "but that man on the table couldn't."

It's very difficult to convince a child that television doesn't always represent the truth. The toys in commercials look magical and exciting as they talk and move around on their own. It takes years for a child to develop some skepticism about these advertisements. One young boy insisted that sugared cereal was good for him because television had told him so. His mother explained the purpose of commercials, but he still believed what he'd heard. Although parents usually can't change their young child's thinking, they can let him know their own opinions: "The cereal on TV looks good, but I think it's too sweet for breakfast." "TV makes it seem like Superman's flying, but he really isn't."

Just as a child believes what he hears on television, he also believes what other people, including other young children, say. If his friend says, "There are bugs under your rug," or, "The moon is a dead planet," or, in a moment of anger, "You're not coming to my party," the listener accepts the statement as truth without questioning the other child's knowledge or motives.

Words are taken literally and have tremendous power. That's why a young child gets so upset when he's called "a dummy"; he feels he must shout back, "No, I'm not," or gets someone else to reassure him. Children, especially those under three, usually can't separate names from objects and people. A mother told her son that he was handsome and he said, "No, I'm not. I'm Jimmy." It takes time for children to realize that names are not parts of things but are separate and often changeable.

They can be confused not just by what they hear and see, but by what they imagine and dream. They aren't sure what dreams are or where they come from: do they come from the sky? the bed? the toys the child sleeps with? through the window? Frightening dreams seem very real and vivid dreams seem part of real life. One child, who had dreamed that an airplane landed in the park behind his house, woke up believing the plane was really there. When his father tried to convince him otherwise, he refused to listen. The father finally took his son to the park to show that there was no plane.

You can find out what your child thinks by questioning him, listening to him, and observing him. You will find that his thinking is different from that of adults and that he believes many things that aren't true. As long as he bases his thinking on appearances and his own experience, you may not be able to change his mind on many issues, but as he nears elementary school age, his logical understanding of the world will increase.

Why isn't my child more reasonable?

A father handed his daughter and her friend cups containing equal amounts of raisins. The daughter looked at both cups and said, "Alison has more. I want more."

"But I gave you each the same amount," her father protested. The girl refused to accept the facts and continued to argue for more raisins.

Struggles often develop over such issues for children less than five years old. They base their reasoning on how things look, not necessarily on how things really are. If something appears right to a child, she'll accept it, even if her acceptance defied logic. One child wanted a whole cup of juice, but her mother only had half a cup left. The child fussed and refused the drink until her mother poured it into a tiny cup. The small amount of juice filled the little cup and the child was happy, even though she still had the same amount of juice she had just refused as inadequate.

Parents can become frustrated when their children don't think logically. A parent can count out jellybeans to prove that all the children at a party have the same number, but the children often will not believe the shares are equal unless they "look" equal. A spread out pile may seem bigger than a compact one; a tall, thin container may appear to hold more than a short, wide one. Parents can demonstrate this prelogical thinking with a simple experiment. They can line up pennies in two identical rows, then spread one of the rows out. A child under six or seven will say that the wider row now has more pennies in it, even though she saw that no new pennies were added.

It's difficult, if not impossible, to change a young child's reasoning before she's developmentally ready to think logically. Once you realize that your child thinks differently than you do, you can understand why she so often rejects what seems perfectly reasonable. By the time she's five or six, you will see dramatic changes in her thinking and reasoning abilities. Until then, you might have to accommodate her at times, rather than struggle to change her mind. A father whose child wanted more ketchup on her plate, even though she clearly had an adequate amount, simply spread the ketchup out so it looked like a larger amount. He avoided an argument, and she was completely satisfied.

Why doesn't my child think about other people's feelings?

A three and one-half-year-old interrupted his mother's phone call. "Can I go outside?" She motioned for him to wait a minute, but he persisted. "Mom, Josh is outside. Can I ride my bike?" When she whispered for him to be quiet until she was off the phone, he walked away, but was back almost immediately. "Now can I go?" After hanging up, she felt frustrated with the interruptions and wondered why her son couldn't be more considerate and patient.

Children under the age of five or six have a difficult time thinking of other people's feelings. Young children, as researcher Jean Piaget pointed out, are egocentric; they focus on their own immediate needs and interests, and consider only one side of any situation—their own. They don't do this to be selfish, although that's often the result. They are generally incapable, during their early years, of putting themselves in another person's place or imagining how other people think. Egocentrism is a normal, although difficult, part of child development.

Parents see egocentric thinking and behavior when children play. One child will grab another's toy, others will hit and call each other names, two children will discuss the faults of a third who stands next to them. When young children play board games, they often cheat, not caring about their opponent's chances. A child who drew an unfavorable card while playing a game said, "I'm just not listening to this card."

Parents try to change their children's actions and teach their children to stick to rules. "Don't hit, you'll hurt him," "He was using that," "You should include her in your game." Yet children have limited control over their thinking and often forget to (or just can't) consider others.

Frequent struggles over a child's self-centered ways can be very frustrating for parents. They may wonder if he is particularly unpleasant or if he acts selfish to "get at" them, and they may also wonder if they've set firm enough limits: "Do other children act this way?" When, for instance, a child doesn't let his mother rest ("Mom, look at my picture!") even when she's not feeling well, she may wonder if her child has any considerate feelings at all.

Although at times your child may act egocentric because you have not set sufficient limits, more often he'll behave this way because he's not yet able to consider other people's needs. Your expectations for his behavior should take into account this stage of development. If you always expect him to be polite and considerate, you and he will find yourselves in constant conflict.

It's very important that you establish limits for your child and try to teach him appropriate behavior. But you should also try to be flexible and patient as he grows through this stage and gradually learns to think about others' feelings and points of view. Of course, it's unrealistic to think you can always be understanding. You often may become angry at his thoughtless behavior, but understanding that this is a part of normal development is helpful. One mother became particularly upset and embarrassed as she heard her daughter tell a boy who could not come to her birthday party, "Oh, goody. Now we'll have enough chairs." Expect to hear such statements, but also be assured that eventually your child will learn to be more considerate.

I want to tell my child about pregnancy and birth. What should I say?

"Mom, how did the baby get in your stomach?" "How did I get born?" "Am I going to have a baby, too?" Parents are sometimes caught by surprise as their three- to five-year-old begins asking questions about sex and childbirth. They wonder how much to tell their child, and when to tell her. Some books and specialists advise parents to give young children all the facts about sex and reproduction, but children often are unable to absorb and comprehend such information. Learning about and understanding reproduction is a gradual process that continues through the childhood years.

Young children usually have their own ideas about how the human body works, based on their observations and experience. Before parents talk to their child about pregnancy, they should ask what she thinks so they know where to start the discussion: "How do you think the baby got inside of me?" Many children believe that eating too much causes pregnancy and that a woman gives birth in the same way she has a bowel movement. A child who's heard that a baby starts from a special seed might think that pregnancy comes from eating seeds. Parents may discover that their child is afraid of pregnancy, since children often fear things they don't understand and things they imagine. By asking questions, parents find out about such thoughts and discover how to reassure her.

Before you offer your three- to five-year-old the facts about pregnancy and birth, wait for her to ask questions. There's no need to volunteer information if she's not yet curious about the subject. And when she does ask, don't overwhelm her with information. Start with simple explanations: "The baby grows in a special place inside the mother." Such a statement may satisfy her only for a few minutes or for six months. Wait for her to ask for more before you continue your discussion; don't feel that you have to tell all the facts at one time.

If you do explain too much too soon, she may become confused or upset. One five-year-old girl, after hearing the details of childbirth, declared, "I'm never going to have a baby." A three and one-half-year-old, who had been enrolled in a sibling childbirth class where he heard all the facts about birth, still believed that "Mom's stomach unzips so the baby can get out." Both these children were too young to handle the information. If your child seems curious about pregnancy and birth, explain the facts in simple terms that you think she can understand. You will satisfy her curiosity without overwhelming her. Then, when she's older, she'll have an easier time understanding, cognitively and emotionally, the facts of pregnancy.

FEARS AND IMAGINATION

Out of sight, out of mind—does every baby think this way?

Until a child is nine months old, he believes that objects and people exist only if he can see them. At six months, if you take a toy away from your child and hide it behind your back as he watches, he'll act as though there no longer is a toy. In the same way, when you leave his side to go into another room, he may believe you no longer exist. Your disappearance frightens him, which explains the anxiety and tears you see.

When you play peek-a-boo with your baby, you reenact the anxiety and relief he feels each time you leave and return. You hide behind your hands or a blanket and he believes you are no longer there. He may even become momentarily upset and whimper. When you suddenly reappear and say peek-a-boo, he laughs with delight to have you back.

By nine or ten months, a child begins to have some idea that objects exist even when he can't see them. At this age, he may look for a hidden toy if he saw you put it behind your back or under a pillow. But at times he may still react with fear and uncertainty when you leave him because his understanding of people's permanence is not fully developed and won't be until he's two or two and one-half years old.

When will my child no longer be afraid to have a haircut?

It's hard to give a haircut to children under two because they wriggle around so much, and it's hard to cut the hair of children over two because they're often afraid of haircuts, and struggle and resist. Two-and three-year-olds have a general fear of bodily harm and often believe that haircuts hurt, that their hair won't grow back, that shampoo will get in their eyes and sting, and that they will be helpless sitting in front of a stranger with scissors.

You should talk to your child about getting a haircut, and reassure her. She may feel less anxious if she has a doll to play beauty shop with. As she washes and cuts (or pretends to cut) the doll's hair, she may begin to feel in control of a situation that frightens her.

If your child is very young or quite frightened of haircuts, you may want to cut her hair at home. You or a relative or close friend can do this as she sits in her high chair and plays with some of her toys or watches you in a mirror. Since it's hard for young children to hold still, and since you may not be an experienced stylist, you shouldn't expect your child's home haircut to be perfect.

When your child is three or four, you may want to take her to a professional stylist. For a first haircut, go to someone recommended by other parents or someone who specializes in cutting children's hair. Before you bring her in for an appointment, you might want to observe the stylist and talk to him or her about your child's anxiety.

Your child might feel comfortable going to the same barber shop or hair salon you use. She may have seen your stylist at work already and be familiar with the surroundings and the people in the shop. Taking her with you when you (or your older child) get a haircut is a good way to help her get over her fears. If she resists professional haircuts but you're determined to take her to a stylist, try to distract her with an interesting object or by promising her a treat. One mother held her son on her lap during haircuts when he was under two, and when he was over two, she tried to distract him with a few play things.

When your child is five she may develop clear opinions about hairstyles. She may prefer a particular look: long hair, short hair, bangs, a ponytail. One boy told his mother he wanted a curl on his forehead "just like Superman's." If you don't agree with your child's choice, the two of you may struggle before each haircut. Try to remember your own childhood arguments about hair, and how it felt to have no control over your looks. If you let your child have some say in how she wears her hair, trips to the stylist usually will go smoothly.

Should I prepare my child for doctor appointments?

Many children have negative feelings—based on past experience and fearful imaginings—about seeing a doctor. If your child is afraid of doctors, you might be tempted to keep an appointment from him; you may even consider starting out for the office without letting him know where you both are going. Although this may seem like a good way to keep him from getting upset, deceiving him is a mistake. You deprive him of time to prepare for the visit, and you may increase his fear. He might believe that you didn't tell him about the appointment because there was something to be afraid of. It's always better to let your child know in advance about an office visit.

If your child is under two years old, you may have a difficult time preparing him for the appointment. A child this young, who won't fully understand the reasons for his visit, may enter the doctor's office calmly and then cry or feel anxious when he goes into the examining room. Many parts of a standard check-up are uncomfortable: the child gags as his throat is checked, he feels momentary pain during blood tests and inoculations, he's measured and tested with cold instruments. No matter how well-mannered the physician is, the examination can be an unpleasant and therefore fearful experience.

During an examination, you can offer comfort and reassurance to your child: "I'm right here beside you," "I know you don't like to have your ears checked," "The doctor's almost done." But such words won't usually relieve the child's anxiety, especially when, as sometimes happens, you're physically restraining him so the doctor can continue the examination. Sometimes a child in this situation will feel comforted if his toy or blanket is nearby.

You'll be more successful preparing your child if he's between three and five years old. He'll be better able to understand what happens during an exam and to verbalize some of his anxieties. Talk ahead of time about the appointment. Tell him briefly about the procedures, the instruments the doctor will use, the toys in the waiting room, and the set-up of the examining rooms, but try to present this information in a way that won't frighten him: "Do you remember the table in the examining room? I can read you a story while you sit up there and wait for the doctor." "There are cups in the examining room so you can get a drink of water." If an injection is scheduled, say, "Your shot might hurt, but only for a moment."

When your child expresses his fears, accept them; don't pressure him to "be brave" or "be good." When he knows that he can say "ouch" or cry, he may feel less upset about getting an injection or having his ears and throat checked.

He may tell you he doesn't want to take his clothes off in the doctor's office. This is a common worry for children four to five years old. Let him know he may have to undress, but talk to your doctor about the situation. Many pediatricians will accommodate a modest child by weighing or examining him while he's partly clothed.

Your child may relieve some of his own anxiety about appointments by playing doctor. When he takes the role of doctor, he's in control as he re-experiences some of the uncomfortable and frightening things that have happened to him. Children usually play doctor by giving pretend injections and using bandages, but occasionally they undress and examine each other. This is a common, innocent occurrence, and you should try not to make your child feel ashamed for playing this way. Just gently set limits about keeping clothes on.

No matter how well you prepare your child, he may remain anxious and afraid. Some children are just more worried than others about appointments and doctors. As long as he is fearful, the best you can do is accept his feelings, give him honest information about what to expect, and offer him reassurance.

What should I tell my child about the dentist?

Because the mouth is a source of pleasure for a young child, when he feels discomfort or pain in his mouth (from teething, sore gums, etc.) the experience can seem intolerable. And he may strongly resist a visit to the dentist, even though he will only feel mildly uncomfortable there.

Most children first go for a dental check-up when they are three or three and one-half years old. A younger child will go if he has a problem with his teeth or gums. Although a child under three probably will not understand what a dental visit is about, his parents should still try to prepare him by describing, in a simple way, the dentist's procedures:

"He's going to look inside your mouth and check your teeth." At the office, a very young child might cooperate if he's examined while sitting on his parent's lap. If this isn't possible, his parents should at least stay nearby to offer reassurance.

A child who's three or older is usually able to cooperate and follow directions well enough to be examined by a dentist. When he is going for his first check-up, tell him what to expect. Try acting out a visit to the office if you think your child is fearful. You can read him picture books on the subject or call the office before the appointment and ask how to help your child feel less anxious.

Despite your preparations, your child may still enter the dentist's office feeling scared, and what he sees and hears there may make him feel worse. The sound of the drill can be frightening, and the dentist's instruments look sharp. When your child is sitting in the chair, he can feel vulnerable and afraid since he doesn't have control over what goes into his mouth. Encourage him to express his feelings and ask the dentist questions: "Will that hurt me? When will you be done?" If you've chosen a pediodontist or dentist who's sensitive and likes children, he or she will reassure your child and explain the procedures in advance, and perhaps providing a mirror so your child can watch. You or the dentist might be able to distract your child by talking about the "treasure" he'll take home after the appointment.

It sometimes happens that parents are more afraid of dental examinations than their children are. If you're apprehensive about dentists, try not to pass your anxieties on to your child.

Why does my child have an imaginary friend?

Many parents worry when their children, usually between the ages of three and five, create imaginary friends. Parents wonder, "Why does he need one? Can't he tell the difference between a real person and a pretend one?" And while they are sometimes amused by their child's concerns ("Watch out! You'll sit on Herman!"), they're more often frustrated.

Yet, an imaginary friend is an important and creative part of growing up for many children. The friend helps a child deal with emotions and problems that he might otherwise not be able to handle. For example, he might invent a companion as a way of relieving loneliness when he moves to a new home, leaving his real friends behind. Or the imaginary friend might help him deal with a new baby in the family, the start of day care or nursery school, or tension at home. Sometimes he creates an imaginary animal, such as a dog, to help overcome a fear of real dogs or because he wishes to have a dog.

If a child feels overly controlled or unaccepted by his parents, he may invent a companion who's very accepting and who always likes him. He may even become a demanding "parent" to his friend, whom he imagines to be a powerless child: "Herman, that was very bad. You shouldn't have done that."

Sometimes a child will use an imaginary companion to relieve himself of guilt. Since a child who's done something wrong fears discipline and the loss of his parents' love, he may deny his misbehavior even when he's been caught. If he greatly fears rejection, he may blame his imaginary friend for his own misdeeds. That way he will not have to deal with criticism, responsibility, or bad feelings about himself: "Herman took the papers off your desk," or, "Herman made me do it." In such a situation, parents can say, "I can't allow you or Herman to play with my papers," or, "You messed up the papers on my desk and I want you to help me clean them up."

If your child has an imaginary friend, you may wonder what to do about it. Should you set an extra place at the table, as your child requests, or will your acceptance of the companion just prolong the fantasy? Compromise is the best solution. It's certainly all right to go along with some of your child's requests for his imaginary friend. And as long as you are patient with your child, it's also all right to set limits: "You may talk about your friend, but we're not going to change our routine for him right now." If you're worried because your child believes in an imaginary character, keep in mind that we encourage children to believe in the Tooth Fairy, Santa Claus, and other pretend characters. The main difference between these and your child's friend is that the friend is your child's own creation.

If you think your child is involved in fantasy because he feels powerless, consider the amount of freedom you allow him. You may want to give him more opportunities to express his feelings and to explore. And if your child seems lonely because of a recent move or the lack of nearby playmates, help him to find real friends who can eventually take the place of the imaginary one.

As your child grows, he will give up his pretend companion, gradually taking on the qualities and responsibilities he assigned to his friend. In time, he and you will look back on this short phase as simply an interesting part of growing up.

Why is Halloween difficult for my child?

Young children regard Halloween with a mixture of excitement and uneasiness. On one hand, the holiday means candy, dressing up, and a full day of fun with friends, but on the other hand, it means strange sights, frightening sounds, and darkness. The ambivalence that children feel about the two sides of Halloween carries over to most aspects of the holiday, including anticipation, picking out costumes, and trick-or-treating. And parents have ambivalent feelings too about the issues of safety and eating sweets.

Before Halloween begins, some parents find that their child's behavior changes. She may become more silly or aggressive or may whine more than usual, asking again and again, "When's Halloween?" Much of the difficulty before the holiday centers around her desire to wear her costume. If she's allowed to dress up in it before Halloween, she may have an easier time waiting for the enjoyable as well as the scary activities to begin. She also may feel less anxious if she can mark off the remaining days on a calendar or tear one piece off a paper chain for each day left before October 31.

Some parents, as part of the pre-Halloween excitement, buy holiday books. Yet these books often have pictures and ideas that can frighten young children who believe that what they see in a book is real. If a Halloween story is too frightening, parents can change the words as they read, or try creating their own family picture books.

The most exciting part of Halloween is usually picking out and wearing a costume. Children enjoy dressing up because they can experiment with fantasy and try out different roles: they can be television characters, superheroes, or grown-up workers. Children often change their minds about which costume to wear and sometimes argue with their parents about costume choices. In most cases, parents should let their child choose her own disguise.

Some children are afraid of costumes, especially ones designed to be frightening. Since young children don't fully understand the difference between reality and make-believe, they are not convinced that a scary ghost or a monster is only pretend. Even when they know the person under the disguise, they may respond to the costume with fear.

Because of their fears, some children don't want to dress up. This can make parents feel uneasy as they wonder why she doesn't like Halloween. Parents in this situation should try to remember that all children are different—ones with older siblings may feel more comfortable in costumes, and outgoing children may enjoy dressing up more than reserved ones do. The age of a child makes a big difference, and older children, who are better able to understand that a real person is behind each mask, enjoy holiday costumes more.

If your child is afraid of costumes, reassure her. You can say, "Costumes look scary, but they're only pretend. People pretend to be ghosts just like you pretend you're a fire fighter." Sometimes such statements work, but often they don't. If your child is afraid, and you've tried unsuccessfully to lessen her worries, don't pressure her. She'll grow out of her fears when she can understand what's real and what's not.

Sometimes a child will wear a costume but not a mask. Masks partially cover a child's eyes and face, and this may intensify her fears. Try using face makeup instead of a mask, or help your child make a mask that she can hold rather than wear. Such a mask will let her exert quick control, and may make her feel more comfortable.

When Halloween night comes and most children's costumes are on, the trick-or-treating begins. Your child may find this to be a difficult part of the holiday. It's dark and there are many people outside, all looking like strangers, many looking very spooky. A child who finds costumes frightening may be overwhelmed by the sight of so many disguised trick-or-treaters.

Your child may be afraid to trick-or-treat at other people's homes. All year long you've told her not to talk to strangers or go to unfamiliar houses, yet on Halloween night it's suddenly acceptable to go and ask for candy. A neighbor's house may seem strange if your child has never been inside. And your child may be afraid either that people will answer their doors wearing scary costumes or that she'll have to stand at a doorstep with other children dressed in frightening disguises.

Your two- or three-year-old may hesitate to trick-or-treat because she's never done it before. And if your child is shy, she may not want to talk to neighbors, even if you coach her. And many children don't like to be focused on by people, especially strangers, who admire their costumes.

There's another side to trick-or-treat anxiety—your concerns about your child's safety. Because of frightening news stories, many parents warn their children about unwrapped candy and spend time looking through their children's bags for open or suspicious food. In order to avoid the possibility of unsafe candy, some parents decide to skip trick-or-treating altogether, instead trying community parties, costume parades, home parties, or Halloween craft treats.

If you do allow trick-or-treating, you'll have to decide what to do with all the candy. Some parents let their children eat a few pieces on Halloween night; others let them eat whatever they want. The days following the holiday can be difficult if your child doesn't lose interest in her candy. If you choose eventually to throw the goodies out, let her know ahead of time so she can pick out a few special pieces to save. Through all of this it might help you to realize that, while Halloween can be an exciting time, it's not always easy for the families of young children.

What can I do about my child's fear of monsters?

All children have bedtime fears. They worry about a monster in the closet, an alligator under the bed, or a skeleton at the window. Such frightening images are part of a child's internal world. At night, when the stimulations and distractions of the day are over, he may begin to focus on this world and on the anxious thoughts and feelings that were stirred up during the day. Worries about a new school, a move, or parents' arguments can cause him to feel afraid. And bedtime darkness makes him feel even more scared and vulnerable.

Fears of monsters, witches, and other bad things sometimes originate with a child's own anger. Adults seldom remember the intensity of childhood emotions. Anger is often rage—the determination to have, to control, and to do for themselves is very strong in children. And because they are egocentric, children assume that adults feel the same things they do. A child who's angry enough to hurt someone or destroy something may believe that the powerful adults around him, like monsters, feel angry enough to hurt him. This is a scary proposition.

Because a child isn't comfortable with hostile thoughts aimed at his parents, he unconsciously projects his own feelings onto them or onto monsters. Instead of thinking, "I'm so angry at Mom and Dad," he thinks, "Mom and Dad are angry at me." The result of this projection can be an increased fear of monsters and other frightening creatures.

The specific scary images that frighten a child can be introduced by a television show, a movie, a fairy tale, or even a picture in a book. Some parents who try to alleviate their child's fears by showing him a book about nice monsters may actually be giving him something else to be afraid of. This can happen because he has difficulty distinguishing what is real from what is not. Once he sees a picture of a monster, even a harmless one, he may be convinced that such a thing exists. Therefore, parents may want to keep a sensitive child from seeing scary books, television shows, or movies.

If your child tells you he's frightened of monsters, try to reassure him. For example, you can say, "Sometimes children think that monsters are real, but I know there are no such things. You're very safe here." Be careful not to pressure him into agreeing that his fears are irrational. And don't dismiss his fears by saying, "Don't be afraid." Children who are told their fears are silly will continue to feel afraid, but may not openly express themselves because they anticipate being ridiculed or shamed. Instead, they may cry, cling, or have frequent scary dreams.

Try to get your child to express his fears, since talking can help him deal with them. The inability to discuss fears can make them feel more real and give them more power. You might ask him, "What does a monster do? What does it look like? Can you draw a picture of it? Where did you think you saw it?" Such questions will help you learn more about what frightens your child. When he's scared, you may have to spend more time than usual sitting with him, reassuring him at bedtime. You may feel more patient about this if you remember your own childhood fears. Although you may have received assurances from your parents, you still believed that frightening things lurked in the closets and under the bed.

No matter how long you sit with your child, talk with him, or comfort him, he won't give up his fears easily. You can help him best by consistently being available to reassure and comfort him.

Why is my child afraid of Santa Claus?

A beautifully dressed two-year-old waits in line to see Santa Claus. When it's her turn, Santa says, "Come here, little girl," and the girl's parents say, "Go sit on his lap." She listens, looks at the smiling face in front of her, and bursts into tears. She's afraid of Santa.

It surprises people to learn that many children fear such a friendly character. After all, from a parent's perspective, Santa represents love and the spirit of gift giving. When a child resists sitting on kind Santa's lap, her parents become embarrassed and easily wonder, "What's wrong with her?" They may try to force their child onto Santa or use threats and bribes: "If you sit on Santa's lap you'll get a lot of toys for Christmas."

Even when parents are patient, they're usually unsuccessful in getting their child to come in contact with Santa. Young children struggle and resist him out of fear, and it's almost impossible to convince them not to be afraid.

Most children under the age of five believe that what they hear and see is real. They regard their own perspective as absolute and for them, Santa is real. They see him in shopping malls, they read and sing about him, and their parents talk as though he truly existed.

This Santa, with a rather deep voice and a beard that covers most of his face, can be scary-looking and unpleasant to a young child. Since she's in contact with Santa only during the Christmas season, he's unfamiliar and children do not go to unfamiliar people with ease. She's not sure he's nice and her parents aren't always reassuring about his looks. While they tell her that a Halloween character or a clown is only someone dressed in a costume, they don't say that Santa, too, is wearing a costume. They don't want her to know.

A young child's belief in a real Santa can take on a mysterious quality, giving Santa tremendous power. Santa "knows" when she is good or bad, and he decides which gifts she will receive. He seems omnipotent, flying through the sky, entering her home when she's asleep, watching her all the time. It can be frightening for her to think about Santa coming at night and when she learns that he arrives through the chimney she begins to wonder, "How will he fit? What if he falls? How does he get the toys down the chimney?" If there is no chimney, "How will he get in?"

A child may worry about being judged by Santa, who will decide if she's been good enough to receive gifts on Christmas. And her parents, not realizing she's already under a lot of pressure during this time of the year, may say, "You'd better be good or Santa won't bring you a present." Adults often use this line when they're frustrated with children's behavior, but it adds a threatening note to the fun and excitement of Christmas gift-giving. A child who hears this threat repeatedly may become anxious, silly, aggressive, or fearful.

Realistically, a child cannot live up to Santa's or her parents' expectations of good behavior. Young children struggle when they have to pick up their toys, they don't like to go to bed, they usually don't brush their teeth or wash their hands and faces without being reminded (at least twice), and they usually don't help with day-to-day chores. It's not that children are "bad," it's that parents' and Santa's expectations are unrealistic.

Given Santa's power to judge, his unusual appearance, and his ability to see and be everywhere, it's not surprising when a young child has ambivalent feelings about approaching him. She wants to tell him what to bring for Christmas and she wants to please her parents, but she's afraid.

Fortunately, if your child fears Santa, there are a variety of things you can do ahead of time to help her feel better. The most important is to reassure and prepare her by talking about Santa, mentioning his size, voice, and clothes. You can explain that he is friendly and enjoys talking with children about Christmas. You also can try letting your child go up to him with a sibling or friend. Be selective about the Santas you visit, asking your friends about their experiences at various shopping centers, and watching a Santa to see how he acts with young children. A Santa who doesn't put too much pressure on children will make you and your child more comfortable.

Finally, consider your child's age and personality when deciding how far to go during the Santa visit. A shy child might display more apprehension than an outgoing child. A one and one-half- or two-year-old will be more frightened than a three- or four-year-old. Children with confident older siblings can often be convinced that Santa is nice and likes children.

Whatever you try, your child may still cry and refuse to go to Santa. If this happens, step back with her and try to find a good alternative activity such as waving to him or sitting down to watch. In a year or so there are bound to be changes in her attitudes, and even though she cries this year, she may have fun visiting Santa next Christmas.

TOYS, PLAY, AND SOCIALIZING

Which toys are appropriate?

Play is an essential part of growing up. While a child plays freely, he satisfies his curiosity and finds out how to use objects; he learns to plan and classify; he begins to evaluate, predict, question, discover, draw conclusions, and solve problems; and he also learns how to interact with his peers and imitate the people around him. A child whose play is not controlled and channeled by adults ("The colors in that painting should really be blue and green." "If you pile any more blocks up, your building will fall.") gains confidence through play and rarely has a fear of failure.

Some parents minimize the importance of play, looking instead for "educational" or prepackaged activities for their child. But he doesn't need these in order to learn. Parents best nurture his drive to learn by following up on his interests, giving him many opportunities to play, and providing appropriate toys and materials.

The following are simple suggestions for age-appropriate toys and activities. The list is by no means complete, and toy stores are filled with new and traditional items. The ages listed here are quite flexible. One child will enjoy a toy at eighteen months, while another child won't play with that toy until he is two or three years old. Some return again and again to toys they used when they were younger. And a child with an older sibling will get an early introduction to toys intended for older children. As your child grows, he'll let you know which toys interest him and which activities he wishes to pursue.

Birth to six months

An infant likes to look at objects around him. By three to four months, he may be accidentally batting toys with his hands or feet, and by four to six months he may intentionally try to touch and grasp objects. During the earliest months you can hang mobiles from the crib or ceiling, put a safe mirror against the side of the crib, or secure a colorful pinwheel to the hood of the baby stroller. Once he grasps objects, you can provide soft toys that can safely go in his mouth and that won't harm him if he bumps against them: a rattle or squeaking toy, teething beads, toys with faces.

Six to twelve months

Once your baby can sit up, attach a busy box to the side of his crib. He'll enjoy one with buttons, dials, pop-ups, and other things he can control. You also can give him kitchen items to play with such as pots and pans, plastic bowls and spoons, and a spill-proof container filled with water that he can shake and watch. He'll like cuddly dolls, squeeze toys, soft cars and trucks, large balls, hollow blocks made from heavy cardboard, and cloth or cardboard books. You can make books for him by slipping pictures into a photo album.

Twelve to eighteen months

Your child will enjoy trucks or cars he can sit on, push-and-pull toys, doll carriages, plastic lawn mowers, wheelbarrows, a two-step kitchen stool he can stand on to see high places, pounding boards, toy telephones, music boxes, rocking toys, outside and indoor climbing equipment with ladders and slides, and adults' shoes he can walk around in. He'll also like simple toys he can take apart and plastic bottles with tops to take off and put on.

Eighteen to twenty-four months

Your child will enjoy stringing large wooden beads, screwing and unscrewing bottle caps, using a punching bag, pushing a toy shopping cart, using plastic tools, playing with balls of different sizes and shapes, arranging magnets on the refrigerator, and playing with stuffed animals. He may be happy for long periods playing with sand or water if he has shovels, pails, measuring cups, sieves, funnels, and plastic bottles to use. Although he will not be able to pedal yet, he may enjoy a Big Wheel or a small bike without pedals.

Two to three years

A child this age may enjoy rubber, plastic, or wooden animals, dolls and dolls' accessories; a play stove, refrigerator, and sink with dishes, pots, and pans; dress-up clothes; a play house; a doctor's kit; large blocks; cars, trucks, a play firehouse and fire engine, and a toy garage and gas station. Most two- and three-year-olds can use pens, paint, crayons, chalk (fun to use on the sidewalk), big paint brushes to use with water outside, and when closely supervised, child-size scissors. Your child will probably have fun jumping on a mattress that's flat on the floor, kicking a deflated ball that can't roll away from him, and riding a tricycle. He'll also like using puzzles, playing musical instruments, and listening to CDs or tapes of folk, classical, or children's music.

Four to five years

A child this age will like using arts and crafts materials such as pens, pencils, markers, scissors, tape, glue, string, play dough, clay, watercolors, tempera (which can be mixed with soap flakes to help prevent stains), and finger paints. Wagons, Big Wheels, and bikes with or without training wheels are fun, as are balls, bats, Frisbees, bubble blowers, kites, bowling pins, balance boards, old tires to swing or jump on, and bean bags to toss. Some of the most popular games for this age group are Candy Land, Hungry Hungry Hippos, Sorry, various matching games, Fish, and Old Maid. You can try offering your child practical things to play with, such as flashlights, magnifying glasses, whistles, simple tools, old household objects he can safely take apart, or a bank and coins; rakes and snow shovels; a funnel, pump, and eggbeater to use while playing with water and bubbles; and a large plastic needle for sewing burlap. Your child may enjoy building with Tinker Toys, Legos, and all kinds of blocks, and may want to make forts and houses out of blankets or large cardboard boxes. You can help your child make a puppet theater from a table turned on its side; he can run the show with play tickets, play money, and a toy cash register. A child this age is influenced by his friends and by TV and may want whatever toy other children have.

When you provide toys for a child of any age, avoid giving too many that limit creative play. So many toys can only be put together and used in one way, and if your child spends all his time with such toys, he'll have little chance to make his own creations. Instead, look for toys that can be used in a variety of ways, and ones that allow him to use his imagination. For example, instead of buying kits of shrinkable plastic with predrawn pictures, buy the same plastic, without the drawings, at a craft store. Then your child can make his own designs.

As you buy toys, you may find that your child becomes intensely interested in a new plaything for several weeks and then loses interest. This is common, although it may be disturbing if you've spent time and energy shopping for the right toy, one your child said he "wanted so badly." He loses interest for several reasons: he may have quickly exhausted all the toy's play possibilities, he may have mastered the toy, figuring out how it works, or he may be frustrated because it isn't made well or is difficult to use.

To get more use from your child's discarded but almost new toys, put them away in a closet for several months. When you take them out, they'll seem unfamiliar to your child, and he may become interested in them again. He may even think of new ways to play with them, since his interests and his play are always changing.

A doll for my son? A truck for my daughter?

There are toys that all children use—balls, puzzles, blocks, clay, crayons, board games—and there are "boy" toys and "girl" toys. Some parents try to avoid stereotyped or sexist toys and allow their children to choose playthings from the full range available. But other parents are uncomfortable when their children play with nontraditional toys. These parents, who do not buy cars and action figures for their girls or baby strollers and tea sets for their boys, fear that playing with toys intended for the opposite sex weakens a child's identification with his or her own sex.

Some parents may discourage their daughter when she acts like a "tomboy" or shows an interest in aggressive, supposedly masculine toys. But parents who pressure her to follow traditionally feminine pursuits may limit her potential.

Parents of boys also can restrict their child's development by demanding only masculine activities. Nursery school and day care teachers often hear parents tell their sons that the classroom's housekeeping area is "just for girls." Yet, there's nothing wrong with a boy who wants to play house or dolls. Boys need to learn how to nurture just as girls do, and an interest in playing house is normal.

Some parents who don't mind if their children play with nontraditional toys still feel uncomfortable buying such toys. One mother was pleased that her son played with dolls at his friend's house, but couldn't bring herself to get him a doll when he asked. Similarly, a parent didn't mind her daughter's use of war toys in the neighborhood, but resisted buying her a tank of her own.

Some parents who have children of both sexes encourage their sons and daughters to share toys, thus allowing nontraditional play. Other parents buy each sibling a few toys intended for the opposite sex so that brothers and sisters can play well together. One little girl had her own set of mini cars to use whenever her brother's playmates came to the house. She joined in the boys' games and her parents avoided the struggles that come when one child is excluded.

When a child is under the age of three or four, he or she will probably be attracted to toys of interest to both sexes, but by the time children are five, they clearly identify which toys "belong" to which sex. One five-year-old girl noticed a two-and-one-half-year-old boy wearing nail polish and she began to question him about his interests: "Do you like Barbie? Do you like robots?" When he answered yes to both questions, she turned to her mom and said, "He's girlish-boyish."

Parents who encourage a child to play with whatever toys he or she likes—regardless of sex stereotypes—often are surprised when their child chooses the traditional "girl" or "boy" toys anyway. Girls are drawn to dolls, toy houses, and dressing up, while boys are attracted to cars, war toys, and space toys. Girls enjoy playing baby and house; boys like playing pirates, fire fighters, and spacemen. Certainly the media have a powerful influence here. Advertisers clearly market their toys for a particular sex, and children never have a chance to see nontraditional play on commercials. But even considering the influence of television, children seem to have their own innate interests in typical, traditional play.

Given this strong drive girls have to play with "girl" toys, and boys with "boy" toys, there's no need for parents to worry when their child shows an interest in toys for the opposite sex. And there's no reason parents should not buy nontraditional toys if their child wants them.

In rare cases, parents might observe that their child seems particularly dissatisfied with his or her gender. A child who consistently tries to play and act like a member of the opposite sex may sense his or her parents' disappointment ("I wish he'd been a girl!"), may be reacting to family stress, or may be influenced by genetic factors. If you're concerned about your child's behavior, keep an eye on the situation and in later years seek additional information and guidance on gender issues.

How can I get my child to be interested in homemade toys?

Although stores offer a multitude of toys, you can create kits and playthings that provide enjoyment and encourage children to be creative. The following are suggestions for games, toys, and gifts for two- to five-year-olds. The kits take time to assemble, but probably no more time than searching the stores for the "right" toy. And your child will have fun helping you put these playthings together and decorating storage boxes with crayons or contact paper. Choose materials that are appropriate for your child's age and supervise as he plays.

Art box
In a plastic or cardboard shoe box, place any of the following supplies: colored pencils, magic markers, crayons, chalk, yarn, string, pipe cleaners, watercolor paints with brushes, small sheets of paper, glue, tape tissue paper, felt, scraps of fabric, a ruler, old greeting cards, Popsicle sticks, strips of cardboard or balsa wood, scissors, and a hole puncher.

Play office
In a large plastic or cardboard file box place any of the following: a calculator, a clipboard, a looseleaf binder with paper, stationery, folders,

pencils and pens, envelopes, paper clips, an eraser, stickers, stamps and a stamp pad, and rubber bands.

Tool box

For three-year-olds and up, make a kit including: a hammer, nails, a screwdriver, a wrench, pliers, nuts and bolts, measuring tape, sandpaper, a child's saw, and styrofoam pieces to put nails and screws in. Wood scraps can often be found for free at lumber yards. You can drive nails and screws partway into a piece of wood 12″ x 6″. Then, a young child can hammer and unscrew these safely. Children should be supervised by an adult when they use the tool box.

Play dough

To make your own play dough, use the following ingredients: 1 cup of flour; ½ cup of salt; 2 teaspoons of cream of tartar; 1 cup of water; 2 tablespoons of oil; 1 tablespoon of food coloring (optional). Combine the first three ingredients in a large saucepan. Gradually stir in the water mixed with the oil and food coloring. Cook over medium heat, stirring constantly until a ball forms. Remove the dough from the heat and knead it until it is smooth. The dough can be stored in plastic bags or containers, and put in a kit with cookie cutters, a rolling pin, small cups, an empty egg carton, empty thread spools, plastic knives, or other objects that would be fun to use with dough.

Sewing kit

In a cardboard box or a lunch box, place: cardboard, poster board, large plain file cards, a hole puncher, string, buttons, a plastic needlepoint needle, yarn, burlap, and scissors.

Forest ranger or camper kit

In a knapsack or cardboard box, store: a canteen, a flashlight, a compass, nature books, binoculars, a whistle, sticks, water bottle, a small cook pot, a magnifying glass, a hat, and boots.

Hair stylist's supplies

In a large plastic bag or box put: a mirror, rollers, hair pins, a blow-dryer (toy or real with the cord cut off), combs, brushes, towels, magazines, empty plastic shampoo bottles, emery boards, play makeup, jewelry, a pencil, paper, and play money.

Painter's kit

You can use a bucket to store: a hat (which you may find for free at a paint supply store), different sized brushes, a paint roller, an old piece of sheet for a drop cloth, a rag, and sandpaper. Your child can paint outdoors with water.

Firefighter's equipment

This kit, which can be stored in a big cardboard box, can include: a fire hat, raincoat, boots, an old cut piece of garden hose, a pretend walkie-talkie, goggles, and gloves.

Doctor's kit

In a box or bag, place: cotton balls, a play thermometer, empty pill bottles, labels, paper, pens, an old white shirt, bandages, Band-Aids, plastic syringes, and a toy stethoscope. Some of these supplies may be obtained for free from your pediatrician.

Sets like these also can be made for police officers, scientists, nurses, shoe salespersons, grocers, astronauts, magicians, and waiters/waitresses. You can vary the contents as your child grows and changes. If you decide to give one of these homemade toys as a gift, let your child help with the wrapping. She can color on white tissue paper or newsprint and make her own card by folding paper in half and decorating it or making a card on the computer.

Do coloring books limit creativity?

There are many kinds of coloring books available, such as cartoon books, "educational" books, animal and history books. They all are based on the same activity—a child colors a predrawn picture. Although this may seem enjoyable to an adult, a young child who spends too much time with coloring books may miss out on the chance to create his own artwork and know the enjoyment of drawing.

Parents sometimes buy these books because they think coloring within the lines will improve their child's hand-eye coordination. Yet, so much of what he does involves hand-eye coordination. When he picks up a raisin, puts together a puzzle, builds with blocks, or zips a zipper, he's improving his skills. He doesn't need a coloring book for practice.

Some parents believe that a child will learn to complete tasks if he works in a coloring book. But often, he is unable to stay within the lines and becomes frustrated. A child between three and five may feel like a failure when he sees how "messy" his coloring looks. And parents may be more critical of his work when the task is to color within the lines rather than to draw whatever he likes. Eventually, he may lose his interest in drawing and coloring: "I'm just not good at this."

Children are often given pre-made or partly completed artwork in nursery school or day care centers. They shouldn't then spend most of their arts and crafts time at home with predrawn coloring books. Parents should limit their child's use of coloring books until he is at least five- or six-years-old. At that age, he will be better able to color within the lines and may find the activity more satisfying. But even then, the use of coloring books should be limited.

The best kind of artwork is the child's own. Your three- to five-year-old will enjoy using pens, pencils, markers, and crayons to color on blank paper. When he has a chance to draw what he likes, the drawing will be a part of him, and his pictures of people, animals, boats, and so on will be unique. Of course, some children are more interested in arts and crafts than others, and some will show more skill. But all children enjoy drawing if they feel successful. And as one four-and-one-half-year-old said, "When you draw and draw, you get better."

Keep art supplies available so your child can color when he wants to. He can draw on plain paper, scrap paper, newsprint, paper plates, lunch bags, and grocery bags. If you have a variety of pens and pencils, he can pick the ones that are most comfortable to use. Many young children who have trouble drawing with crayons do much better with pens and markers.

My child wants to play with toy guns. Should I let him?

Many preschoolers—especially boys—still want to play with toy guns despite all the frightening news about gun violence. They enjoy squirt guns, space guns, cap guns, and rifles, and they're impressed with how toy guns can shoot water, flash, and make loud noises. If a toy gun isn't available, a child will make one out of wood, a stick, a straw, even paper. And if he can't make one, he'll shoot with his thumb and finger.

A child is attracted to toy guns because they give him a sense of power and control. In his everyday life, he is relatively helpless, but when he holds a toy gun (which looks real to him), he feels he can protect himself while telling other children what to do: "Stand over there and put your hands up." Children like to play roles: firefighter, mother, father, nurse, doctor, policeman, cowboy, bad guy. Children see armed guards at airports, hear news about fighting and terrorism, see shooting all the time on television and in computer games, and they act out what they see. The good and bad guys have guns, and when the good guy shoots and wins, he's a hero.

There are parents who are comfortable letting their children play with toy guns. Some even encourage it. Many parents have mixed feelings. They don't like gun play, since they know the danger and violence associated with real guns, and they want their children to play less aggressively. But even many of these parents eventually give up and let their children use toy guns. The parents find that, despite their arguments and their efforts to involve their child in other activities, he may still want to play with toy guns, and if he doesn't have one, he'll improvise one.

You may decide not to let your child use toy guns, or to use them only in a limited way. If toy gun use in the house bothers you, tell him to go outdoors. Tell him not to shoot at people who don't agree to play, and not to aim a toy gun in someone's face. Gun play may be difficult for you to watch, since it imitates a frightening part of life. Yet, gun play doesn't seem to encourage general aggressiveness. In fact, it can be an outlet for naturally aggressive children.

As long as your child plays with toy guns in moderation, there's no harm in the activity. He'll probably stay interested in these as he goes through his elementary years. If you see gun play becoming your child's dominant activity, you need to try to figure out why. Does he feel unaccepted at home? Does he feel verbally or physically under attack at home or at school? A child who engages in excessive toy gun play may feel powerless or rejected. Pay more attention to him at home and try distracting him from toy guns by introducing him to alternative activities and organized games.

Should my child play with children his own age?

All young children, even those under a year old, love to be around other children. When children one and one-half years old and younger play together, they usually get along well. They play side-by-side, independently engaged but enjoying each other's company, and there are few arguments over sharing. Occasional disagreements pass quickly because these young children can be distracted easily.

By the time children are two or three years old, however, playtime is full of arguments for playmates of the same age. They struggle with each other over possessions, sharing, and autonomy, and constantly shout, "That's mine!" A parent often has a difficult time watching children this age play together. They don't pay attention to each other's needs and don't give in without fighting. When children turn four, they do get along better, although there's often a streak of competitiveness as each tries to exert power.

Play is generally much smoother when children of mixed ages play together. A group made up of two- to five-year-olds will struggle less because each child is at a different developmental stage with different needs. A younger child will watch and imitate an older one, asking for help with games and tasks and getting information. An older child, who is less possessive, will give in to the younger ones, offering help and leading games.

Although parents are usually comfortable when their young child plays with an older friend, they're not as sure when their older child plays with a younger one. Parents may feel that he will be bored with younger children or will be brought down to their level. But a five-year-old playing with three-year-olds will stimulate himself, depending on the activities he's involved in. He'll play elaborate games with the simple toys available, lead a complex game, or create his own arts and crafts projects. He might enjoy the chance to play again with toys he's outgrown. And he may feel good playing around younger children because he can be helpful and knowledgeable and direct his friends' play: "Let's put the blocks here and build a castle." "The puzzle piece goes there." "Do you want to hold my hamster? Be gentle, he has fragile bones." His own confidence will be boosted when he can teach and lead.

Sometimes there are problems with mixed age groups. An older child may engage in elaborate play that the younger one doesn't understand, and both children may become frustrated. And some older children may feel compelled to boss a younger child, knocking over his buildings and grabbing toys. When such children (who are often reenacting what happens to them when they play with an older sibling or friend) sense they are bigger than the children they're playing with, they try to exert power. Parental supervision is needed in such situations to keep the play between younger and older children peaceful.

When you arrange playtime for your young child, encourage him to choose playmates who seem right for him. At times you may find it works best when he plays with children his own age; at other times you will want him to practice relating to and accepting children of different ages. After all, in the family, in the neighborhood, and out in public, he will be involved with people of all ages. What is more important than the ages of playmates is how well the children get along.

What about playgroups?

Parents probably benefit from playgroups more than their children do. Parents of very young children often feel isolated, so they welcome a chance to meet with other adults, compare child rearing stories and advice, and observe how other parents handle their children. Of course the children also can benefit from a playgroup, and as they get older, they enjoy seeing their friends regularly and playing at each other's homes.

If you're interested in starting a playgroup, talk to other parents about the possibility. Ask your neighbors and friends or look in grocery stores, houses of worship, and newsletters for notices from other interested parents. Although playgroups are most convenient when the participants live near each other, groups often form between people in different neighborhoods.

Your playgroup will probably work best with three to five children of mixed ages. If all the children are two and one-half, there will be a great deal of arguing over possessions, but if some are two and some are four, group meetings will be more harmonious. The youngest child will be happy playing alone next to the others, and the oldest ones will be more likely than the two-year-olds to share toys.

Many playgroups are successful meeting in the morning, although some meet between 3:30 and 5:30 in the afternoon, normally a slow time for at-home parents with young children. Other playgroups meet on the weekends so parents who work full-time can participate.

Your playgroup will probably get together once a week, meeting at each member's house in turn. In some groups, every parent comes every time, while in others, parents rotate attendance so that in a group with six children, two parents attend any one session while four have the time free. The success of this rotating method depends on the ages and personalities of the children, and how well the families know each other. Some young children do not want to be separated from their parents and may cry for a few minutes or for the whole play session, particularly if the parents in charge are not familiar.

Before your playgroup begins meeting, get together with the other parents involved and develop rules and standards for practical issues. What kind of snack will be served? What happens when children fight? Who should bring toys? How will you handle the problem of sharing toys?

Your playgroup will be most successful if the parents involved share similar interests and attitudes, especially regarding parenting, since conflicts can arise when one group member accepts behavior that bothers another. As long as the adult members of a playgroup are basically compatible, they should be able to talk about their differences and try to work out solutions to the group's problems.

My child likes to talk on the telephone. How do I handle this?

Children like to do what their parents do, and parents spend a lot of time on the telephone. Even before a child is two years old, he'll imitate his parents by using a toy phone, holding a real phone, pushing the buttons, and making sounds. When he's between two and three, he'll want to talk on the phone and, given the chance, he may do comical things. He might listen and nod without saying a word, or he may hold objects up to the phone so his listener can see them since he assumes that if he can see something, everyone else can. One two-year-old had his aunt hold on while he got his pet gerbil. "See," he said, holding the animal up to the receiver, "he's moving around."

Children like to imitate their parents by being first to answer the phone. Parents who want to avoid this situation shout, "I'll get it," but sometimes their child also shouts, "I'll get it," and races his parents to the phone. When a two-year-old answers, he might just hold it, saying nothing. A three-year-old might pick up the phone and say, "Who is this?" or "What do you want?" and a four- or five-year-old who is given a message by a caller will probably forget it. At these young ages, children's conversations are all about themselves. Once they've said what they want to say, they may simply hang up without thinking or caring about the person on the other end.

Children are fascinated by the telephone not only because their parents use it, but also because it has a magical quality. It's both tool and toy, and it lets a child share his thoughts with other people, something children like to do. They also like to talk on the phone because they don't want to feel left out. If parents are having a conversation, children want to be in on it and they want the attention their parents are giving to whomever is on the line.

Parents often are frustrated when their child wants to talk, especially when they're engaged in important calls. He might yell and have a tantrum if he's not allowed to talk, and such noise can embarrass parents. If he becomes too disruptive, his parent might have to end an important call prematurely, hoping that the person on the other end is understanding. Although parents can gradually teach a five- or six-year-old not to interrupt important calls, explanations do little good with younger, egocentric children. Sometimes they can be distracted by a silent offer of toys or food, but more often they just keep interrupting.

Parents may feel particularly embarrassed if their child answers an important phone call. One mother expected a business call from a man named Paul Jones. Her son picked up the phone, listened, and then shouted, "It's Paul Bones. Who's he?" A four-year-old can be taught to answer the phone politely, but parents of younger children have to be tolerant and hope their callers understand children's behavior and have a sense of humor.

One way you can accommodate your young child's desire to answer the phone is to ask relatives or friends to call at prearranged times; then you can safely let your child answer and talk. If you have an adult who enjoys making such calls, you may be able to keep your child from interrupting you. Tell him, "As soon as I'm off the phone, we'll dial Aunt Ellen and ask her to give you a call."

If you're having a phone conversation with the parent of a child the same age as yours, ask if your child can talk for a few moments. The other parent will certainly understand and may want to put his or her own child on to talk to you. And since children like to talk to each other, your child may especially enjoy a chance to call one of his friends.

Why does my child get anxious before holidays and birthdays?

"How long 'til my birthday?"

"When is three weeks up?"

"Is it Halloween yet?"

Parents hear such questions whenever special occasions approach. Children have a hard time waiting, and since their concept of time is different from an adult's, they ask about holidays over and over again. Parents can tell their excited child that Christmas is four weeks away and almost immediately, she will ask again, "How long before Christmas?"

She begins anticipating a holiday as soon as preparations begin. Her day care or nursery school class might make Valentine cards weeks in advance, and her friends might discuss Halloween costumes long before October. Christmas preparations sometimes begin before Thanksgiving, giving children a great deal of time to watch holiday commercials, see store decorations going up, and think about presents.

When there's a long period of anticipation before a special event, children get anxious and excited and may go through behavior changes, becoming sillier, more active, and more likely to whine. Children who are admonished to "be good" in order to get birthday or Christmas gifts may feel pressured and become more aggressive. It's very hard under any circumstances for a child to be consistently good, and when she's anxiously anticipating a holiday, behaving well is that much harder. Some parents find that their child's behavior improves if they ease up on the holiday pressure, perhaps giving a surprise treat ("Just because I love you") to slow the build-up.

Parents also can try to help their child deal with the waiting period by giving her a calendar to mark off, or by making a special paper chain. Each day for a week or two, she can tear off one link; the day all the links are gone is the day she's been waiting for. These devices help some children stay calm, but generally children remain very excited. Parents should be patient with the excitement and expect that their child will continually want the celebration to begin "now." They can sympathize if they consider their own feelings before special parties or vacations.

Your child may get particularly worked up before her birthday. Since party preparation takes time, you may start planning the celebration weeks before the date, while your child considers whom to invite and what presents she'd like. She may be very excited about the gifts and party or she may have mixed feelings about being the center of attention and may decide, as one five-year-old did, "Nobody should sing 'Happy Birthday' to me at my party." She may worry ahead of time about having eight or ten friends over at once, and may be concerned about sharing her toys and letting the guests see her presents. One child, concerned about her anticipated gifts, said, "At the party, no one can come and play in my room." Although there is no way to keep your child from feeling excited and anxious before her birthday, if you anticipate her feelings, you will be better able to reassure her.

Why doesn't my child want to share?

"It's mine!" screams the young boy, yanking a toy from another child.

"That's not nice," his mother says. "Michelle is your friend and I want you to share with her."

"No, it's mine!"

At times almost all young children have trouble sharing. Even eighteen-month-olds argue over toys, although conflicts generally peak between the ages of two and two and one half. Episodes of screaming, crying, and even biting are not uncommon when children struggle for a toy. Sometimes the severity of the anger and anxiety that young children exhibit is incomprehensible to adults. One mother who took care of several young children described her daughter's behavior during this stage as horrifying: "When Tali was two she would stand at the front door with her arms spread out and yell, 'MINE'!"

What parents should try to understand is that a child's possessions are important to him and that he feels violated if another child handles them. When a friend comes into a child's home, the child suddenly is asked to give up his toys, to share with someone who usually doesn't ask before using something. His biggest fear is that he will lose his toys, or that they will no longer belong to him. That's why he screams and tugs at a possession, crying, "It's mine!"

Because a young child's thinking is egocentric, he sees things only from his point of view and is unmoved by his parents' logical reasons for sharing: "Your friend wants to use this toy. How would you feel if he didn't share with you?" The question doesn't make sense to children these ages and it won't change their behavior. A child also won't be moved by his friend's obvious distress at not having a chance to share a toy. One three and one-half year old child became interested in her toy vacuum cleaner only after her friend took it out of the closet to use. A struggle ensued between the two children until the mother intervened. "Jesse was using the toy first. How would you feel if your friend Niki took her toys away from you while you were visiting her?" The child stood quietly with a blank look on her face and said, "It's my vacuum cleaner." Such lack of concern for another's feelings may be difficult for parents to accept because adult thinking is so different from a young child's.

Parents who are frustrated or embarrassed by their child's unwillingness to share may blame themselves or have negative feelings about their child, considering him to be bad or selfish. After watching him grab a toy, parents may become angry and try to force him to share. But once they realize that trouble with sharing is a normal aspect of development, they usually feel more comfortable and tolerant. Talking to other parents about sharing also may help. It's helpful to remember that sometimes even adults have problems sharing. People argue over parking spaces and cut each other off during rush hour. And an adult need only imagine a visiting friend opening drawers and looking at personal belongings to understand how a child feels.

Understanding your child's difficulty with sharing may bring some comfort, although you'll still have to deal with struggles over toys. Unfortunately, there are no magic answers to the problems of sharing, but there are things you can try to lessen the tension. First, you can prepare your child. If a friend is coming to visit, say, "When Michelle comes over she'll want to play with your blocks, your puzzles, and the sliding board." Ask Michelle's parents to send along a little bag of toys for your child to play with. Don't expect your child to share all his toys when a friend visits. You may want to put away a few special possessions, or explain to visitors that there are some toys he doesn't want to share.

If he grabs everything away from his friend, tell him, "Michelle's using that now and when she's finished, you can use it." Then tell Michelle, "When you're done with that toy, please share it." Sometimes you may want to set time limits for taking turns, but understand that your child may be frustrated by having to give up a toy he's playing with or trying to master. Imagine that you're attempting to make a cake. You take out the ingredients, start to mix them, and then hear, "Time's up! It's Sharon's turn." You'd indignantly reply, "I'm not done yet!" and even a few minutes more wouldn't help. That's how your two- to five-year-old feels when forced to stop what he's doing and take turns.

When the struggle over toys becomes intense, you can try to interest your child in playing with something else. Or it may help to offer him choices: "Which toy would you like your friend to use—the ball or the puzzle?" If he can't choose, you choose for him. You may have to distract him by playing with him yourself or reading him a book. Although this can be frustrating, especially if you're involved in conversation with another adult, you should recognize that conflicts among young children, and the resulting interruptions, are unavoidable.

Parents often find that sharing is easier if children play outside, if they play at a friend's house rather than at their own house, or if they are involved in something together, such as coloring, using play dough, or painting. Whatever you try, though, sharing will probably still be a problem. As you set limits on the struggles, reassure your child that you understand what a difficult time he's having. And remember to model the behavior you want him to adopt. If you are giving, if you share courteously, your child will eventually copy you. Children learn more from parents' examples than from parents' admonitions.

By the time your child is three or four years old, you'll notice a general change in his attitude toward sharing. He'll show less anxiety when a friend uses a toy and will begin to say, "Here, you use this," or "Let's both play with these." When he's four or five, he'll begin to place more value on friendship. Eventually, he may be sharing more openly than you'd like, and you may find yourself saying, "Don't let him use your bike—he might ruin it," or, "Don't let her take that toy home with her." In the meantime, though, you can help your young child get past his difficulty with sharing by being patient, understanding this developmental phase, and not applying too much pressure.

How do other children act when they're angry with each other?

"Katie, let's play house. I'm the mommy, you're the baby."
"No, I'm the mommy, or I won't be your friend."
"Then you're not coming to my birthday party."
This exchange is typical of what preschoolers say when they argue. They may play well together and then suddenly tell each other, "I hate you," or, "You're a dummy." Young children, whose emotions are close to the surface, concentrate on their immediate wishes and needs. And because they're egocentric, they don't consider each other's feelings but let their anger come out in harsh words or actions. Some children give in when spoken to in this way, while others either fight back and persist until they get their way, or try to find an adult to help.

Parents wonder what to do when children are angry with each other. They should begin by setting limits on their child, who is egocentric and needs this adult guidance; on her own, she doesn't think about others when she's mad. However, if parents restrict her expressions of anger too much, she may end up believing that anger is bad and inappropriate. When she's kept from expressing her feelings, they'll be released in other ways. She may become destructive with her toys or while playing, manipulative with her parents or friends, or tricky as she tries to get other children to do what she wants. She needs a chance to let her anger out, and even if her parents don't like to hear her say, "I hate you! I'm not playing with you," they should realize that children are not very good at expressing their exact thoughts. Harsh words are sometimes a young child's way of letting her strongest negative feelings be known.

When it seems appropriate, parents can let arguing children try to work out their differences themselves as long as no one is getting physically injured or having his or her feelings terribly hurt. Children are sometimes surprisingly good at settling their arguments and can gradually learn to work problems out with one another. A child who seldom has a chance to settle her own arguments may become a "tattle-tale," dependent on her parents for help even with minor difficulties.

Parents who see that children cannot resolve arguments alone can offer suggestions. "Why don't you both pretend you're mommies and let your dolls be the babies?" If one child shouts something mean to another, parents should avoid saying, "That's not nice!" and instead say, "You're really mad because Tanya doesn't want you to play now. Why don't you tell her that?" Even if angry children ignore parents' suggestions, the very presence of adults will have a restraining effect. Children tend to be less aggressive with each other when parents are nearby.

You can lessen your child's involvement in arguments by avoiding situations that usually lead to problems. For instance, your child may play well with one child at a time, but not when a third joins in. Three can be a difficult number—two friends will often pair up and exclude or attack the third. If you can't avoid this situation, give all three children frequent reminders about getting along and including each other in play. If your child consistently argues with one particular playmate, limit their time together or tell them, "You have to find a way to get along with each other or I'm not going to let you play together." Your young child's anger, no matter how momentary, is very real and very strong. Allow her emotions to be heard, but when necessary, help her control her anger by setting firm limits.

BEING NICE

Why is my child uncomfortable kissing relatives?

In most families, children are expected to kiss their relatives hello and good-bye. When a child does this spontaneously, his parents are pleased, and when he doesn't, they usually prompt him, "Give Grandma and Grandpa a kiss. They haven't seen you in such a long time." Parents know how nice it feels to be kissed by a child. They want their child to be liked by relatives, and they feel that they'll be judged unfavorably if he child doesn't give a kiss.

Yet, many children are uncomfortable kissing their relatives and often don't want to do it. This can create an awkward situation, especially when a relative feels rejected by the child or feels that he's not excited to see her. And if the relative has brought him a gift and still doesn't get a kiss, she might feel particularly frustrated and begin to say negative things such as, "What's the matter with him? Is he shy?" His uneasy parent may urge him to "give Aunt Sue a kiss since she gave you a present," and Aunt Sue may say, "I'll take my gift back home with me." All of this can put a great deal of pressure on the young child, who will usually give in if harassed enough. But the resulting discomfort for him and his parents is often not worth the struggle.

A child who resists giving a kiss is probably not rejecting a relative. Most children are excited about seeing family members, but feel uneasy giving a kiss hello for any of a number of reasons. A child may just not be comfortable with the physical contact of a kiss, or, feeling shy and self-conscious, may reject kissing because he doesn't like to be focused on. He may want to stay close to his parents, even cling to them, until he feels adjusted to the visitors or to being in a relative's house.

Sometimes a relative is one the child rarely sees, and he resists kissing because he needs time to get used to a strange face. A few children have private or magical concerns about kissing. One five-year-old worried that he would "turn old" if he kissed his aunt, while another child reported that she didn't want to kiss her relatives because "people give you germs on your lips." And at times a child won't give a kiss good-bye because he doesn't want a visit to end, although he may not explain this.

If you're faced with a resisting child, try to let the kiss go—most children just need time to ease into a visit and feel friendly. Instead of insisting, suggest other options for your child. He could tell his relatives about something that has recently happened, demonstrate a new skill, or show them a favorite possession. And even if he won't kiss, he may willingly "give five," shake hands, blow a kiss, or give a hug good-bye.

We can all remember being small and having a relative pinch our cheeks or demand a kiss. If we recall how we felt then, we can understand our own children's reluctance to give kisses, and can help them find other ways to begin and end enjoyable visits with relatives.

Is it all right for her to call me by my first name?

It's very common for a first-born child between the ages of eighteen months and three years to call her parents by their first names. She imitates what she hears and since her parents and their friends, neighbors, and relatives all use first names when talking to each other, she uses first names too. Even if her parents call each other "Mom" and "Dad," she may still use first names because those are the ones she hears most often.

Many parents don't mind if their child occasionally uses first names, although some consider anything other than "Mom" and "Dad" disrespectful. When a child uses her parents' first names, however, she intends no disrespect—usually she's just mimicking what other people say. Over time, this imitative behavior will diminish and the child will stop using her parents' names.

If you're bothered or embarrassed when your child calls you by your first name, remind her to say "Mom" and "Dad." But remember that it will be hard for her, especially if she's under two, to call you "Mom" and "Dad" consistently, since she doesn't usually hear other people call you that. If you have a second child, you'll notice that he or she rarely uses your first name. That's because there's an older sibling to copy, and because the second child is used to hearing "Mom" and "Dad."

A common question related to first-name use is, "What should my child's friends call me?" Some parents are most comfortable with first names and believe they're easier for young children to remember and use. Other parents want to be called "Mrs." or "Mr." Choose whichever makes you comfortable and let your child's playmates know what you'd like to be called.

What can I do about my child's whining?

Hearing a child whine is very annoying. Young children often whine when they're tired, hungry, angry, or frustrated, and once they start, it's difficult to stop them. When parents ignore their whining child, he usually just continues until they finally speak to him. And even those parents who try to be patient or who believe it's best not to focus on a whining child often end up shouting, "Stop whining!" One mother constantly scolded her four-year-old, "What did I tell you about whining? Use a grown-up voice!"

There are no easy ways to keep your child from whining. You can try redirecting his attention, although your attempts at distraction may be unsuccessful. You also can try letting him know, without attacking him, that you're unhappy with his tone. When you say, "You're whining!" or, "Stop whining!" you imply blame. Instead, try expressing your feelings in a less negative way, without using the word "whining" at all. Say, "When you ask me in that way, I don't want to do anything for you," or "You'll have to ask me in another way."

Sometimes, particularly if your child is three or younger, you won't be able to understand what he says when he whines. You can tell him, "You'll have to ask me in a voice I can understand," or, "When you talk to me that way, I don't feel like listening to you. Can you find another way to tell me what you want?" You may not be able to stop a three-year-old's whining until you discover what's causing it. Sometimes a child with an older sibling whines because he feels he can't compete with his brother or sister. He turns to whining and baby-talk in order to be noticed and to take on the qualities of a baby, who, he feels, couldn't be expected to act like the older sibling.

By the time your child is five, he should be better able to express himself and understand the limits you place on his whining. If he whines continuously despite your efforts, he may believe whining is the best way to get what he wants. You may need to listen to him more and give him more time and attention.

How do I react when my child says, "I hate you, Mommy"?

When a young child gets angry with her parents, she shouts, "I hate you. You're dumb!" This outburst might come after her parents have said she can't go outdoors or have a friend over or do something else she wants to do. A preschooler has a hard time putting her exact feelings into words. She doesn't know how to say, "Dad, I think you should allow me to stay up later tonight because..." or, "I'm angry with you because you said..." She's too young for such articulation and too young to show respect. Instead, she expresses her anger by saying, "I hate you."

Most preschool children say, "I hate you," to their parents. Some parents accept and understand these words as the beginning of their child's expression of negative feelings. But all parents can feel betrayed when their child, after receiving love and attention, turns on them over a minor disappointment. It can be frustrating when adult reasoning, logic, and caring fail to keep a child from yelling, "You mean mom." Many parents are tolerant when their two- or three-year-old yells, "You dumb mom," but feel less understanding when their four- or five-year-old says, "I hate you." A child's words can feel threatening to parents who don't like their children to be angry with them.

Parents who can't stand to hear "I hate you" often say, "That's not nice! Don't let me hear those words again." But the child needs to release her angry feelings somehow, and if she isn't allowed to express them verbally, she'll find other, perhaps more destructive ways. She might turn to aggressive behavior such as biting or hitting, or she might take out her anger by becoming deliberately slow, acting excessively silly, pretending she doesn't hear her parents, or finding other ways to annoy them. However, if her angry feelings are acknowledged and allowed to be expressed, she eventually will learn to state her feelings more appropriately.

If your child says, "I hate you," offer her other ways to tell you how she feels. Suggest she say, "I'm mad at you," "I'm angry," or, "I don't like what you did." Acknowledge her feelings, but say, "I want you to tell me in different words."

Children are natural mimics. Your child uses the word "hate" because she hears it so often. Adults say, "I hate this dress," or, "I hate it when people do that." It's natural for your child to use the word to express her dislike of something or someone. You can take advantage of the fact that she's a mimic and gradually teach her to express her anger in acceptable ways. When your child says, "I hate you," rather than make an issue of it, simply restate her words. Say back to her, "You're really angry at me, aren't you. You don't like it when I say it's time to come in." If she hears you express her anger in this way, she gradually will begin to use similar statements herself.

How can I teach my child to respect others?

There are two ways a child learns about respect. He listens to what his parents say about respectful behavior, and he copies the way they actually act. Ultimately, he'll learn more from their actions than from their words. If they treat him and others courteously, he'll eventually copy their behavior. But if they speak harshly to him—"Get over here now!"—and consistently belittle him when he expresses his needs or makes mistakes, he will not learn to treat others with respect, even if his parents admonish him to behave well.

Day care and nursery school teachers sometimes say they can tell how respectful parents are by listening to children playing in the housekeeping corner. When two preschoolers pretend they have a crying baby, one might say, "Let's pick her up. She's crying," while the other might reply, "You get out of this house right now and take this crying baby with you."

A young child doesn't automatically know how to act appropriately. He has to have good models and be taught and frequently reminded because he's egocentric and easily forgets about other people's feelings when his own needs are strong. Parents often feel defeated after telling their child again and again to be nice to others, only to see him act selfishly again. At such times, they should remember that learning to show respect is a slow process and that it's natural for young children to think mainly of themselves.

If you feel constantly unhappy with your child's disrespectful behavior, perhaps you should re-evaluate your expectations of him. It's possible that you're asking for more than he's capable of giving. The younger he is, the less likely he is to control his emotions and put himself in someone else's place. Therefore, it's necessary for you to put limits on his behavior, "You can't say such mean words to your sister."

Look for ways you can model respectful behavior: "Let me pick you up so you can see better." "Let's go over there and thank that man for helping us." When children are respected, they internalize feelings of self-worth, believing that their ideas, needs, and desires are important. Over time, your child will give back the kind of respect you've given him, and you'll see him begin to consider other people's needs and feelings.

Should I ask my child to say "please" and "thank you"?

"Jennifer, how do you ask for something?"
"Now what do you say to Uncle Marty?"
"What's the magic word?"
A child who's questioned like this may mumble a faint "please" or "thank you," and her parents may feel somewhat reassured. But they also may wonder why they have to constantly remind her to use polite words.

When children say "please" and "thank you" without being prompted or coerced, parents feel a sense of satisfaction. They're proud when their child is polite in public, and they feel good when she's polite at home. Children make so many requests throughout the day: "Get me a drink!" "Give me a napkin!" "Tie my shoe!" If a child prefaces these statements with "please" and remembers to say "thank you," her parents will not feel so overwhelmed and will have an easier time responding to her constant needs.

So why don't most young children say "please" and "thank you" spontaneously? And why do many parents find themselves in situations such as this: a mother preparing to leave a neighborhood party tells her three-year-old daughter, "Say 'good-bye' and 'thank you' to Mrs. Miller." The daughter turns away and refuses to speak as seven mothers stare at her. The mother tries again, then thanks the hostess herself and leaves, feeling defeated and embarrassed by her child's impoliteness.

Yet, when children forget or refuse to say "please" and "thank you," they're usually not being impolite. There are several explanations for their behavior. First, they have a difficult time grasping general rules, including ones about responding in socially appropriate ways. A child who's told to say "thank you" when given something at Grandma's house may not connect that experience to a similar one that happens later at a neighbor's house. Although she is again being given something, she's too young to understand that she should respond as she did earlier.

Another reason children may not use polite words is shyness. While some children respond to prompting, others are just too self-conscious, especially when adult attention is focused on them. A shy child may refuse to say "please" or "thank you," and this can lead to a struggle if her parents try to force the issue.

Finally, a child may be too preoccupied to say "please" and "thank you," especially if she's just been given a new toy or has an urgent request. She has a difficult time thinking about and considering other people's wishes, and saying what her parents want her to say may be the furthest thing from her mind when she's excited.

Sometimes parents who constantly remind their child to say "please" put themselves in a bind. They may inadvertently convince her that all her wishes will be granted if she uses what, for her, may actually seem like a magic word. For example, in a toy store she may say, "Please, Mom, please. Will you buy this for me?" When her parents explain why she can't have the toy she just politely asked for, she may not understand (or not want to hear) their reasoning: "But I said please!" Since her parents want to encourage politeness, they may be reluctant to say "no." Inevitably, she will receive a confusing mixed message—saying "please" sometimes gets her what she's asks for and sometimes doesn't.

If your child does not often say "please" and "thank you" on her own, there are a number of things you can try. Watch for the times when she does use polite words and reinforce that behavior by saying, "I really like the way you asked for that." If you know that your child is too shy to say "thank you," you can do the thanking for her, which may make you both more comfortable, and let you model polite behavior for her. And if you're unhappy with the way she's asked for something, say, "When you ask me that way, it doesn't make me want to give you the juice," or, "You'll have to find another way of asking." Such statements give her an opportunity to say "please" or to change her tone of voice.

Tone can be very important. As adults, we're usually more concerned about using a polite tone than about always attaching "please" to our requests. When your child makes frequent demands ("Zip my jacket!") you may be so frustrated with her tone that you find yourself harshly demanding politeness ("PLEASE!"). If she mimics that harsh "please," you still won't like the way she sounds. But if instead of demanding a "please" you model the right tone, she may understand what you want and respond more pleasantly.

Finally, remember to say "please" and "thank you" when you ask your child for something or when she's done what you've requested. All too often we make demands of children without ever saying "please" and "thank you" to them. When your child hears you speaking politely to her and to other children and adults, she'll begin to do as you do, and increasingly say "please" and "thank you" on her own.

Should I always make my child say "I'm sorry"?

A mother who sees her son hit his playmate says, "That wasn't nice. Now tell your friend you're sorry." The boy reluctantly mutters, "Sorry," but it's clear he feels no remorse. In fact, he probably believes he did nothing wrong. Young children are egocentric and often focus on fulfilling their own needs without considering other's feelings. At times, they grab, hit, knock over each other's blocks, say unkind things, and refuse to share. Parents who don't want their child to do these things should set firm limits on inappropriate behavior rather than coerce him into making insincere apologies.

When a child is forced to apologize, and when saying, "I'm sorry," is the main consequence for unacceptable behavior, he may decide that it's worth hitting other children or knocking over their toys. All he has to do is apologize afterwards and he may be excused.

Parents often enforce an apology because it's a quick and easy way to deal with misbehavior. Yet, parents know that hearing their child apologize can at times be unsatisfying, particularly if he has done something dangerous such as throw sand in a playmate's face. They may try to talk to their child about his unacceptable action and he may respond, "But I already said I'm sorry." However, when they don't overemphasize apologies, he can't so easily "get off the hook." He has to find other ways to resolve conflicts.

The real motivation for a child to change his behavior comes not from the fear of having to apologize, but from the fear of disappointing and angering his parents and, as he gets older, his friends. A child who doesn't want his parents to get angry at him may apologize on his own for misbehavior. Such an apology comes from within him and is much more sincere than an apology the he's forced to make.

Parents may wonder why their child doesn't make genuine apologies more often. Sometimes he's too embarrassed or ashamed to admit wrongdoing and at other times he may not like being put on the spot. He may deny his actions either because he actually believes it's true or because he fears his parents' reactions and disapproval. Often, young children have strong feelings of autonomy and resist doing what their parents want them to do.

When your child hurts another child, focus on setting limits. Rather than saying, "You hit her, now apologize," say, "I'm not going to let you hit her," or, "You may not want to play with her, but I'm not going to let you hurt her." If your child is four or five years old, have him help remedy a situation: "Since you pushed over your friend's blocks, you have to help her put her building back together." You can also model considerate behavior by apologizing for him: "I'm sorry he pushed over your building. He's going to help you build it again."

The older your child gets, the more easily you can discuss angry feelings with him. Listen to his reasons for misbehavior, no matter how far-fetched they seem. Before he can offer sincere apologies, he needs to believe that he can explain his side of a disagreement. Children (and adults) who feel unheard often defend themselves and, unless coerced, refuse to apologize even when they know they're wrong.

Since your child imitates your behavior, remember to apologize to him when you overreact, bump into him, or take him away from play to rush out for your own reasons. If you apologize whenever the situation calls for it, he will eventually copy your words and actions.

What should I do about bathroom language?

"Billy, what are you going to be for Halloween?" asks Jane.

"Doo doo face," says Billy, and both children laugh.

Young children think it's funny to say such words as "doo doo," "pee pee," "boobies," and "butt." The words are not quite "bad," but to children they have their power. They use bathroom language when they feel silly or need a quick way to be funny and make their friends laugh. The words also provide a way of releasing tension and getting attention. A child might use bathroom words more than usual when there's a new baby in her family, when she's unhappy in day care or school, or when she wants the attention of a friend who's playing with someone else. Using these words often does bring a child instant attention from adults and friends.

Different parents have different reactions to bathroom language. Some just shrug their shoulders and ignore the words. Others are annoyed or embarrassed and wonder where their child learned such language. They worry that she will be reprimanded by a teacher or caregiver, and wonder if her use of bathroom language is a reflection on their parenting.

You should feel reassured to know that all children use bathroom words, which they hear and repeat on the playground. It's almost impossible to delete the words from your child's vocabulary. The best you can do is set limits by saying, "I don't want you to talk that way in the house," or simply, "I don't want to listen to you using those words." But don't dwell on the fact that she's using bathroom language. This is just normal preschool silliness.

My child uses profanity. How do I respond?

Parents often forget that children are active listeners and imitators. If parents use profanity (and most do, either regularly or during moments of anger), so will their children. And children are surprisingly good mimics. They swear with their parents' tone and intensity, and they use curse words in the appropriate contexts. Young children pick up profanity, which they also hear from playmates and on TV, just as they pick up other phrases.

When people respond with surprise to a child who's used a curse word, or when they say, "That's bad," the child learns that profanity has power. He may continue to use swear words to test out their shock value and to try to understand what makes certain words bad.

Parents are usually alarmed by their child's swearing. They fear embarrassment and worry that he will be blamed for teaching profanity to other children. Parents also fear that his cursing will reflect on the entire family, and that people may assume such language is used and condoned in his home. Because of these fears, many parents become angry and react strongly when their child uses profanity. But they should be careful not to blame him for his natural tendency to imitate what he hears.

If your child uses swear words only occasionally, there's no need to be concerned. But if he uses such words often, there are several things you can do. The most important is to stop using profanity yourself. If he no longer hears the words from you (or from the TV shows you let him watch), he'll probably stop cursing. You can also explain that you don't want him using profanity, and you can set firm limits on his language. As long as you don't overreact, he'll probably give up profanity once the novelty wears off, although during the elementary years he may experiment with it again.

How can I help my children get along with each other?

Family dynamics change drastically when a second child is born. While parents give constant care to their infant, their older child often reacts negatively because of the major adjustments she has to make. Reactions vary, of course, with the age of the older sibling. A four- or five-year-old will be much more independent and understanding than a one- to three-year-old, but all older siblings will have some negative feelings. The way parents respond to their older child's feelings about the baby often sets the tone for the children's future relationship.

Some parents who pressure their older child to love the baby try to censure their child's feelings: "Don't say that about your little brother—it's not nice." "Be gentle with the baby." A child who's not allowed to share her negative feelings with her parents will continue to have those feelings; she'll just express them in other ways. She may not take her anger out on her parents since she, like all young children, fears losing their love, but she may take her anger out on her sibling.

The older child needs the freedom to express her negative feelings so she can resolve them. If her parents allow her to say, "Take the baby back to the hospital," and show that they understand her situation by saying, "It's sometimes hard, isn't it, to have a new baby in the house. Mommy and Daddy can't give you all the attention we used to, but we love you and know how you feel," the child will be reassured. She'll begin to accept and even like the baby once she knows that she can express her dislike without risking her parents' love. The more she's accepted and reassured, the more likely she is to develop positive feelings about her sibling, although there will always be some negative emotions as well.

Your older child will begin to feel good about her sibling when the baby starts smiling, giggling, and seeking her out: "He likes me!" You should support and encourage this early interaction by saying, "Yes, he really does like you. He seems to think you're funny and nice." At this point, she might enjoy helping you take care of the baby.

As your children grow, you'll have to consciously encourage them to respect each other. When they show consideration, give them positive feedback: "That was nice of you to pick up his toy." "Thanks for letting him play with you and your friend." If you treat each of your children with love and show that you accept them and their similarities and differences, they will respond positively.

Don't make one child seem more important or more deserving of consideration than the other. If you say, "Let him do it—he's younger," or, "She's older, so she can go," or, "She's better at it, so let her go first," you will give your children reasons to feel resentful and jealous, and you will encourage a cycle of competitiveness. And if you say, "The baby needs to be carried, but you're big enough to walk," or, "Don't play with the baby's toys. You're too old for that," your older child will feel anger that will be directed at her younger sibling, not at you.

At times you may sympathize with your older child, but be careful not to encourage her negative feelings. Listen to her complaints about her younger sibling, but don't say, "Yes, he really is a nuisance, isn't he?" She will consider your comments a license to feel and say what she wants about her sibling, and your younger child may end up feeling rejected.

Be matter-of-fact about the different things you do with your children: "She's going to bed later because she slept later this morning." "I'm putting this together for him because he doesn't understand how to do it." If your children are four or more years apart, there will be many times when you treat them differently. The older one will be allowed to watch a special television show or stay outside by herself while the younger one won't. In such cases, don't present the older child's activities as "better," or as privileges, since your younger child will interpret the privileges to mean, "She's better than I am." Discourage them from feeling competitive about what they're allowed to do. Rather let them both know, "This is just the way things are right now." Each child does what's appropriate.

When your older child wants to play alone or with his friends, you may have to distract your younger one by reading to him or having one of his friends over. The older child needs her privacy and her possessions, but at times she also has to give in and let her younger sibling join in the play. You may be tempted, if your children are at least four years apart, to make the older one responsible for entertaining her sibling. However, this is unfair to the older one, who may resent having someone "follow me around all the time." Forcing one child to stay with the other will probably increase the bad feelings between them.

If they are one to three years apart, they'll share many of the same interests, toys, and friends—a situation that can lead to conflict. When a friend comes to play, encourage them to include everyone. The child who brought the friend can have more control over the games, but siblings should be allowed to play. Although the child who must share her friend may be resentful at first, she'll soon focus on playing. If you let one of your children exclude the other from all play, the one left out will develop strong negative feelings about his sibling.

If your children are close in age and argue over toys, try to downplay the issue of possession. Rather than say, "That's his toy," encourage them to share and trade their playthings, and provide some toys that will interest both. If your younger child wants to play with something that belongs to his sibling, distract the older one for a moment so the younger has a chance with the toy. Then thank your older child for sharing, even though she did not do so intentionally. Similarly, distract the younger child so you can return his sister's toy, and tell him, "Isn't it nice she let you play with this for a little while?"

In spite of all you do to encourage a good relationship, your children will still argue with each other, probably some every day. Allow them to work out some of their minor problems themselves and try not to take sides. Too often parents end up blaming quarrels on the older child "who should know better." When this happens, she gets angry at her parents for scolding her, but she takes out her anger on her sibling because he is a safer target. Try to understand and accept that some arguments are inevitable. And take comfort and pleasure in the times you see your children showing genuine love and consideration for each other.

How can I teach my child to be gentle with his pet?

It's not unusual for a young child to handle his pet roughly and play with it in inappropriate ways. He may touch its eyes, pull its fur, put his fingers in its ears, and even sit on it. One child carried her hamster in her purse, while another was delighted to let his pet gerbil "have fun rolling down the steps."

Parents frequently react to such mistreatment by saying, "How would you like it if someone did that to you?" One veterinarian became so irritated by the way his daughter carried the family's new dog that he carried his daughter around the same way to show her what such treatment felt like. However, logic and examples have little effect on children under five, who have a difficult time putting themselves in another person's (or pet's) place.

A child doesn't mean to cause harm when he mishandles his pet. He just intends to play with it and explore it, and he doesn't understand the consequences of his actions. In fact, most children are very fond of their pets, and some develop strong emotional attachments to them, since pets can serve as comforting companions. One child, seeking acceptance after his father disciplined him, hugged his cat and said, "You like me, you're my friend." Children often share feelings with their pets: "Mommy won't let me go outside and I want to."

Your child may feel a great deal of affection for his pet, but if he's under five years old, you have probably seen him mistreat the animal. In order to protect the pet, show your child exactly how to handle it and be prepared to remind him often about appropriate holding and touching. You may also have to set consequences: "If you handle the dog roughly, you won't be allowed to play with him."

If your child is four or five years old, consistent reminders and firm limits should sometimes work, but if he's three or under, he's too young to remember how to play with a pet safely. In any case, you'll have to supervise closely whenever a child these ages is playing with an animal. Because watching a young child and a pet takes a lot of time and energy, many parents decide not to get a pet until their child is at least five years old. That way, he will be old enough to take responsibility for some of the pet's care and will better understand how the pet should be handled.

CARETAKERS AND EARLY EDUCATION

How can I choose a good pediatrician?

Every family wants a pediatrician who's dependable, competent, caring, and easy to talk to. Some doctors are all of these things, and others are not. Therefore, when parents are looking for a pediatrician, they should (to the extent allowed by insurance) take the time to visit several doctors, seek recommendations, and ask questions. Because the family's relationship with its pediatrician will be a long and involved one, it's important that parents choose their child's doctor carefully.

To get the names of pediatricians you can interview, ask for recommendations from friends, relatives, your obstetrician or midwife, and your insurance company. Check with local hospitals and the referral services of local medical societies. Once you have the names of several pediatricians, set up appointments to visit. It's always best to see at least two doctors so you can compare them before you make your decision. Some charge for consultations, so ask about fees.

When you visit each pediatrician's office, look around. Are there toys and books available for children? Is the floor clean enough for a baby to crawl on? Are sick and healthy children and newborns separated? Do the receptionists and nurses seem pleasant?

When you talk to the doctor, ask questions and pay attention to how she responds. Does she answer you fully in terms you can understand and does she listen to your point of view? Do you feel comfortable with her? How do you think she relates to children?

Here are some of the questions you might want to ask during your interview: where and when will the pediatrician examine your newborn? How does she feel about breast feeding and bottle feeding, and does she approve of the feeding method you've chosen? Does she make herself available to discuss nonmedical issues such as pacifier use, sleeping habits, and nutrition? Does she have regular call-in hours when you can ask questions over the phone? Is there a fee for phone consultations?

As you consider which pediatrician to use, think about such practical issues as the distance from the office to your home, the office hours (some pediatricians have extended hours for working parents), the doctor's fees, her procedure for emergency visits, and how her office handles insurance. If she practices alone, find out who covers for her when she's sick or on vacation, and try to meet that doctor briefly. If the pediatrician you interview is part of a group practice, ask if you can choose one of the doctors as your primary pediatrician.

Choose a doctor you feel comfortable talking to, since you will frequently consult with her about your child's growth and development, as well as medical problems. You may find that after you start taking your child to a pediatrician, your feelings about that doctor will change. You may not have known at the time you first interviewed her that you would be facing such issues as thumb-sucking, sleep problems, or late toilet use. Now you discover that her opinions about these issues are contrary to yours. She may, for example, be against giving bottles to a toddler, while you think it's acceptable.

In such situations, parents who feel intimidated by their pediatrician choose to hide their child's habits when they come in for appointments. They leave their child's blanket, pacifier, or bottle at home, rather than face the doctor's disapproval. Such parents may eventually grow distant from their pediatrician, seeking her advice only on medical issues. Other parents in the same situation may become more open with their doctor, letting her know just how their child behaves and discussing differences of opinion on parenting issues. If you find yourself disagreeing with your child's doctor too often, you'll have to decide whether to work out a compromise or switch pediatricians and start a new relationship.

How do I find a good occasional baby-sitter?

It can be difficult for parents to find a teenage baby-sitter they feel comfortable using. When they leave their child for an afternoon or evening, they want to know that he'll be happy and safe. Yet it's hard to tell from a quick conversation or a few minutes' observation whether a sitter will be responsible. The best way for parents to select a sitter is to ask for recommendations, get to know the sitter, and monitor carefully the way she performs the job.

To find potential sitters, ask friends, neighbors, relatives, and co-workers for recommendations. You also can ask local high school teachers or counselors for suggestions. Good sources of names are sitters who may be too busy to work for you but who can pass on names of friends. Whatever your source for baby-sitters, get suggestions from people you trust. Also, as you seek referrals, keep in mind the ages of baby-sitters. Parents of infants may prefer an older teenager while parents of four- and five-year-olds may be comfortable enough with a twelve- to fourteen-year-old sitter who will keep their child entertained.

After you've contacted a potential sitter, invite her to your home so you can observe her with your child. Ask questions about her activities, schoolwork, and friends. She'll be pleased that you take an interest in her, and from her responses you'll get to know what she's like. Watch as she interacts with your child. Is she friendly, playful, nurturing? How does your child respond to her? One father was delighted when the girl he was interviewing spontaneously took out her keys and jiggled them in front of his whimpering eighteen-month-old, calming the child. If the sitter is young or inexperienced, you may want to meet her parents—and they may want to meet you.

If you decide to use the sitter, have her arrive early on the day she'll watch your child so you can give her instructions. Teenagers need strong guidance and limits, so be prepared to tell your sitter in detail what your expectations are. Describe how you want her to handle feeding, playtime, television, toilet use, and bedtime, and write down your instructions so she can refer to them later. Make it clear if you don't want her to talk on the phone, invite her friends to your house, or take your child outside.

Before you leave, let your sitter know how you can be reached and leave emergency phone numbers. You might want to write down a list of activities your child enjoys, and another list of things to do (take out play dough, read books) if he gets silly or hard to handle. A four- or five-year-old may spend time testing a new sitter and feeling a sense of power: "This is my house, my food, my TV." Let your child know ahead of time that you expect him to behave appropriately, and let your sitter know that it may take time for him to feel comfortable.

If he has a difficult time separating from you, you might feel tempted to leave without warning him or saying good-bye. But if you do this, you'll probably increase his anxiety. It's better to tell him you're going and have the sitter comfort him as you leave. If he'll be asleep when you go, tell him before bedtime, "While you're sleeping, Kim will come and baby-sit for you." You also can take time before the baby-sitter arrives to tell your child about the fun he and she will have. If you let the sitter do special things with him—give an extra dessert, play a new game—he may be less anxious about your leaving.

While you're out, call home to see how things are going. Occasionally, your sitter will tell you that your child isn't feeling well and you'll then have to cut your evening short. This can be frustrating and at times upsetting. But it will happen less and less as your child gets older.

Trust your instincts. If you feel that something happened while you were away, try to find out about it. If your child seems unhappy with a sitter, try to learn why. You can ask a three- to five-year-old, "What do you like about Michelle? What don't you like?" Although you may hear some exaggerated stories, you should take him seriously when he says, "She yells too much," or, "She tries to scare us." If you're unsure about a sitter, ask a neighbor or relative to come by and check next time the sitter is at your house. And if you feel that a sitter is not responsible, stop using her and look for someone else. In order to enjoy your time away from home, you have to feel good about the person watching your child.

How can I choose the best day care center or nursery school for my child?

Every day care center and nursery school is different, and parents have to search carefully to find a good place for their child. Schools might claim (as Montessori, Waldorf, co-op, and religious schools do) that their programs are based on familiar philosophies, but parents have to see how the philosophies are actually implemented. The personalities of staff members, the physical layouts, and the day-to-day programs are what determine a school or center's quality. The only way for parents to make an informed choice is to observe a number of programs.

Parents who want a program that meets three mornings a week and parents searching for a day care center open twelve hours a day will be looking for the same qualities. All parents want caring staff members, a pleasant facility, and a flexible program that will meet their child's needs for the one to four years she will attend. The difference for parents looking at full-time day care is that their child will spend most of her waking hours at the center they choose. Therefore, the selection of a quality day care program is essential.

As you look for child care facilities, narrow your choices to centers that are easy to get to. If you're considering nursery schools, you'll probably want one close to home, while you might find a day care center more convenient if it's close to your work. Narrow your choices further by asking friends, neighbors, and coworkers for recommendations. Then visit at least two or three programs before making a decision.

When you go to a center or school, think about the physical space. Are the rooms inviting, clean, and safe? Is there ample room to play inside and is there play equipment outside? Are there places in the classroom where your child can play quietly? Are there a variety of toys and materials within easy reach? Where will your child take naps, and where can she go if she doesn't nap? Does the overall environment seem exciting?

Watch the teachers and aides carefully, since they set the tone for the program. Do they seem to enjoy their jobs and relate well to each other? Do you like the way they interact with the children? Good teachers will be warm, understanding, and respectful of children. Do they seem reassuring and flexible enough to let a child follow her own interests? Are you comfortable with the way they set limits and carry out discipline in the classroom?

Try to imagine your child in the programs you observe. How would she react? Are the teachers' expectations appropriate for her? Would the schedule allow her flexibility? What if she wanted to continue with one activity when the teachers had scheduled a switch to another—would she be allowed quietly to finish what she was doing?

See if the teachers pay enough attention to the children in the room. One parent saw a teacher who was so involved with a small group working on the day's curriculum project that she ignored the rest of the class. When the teacher finally became aware of an argument in the block corner, she was too late to help a child whose building had been destroyed.

Consider how many teachers there are at the center or school, and the makeup of the groups. Young children need a lot of attention and comfort. Older children need fewer adults, but the teacher-child ratio in all cases should seem satisfactory to you and meet local licensing standards. Are there mixed age groups in a single classroom, or are children placed with others the same age? You may prefer one arrangement over another.

Pay particular attention to the school or center's program. Too many are highly structured and goal-oriented, arranged with parents' and not children's needs in mind. Many teachers say, "Parents want academics. Parents expect projects." But when academics are over-emphasized, children lose opportunities to play, experiment with different materials, and come up with discoveries and their own answers to problems. In an effective program, children have plenty of time to explore on their own and teachers value active play and socializing.

Look at the children's artwork. Most nursery schools and centers have children do one or two art projects a day. Is the work displayed at a child's eye level? Are all the projects precut by the teacher? Do all the finished projects look alike, or are they truly products of the children's effort and creativity?

Finally, see if the activities are appropriate for the children. One group of two-year-olds was expected to dye Easter eggs in school, but the children were clearly incapable of following the necessary steps. Rather than drop the activity, the teachers did all the dyeing themselves.

Teachers should build on children's interests and abilities, not give them tasks they can't perform. Look for a program that stresses exploration and discovery and teachers who will follow up on your child's own interests and abilities.

What if I don't send my child to preschool?

Stay-at-home parents feel pressure to send their child to preschool since most children go to some sort of program and child care professionals generally recommend it. Parents who keep their child home until elementary school often face the disapproval of friends and relatives. People ask, "How will he learn to socialize?" "Isn't he ready?" "How can you get anything done with him around all day?" "Aren't you afraid he'll miss out?" "How will he be prepared for kindergarten?"

There are a number of good reasons why a child might not go to preschool. When there's a new baby in the family, some parents keep their older child home so he won't feel rejected or pushed out. The expense of nursery school deters other families, either because they can't afford the fees or don't think the experience is worth the cost. Some parents are unable to find a nursery school that seems appropriate for their child, and some want to be with their child full-time until elementary school begins. Finally, some parents keep their child at home because they welcome the freedom: when there are no school schedules to follow, parent and child can wake up when they want, go on outings together, and stay outdoors as long as they like.

A child who stays out of nursery school will not be harmed socially. He'll have chances to play with siblings, neighborhood children, and friends who attend part-time or half-day programs. His parents also can enroll him in once-a-week recreation classes and set up a visiting arrangement with other children who don't attend nursery school.

When a child does go to nursery school, his parents often marvel at how he changes. He seems more cooperative and knowledgeable, and they attribute his growth to the school. But parents whose children stay at home also see these changes. Young children naturally mature and develop as they get older, and a four-year-old who stays home will have the same interest in learning and playing as a four-year-old in a preschool.

A child who stays home will be busy and involved, especially if his parents provide an environment in which he can explore, play, read, go on outings, and create—all the things done at school. He'll learn about his world because, like all young children, he's curious. Preschool can be a very positive experience, but it isn't a necessary one.

If you decide to keep your child at home for the preschool years, you may wonder how he'll adjust to kindergarten. As long as you prepare him by visiting the school ahead of time and talking about kindergarten activities, he is likely to do just as well as a child who attended preschool. Kindergarten is a new experience for all children, and they all go through a period of adjustment.

During the years that your child is at home instead of in preschool, people may ask him, "Where do you go to school?" and other children will tell him about their schools. Your child, particularly if he is four or five, may wonder why he isn't in school, and may feel somewhat alienated from his friends. Many children, however, are not affected by the questions and comments of others and confidently announce, "I don't go to school," or, "I learn at home." If your child does express a desire to go to nursery school, you may want to look for a program that meets your needs as well as his, or you may decide to tell him that he'll go to school when he's old enough for kindergarten.

Although the decision to keep your child home may be a difficult one, you might be surprised by unexpected support. One mother, expecting a lecture, reluctantly told her pediatrician she was not sending her child to school. The doctor shocked and delighted her by not only praising her decision, but telling her that he and his wife had kept their children home and that the experience had been very positive.

How should I prepare my two- to four-year-old for day care or nursery school?

When a child begins day care or nursery school, she and her family face the issues of separation and independence. A four- or five-year-old will probably go off without much difficulty, but many children under three have a hard time leaving their parents. Parents can make the transition from home a little easier if they talk to their child about what will be happening and patiently reassure her.

You can begin preparing your child several weeks before her new program starts. If she previously went with you to visit the school or center, remind her of what she saw: "Remember the blocks and puzzles you played with there?" If she's never seen the school, describe the building, the toys, and the activities. Let her know about snacks, lunch, and naps, and reassure her that the school has bathrooms and places for her coat and other belongings. Mention the name of someone she knows who will be in the program with her; if she doesn't know anyone in the school, tell her there will be many other children her age there. If you know who your child's teachers will be, tell her their names.

If your child is under two, you won't be able fully to prepare her for nursery school or day care because she won't understand much of what you tell her, although you can still describe whatever you think will interest her. She will basically have to experience the new program and the separation firsthand. You and your child's caretakers will have to be understanding and nurturing as she adjusts in the early weeks of school, and you may have to be flexible about your own schedule so you can take her home early if necessary.

On the first day of school, before you leave home, talk to her about the separation that's coming: "After we get to the classroom, I'll stay for a few minutes and then say good-bye." Tell her what time you'll be coming back and what your driving arrangements will be. If she'll be in a car pool, tell her who will drive. For the first few days of school you may want to do the driving yourself to help her adjust to her new situation.

Be patient as you say good-bye to her the first few days. Many children, especially those under three years old, have a difficult time leaving their parents, particularly if the program lasts a full day. Your child may want to say good-bye several times, or she may cry. Don't threaten her or say, "Be good and stop crying," or, "Be a big girl." She needs support, not pressure. You might be able to eliminate some of her anxiety by letting her bring along a favorite toy or blanket. Try arriving at school fifteen minutes early so you can spend more time with her before you go. Or give her a special little treat when she gets in the car or a "love" note or picture to carry into school with her.

You should not try to sneak out of the school without saying good-bye, even if you think such an action might keep your child from crying. Eventually she will notice you're gone and may become frightened and upset. Although it's painful to see your child cry as you go, you should still say good-bye to her. You might feel better if you wait outside the classroom door, listening for a few minutes until she's calmed down.

As time goes by, she may continue to have trouble leaving you at the school door. Children two years old and younger don't understand that you'll return, no matter how often you tell them. This may make them anxious in the morning and off and on throughout the day. Consult with your child's teachers. They may be able to help by giving your child extra comfort and reassurance, and getting her involved in activities.

It might take your child several weeks to adjust to school or day care, and during that time you may see some changes in behavior such as bed-wetting, nightmares, decreased appetite, more frequent whining, and reluctance to go to school. Getting used to a program is more difficult for some children than others, but most children are affected in some way during the early days of a new situation. You'll have to be patient and understanding as your child adjusts.

If, after several months, she's still showing behavioral changes and seems unhappy, talk to her teachers and stay to observe the program. You might even drop in unexpectedly to see how she is, and to try to find out why she isn't enjoying herself. As you watch her, ask yourself the following questions: does she seem to have friends she enjoys? Is she one of the youngest children in the group? (If she is, she may feel less confident and accepted.) Is she getting enough attention from her teachers? If the program seems inappropriate, take her out and find a better one. But if you're unsure, wait a bit before making your decision. Your child just might need an extra amount of understanding and time to adjust to day care or school.

I'm having a difficult time adjusting to day care. What should I do?

When parents work full-time outside the home, they often send their child to a day care center. Yet, eight to twelve hours a day, five days a week is a long time for parents and children to be apart, and the separation takes an emotional toll on parents. They miss their child, particularly when he first begins a program, and they worry about the care he's receiving. Is he happy? Safe? Are his teachers taking an interest in him? Does he have friends?

Parents may feel guilty because they fear that day care will have a negative effect on their child. If they see his behavior change, they wonder if it's because of his program. They feel bad about not spending enough time with him, and a mother, especially, may wonder whether she should have gone to work full-time in the first place. Even when parents and child are together in the evenings, the effects of work and day care continue. There's never enough time together at home and parents who want time for themselves feel guilty about not paying enough attention to their child.

If you're concerned about having your child in a full-time program, your feelings are natural. There are things you can do to lessen your guilt and worry and to solve some of the child care-related problems you experience. The most important step is to reassure yourself about your child's well-being by staying in close contact with his teachers. Call the center periodically and find out how he's doing. If the teachers agree (and they should), ask that he be brought to the phone so you can talk to him. When you have a chance, drop by the day care unannounced so you can observe him at play. You will feel better if you see him happily involved.

If you suspect that he's not happy, don't ignore the problem, even if you feel desperate about the need for child care. It takes a great deal of effort and energy to become involved in your child's day care situation; some parents avoid or deny all problems because they don't have the time, desire, or energy to cope. Others are afraid even to question their child about his day for fear he'll say something negative.

If you're worried about your child's adjustment to day care, you have to become involved enough to help him. Make sure the quality of his program remains high—don't compromise. Spend as much time as possible with him when you're home in the evenings and on weekends. Look to other parents for support and advice. Finally, reconsider your need to work outside the home or to work full-time. You and your child could benefit greatly if you were able to stay home with him as much as possible during the few short years before elementary school.

When should my child learn ABCs and numbers?

Many preschool and day care programs claim to be "academic," teaching very young children to count, recite the alphabet, and learn various concepts. Such emphasis on educational activities is part of a larger, society-wide push to have children learn more, faster. Publishers put out educational books and software; toy companies manufacture educational games; television shows teach the alphabet and numbers. Because of pressure from friends, neighbors, some child development professionals, and the media, many parents feel concerned if their two-, three- or four-year-old hasn't yet learned shapes, colors, letters, and numbers.

It's possible to teach a young child to memorize and then recite back almost any short list, including the numbers from one to ten and the alphabet. But comprehension of such concepts doesn't usually begin until she's four to six years old. A three-year-old may know that saying "1, 2, 3, 4," is called counting, but she probably won't understand that the number 6 represents six objects. To her, learning the alphabet is like learning to recite in a foreign language without knowing the meaning of the words.

A child can't be taught to understand concepts before she is ready. Gradually, as she experiments with objects, questions her parents and other people, observes her environment, and explores, she'll learn what words and numbers mean. If her natural curiosity is encouraged and she has materials to experiment with, she'll learn concepts easily.

But too much emphasis on early education may discourage her and diminish her natural drive to learn. Parents should wait until their child shows a spontaneous interest in letters, words, and concepts, then follow up on what she can do.

There's no need for schools and parents to provide excessive amounts of educational materials for young children. Colors, shapes, numbers, and words are part of whatever children do, so they learn about these things naturally. Every day, a child hears, "Put on your blue shorts," "Do you want the red or the green crayon?" "Here are three crackers," "Look at that big truck." She has constant exposure to such concepts as same and different (milk is different than juice, Mom is different than Dad), soft and hard, big and little. She hears adults counting, sees them reading, and observes letters and numbers everywhere. She gets a natural jump on literacy when her parents read to her daily, patiently repeating her favorite stories.

You will gradually hear your child ask, "How many is this?" "What color is this?" "What does this say?" She'll begin to count out loud, at first getting the numbers out of order, and she'll write letters on paper, often creating nonsense words or writing her name backwards. Try not to correct her, but rather encourage her to keep counting and keep writing. She'll learn at her own pace—without pressure—because she's interested and self-motivated. Then, starting with kindergarten and first grade, you'll see her make great strides in literacy and math.

Why do so many children have Attention Deficit Disorder?

ADD has become a common—and at times controversial—childhood "disorder." Children are diagnosed with it when they have trouble paying attention to tasks, especially ones they're not interested in. While a preschooler may be identified as having ADD, more often a child is diagnosed during the early elementary years, when his teachers or parents begin complaining about how distractable he is: "He just doesn't focus." "He's too hard to handle."

There's no consistent chemical evidence for ADD, and while it's certainly a real disorder, a growing number of people feel that it's over-diagnosed by pediatricians, therapists, and even educators. Children who truly have ADD typically have additional neurobiological difficulties, including visual, auditory, or motor problems. But any child who says, "I forgot," and who dawdles before going to school, procrastinates over homework or chores, is boisterous or temperamental, or gets involved in something other than what he's directed to do could potentially be labeled ADD and medicated for the condition.

One mother reported two examples of what she believed was ADD behavior in her five-year-old: "He sits at dinner with one leg hanging off the side of the chair, and he doesn't listen when I tell him to stay close by me in the mall." When asked what she does about these things, she responded, "Nothing! He has ADD so he can't help it."

Too often, the diagnosis of ADD and the medication that follows are either a catch-all method of dealing with a seemingly difficult, but normal, child or an excuse for not setting firm limits, spending time with him, and meeting his needs at home or at school. Parents and teachers worried by the increase in ADD need to know that there are a variety of other, more common reasons why a young child would have trouble listening to adults or paying attention to his responsibilities.

Many children are simply spirited by nature, or they may act out in aggressive ways because they're not receiving enough calm, positive attention. A child may feel stress because of his parents' divorce, a new sibling, or school pressures. Often, parents haven't helped their child learn to get along with others, and haven't given him enough guidance and discipline.

A rarely discussed contributor to ADD-like behavior can be day care, where many children, starting at age two, follow a rigid schedule initiated by teachers. Frequent changes from one activity to another mean a child can't focus for long periods or get involved in something interesting without constant interruptions. The schedule basically trains him not to pay careful attention.

Here is a typical day for a young child in a day care program. He may wake as early as 5:30 A.M. so his family can leave home by 6:00 to get to day care by 6:30. He's rushed as he gets dressed, and there's no time to play before driving off. Once he arrives at the day care center, his schedule is packed (only naptime lasts longer than an hour).

6:30 A.M.	Arrives and says good-bye to his parents whom he won't see again for ten to twelve hours.
6:30–7:00	Breakfast
7:00–8:00	Table games, puzzles, quiet activities
8:00–8:30	Story
8:30–9:15	Art activity
9:15–9:45	Snack
9:45–10:30	Outdoor play
10:30–11:15	Circle time with teacher-directed activity
11:15–11:30	Wash up and prepare for lunch
11:30–12:00	Lunch
12:00–2:00	Nap
2:00–2:30	Snack
2:30–3:15	Outdoor play
3:15–4:00	Free play
4:00–4:30	Story
4:30–5:00	Music
5:00–6:00	Table activities, puzzles, Legos, clean up, and preparation to leave.

At 6:00 P.M., the child is picked up and taken home or on an errand. His family arrives home between 6:30 and 7:00, and he plays or watches TV until dinner. Then he plays for a short while before bath, story, and bed at 8:30, or later if he had a long nap at day care.

Children do this day after day, often for four or five years. While the day care schedule may seem to keep them busy and enriched, it actually operates counter to their needs. According to developmentalist Erik Erikson, preschoolers have important tasks at this developmental stage: they need to initiate ideas; plan, carry out, and persevere in activities; and set goals. This is how they learn to focus, concentrate, and follow through.

Yet, children in many day care programs are not focusing and following through enough. All day, they're required to share or give up whatever they're using before they're done. They often don't have time to finish what they start before teachers interrupt to get them ready for the next activity. The starting and stopping and the lack of flexibility keep them from learning to concentrate for extended periods. The frustration can make them uncooperative and fidgety. By the time a child gets to kindergarten or first grade, his teachers may be pointing out his ADD-like behavior.

If you suspect your child has ADD or if he's already been diagnosed, don't give him medication unless you and your physician believe it's absolutely necessary. There are many other strategies you can try first. If he's in day care, look for programs with more flexible schedules. Limit TV, video game, and computer time; instead, spend more time with him, playing together and paying attention to his interests. Highlight his capabilities, nurture his curiosity, and give him opportunities to initiate activities. Slow down, let him finish what he starts, and don't stress clean-up over discovery and creativity.

You also need to make discipline a priority. Set clear limits on his inappropriate behavior, follow through with consequences, and redirect him toward more positive activities. Look for underlying reasons for his misbehavior. Help him learn to control his impulses, and consistently teach him right from wrong.

All children have some trouble concentrating, especially when they'd rather be doing something else. If your child shows ADD-like behavior, it will take time for him to learn to focus on important tasks. But with your involvement and patience and his teachers' cooperation, he should eventually be able to follow directions and pay attention without needing medication.

What should I look for in recreation classes?

Parents enroll their child in community recreation classes so he can pick up new skills and enjoy himself. Sometimes these classes are well-run and satisfying, but other times they're poorly taught and disappointing. In order to choose classes wisely, parents should try to observe programs before registering, and consider which activities are most appropriate. Then, once class sessions begin, they should monitor the program and help their child adjust.

Before you sign up for a class, watch a session taught by the instructor your child will have. Although it may be difficult for you to arrange an observation, it's worth the effort. Many recreation programs sound exciting when described in catalogs and brochures, but turn out to be boring or inadequate. If possible, take your child along so he can let you know if he's interested.

As you watch a class session, ask yourself these questions: how structured is the program? Does it look like fun? Do the children seem to be enjoying themselves? How does the instructor respond to a child who's hesitant about joining the group? Is there unnecessary pressure on children to conform and achieve? Does the teacher seem to nurture creativity? Does she say, "I like the way you did that," rather than, "You can do better than that?" Does she accept a child's limitations? How large is the class? Do children get a chance to show the teacher what they can do? Do they have to spend much time waiting for turns?

If you decide to enroll your child in a class, briefly prepare him for the first session. Talk to him about the instructors, the equipment, the clothes he'll wear, and any friends who'll be in the class. Let him know about transportation arrangements and where you'll be while the class meets. And since most children wonder about the availability of bathrooms, tell him that the recreation program has bathrooms.

On the first day of class, you'll notice that some children quickly join in the activities while others have difficulty adjusting. If your child is reluctant to get involved, you might feel discouraged and embarrassed, especially if the other class members are having an easy time. You might also feel alone, questioning your parenting abilities and wondering what you've done to make your child shy and unwilling to participate. You might feel angry at your child, particularly if it was his idea to take the class.

In such a situation, a supportive teacher can help by smiling, waving, coming over to talk, and generally letting your child know he's accepted even if he doesn't choose to participate right away. You'll also feel more comfortable if the other parents in the group are supportive rather than judgmental. While you're encouraging your child to participate, try not to pressure him but rather accept his hesitancy and, if necessary, sit with him until he's ready to join the group.

In later class sessions, he may continue to resist joining in or may become disenchanted with the program. Perhaps the instructor overwhelms him, the other children seem too big, he's not ready to separate from you, the teachers' (or your) expectations create too much pressure, he's unwilling to join in because you're watching, or the class is not what he thought it would be. He may have had his own fantasies about the program, imagining he'd be free to jump on the trampoline, do somersaults, or improvise his own craft projects. But most programs allow little freedom—children are told what to do and how to do it, and they spend a lot of time waiting for their turns.

It's not unusual for a child's interest in a recreation program to dwindle as the weeks go by. You may hear, "I'll go another day," or, "I don't want to go." Often because of a rigid structure or intense competition, the classes stop being fun. Think back to your own experience with recreation programs. The classes that you enjoyed and continued to attend were ones that provided fun, acceptance, and positive feedback. The ones you disliked made you feel unaccepted and pressured.

If your child wants to drop out of a recreation class, discuss the situation with him and then with the instructors. They can help you decide whether you should spend some sessions helping your child adjust, or whether he should stop attending. Don't force him to continue in a class he's not enjoying, since such pressure is likely to increase his resistance to all classes. And don't worry that quitting will make him an habitual "quitter." He's too young to have understood what he was getting into, or to need a lesson in perseverance. Just continue to expose him to a variety of experiences and activities so he can figure out what interests him and develop new skills.

Is my child ready for kindergarten?

As a child approaches the end of his preschool years, his parents begin to consider his readiness for kindergarten. Some parents confidently envision their child in kindergarten, but others, particularly those whose children have mid- to late-in-the-year birthdays, wonder if he's ready for this major step. There are school districts that require children with late birthdays to wait an extra year before starting kindergarten, but most districts let parents choose whether to enroll their child during his fifth or sixth year. Because a child's success in the first year of school lays the foundation for later success, the decision to send a child to kindergarten must be made carefully and in his best interests.

Parents sometimes assume that a child who's been to day care or nursery school is automatically prepared for kindergarten, but it's a different experience in a number of ways. Children in kindergarten are expected to spend scheduled amounts of time sitting and working on specific academic skills. Although play is considered part of the daily program, emphasis is placed on group and individual academic work and on following a set curriculum. Kindergartners become part of a large school community that operates under new rules and expectations. And children find that their parents, who are excited about kindergarten, may begin to put emphasis on "doing well."

Chronological age is the major factor determining kindergarten readiness, but naturally there are related factors parents should consider: cognitive or intellectual development, social and emotional development, and physical size. If a child is five to eleven months younger than other kindergartners, he may display behavior that's significantly different from his classmates'. Even if he's advanced in one area of development such as academics, he may generally be functioning at a level lower than expected for his age group.

Another area of concern should be social and emotional development. A child who's socially or emotionally immature may have a difficult time accommodating to his teacher's demands. He may seem unwilling to behave as kindergartners should, when actually he's unable to act more mature. He may have a hard time working and playing cooperatively with his classmates and this may cause him to be labeled a "behavior problem." Naturally, if he's labeled this way, his self-image will be affected, and ultimately, he may continue misbehaving because he feels frustrated and angry over his inability to do what's expected of him.

A child who lags behind socially but is advanced academically poses a dilemma for his parents, who may be concerned about holding him back an extra year. They may think he will not be challenged in academic areas if he waits and attends kindergarten with younger children, yet, if the imbalance between social and intellectual development is striking, he's probably not developmentally ready for kindergarten.

To evaluate overall readiness for kindergarten, parents should first look at their child's cognitive development. When a child is functioning academically below kindergarten level, he sometimes can be helped through individualized instruction from teachers and specialists. But the child who's lagging behind often has a hard time catching up because learning in certain areas is too difficult for him. Despite the instructional support, he might think he's "not as good" as his peers, and he may feel unnecessary stress because he can't cope with the demands of school. When this happens, he'll probably show signs of disliking school, say he hates school, or exhibit behavioral problems. Academic struggles in kindergarten often establish a pattern that can continue for years.

Another factor parents should consider is size and physical development. When a child is several months younger than the average kindergarten student, he also may be smaller than his classmates. Size and age are important to young children, who frequently check each other to see who's tallest or oldest. And since children often begin to lose their teeth during the kindergarten year, a younger child might be frustrated and unhappy if he doesn't lose teeth when his older friends do. Being the youngest and smallest can put a child in a vulnerable position in the classroom, although this naturally would be more of a problem for a child who's reserved and quiet rather than boisterous and outgoing.

If you're unsure about your child's readiness for kindergarten, seek opinions from others, including professionals. If your child has been to day care or nursery school, the first people you contact will probably be his teachers. Since they have a basic understanding of kindergarten requirements and have had many opportunities to observe children, they'll be able to advise you. As long as you like and trust them, their judgment may be very helpful. If you continue to have questions, seek the opinion of a developmental specialist who assesses school readiness. Your pediatrician also may be of help in addressing your concerns. Friends who have held their children back a year can share their thoughts with you, and elementary school counselors or principals will discuss the issue and offer information on kindergarten readiness.

Most parents who have held their children back a year have not regretted the extra time for growing and maturing. The child who starts kindergarten when he's developmentally ready is better able to meet academic demands and get along with others throughout his schooling. When children don't have to struggle to keep up, they develop a strong sense of self-confidence, and this provides a good foundation for the school years.

Part Two

The Six- to Nine-Year-Old

"Is my child overscheduled?"

"Do other kids keep their rooms neat?"

"How can I tell if my child's doing well in school?"

"When should I give an allowance?"

The early elementary years are an exciting time of change for kids, and a busy time for parents who must keep up with their own and their children's schedules. Children begin school, form strong friendships, participate in after-school activities and organized sports, and become more responsible and independent. They mature and develop self-control. However, at times they also feel insecure and inferior.

These are the industrious years. Kids are increasingly involved in academic learning and pursuing their interests, whether soccer, piano, swim team, dance, participating in outdoor games, starting a collection, and on and on. They're discovering what they're good at and what they need to work on. They're picking up skills and knowledge, and learning lessons in sportsmanship, teamwork, creativity, practice, and commitment.

They're also becoming less egocentric and better able to understand and sympathize with others' points of view. Since they need practice imagining themselves in another's place, you need to remind them about people's feelings and talk often about getting along.

You continue to be the major influence in your child's life, and your involvement with him is essential during these years. Your challenge is to keep being a positive role model, setting limits, discussing your expectations, and listening to him.

GRADUAL CHANGES

Why does my child still have trouble at bedtime?

Many parents believe that six- to nine-year-olds should go to bed on their own without arguing, and when their own child doesn't, they feel frustrated. They get tired of saying, "Brush your teeth." "Now put on your pajamas." "Now put your clothes away." They also are bothered if she dawdles or gets up once she's been put to bed.

Independent bedtime habits develop slowly. Most children can fall asleep without having their parents stay with them, and many can take care of their middle-of-the-night needs: going to the bathroom, getting a drink, finding an extra blanket. However, it's still common for young children to need help at bedtime. Most require prodding at night and some won't get ready at all unless their parents guide them through almost every step of the process. All these reminders are necessary because they have difficulty separating themselves from their activities. They'd much rather continue playing or watching TV. And because bedtime is of no interest to them, they're easily distracted and need to be kept on track. The procrastination that bothers so many parents is the result of the young child's inability to focus on something she doesn't want to do.

Children this age also need their parents for bedtime rituals, which continue to be important. Some kids can't go to sleep without a story, a conversation, or a hug and a kiss. In busy families or on rushed days, bedtime may be the only time parents and children have quiet contact.

While most children need some parental help at night, if your child has consistent trouble at bedtime, try to find out why. Observe her and talk to her about the problem. Depending on her age, there might be a simple explanation. Perhaps she's hungry and needs a snack in the evening. She may avoid bedtime because she's afraid of imaginary creatures or the dark and wants to put off going to sleep as long as possible. If that's the case, spend fifteen minutes or so in her room while she falls asleep; try keeping a light on at night or suggesting that she sleep with a personal treasure or newly received gift. She may also sleep more securely in a room shared with a sibling.

Your child may have trouble because she simply isn't tired. Some parents, understandably eager for time alone in the evenings, set early bedtimes without considering their child's actual sleep needs. If you know that your child isn't sleepy, you can send her to bed later or set a flexible bedtime, including later hours on weekends. As an alternative to changing her bedtime, you can stick to the early hour but allow her to do something quiet in her room, such as read, draw, do a puzzle, or listen to music before she falls asleep.

If her bedtime problems just seem to be habitual, you'll have to set limits and tell her the consequences of too much dawdling: "If you don't get ready quickly, you won't have time to play before bed." "When you take so long to get in bed, I don't have time to read to you." It's important to anticipate evening struggles rather than let annoyances build up to an angry battle of wills.

You also can try rewarding your child for getting ready on time: "If you're in bed in five minutes, I'll let you listen to a tape before you fall asleep." One child would get ready quickly in order to hear favorite stories about her family.

Bedtime will be less stressful if you try to be patient and remember that your child will gradually assume her own bedtime responsibilities. Meanwhile, as long as she responds to your reminders and does get ready, you don't have to worry or feel defeated. If there are evening arguments, try to resolve them with a bedtime talk. Discuss what happened that day, tell your child about something exciting that's coming up, suggest that you both try a little harder to cooperate with each other, and remind her of how special she is.

Sometimes our child wants to sleep in our bed. What do we do?

Some children still periodically climb into their parents' bed. Kids who formed this habit during their early years may take a while to grow out of it. Originally they had a strong emotional need to be with their parents at night. After the need is gone, the habit may linger.

Many parents are not concerned about the practice, primarily because their child goes to sleep in his own bed as independently as other kids his age do. Although he spends many nights on his own, he still sometimes prefers, with gradually decreasing frequency, to be with his parents if he wakes during the night.

Some children seek comfort with their parents because they've had a nightmare or they aren't feeling well. Others find their way into their parents' bed during times of stress or after their parents return from a vacation. If parents' busy schedules leave little time for him, he may want to sleep in their bed as a way of having contact with them. Most often, however, children climb into their parents' bed out of habit. The habit will eventually disappear during these years.

If you're bothered by your child's continuing nighttime visits and want to end them now, talk to him about the situation. He's old enough to understand and accept your expectations. Tell him, "Since you're getting older, we want you to sleep in your bed for the whole night. If you need us during the night, come and let us know." He may follow your wishes immediately or slowly adjust to the new routine.

If he resists sleeping in his own room, try to find out why. One set of parents discovered that their daughter came into their bed at night to stop them from arguing. Ask your child what he thinks will help him stay in his own bed. Suggest that he sleep with a stuffed animal or an extra light. You might even try rearranging his room to make it more comfortable. More than anything, he will be helped by your reassurance.

What can I do about picky eating?

"Sit there until you finish your peas."
"If you don't have room for salad, you don't have room for dessert."
"Just take three more bites."
"If you don't eat what's on your plate, you won't get anything for the rest of the night."
Parents say and do all sorts of things to get their children to eat. Some threaten, others bargain, and some make their children sit at the din-

ner table for hours after the rest of the family has left.

As most parents find out, coercion doesn't "cure" a picky eater. Parents need only think back to their own childhoods. They were probably forced to try a food that was unappetizing or to finish eating when they were already full. Some people never get over such experiences; one father who was forced to have spinach as a child still won't eat it.

Picky eating is usually the result of stress and arguments about the quantity and variety of food. Parents who pressure their child at mealtime may make her lose her appetite. A child who has no control over what, when, and how much she eats feels powerless and frustrated—as an adult in the same situation would. She may angrily demand certain foods or react passively by picking at what's on her plate and taking tiny bites. In either case, she's not consciously trying to manipulate her parents, but rather acting out her sense of helplessness.

Picky eaters may avoid tastes and textures they find unappealing. In some stressful situations, a child may be psychologically unable to eat certain foods. One girl found cooked vegetables so repulsive she cried at the thought of eating them.

Picky eaters also may refuse to try new foods—perhaps they've been pressured too often to taste something different. A child who has faced frequent arguments about trying or finishing new foods finds it safer to stick to the few dishes she likes.

Parents may inadvertently create a picky eater if they pressure their child to eat large quantities of food or finish what's on her plate. A child with a small appetite can't help but feel upset if she's urged to eat more, and more often, than she wants.

When parents try to coerce her into eating, the results usually are negative. First, meals become unpleasant times of arguments and power struggles. Also, children resort to sneakiness, either taking the foods they want (usually sweets) or secretly disposing of foods they won't eat. Some children hide their unwanted food into their napkin, then throw the napkin away. One child managed to slide her peas behind the refrigerator. Another put bits of food on her father's plate when he wasn't looking. And there are always children who feed their food to the family pet.

If your child is a picky eater, the first approach you should try is removing mealtime pressure. Although your goal is to keep your child well-nourished and healthy, you shouldn't force her to eat. Children who willingly eat well-balanced meals and try a variety of foods usually have been fed with a low-stress approach. From an early age, they've been allowed to pick and choose, without pressure, from an assortment of foods that are acceptable to their parents. If you create such an atmosphere in your home now, your child's eating habits likely will improve.

First, let her determine how much she wants to eat. Since her eating patterns are well-established, you have a realistic idea of her appetite. Don't urge her to eat more than she usually does. She'll eat enough to keep from being hungry. If you believe she's underweight or exceptionally small, don't force her to eat extra food. Instead, discuss your concerns with your pediatrician, who may offer suggestions or otherwise reassure you.

When possible, prepare foods that you know your child will eat, and don't pressure her to try new foods. Once she feels she can accept or reject something new without angering you, she may be more willing to taste what you offer. You also can try giving her choices—if she doesn't eat carrots, offer her another vegetable or a different healthy food.

Be careful not to humiliate or tease her about being a picky eater. If you let her know you accept her eating habits, she'll feel more relaxed at mealtimes. You may be embarrassed if she acts picky when eating at someone else's house, but you can help ease the pressure there, too. Usually, others will pay no attention to what she eats. If your host asks ahead of time, let her know that your child has a small appetite or eats only certain foods. Most people are understanding of children's needs.

If you eliminate mealtime stress and your child is still excessively picky, look further for reasons. She may feel overly controlled in other areas of her life and may try to exert some power by rejecting food. It's also possible that she will remain a picky eater no matter what you do. Some people, including adults, are just very particular about food.

It takes patience to deal with a picky eater, but the rewards can be great. Once your child believes she has some control over what she eats, both she and you will feel calmer. Then, instead of focusing on what and how much she's eating, your family can concentrate on enjoying mealtimes together.

What should I tell my child when he says, "Everybody else has lost a tooth"?

Losing a first tooth is a milestone for children. From kindergarten on, they look forward to the event as a sign that they are truly growing up. Adults often forget how important the experience is and how devastated a child can feel if he's one of the last in his group to have a loose tooth.

If your child is upset because he has "slow teeth," spend time listening to him and reassuring him. Even though his problem is a mild one, don't lightly dismiss his unhappiness because his feelings are very real. He wants to experience what his friends and classmates have gone through. If he has older siblings, he's seen them get money or a gift along with a lot of attention for losing teeth. It's natural that he wants to be part of this.

He may have a kindergarten or first grade teacher who makes a fuss over lost teeth. Some classrooms have colorful wall charts showing how many teeth each student has lost, and some teachers offer special privileges on the day a tooth comes out. This can be hard for some kids, especially those with end-of-the-year birthdays who are likely to lose teeth later than their older classmates. If your child is unhappily waiting for his first loose tooth, such school activities may make him feel worse.

Fortunately, you can promise him that he'll lose a tooth. While you wait, you can read him some comforting books about other children in his situation. One mother wrote soothing notes to her child, saying that the tooth fairy knew all about him and would be visiting one day. Other parents suggest that their six- or seven-year-olds wiggle their front teeth looking for a hint of movement. Even if it takes months for a tooth to fall out, a child will feel better as soon as he detects a bit of looseness.

Occasionally, the first tooth a child loses is one a dentist extracts. If your child has to go through this procedure because of dental problems, talk to him about what will happen. If he's anxious, let the dentist know and ask for help in reassuring your child. If your child wants you close by during the extraction, plan to stay with him. However, if you anticipate an outburst, you might want to send him off with just the dentist and assistant. Some children are more in control of their emotions when their parents aren't with them.

Before and after the tooth is pulled, tell your child about the "treasure" he'll get at the dentist's office and the surprise he'll find under his pillow. Even though the extraction is unpleasant, when it's done, he'll still have the excitement of having lost his first tooth.

Should my child believe in the tooth fairy?

Children under seven generally follow their parents' lead when it comes to believing in imaginary characters. If parents encourage their child to believe the tooth fairy is real, she's likely to go along with them. And if they tell their child there is no such thing as the tooth fairy, she'll accept that as fact.

Of course, she may figure the truth out on her own, especially if she's awake when her parents put money under her pillow. "Dad, I saw you! You're the tooth fairy!" Some kids hear the truth from older siblings. However, having older siblings can sometimes make a child believe more firmly, since tooth fairy visits have been part of household lore from the child's early years.

Children often ask each other, "Do you believe in the tooth fairy?" While they may take different positions, they rarely quarrel about the issue. Instead they'll say, "Jermaine believes in the tooth fairy but I know it's my parents," or, "Sarah doesn't believe in the tooth fairy but I do!"

Children who do believe in the tooth fairy sometimes worry about getting the rituals right. If a child's misplaced her tooth at school or at a friend's house, or if she didn't notice it fall out or swallowed it, she may be afraid the tooth fairy won't visit. Another common fear is that she won't get to keep the tooth; many children are interested in their teeth and don't want to give them up to the tooth fairy.

When your child has one of these concerns, let her know she'll receive a gift under her pillow whether the tooth is there or not. If you want her to continue believing in the tooth fairy, suggest that she leave the fairy a message explaining the special circumstances.

At some point your child may ask, "Are you the tooth fairy?" Ask her what she thinks. If she really knows the truth, explain that you are and then add, "It was fun to pretend a fairy was leaving you gifts," or, "I enjoyed thinking about the tooth fairy when I was little, and I thought you would too."

If you choose not to teach your child to believe in the tooth fairy, the two of you can still have fun with the idea. You can both pretend the fairy is real and you can leave your child funny notes "from the fairy." If you don't want to talk of a fairy at all, you can leave a special treat "from Mom and Dad" under her pillow.

Magical thinking slowly disappears during the elementary years and eventually all children realize the tooth fairy isn't real. Still, the myth is an enjoyable one whether your child believes or just plays along. Getting a treat—money, stickers, baseball cards, or a small toy—makes losing a tooth even more special.

When will my child give up thumb-sucking?

As children get older, it gets harder to accept some of their habits. Thumb-sucking in particular bothers many parents who find it embarrassing and frustrating. While they tolerate thumb-sucking in a preschooler, they believe it's inappropriate for an older child.

A six-year-old who sucks his thumb probably does so less often than he once did. This is partly because he's now occupied with school, after-school activities, and friends. Most children these ages are inclined to suck their thumbs in private or when they're with family members.

Even though thumb-sucking decreases with age, most parents want their child to give up the habit completely. Parents may argue with their child over thumb-sucking and end up in angry confrontations and power struggles. Some parents back off for a while and others give up in anger, at a loss for what to do.

There are a number of reasons a six- or seven-year-old (or one who's even older) sucks his thumb. It may be a well-established habit he hasn't felt pressured to break, or he may not be emotionally ready to stop. He may suck his thumb at night to help himself fall asleep. If he feels insecure at school he may seek comfort through thumb-sucking, or he may do it when he faces family situations he can't control such as sibling rivalry, divorce, or constant tension.

Sometimes a six- or seven-year-old gives up thumb-sucking in response to teasing and peer pressure: "Ooh, you still suck your thumb. That's for babies! I stopped sucking my thumb when I was four!" However, a child with a strong thumb-sucking habit may not respond at all to negative comments or care if other people watch him.

To help your child give up thumb-sucking, first talk to him about it. Pick a time when you're both calm and tell him your feelings and ideas. Acknowledge his desire to keep sucking his thumb but let him know how much you want him to stop. You can ask for his suggestions: "How can we help you give up this habit?" Remember that while thumb-sucking is a problem for you, it may not seem like one to him.

You can suggest that your child wear a bandage on his thumb to remind him not to suck, or you can gently signal him when he puts his thumb in his mouth. This is more effective than abruptly pulling on his hand or angrily saying, "Take your thumb out of your mouth!"

Try distractions that occupy his hands—playing with clay or helping in the kitchen. You might want to work out an agreement. If he stops sucking his thumb, he gets a reward. One family kept a daily chart for their daughter, and after a week of checkmarks for not sucking her thumb, she got a special game.

Ask trusted friends for suggestions. And if one technique doesn't work, try another. One family bought their child a fancy glove to keep her thumb covered. Some parents paint a foul-tasting liquid on their child's thumb, or have the dentist place a special tooth guard in their child's mouth. Don't try either method without getting your child's permission. You should never force such methods.

As you help your child give up his habit, create an atmosphere of respect in your home and try to keep him from feeling humiliated or embarrassed because of his thumb sucking. Then don't let your other children make fun of him. If he seems particularly anxious, he may be feeling too pressured. You might want to slow down your attempts to eliminate his habit, or hold off for a few weeks.

Throughout this process, give lots of positive feedback: "You're really trying hard. I appreciate what you're doing." Don't be surprised if steps forward are followed by steps backward. It's not easy for him to give up thumb-sucking, especially if the initiative is yours and not his.

Should I tell my child the truth about Santa?

Most young children believe in Santa Claus. They think he's real, he comes to each home, and he brings all the Christmas presents. From earliest memory, kids are taught to believe in him and they rarely have reason to doubt until they turn six or seven. Even at those ages, many are convinced Santa is real.

Parents who encouraged their preschoolers to believe in Santa may have second thoughts when their kids get older. Is it right for a third-grader to believe Santa is real? Should parents tell the truth? Some want their children to hold onto the belief as long as possible, but other parents feel uneasy about misleading their older children.

By elementary age, most children have heard people say Santa isn't real. Young friends say, "Santa is really your parents." Older siblings tell younger ones, "Mom and Dad are the ones who buy the presents." While some children discover the truth this way, some are unaffected. Their belief in Santa can't be shaken: "Santa's real at my house. He really comes and brings the presents, and he even eats the cookies we leave him." In fact, children with very strong beliefs may reconvince doubters: "You're right. Santa does bring the presents."

Some children have a hard time giving up their belief in Santa. After all, he's a wonderful, mystical person who brings gifts and pleasure. By the time a child is six, her vision of Santa is all-good and she no longer fears his judgment and his unusual appearance. She may hold onto her belief in him because it's so comforting.

To find out what your own child thinks, ask, "Do you believe Santa's real?" You may be surprised to learn she already knows the truth. Some children hesitate to share their knowledge because they fear they'll disappoint their parents. If your child says she doesn't believe in him, question her a little further to find out what her feelings are: "You believed in Santa for so many years. What made you change your mind? Who do you think delivers the presents?" Most likely, she'll answer, "YOU!"

If she still believes in Santa or is only beginning to doubt him, you may be afraid of destroying her fantasy. Yet many six- to eight-year-olds are ready to find out the truth, even if they're a bit disappointed. The truth can't ruin Christmas for your child, because all the enjoyable and meaningful rituals will continue.

You might be reluctant to discuss Santa because you're uncomfortable explaining why you misled your child. If she asks why you didn't tell her the truth, or if she seems to doubt what you tell her now ("Are you sure you're telling the truth? There really is no Santa?"), explain that having kids believe in Santa is a special part of the Christmas tradition. "When you first saw Santa, you thought he was real. We decided to go along. But now you're asking questions and you're old enough to understand." Explain that your family won't have to give up the spirit of Santa just because he isn't real. Talk about what Santa represents—love, kindness, caring, and the spirit of giving. As your child gives up her long-held belief, show her that the values Santa represents will always be an important part of Christmas.

"When I grow up I'm going to…" How do I respond?

"I'm going to be a famous basketball player."
"I'm going to live in a mansion and have a limousine."

"I'm going to be president."

Children between six and nine see unlimited possibilities. Their thinking is still magical, and they believe they'll accomplish whatever they desire. Although they're beginning to reason logically and organize their thoughts, they live in the "here-and-now." If a child enjoys ice-skating, it seems logical to him that he can become a famous skater.

Kids think about the future, but they don't think the way an adult does. They can't put themselves in the place of someone who has worked hard to accomplish a goal. They don't think about obstacles, expenses, time, or limited abilities. Instead, they have an innocent optimism that leads to dramatic conclusions: "When I grow up, I'm going to be a star!"

When your child tells you his grand plans, don't feel you have to set him straight. One father, hearing that his daughter wanted to become an actress, lectured her on the practical side of working in the theater. She burst into tears.

Respect your child's confident statements and try to learn more about his values and thinking. If he says he's going to be rich, ask, "What will you do with all that money?" He might list what he'll buy, but he might also say he'll share the money with poor people. One child who said he was going to build a "Kids' World Park" gave details about accommodating kids with disabilities.

Childhood is short. Through the years, your child will discover his own limitations and learn how the world really works. His innocence will gradually fade as he comes to terms with life's realities. You do him no harm now by allowing him his fantasies and listening to his big dreams.

GROWING INDEPENDENCE

What do I do about my child's desire for more independence?

The early elementary years are a time of growing independence. Children generally have an easy time being away from home during the school day, and they often want to play with friends or participate in organized activities in the afternoons. On weekends they may balk at joining a family outing, preferring to spend time pursuing their own interests or being with friends. Kids this age also want less parental supervision. They want to ride their bikes to the playground, walk to the community pool, and stay outside longer.

Parents greet this push for independence with ambivalence. They want their children to become capable, competent people who can take care of themselves. At the same time, the path to independence isn't smooth and the process of letting go isn't easy.

Primarily, parents worry about their child's safety. As she strives for independence, they constantly have to consider her welfare. Some decisions are easy: a seven-year-old is too young to ride her bike on a busy street. Other decisions are more difficult. Is she ready to walk alone to her friend's house? Can she go to a neighborhood playground without an adult? Kids of this age are confident enough to argue heatedly, "I want to go! Everybody else is allowed to!" They feel justified in pushing their points. They know what they want, and parents have the tough job of determining how much independence to give and when to give it.

Parents also have to deal with their own feelings of frustration and sadness. The frustration comes from gradually losing control. No matter how often a preschooler says, "I want to do it myself!" her parents are still firmly in charge. The six- to nine-year-old has a stronger will, a stronger sense of herself, and a growing need to make some decisions for herself. Parents also have a sense of sadness as she begins to separate from them. Certainly there's pride as she matures and becomes more independent, but there's also a feeling of loss. The child who had depended totally on her parents is now growing up.

As you deal with the issue of independence, you'll make constant adjustments. Sometimes you'll be surprised at how mature your child seems. One mother was amazed when her formerly reluctant seven-year-old went off confidently for a weekend at a friend's. Until recently, the girl wouldn't spend a night away from home without lots of kisses, hugs, and assurances from her mother.

Sometimes you'll be surprised at how dependent your child suddenly seems; in development there are always steps backwards. Mixed with your child's growing independence is a strong need for your guidance and positive feedback.

If you're finding it hard to let your child do more for herself, consider the benefits of independence. If you allow her some of the freedom she wants, she'll feel confident about her ability to take care of herself. Let her ride her bike in the neighborhood. Let her make choices—how to arrange her room, for instance—and she'll feel good about decision-making. And if you let her help you with some challenging tasks, you'll encourage her sense of competence. For example, let her help you trim the bushes or plant flowers. In the kitchen, let her slice the vegetables, mash the potatoes, or prepare dessert. These are more rewarding activities than such usual jobs as setting or clearing the table.

As she pushes for independence, you may be puzzled (or irritated) to find she doesn't take on more personal responsibility. You still have to remind her about chores and simple tasks: "Do your homework." "Straighten your room." "Get ready for bed." From her point of view, these are not top priorities. What's important to her is running around outside, doing an arts and crafts project, reading a good book, or playing a game.

As you tackle the difficult job of deciding how much independence to give, talk to other parents and ask yourself questions about your child. How mature is she? Can she safely cross the street? Would she dart into the street after a ball? Do her friends follow common-sense rules? Would they encourage her to misbehave?

Consider your child's age and the ages of her friends. Six- and seven-year-olds need a lot of supervision while eight- or nine-year-olds are capable of spending more time on their own. In general, early elementary-aged children need to be checked on. First, there are safety concerns. Seven-year-olds allowed to go off by themselves may be harassed by older children. A six-year-old skating alone may fall and have no one to help her.

Kids also need supervision for social reasons. They may become angry with each other and fight. They may also exclude one another from play and need some reminders about getting along.

After you've considered your child's maturity and age, judge her requests for independence separately. If she wants to go to the playground, will she walk or ride her bike? Will she be with a friend or an older sibling? How long will she be gone?

You know your child and her patterns of behavior. If your instinct says she shouldn't go on her own, don't give in to your child's demands. You may feel over-protective at times, but it's better to be cautious. Try to interest her in another activity, or put your own tasks aside and take her where she wanted to go. She can play happily at the park while you sit reading nearby, comfortable knowing she's safe.

If you and your child argue a great deal about independence, take time when you're both feeling calm to talk about the problem. Tell her, "It seems like we yell a lot about things I won't let you do" and give her the reasons for your decisions. When she's angry, she may not understand why you say no and may assume you're trying to be mean. Calmly explain your concerns, then listen to her. Let her know you're paying attention: "It sounds like you think I've been unfair." Communicating on the subject of independence will help you understand each other and get along better.

Why isn't my child more responsible?

"Why do I have to tell you over and over again to put your clothes away?"

"You should have started your homework earlier!"

"Taking care of the gerbil is your job."

"Don't race your bike down the sidewalk like that."

All parents want their children to be responsible. They want them to be considerate of others, do their schoolwork carefully and on time, take care of pets, follow safety rules, and do household chores. When children don't act responsibly, parents become frustrated: "When will he ever learn to do the right thing?"

It is helpful to know that responsibility is tied to a number of other traits such as thoughtfulness, common sense, generosity, and empathy. Responsibility requires maturity, alertness, and a social conscience. While a nine-year-old may be quite responsible, a six-year-old is just learning to think about the consequences of his actions.

In order to become responsible, a child needs good role models. His parents set the standards he'll follow. If they emphasize the importance of doing a good job and caring about others, he'll pick that up. He'll often behave politely at a friend's house and attentively at school.

The process of learning is neither quick nor smooth. Six- to nine-year-olds need many reminders, particularly about personal grooming and household chores. Since a child rarely enjoys or cares about these tasks, he isn't motivated to do them. This is understandable; even adults don't like to consistently clean, shop, make repairs, and pay bills.

Kids also don't understand the reasons for many tasks. Making a bed may not seem important: "I'm just going to mess it up again tonight." Even when parents explain why jobs are necessary, their child might resist: "It's not fair that I have to take out the trash. I'm not the one who filled up the bag." "Why should I put the game away? Shannon took it out." "Nobody will care if my hair isn't combed."

Parents may feel less frustrated if they accept that reminders are a necessary part of teaching a child to be responsible. One mother, angry over repeatedly having to ask her child to clear his dishes after eating, decided to take a realistic approach. Instead of loudly reprimanding him ("Why can't you ever remember to put your plate in the sink?"), she simply incorporated reminders into her mealtime routine ("Don't forget to clear your dishes"). She felt calmer, he felt less pressured, and the job got done.

Reminders are important in all areas of responsibility. Children need to be told, in nonjudgmental ways, about safety, consideration for others, schoolwork, and family obligations. For some responsibilities, such as chores or homework, a chart might be useful. Each day, a child checks off the jobs he's completed. Even with a chart, though, most kids still need reminders. The mother of a second grader tried offering a reward each time her daughter did her homework, made her bed, and got herself dressed without reminders. However, this mother's expectations were unrealistic—a child this age just can't consistently keep track of this many obligations.

If your child continually fails to be as responsible as you'd like, re-examine your expectations. You might be asking him to do too much. Try eliminating one or two of the less important tasks he struggles with and see if he doesn't become more responsible about the remaining obligations. Also, be sure to leave him free time to play and pursue creative projects; if he has to spend a big portion of his time on tasks that don't interest him, he'll be too frustrated to do his best.

In teaching responsibility, as in many other aspects of parenting, you'll find your child becomes most cooperative when you get involved. Help him clean his room, offer to trade jobs so he can water the lawn while you pick up the toys, occasionally sit beside him paying bills or writing a letter while he does homework, put on your seat belt as you tell him to fasten his, have him help you on a charity project.

If he's able to behave responsibly after you've given him reminders, he's on the right track. Although you may wish he'd learn more quickly, be assured that you'll continue to see progress as long as you patiently reinforce responsible behavior at home.

Why is it hard to talk about money?

Money is an emotionally charged subject. Many adults are uncomfortable with their financial situations and therefore reluctant to discuss money with their children. Some parents have feelings of guilt, anger, or confusion stemming from their childhood experiences with money. They may go out of their way to create a different climate in their own homes or may treat their children exactly as they were once treated.

Children's lifelong attitudes toward money are based on what they learn at home; they'll pick up their parents' feelings whether finances are openly discussed or not. For that reason, parents should give careful thought to talking to kids about money.

People often wonder how open they should be about the family's finances. Should children have all their questions answered? Do they need to know how much the house cost, how expensive the car is, and how much the family paid for last summer's vacation? Finances are a very private matter for most adults, and it's difficult to know how much to share with a child.

At the least, kids should feel it's acceptable to ask questions, and they should have their questions answered in a way that will satisfy rather than frustrate them. That doesn't mean parents have to provide all the details. However, they shouldn't make money a secretive subject. No child should constantly hear, "I'm not telling you how much I get paid," or, "Don't ask. It's none of your business." It's fine for parents to say at times, "The price of this feels private to me. I really don't want to share it with you." Then, at other times, they can be open about costs.

When children ask about money, their parents have an opportunity to start a discussion: "How much do you think our house cost? Do you know how much people pay for houses?" Parents can use financial questions to introduce subjects such as borrowing and saving.

Such discussions are valuable because young children have only vague ideas about money. They try to organize the little they know into general theories: "If you don't have enough money, just tell your boss." "Go to the bank and they'll give you more money." "Sue somebody and you'll get a lot of money." "Just trade in your change for dollars and you'll have a lot." A six- to nine-year-old has little understanding of buying power. Twenty-five dollars may seem like a lot and the $150 a week her mother spends on food may seem a fortune. A child this age also assumes that bigger means more expensive and she may not understand that a small piece of jewelry can cost more than a piece of furniture.

It's difficult to give kids a clear picture of where money comes from, how it's spent, and how financial decisions are made. A child, not seeing the difference between necessities and luxuries, watches her parents purchase shampoo, food, clothes, and gasoline. She assumes they can buy whatever they want. Then, when they place restrictions on her purchases, she may feel confused and unfairly treated.

Children are quite sensitive to their parents' financial concerns. When parents argue or worry openly about money, kids worry, too. A child may feel responsible for financial disagreements because her parents have told her the things she wants are expensive. She also may feel guilty if her parents say, "We buy you nice clothes and you don't even wear them," "Stop asking for new toys. You've got plenty already."

On the other hand, children can make their parents feel guilty. When a child says, "Benjamin has new skates and so does Eve. Why won't you buy me some?" her parents may feel inadequate and unable to make her happy. It's important that they keep such demands in perspective. All young children want what their friends have. Parents should buy or not buy according to their own values and circumstances. They can tell their child, "You'd like to have what Eve has, but we're not going to buy it," or, "We have different buying rules in our home." They should try to answer their child's requests for purchases appropriately and realistically, without becoming angry or defensive.

Talking to your child about money is not easy. Try to respect her point of view, understanding that her knowledge will increase as she gets older. She's not capable of adopting your financial concerns, and you shouldn't expect her to. If you work outside the home, don't burden your child with guilt by making such statements as, "We work hard to pay for your things." Listen to her questions and engage in conversations (without lecturing) about money. And decide on what attitudes you want to teach her. How do you ultimately want her to feel about earning, spending, and saving?

Should I give an allowance?

In theory giving an allowance is a good idea, and this is a good time to start. Many parents of six- to nine-year-olds want their children to begin learning how to save and spend wisely.

There are two main ways in which an allowance is given: conditionally and unconditionally. An unconditional allowance is handed out automatically every week. A conditional allowance is only given after a child successfully completes certain requirements. Chores are the usual requirements, but sometimes conditions are related to school work or general behavior. One parent who gives her child a conditional allowance said, "I want him to learn how the world works. You get paid for what you do."

When an allowance depends on a child's performance, there can be family conflicts. Children may remember only half of their chores or may argue that they're too tired or busy to do all that their parents want. Parents have to constantly remind a child, "If you don't clear the table, you won't get your allowance." "No money if you don't fold the clothes." In addition, he may complete his task, but not to the satisfaction of his parents. They have to continually monitor and judge.

When kids are threatened with losing their allowance, they often do as their parents desire. However, they sometimes try to negotiate. One boy regularly got two dollars a week for making his bed and cleaning his room. When he wanted to miss a day, he started bargaining: "Just give me one dollar this time." When the negotiating got out of hand, her parents switched to an unconditional allowance and used other tactics to encourage him to keep his room neat.

Some parents use an allowance to try to control their child's behavior. He may gain or lose money depending on how obedient he is or how well he does at school. While this may work, it may lead to anger and frustration. If he hears, "You forgot your math book. You're losing 50 cents this week," he may feel unfairly penalized. Receiving an allowance should be a positive experience, not one associated with anger and feelings of helplessness.

While some families have success with a conditional allowance, others eventually give it up because of the struggles and attitudes they see their child adopting. One parent said her son refused to pitch in and help with anything other than his assigned chores unless he was paid extra.

However parents decide to give an allowance, they should strive for a system that makes them and their child feel good. If one method doesn't work, they can try another.

At times, children are very interested in money, asking for an allowance at the earliest possible moment each week and eagerly counting their savings. At other times, they may forget their allowances for weeks. Some families have a regular day when the allowance is given, while others are very casual, giving children money at irregular intervals. Again, any method is fine as long as family members are comfortable with it.

A big question for parents is how much money to give. There are no general rules, and amounts vary from family to family. When parents are in doubt, they can find out how much other children are receiving. Families in a neighborhood or parents of close friends sometimes agree to give their children equal amounts.

Many parents open a bank account for their child when they start giving him an allowance. They want him to learn about saving and put at least part of his money away. Yet, it's often hard for them to know how much should be saved and how the savings should be used. While they should encourage savings, they should also allow their child to make his own decisions about his allowance. He'll certainly make mistakes, but he'll learn valuable lessons from the experience.

For instance, if he wants a toy his parents aren't willing to buy, he may decide to save and buy it with his own money. If he does manage to accumulate enough, they should praise him for his patience even if they doubt the wisdom of his purchase.

It takes time for children to learn to manage money wisely. You may be frustrated if your child wants to spend each week's allowance on gum, baseball cards, or comics. You don't want him to waste his money, yet you do want him to have control over what is, after all, his. You'll have to strike a balance, letting him make some mistakes as long as he doesn't violate your family's basic ideas about buying and saving. Keep in mind, too, that most adults make unnecessary, frivolous purchases from time to time.

To encourage your child to be more responsible about money, have him occasionally donate a small amount, perhaps at the same time you're making a donation to a worthy cause. He can use his money to help buy toys for needy children or give a cash gift to a charity. Although he may initially resist, he'll soon feel good about his donations, especially if you praise him for helping others.

Suddenly my child is clothes-conscious. What happened?

"Cool! Awesome! Can I buy this shirt? All the kids at school wear this kind."

As boys and girls reach the middle elementary years, they define themselves more and more by the clothes they wear. It's not unusual for them to have strong preferences for certain styles and colors. They copy what their peers and older siblings wear and they pick up messages from TV, magazines, movies, store displays—even dolls dressed in the latest fashions. Because clothing sales are big business, retailers and manufacturers bombard consumers with images of contemporary styles, and kids can't help but be influenced.

A child most often wants to wear what other children wear. If she looks too different she may feel vulnerable or threatened and may be teased. Parents, too, sometimes prefer their child to dress as her friends do. Looking like the rest of the group gives a sense of belonging.

Children's style preferences vary; what's popular in one city or school or neighborhood may not be in another. Some children like conservative looks, some prefer only up-to-date fashions, and others just care about specifics such as shoes or jewelry. The intensity of a child's clothes-consciousness varies also, from caring a little to caring a lot. Most young children are too absorbed in friends, schoolwork, hobbies and after-school activities to make clothing a major preoccupation.

However, a child's opinions about clothes can be strong enough to cause conflict. On the one hand, parents want to buy clothes that please their child, but they're also frustrated if she wants items they find unappealing or expensive. Shopping becomes difficult because it's hard for them to know what will fit or look good on her, and if she'd like their selections. Most parents have had the experience of picking something out and bringing it home to their child, only to have it hang in the closet unused. To avoid such waste, many parents take their child along on shopping trips. This, of course, leads to other problems. Children often dread shopping and trying on clothes. They act angry, bored, or silly, and find it hard to stick to the task.

You can ease many clothing conflicts by offering your child some choices, involving her in the process of choosing what to get, and preparing her for shopping trips. For instance, before you go to a store, tell her what she can get and how much you're willing to spend. That way you and she will have similar expectations. Once you're shopping, have her help hunt through the racks for sizes or colors: "See if you can find a sweater with green in it to go with the pants you like." Let her make some decisions: "You can get this shirt for twenty dollars or you can get two shirts for ten dollars each." If she picks an item you don't like, suggest a modification: "Let's look for something with a smaller design on the front."

If she's firm about wanting only current fashions, you can either avoid arguments by buying some of what she likes as long as you find it appropriate, or you can initiate a compromise. Suggest she pick out pants while you pick out the top. Let her choose a wild sweater and a plain skirt to go with it. Have her pick the styles, and you select the colors. (Fashionable clothes often look far less outrageous in muted colors.) You also can encourage her to concentrate on accessories such as bracelets and hair bands. If she gets some of the clothes she wants, she'll have an easier time accepting your refusal to buy items you can't tolerate.

Keeping the cost of children's clothing down is always important. If your child wants a particular style, look for affordable versions at department or discount stores. A six- to nine-year-old doesn't care about cost, only about having a certain look. At times, if she wants something you consider too expensive, offer to pay half while she pays the rest out of her allowance.

In addition to cost, consider the practicality of your child's clothing. Since she needs to run around and explore, don't buy play clothes that are delicate or hard to clean.

If you are having frequent arguments about clothing, step back and think about the issue. Excessive clothes-consciousness can be the result of power struggles in which parents won't let their children participate in decision-making and children feel they can't give in. Instead of getting locked in a battle of wills, consider your child's opinions and remember that she, like you, just wants to dress in a way that's physically and emotionally comfortable. If you constantly argue about buying decisions, she will continue to focus on clothes. But if you allow her to help choose which to buy, you let her know she's competent and capable of making some decisions for herself. You may sometimes be giving in, but you will be diffusing the issue of clothes-consciousness and helping your child gain self-confidence.

Why won't my child cooperate in the mornings?

"If you don't hurry up you'll be late for school!" Parents say this over and over while they hurriedly prepare breakfast, pack lunches, and get the family ready for the morning commute to day care, school, or work. In the midst of all this activity, six- to nine-year-olds dawdle along, seemingly unaware of the frustration they cause. It can seem to parents that nothing keeps their children from procrastinating—not logical arguments, threats, rewards, or punishments.

One seven-year-old, proud of having gotten up half an hour early on a school morning, used all her time to watch TV instead of getting ready. An eight-year-old who dressed himself after much prodding asked, "Now what do I do?" as if he'd never been told to brush his teeth and pack up his school books. Many children need constant reminders: "Comb your hair." "Put on your shoes." "Stop playing and come down for breakfast."

Most young children procrastinate in the mornings because they aren't interested in rushing off to school. Getting ready is something they have to do, but it's not a priority. They would much rather get involved in an interesting activity such as playing, drawing, reading, using the computer, or watching TV. In addition, they have only a loose sense of time. Ten minutes can feel like plenty of time to finish playing and get dressed. It's parents, not children, who think time and morning routines are important.

Some kids are overwhelmed by the process of preparing for school. Instead of struggling to keep track of the things they must do, they avoid getting ready in the morning altogether. Other children, like some adults, just aren't "morning" people and have a hard time waking up early. In some families, mornings are so stressful that children deal with the tension by pushing aside demands and distracting themselves in play.

Here are some strategies to try if you, like so many parents, have a child who procrastinates. Try waking yourself up fifteen to twenty minutes earlier so your preparations won't be as hurried. With a little more time in the morning, you can relax, share a cup of cocoa with your child, talk during breakfast, maybe take a short walk. Even five minutes of relaxed time together can make the morning smoother.

You also can wake your child up earlier so he has time to play before getting ready. If he seems tired in the morning, a shower may help wake him up. Try setting an earlier bedtime. This helps some children, although others don't wake up well no matter how much sleep they've had.

You might find mornings more peaceful if you change the timing of your chores. Make lunches, lay out clothes, and help your child pack up his homework in the evening so you'll have more free time before school.

Prepare a chart for him listing the things he should do to get ready, and use a timer to let him know when to begin. You can try a system of checks and rewards as motivators.

Perhaps he doesn't clearly know what you expect from him. Calmly but firmly tell him what his morning responsibilities are. At a time when you're not angry, ask him for suggestions: "What would help you get ready?" Explain the consequences of dawdling: "If you aren't outside in time, you'll miss the school bus." "If you don't come downstairs early enough, you won't have time for pancakes."

What works for one family or child may not work for another. You may have tried many techniques and still find your mornings difficult.

In that case, changing your attitude toward your child may help some. Instead of expecting him to take care of himself completely, accept that you'll have to help him along. It may be faster and more peaceful for you to comb his hair than to yell, "Can't you remember anything? I told you to comb your hair!" Identify the tasks he has most trouble with and either offer help, do them for him, or keep calmly reminding him. If you change your tone, he may actually cooperate more because he wants to please you.

As your child approaches nine, you'll see less procrastination in the mornings. He'll be better able to handle multiple tasks in a short time and be more responsible. He'll also care a little more about his appearance so he'll put more effort into getting ready for school.

TOUGH ISSUES

"Why did Daddy's uncle have to die?"

All young children have some experience with death. They may have lost a pet, seen TV coverage of a tragic accident, or overheard their parents talking about death. They may have lost a family member or heard about the death of a famous person. The circumstances vary and so do children's reactions, ranging from curiosity about the death of a celebrity to devastation at the loss of a close relative.

Whatever the circumstances, talking to a child about death is difficult for parents, especially if they themselves are grieving. They may feel overwhelmed by their own sadness and unable to meet their child's needs.

Even when parents aren't mourning a personal loss, their child's questions can make them uncomfortable: "Why did he die?" "Why couldn't the doctor make him better?" "What happens to people after they die?" Parents have no easy answers or quick assurances. In addition, speaking about death forces them to confront their own questions and fears and reminds them of their mortality.

A child reacting to a death feels many of the emotions an adult does: loss, anger, frustration, and resentment. She may feel powerless ("Why couldn't anyone help?") and guilty ("I wish I'd seen her more."). She may blame herself for a death she couldn't have prevented ("If I'd been good all the time, he wouldn't have died").

If your family has experienced a loss, the most important thing you can do is talk to your child and comfort her. Find out what she thinks and, if necessary, correct her misconceptions: "I know it's sad she was sick for so long." "No, it wasn't your fault Grandma died." "Your thoughts didn't cause the accident." Let her share her feelings, and include her in some of your family discussions about the death. She may want to talk about her fears that you or she will die.

Some children don't talk at all about their loss. If your child shows no sign of mourning or if she seems to be coping too well, she's probably holding her feelings in. Talk to her about the person who died and help her express her hurt and anger so her feelings don't become overwhelming.

If she wants to attend the funeral of someone she was close to, consider letting her go. It's better for her to be with you there than to feel excluded or frightened at home. Explain what the funeral will be like. Let her know that people will be sad and many will cry. If she doesn't want to attend, respect her decision. One nine-year-old told her parents, "I don't like funerals and whenever you ask me if I want to go to one the answer is NO."

As she struggles with her feelings, remember that mourning and the feeling of loss can last for weeks, months, even years, depending on how close she was to the person who died. Let her see that you, too, are still adjusting. With time and help from you and others, such as the children's support groups found in religious and hospice organizations, your child will gradually come to terms with her loss. Families that share difficult times often find they are stronger and closer as a result.

What should I say about sex and pregnancy?

"How was I made?"

"Where did I come from?"

Children's understanding of sex and childbirth changes greatly between the ages of six and nine. Six-year-olds are still egocentric thinkers with personal opinions about how things work. They may reject the facts of life in favor of their own ideas about sex. Eight- and nine-year-olds can accept others' thoughts and are better able to understand sex and birth.

Learning about sex is gradual. It begins early, with a child's first feelings about his body. The way his parents respond when he's learning to use the toilet, when he touches his genitals, and when he asks questions about his body contributes to his self-image and sense of sexuality.

By the early elementary years, all children have some information about sex. They've heard it from their parents, their older siblings, their friends, or characters in movies and on TV. Some are just told things, others ask. One six-year-old, watching her mother change her seven-month-old sister's diaper, asked, "So how did you get pregnant, anyway?" Another child picked up a tampon and asked, "What's this for?"

Parents are often startled by how much their child knows. Inevitably, kids pick up a lot by talking and joking with each other about sex. One boy giggled while watching kissing on TV and then explained what "French kissing" was. He'd heard about it from a classmate. A girl told her mother how babies were made: "The S word. You know, SEX! You get naked and have sex." Her older sibling had told her.

Parents should ask, "What do you think?" to find out what their child knows. Once parents are aware of his ideas, they can decide where to start discussions and how much information to give. It's necessary for parents to be sensitive when talking about sex. Many children are not ready for all the facts, and too much information at once can be overwhelming. A six- or seven-year-old may be confused and uncomfortable at the thought of adults engaged in sex. A six-year-old, after hearing about childbirth, said, "I'm never having a baby!" At these ages, some children can accept and understand only small doses of information. Parents should tell a little about intercourse, conception, pregnancy, and birth, then wait for more questions before continuing.

Eight- and nine-year-olds may also be embarrassed by talk of sex, but they understand more. If a child this age hasn't asked much about sex yet, his parents can initiate a discussion. They can begin by asking what he already knows. Some of the information may be right but some may be distorted, and it's important for parents to correct misconceptions.

The tone of these discussions is important. Parents should be discreet and respectful, never laughing at their child's questions or comments. Children need to feel they can come to their parents for straight answers about sex. The trust established during the early years will be important throughout childhood and especially during adolescence. If a child feels reluctant to talk to his parents because he feels ashamed or fears ridicule, he'll gradually stop bringing questions home.

Of course, even the most well-intentioned parents may feel uncomfortable discussing sex. Parents who—verbally or non-verbally—convey their reluctance to talk may inadvertently shut off communication with their child. Parents may want to read about human sexuality before answering their child's questions. Parents also can mention the awkwardness they or the child may be feeling: "I know you're a little embarrassed. I am too. But in our house, it's okay to talk about sex and ask questions."

In addition to talking, you might try another approach to sex education—offering your child books on the subject. There are many available. Read several before selecting ones that seem appropriate, considering his age and maturity. Start with a simple book and, as needed, introduce ones that include more details. You can read the book with him, offer it to him, or simply leave it where he'll find it on his own. Then wait for questions or begin a discussion yourself.

When you talk about sex and pregnancy with your child, you may want him to keep the information from his younger siblings—they might not be ready to hear all the facts. Your older child may try to keep your discussions private, but chances are he'll tell his siblings what he knows. He might want to share his new information with someone, and a sibling is handier than a friend. If this happens, talk to your younger child, correct misunderstandings, and offer explanations that seem appropriate. If he's not interested, don't press the issue. He'll come to you at a later date with his own questions.

Should I tell my child about AIDS?

Many parents would like to avoid discussing AIDS with their child. However, kids are aware of the disease. They hear about it on TV and radio, they see stories about it in papers and magazines, and they hear adults and other children talk about it. They've heard that AIDS patients die. They also believe the disease is mysterious, since they aren't sure why or how people get it. This makes AIDS scary to them.

When you talk to your child about AIDS, you have the difficult task of presenting accurate information without making her unnecessarily frightened. Since children are not likely to pick up the disease, you can be honest but reassuring about her chances of exposure.

Let her ask questions and tell you what she already knows about the illness. Some of her information may be very inaccurate. Some of her questions may be too complex for you to answer without doing some research. Still, open communication is the best way to ensure that she forms a realistic idea of the disease.

She may believe that AIDS is as easy to catch as chicken pox or a cold. Let her know that all viruses are not alike, and that AIDS is very difficult to contract. Give details you consider appropriate for her level of maturity: "People who have the virus in their bodies sometimes pass it on to others." "Doctors can check people's blood to see if they have the disease." "There are things people can do to make sure they don't get AIDS." Explain that AIDS is passed on mainly through sex and through drug users' needles.

Your child will feel less concerned about AIDS if she can discuss it with you. If she doesn't mention the disease on her own by the time she's nine, you might want to bring it up as part of a general discussion of health, safety, sex, and growing up. There are good children's books on the subject that you and she can read together. It also might help her to know that doctors and researchers are actively looking for ways to prevent and cure AIDS.

Should I be worried about drugs?

Schools, parents, and the media try to give children a clear message—drugs are bad. Children hear, "Just say no to drugs," and, "Drugs can kill you." Six- to nine-year-olds accept the message without question and declare, "I'll never take drugs!" "You'll go to jail." "It's against the law." With few exceptions, they have no internal conflict about drugs, they don't experiment, and they don't face peer pressure to try drugs. They're very aware of what's right and wrong and they even know that drinking and driving don't mix. One child, seeing a passing motorist sipping from a beer can, urged his parents to write down the license-plate number and call the police.

It's easy for a young child to say no to the idea of drug use. What parents need to consider is what will happen when their child gets older and is confronted with peer pressure and opportunities. Parents hope that early warnings will keep their child out of trouble, but unfortunately, that's not always the case. However, they should do all they can now to help their child reject impulsive experimentation later.

First, they should behave in ways they want their child to adopt. Too many parents say, "Don't use drugs," and then condone, use, or abuse alcohol or drugs themselves. They need to set a good example. If they drink frequently, kids will accept that as normal behavior. If they smoke, their children may smoke when they get older. Certainly if parents use drugs, their child will be confused about their warnings. Parents may try to hide alcohol or drug abuse, but he will eventually discover the truth. Then he may not only copy their actions, but feel anger and distrust toward them for deceiving him.

At some point, as you deal with the issue of drug abuse, your child may ask if you've ever used drugs. If you haven't, you can comfortably answer the question, perhaps starting a discussion: "What made you curious?" "What did you think I'd say?"

If you did use drugs in the past, this isn't the time to give your child the details. Perhaps you can share more when he's older, but at this point simply give your message that drug use is unacceptable. Telling him anything more will greatly increase the risk that he'll eventually do as you once did.

Keep the lines of communication open. While your child might be enrolled in an elementary school drug education program, don't count on that to keep him safe. These programs are often ineffective because they're aimed at young children who are already convinced that drugs are bad. Programs for pre-adolescents and teens tend to be more successful because they target kids who are actually exposed to drug culture and who are much more cynical about laws and prohibitions.

Your child needs your continuing guidance and support to resist drugs. Answer his questions and talk about the dangers of drug use. Your child will hear about political leaders, celebrities, and sport stars who've been arrested for drug possession or who've died of overdoses; he may be very upset if he admired one of them. Use these occasions to talk about the reasons for drug use and the alternatives people can choose.

As your child grows, you can help him avoid drugs by staying involved and encouraging him to feel good about his abilities and character. There's value in a strong ego. A positive self-image gives a preteen or teenager strength to resist peer influences and comfortably say no to drugs.

During the early elementary years, you'll have few actual worries about drug use. But don't ignore the potential problem. As he reaches the pre-adolescent years, keep talking to your child, reinforcing the anti-drug messages he hears, and helping him become strong enough to resist temptation when he encounters it.

What should I do if my child is being picked on?

At some point, every child is the victim of teasing. Classmates pick on each other: "You don't know how to multiply yet!" "Kevin has a girl-friend!" Siblings insult each other: "You're so dumb!" "Your ears stick out like Dumbo!" Occasional harassment is an inevitable part of growing up. However, when a child is consistently picked on at home, at school, or in the neighborhood, this is a serious situation and parents need to intervene.

Parents often have mixed feelings when their child is regularly picked on or bullied: "Is he really so different from the others?" They wonder if they could have shaped his personality differently. Should they have put more emphasis on fighting back? They may wish their child could tolerate a "normal" amount of teasing or stick up for himself: "It's a tough world out there and you have to learn to get along." Sometimes his predicament stirs up unhappy memories for them: "I used to get picked on for being short."

Despite their feelings, a child who's picked on needs his parents' help. If he's teased too often, his self-esteem will be affected. He may come to view himself as his peers do and believe he deserves to be bullied. Then his behavior will encourage other children to continue taking advantage of him.

Sometimes he actually invites bullying as a way to get attention. If he feels unlikable or friendless, he may believe any recognition is better than none. He might laugh at himself because he sees no other way out: "See, I'm fat as a pig."

More often, kids are singled out because they're vulnerable or perceived to be different. A child may be picked on because of his weight, height, hair style, clothing, lack of athletic ability, or interest. He may be picked on simply because he lacks strong defenders and is therefore an easy target.

Why do any children look for a victim? In some cases, the ones who pick on others have never been consistently reminded to think or care about another person's feelings. In other cases, they may be strong competitors who need to feel bigger and better at everything. Often, kids who bully others are themselves bullied at home. They may be put down by harsh or inflexible parents or attacked by siblings. Feeling powerless, they seek release by treating someone else as they've been treated.

If your child complains about being picked on, first reassure him: "No one likes to be teased. You wouldn't treat someone that way because you know how bad it feels." Let him know that you won't just leave him to fend for himself. Then together, find ways to make the situation better.

Gather as much information as you can. If you suspect he's being victimized, but find him reluctant to discuss it, talk to him about hypothetical cases or your own experiences: "Sometimes kids make fun of someone just because she likes different things." "When I was your age, some boys used to tease me on the bus."

Ask your child how he thinks he might solve his problem. He may come up with usable ideas: tease back, walk away, tell the teacher or another adult, or get a friend to help out. If he's worried that defending himself will get him into more difficulties, discuss his fears: "What do you think will happen if you tease Bonnie back?" Offer encouragement: "I think if you ignore Matthew's teasing, it will make him uncomfortable. He'll probably get tired of bothering you if he doesn't get any attention for it."

Role playing may be an effective method of problem-solving. Create situations similar to your child's: "Imagine I'm Jimmy and I say, 'You stink at throwing a ball.' What can you do or say to stop me from repeating things like that?"

If he's picked on at school, you should contact his teacher. She may not be aware of what's going on, particularly if your child is harassed on the bus or during lunch or outdoor play.

When neighborhood kids tease your child, you can deal with them directly. Watch closely and set limits on their behavior: "You'll have to stop bothering Phillip." "If you want to play here, you can't pick on these kids." If there's an opportunity, you can talk to seven- to nine-year-olds about what it feels like to be picked on and suggest ways they can control their behavior.

You also may want to call the parents of a child who consistently bullies. They may be unaware of their child's actions. Although the discussion might be awkward, work at trying to gain the parents' cooperation: "I hope we'll be able to help each other out."

While you're helping your child deal with his harassers, encourage him to form new friendships. If he's secure in a circle of friends, he'll be less vulnerable to teasing.

If your child continues to be picked on, you probably need to examine the relationships in your family. Does your child allow himself—or do you allow him—to be picked on by his siblings? If so, he may similarly allow himself to be picked on by his peers. Are all people in your family treated equally and with respect? Are put-downs common at home? Are you available to notice family interactions? Do you stress harmony in the family? Are you tolerant of differences among your children? Do you point out your child's strengths and compliment his abilities? Is there too much stress in the home?

If you've tried a number of strategies without success, you may finally have to consider some big changes to remove him from harassment. One couple moved to a new neighborhood with more compatible families and found their child was much happier. Another family, unable to affect the behavior of a group of school bullies, put their daughter in a new school. The mother said, "It felt like we gave her a new start in life."

How can I help my child adjust to moving?

Moving can be exciting. It also can be very stressful. There are upheavals, physical work, and sad separations for the whole family. As parents pack up toys, photographs, and clothes, they often feel nostalgic. As a child says good-bye to his room, his favorite play spots, and his friends, he may wonder what his life will be like.

The success of a move depends on the circumstances involved. Families moving because of divorce, unexpected job transfer, job loss, illness, or death face pressures and burdens not shared by those moving under happier circumstances. A family moving to a familiar neighborhood will have an easier time than one going to a strange city or state.

Parents' attitudes greatly influence the success of a move, since a child will often adopt their viewpoints as his own. If they're cheerful about going to a new home, he'll accept inevitable changes more easily than if they're nervous and upset.

His move will go most smoothly if he doesn't have to change schools. If he can spend his school hours with familiar teachers and friends, he can concentrate on the nice things about his new home: his bedroom, a nearby park, a bike trail. Some parents who make a mid-school-term move to a nearby community let their child finish the year in his old school. That way, he can be comfortable in class while meeting new neighborhood children.

Because parents get caught up in the physical demands of moving, they often don't take time to reassure and support their child. They may believe all kids are resilient and have an easy time adjusting: "Don't worry. You'll be fine." "You'll make lots of new friends." "Second grade is the same no matter where you go." Yet, leaving familiar surroundings can upset any child.

The best way parents can help their child is by listening to him talk about the move. If he can express his fears, anger, and sadness, he'll feel better. If he believes his negative feelings are unacceptable, he'll hide them and express his anxiety in other ways. He may lose his appetite, act moody and sensitive, whine, cry frequently, or fight more with his siblings.

Encourage him to talk about moving. Ask questions: "What's the best part about moving? What don't you like?" "What can I do to make this easier for you?" Show that you understand his feelings: "I know it's hard to leave our house. You'll really miss your friends, won't you?" Talk about the separations he'll experience. He may be upset about leaving grandparents, cousins, a baby-sitter, or teacher. Let him know he can stay in contact with people who are special to him.

Before you pack, take photographs or videos of each room in your house, and ask your child if he'd like to be in those pictures. Help him plan a farewell with his friends. He may want children over for a party or outdoor snacks and games. He may decide to make cards for friends or offer them a treasure from his room.

He may want to help with the packing, or he may want nothing to do with the process. You shouldn't insist on his help. As you pack his belongings, don't get rid of his things without asking him. He may still feel attached to playthings he's outgrown and, if the move is difficult for him, he may not want to part with any possessions: "I'm keeping everything!" If he feels this way, put all the items you'd like to discard in a box, take them to the new house, and, after he has adjusted, ask which ones he'd like to keep.

Immediately after the move, resume important family rituals like bedtime stories, evening snacks, and breakfast with the whole family. Show him his new school and set up an appointment to visit the principal and tour the building. Enroll him in after-school activities or sports where he'll meet new kids while doing things he enjoys. And remember, in the midst of unpacking, he needs extra time, reassurance, and love.

How will my divorce affect my child?

Parents in the midst of separation or divorce can easily feel overwhelmed. They must deal with their own emotional, legal, and financial problems and often have little energy left for their children. Yet, children suffer greatly during a divorce and need special attention just at a time when parents are least able to give it.

When parents are caught up in a divorce, they often don't see their child's distress clearly. They may feel helpless and guilty and, as a result, deny his needs: "He'll be fine." "The kids'll keep busy." "Their father worked such long hours, he didn't spend much time with them anyway." "He was an awful father. They'll hardly miss him."

Kids often don't ask directly for help or reassurance. Instead, they may act sad, angry, and frustrated. Siblings will fight, cry, and whine more, or may do poorly in school. Children who act as though everything's fine are simply keeping their anxious feelings inside.

Divorce can cause lifelong strain for children. They can grow up to distrust all relationships and fear being hurt. The roots of such emotional damage lie in the way children think about and experience divorce.

Often they blame themselves for the separation. They know that parents sometimes argue about child rearing, and they feel responsible for their parents' fights: "If only I'd been good." "If only I'd listened more." Children also believe that their wishes are very powerful. Since they've sometimes had negative thoughts about their parents, they can believe those thoughts caused the divorce.

Related to this is a child's intense desire to have his parents back together. If bad wishes can cause a divorce, can't good wishes reunite two people? Even when the relationship was tense, argumentative, or abusive, the child will likely want them to stay together. And much as parents may want his approval for the divorce, he won't believe that living apart is best. Instead, he'll talk, dream, and wish for a reconciliation, and when one doesn't come, he might feel angry at himself for his powerlessness and angry at his parents for ignoring his desires.

Parents have to deal with these feelings. There should be open communication between them and their children, and a sense that sad and angry thoughts are acceptable. Kids should talk and parents should listen and reflect back what they've heard: "It sounds like you think it's your fault Dad and I don't live together anymore." After a child has expressed his feelings, parents have to continually reassure him.

Children need to ask lots of questions and parents should listen and respond, even when it's very difficult: "Where will Daddy live? Will we see him? Why can't he sleep here? Will he ever live here again?" "If Mom was the only woman in the world, would you marry her again?"

Since he learns that his parents have stopped loving each other, he'll worry at times that they'll stop loving him, too. He needs to hear that both parents love him very much, and that, no matter how angry the parent he lives with is, he or she will never leave him. He'll also want to know he can continue his relationships with grandparents and other relatives who've been close to him.

It's important (now and throughout his childhood) for him to have regular, frequent communication and visits with the parent not living at home. A child loves both parents and will have an easier time adjusting if he sees the one not living with him often. Parents should reject the impulse to belittle each other or try to get their child to take sides. Although this can be very difficult if the divorce was bitter, parents must keep their child's needs in mind. If he's put in the middle of an emotional tug-of-war he'll feel pressured, guilty, and disloyal.

As you help your child, offer him outlets for his feelings and try to smooth the way as much as possible. Talk to his teacher and ask for his or her support. Help your child tell his friends about the divorce. He might be ashamed to talk to his peers about it because it makes him different and more vulnerable.

Offer him books about children dealing with divorce and suggest that he write his feelings down. Be comforting when he cries or asks for extra hugs and attention.

If you're the primary caregiver, you may find it very difficult to provide him with the support he wants. You may be overworked and emotionally drained. At times, tell him that you can't pay attention to him: "I'm feeling sad right now. Can I help you a little later?" He may be considerate for a while, but eventually he'll return for reassurance. You also can try distracting him since, despite the divorce, he'll continue to have outside interests. If you do have to postpone talking to him, remember to make time later.

Since you'll be busy and carrying a bigger work load without your spouse, you might be tempted to put some of the burden on your child. The period during and immediately after a divorce is not the time to give him additional chores or responsibilities. He might especially resent doing jobs his absent parent did.

Whatever you do to try and ease your child's way, understand that you can't fully keep him from suffering because of your divorce. Take his emotional responses seriously and get help for him and for yourself. Many parents and children have found individual or group counseling useful.

SETTING LIMITS

How do I handle discipline?

Disciplining is a difficult job that gets a little easier when children reach the early elementary years. Six- to nine-year-olds have integrated many of the rules they've heard over and over, and they usually behave in socially acceptable ways. As they get older, they need fewer reminders, their impulsive exploration slows down, and they give more thought to what they're doing. They also become more capable of listening to reason. Parents of a six- to nine-year-old can reasonably expect her to consider other people's feelings, behave well in public, give of herself, and share with others.

Of course, the need for discipline continues. The purpose is to get children thinking about their misbehavior so they won't repeatedly do things they shouldn't. Setting limits is still one of parents' major responsibilities. Unfortunately, some parents don't deal with their child's misbehavior. They may be overwhelmed by their own stressful situations or feel they can't control her and thus give up trying. Other parents don't discipline because they're afraid of making their child unhappy or angrier and more unmanageable. Whatever the reasons, parents who don't set limits do their child a great disservice. They also reinforce unacceptable behavior as she quickly learns she can act as she wants without significant rebuke or punishment.

All parents must set limits. Kids need to know what is and isn't acceptable and that there are consequences for bad actions. The consequences don't always have to involve punishment. Often, kids feel a surge of guilt over wrongdoing: "It really was an accident. I'm sorry— I didn't mean to do it." Such uncomfortable feelings may keep a child from repeating certain actions. Her parents can say, "I see you feel bad about what happened on the playground; now remember to play more carefully." When the child's guilty feelings don't deter her from misbehavior, her parents have to state the consequences: "If you don't stop fighting with Cara, you'll have to go to your room." Depending on the nature of her actions, the consequences can be stronger: "If this continues, you can't play with your friends after school." Parents usually know which disciplinary methods work best. Taking privileges away from one child might be effective, while another just needs to hear the threat. Some children respond best to being separated from the family for a "time out" in another room.

Many adults use the same disciplinary methods their own parents used: "They spanked me and I turned out OK. Why shouldn't I do the same to my child?" Yet, if parents remember the feelings they once had—especially humiliation and resentment—they may recognize that there are better ways to discipline children. They should not follow the examples of their own pasts if the examples include spanking, slapping, or verbal abuse.

Effective discipline is neither harsh nor lenient. Harsh punishment, including spanking and other physical punishment, makes children angry and resentful. They aren't motivated to change their behavior, only to sneak and manipulate and try to get away with more misbehavior. They'll think about the unfairness of the punishment rather than their own actions. At the other extreme, discipline that's too lenient is ineffective. A chronically misbehaving child who only has to say a fast "I'm sorry" or tolerate a brief, easy punishment, won't learn to control her misbehavior. Parents shouldn't be too quick to forgive and to renew their child's privileges.

Kids may misbehave because they want more attention paid to their words, interests, and activities. A child who feels left out or unconnected—perhaps because of family problems, a new baby at home, sibling rivalry, or a mother's return to work—may seek negative attention if that's all she can get. For example, one sibling may fight frequently with her brother because she feels he gets more of their parents' time. Then her anger and jealousy might be directed at him.

Sometimes children act out their frustration and sense of helplessness by misbehaving because they're unhappy, insecure, or unsuccessful in school. In such a situation, parents should talk with the teacher, consider tutoring, offer more encouragement, and closely monitor their child's progress and behavior.

As you discipline your child, you should look for the source of her misbehavior; otherwise, you'll spend time treating the symptoms rather than the cause of the problem. You may see dramatic changes in behavior when you give your child more time and positive attention or when you address situations that are troubling for her: a difficult school year, problems with friends, uneasy sibling relationships.

If you're unhappy with your child's behavior, set limits, of course, but also talk to her. When she shares her feelings about specific problems you'll gain insight into her behavior. You also can reason with her: "When you act that way, Matthew feels left out. I don't think you'd feel good if you were in his position." Ask, "What can you do to change your behavior?"

Be flexible and give encouragement and praise to reinforce positive actions. If you worry about how her behavior is viewed by other adults, take comfort in the fact that kids who misbehave at home often don't misbehave when they're out. More struggles take place between parent and child than between child and peers or child and other adults. A child who says, "You're mean!" to her parents usually knows it's unacceptable to say that to her teacher or her friends' parents. All people act and express themselves differently in the comfort of their homes.

Discipline is a difficult issue. If you're concerned about your child's behavior or unsure of your own ability to set limits, take parenting classes on discipline or consult with a professional who understands child development. Such specialists can help guide you in the appropriate direction.

Why is my child so aggressive?

Aggression can be a positive or a negative trait in children, depending on how it's channeled. Some aggressive kids start fights, while others put their energy into sports and hobbies. An aggressive child may be adventurous, taking risks and making discoveries, or he may be merely reckless. He may excel in school by putting extra effort into all his work, or he may do poorly in school because of bad behavior.

Parents don't worry about a child who is positively aggressive. He will be rewarded for his energy, enthusiasm, and drive. What parents do worry about is a child who, at six to nine years old, is belligerent and offensive to others.

Children who were aggressive as preschoolers often show less negative behavior as they get older because their energy is focused on school, friends, play, and organized activities. Still, many early elementary-aged children show occasional aggression and some are consistently rough. Parents need to watch and carefully control children's aggressive behavior.

First, they should clearly tell their child what is and isn't appropriate. A child doesn't know how to act if his parents send confusing messages. Some try to excuse their child's aggression by saying, "Oh, that's just how boys act," or, "At least he doesn't hide his feelings." Such attitudes don't teach him that his negative behavior is unacceptable.

Instead of being ambiguous, they should tell him that fighting, hitting, and using abusive language is unacceptable: "I absolutely won't allow you to behave that way." Parents also should state the consequences of negative behavior so he knows what to expect: "If you treat Nick roughly, you'll have to come inside."

It's important for parents to find the source of their child's aggression. He may be copying abuses he sees or receives at home. If parents fight with each other, their child may fight with his siblings or peers, either to imitate his parents or to alleviate his feelings of fear, anger, and helplessness. If he doesn't believe he can get away with open fighting, he might become sneaky about it. And if he feels his parents won't listen to his feelings or change the way they treat him, he may act out his frustration in aggressive ways.

Some children are aggressive due to problems at school or because they generally feel inferior. They attack others to feel more powerful. Siblings sometimes fight because they think they're being treated unfairly or because their parents actually do treat them in ways that encourage aggression, perhaps by favoring one or belittling another. The roots of aggression are sometimes difficult to find. If aggressive behavior continues over a long period, parents may need the guidance of a professional counselor.

In most cases, however, positive action taken by parents is enough to help a child control his behavior. They can offer him alternative ways to release his aggressive feelings and they can become role models for him.

If your child has a lot of aggressive energy, involve him in activities such as gymnastics, soccer, basketball, or another sport that will offer him a natural physical release for his emotions. When he's angry, he can't hit a friend, but he can kick a ball.

Talk to him about acceptable ways to express his feelings: "When you're angry enough to hit your brother, you have to let him know with words, not actions. Tell him what's making you so mad." "If you feel yourself getting out of control, don't hit—come to me for help."

Let him see how you handle aggressive feelings in your own life. Show him how you talk out your problems, take time to cool off, or go for a walk until you feel calm. Kids imitate their parents and, if you can model appropriate behavior, he will learn from you.

Watch as he interacts with others. He may be aggressive in a playful way, tugging on a friend's shirt, teasing, pretending to be in a wrestling match, or calling out insults. If the aggression seems benign, don't interfere. But such behavior can escalate, and even if the tone stays playful, your child's aggression can become very annoying to others. If you see that happening, firmly step in: "Suzanne doesn't want you to push her like that."

You can try to distract him and his friends with a new activity or different topic of conversation: "Come on in for a snack," "Why don't you show Sandy your new game?" "What did you think of the movie you saw last night?"

If distraction doesn't work, you have to take control. Place limits on his aggressive behavior and tell him you expect him to change the way he acts with his friends. The combination of your anger and your ground rules—"No rough play or hitting"—may help him moderate his actions.

He may simply not yet have the inner controls to halt his aggressive behavior. That may be true even if he wants to change the way he acts. Until he acquires control, he will need you to offer guidelines and set limits.

What can I do about lying?

Parents spend a lot of time teaching their children to tell the truth. Most early elementary-aged children have learned not to tell serious lies, although they may continue to exaggerate and tell "little white lies."

A number of factors help children learn to be truthful. First, most parents put strong limits on lying. Second, kids find that the consequences of lying include the temporary loss of parental acceptance and affection. Since they care very much about pleasing their parents, they're reluctant to risk losing their approval. Third, when children know lying is wrong they feel guilty about doing it. Guilt is an uncomfortable feeling and a strong deterrent to negative behavior. Kids also resist lying when they discover it doesn't get them what they hoped it would. And finally, they learn to be honest when the consequences of lying are worse than the consequences of telling the truth.

All children distort the truth to some extent, usually in minor ways. After all, they're exposed daily to examples of questionable honesty. Parents say, "I'll be off the phone in a minute," and then they talk half an hour longer. Teachers say, "I'll get to you soon," but they leave the child waiting. Television commercials promise exciting toys, but children discover that the products don't actually work or meet expectations. After watching a commercial, one child said, "They're lying about what that doll does and you're not supposed to lie." They also hear adults telling intentional white lies and offering false excuses: "I'm so sorry I can't make the meeting tonight, but I'm not feeling well," or, "Sorry officer, I wasn't aware I was speeding."

The "minor" lies children tell often involved things they don't want to do, such as brush their teeth or take a shower. A child will say, "Yes, I washed my hands," when she hasn't. Kids also commonly lie when confronted with open-ended questions from teachers or other authority figures ("Jason, were you playing around?" "Maria, are you wasting time over there?"). Many children will answer "No" because they hope to avoid a reprimand and believe they won't get in trouble for lying in such a situation. The teacher will usually respond to a child's "No" with only a reminder ("You need to get back to work,") or the offer of a distraction ("You should start on your art project now.").

Another common sort of lying occurs among peers. One child exaggerates or lies about her possessions because she wants to have the same things her friends have. She lies to give herself a sense of belonging. Others lie out of a competitive desire to impress their peers. Parents often overhear six- to nine-year-olds making outrageous claims about their possessions and abilities. Sometimes such fibs lead to fights. The threat of losing friends may be enough to make a child tell the truth.

Although most children distort the truth occasionally, some continue to tell serious, frequent lies. They may do this because they find their parents' discipline too threatening. If the consequences of misbehaving are very harsh, a child will lie to avoid them. And if parents impose heavy punishments for lying about the misbehavior, she may be even more afraid to admit the truth. She may reason that it's better to lie on the chance that she'll get away with it than to tell the truth and face certain, severe punishment. When she is confronted with her misbehavior and her lie, she may still refuse to tell the truth because the consequences are too frightening. She may instead blame a sibling or friend rather than face the inevitable confrontation. Basically, she tries to protect herself by denying the facts.

Parents whose child lies out of fear need to reevaluate the discipline they're imposing. If they can deal with their child less harshly, she may eventually feel safe enough to tell the truth. They should continue to set limits and consequences for lying, but the limits and consequences have to be fair. If they're excessive, she will continue to view lying as the better alternative.

Parents, of course, often find themselves in a bind. They want to punish misbehavior and reward honesty. But if their child is honest about misbehaving, the end result, from the child's point of view, is negative. She still has to face the consequences. Parents have to handle this dilemma by evaluating each situation separately and making a special point of reinforcing honesty.

The way you talk to your child about lying is important. Instead of angrily shouting, "You're lying again!" show some understanding of her position. Say, for example, "I think you made up that story because you were afraid I'd get mad at you," or, "Sometimes people don't tell the truth because they're worried about getting in trouble," or, "I think you lied because you thought I wouldn't let you go to your friend's birthday party." If you've been overly harsh in your punishment, discuss that with her. Tell her you realize you've been getting too upset. Say, "I should be more patient with you." She needs reassurance that you can accept the truth without becoming excessively angry.

If you've eased up on your reactions and she's still lying, look at other aspects of her life. Is she having problems in school? Is she able to make friends? Is she getting enough positive attention at home? Observe her at play and ask her teacher for observations and suggestions. Tell your child what you expect of her and talk about the effects her lies have on other children. As long as her lying isn't excessive, you don't need to worry. Just watch her behavior, reinforce examples of honesty, and continue talking about telling the truth.

How should I deal with profanity?

Children are familiar with curse words. They learn them from peers, siblings, and parents, and they hear them on TV and at the movies. They partly experiment with these words to see the effects on playmates and parents. They whisper the words on the playground and tell stories about kids who got in trouble for saying bad things. Using profanity makes a child feel "tough" and grown up. It can also impress his friends and make him feel part of his peer group.

While most kids are interested in profanity, they also know that it's unacceptable. They've heard their parents' warnings. They often tattle on each other: "Phillip called me the 'B' word today!" "Anton said a dirty word!" They certainly wouldn't use curse words with teachers, and they rarely would with other adults outside the home.

They do, however, occasionally use profanity in their own homes, often in the same ways that adults do, to show anger and frustration.

Unlike adults, though, kids say curse words infrequently, quietly, and with a guilty look that shows they know they're doing something wrong. As long as parents see those signs of guilt, they shouldn't worry about their child' profanity. He's only trying out the words.

Some parents accept the occasional curse word at home, considering their child's experimentation harmless. Others won't allow any profanity in their home. Whatever your feelings, be assured that, as long as he knows profanity is unacceptable, you have no cause for alarm. If, however, he shows no signs of guilt about using curse words, or uses such words frequently, you should give more thought to the issue.

He may use profanity because he needs more positive attention than he's getting from you and his friends. Cursing is a way of getting noticed, and to a child who feels neglected, negative attention is better than none at all. He also might be using profanity because you aren't giving him a clear enough message that it's wrong. Set firm limits on his use of curse words and follow through if he ignores your warnings.

There's one more reason your child may use excessive profanity— he may hear you use it so often that it seems natural to him. In order to stop him, you have to monitor your own language and act as a model for him.

My child seems self-centered. What should I do?

By the time a child is in elementary school, her parents and teachers expect her to be considerate of others. Over the years they've spent a great deal of time (usually unsuccessfully) reinforcing the need to be thoughtful. During those early years, however, the child was developmentally egocentric and therefore incapable of considering other people's points of view. Now, she's old enough to understand, yet she may continue to seem self-centered and selfish, leaving her parents to feel they've failed: "How did we create a child who only cares about herself?"

A look at typical behavior may help parents see that it takes a long time for children to become consistently thoughtful. Many six- to nine-year-olds continue to act, at times, in self-centered ways. They can be uncaring to each other, particularly verbally: "You don't know how to jump rope." "You think you know everything." "I don't want to play with you!" They sometimes make themselves feel better by putting others down.

They may form groups that thoughtlessly exclude others. Sometimes a leader is chosen who assigns tasks and roles to a lucky few and tells everyone else they can't play. Some groups pick on a particular child, seemingly oblivious to the misery they cause.

Children also continue to show self-centered behavior when they become overly competitive. As soon as one child finishes describing her plans or possessions, another may counter with something (real or made up) that is much bigger and better.

Kids don't confine their selfishness to peers. At home, parents hear, "You're the worst Mom in the world." At times, their child may expect kindness but offers little back. She may also hurt her siblings' feelings and exclude them: "You can't play with us when my friends are over."

Why do children act this way when their parents try so hard to teach them thoughtfulness? Development is gradual, but by the time they enter elementary school, most have come a long way from the self-centered behavior of preschoolers.

Parents often set high standards and demand that their child act in mature ways before she's ready. It's right and appropriate that parents expect her to be considerate, but it's unrealistic to assume that an early elementary-aged child will be considerate all the time.

If parents are concerned about their child's selfishness, they should look not just at isolated incidents, but at her overall pattern of behavior at home, school, and while visiting others. Does she generally think about other people's feelings? When her parents remind her about being considerate, does she listen? Does she play what her friends want her to? Is she tolerant of her friends' views? Is she interested in other children's ideas? Does she share? Does she display appropriate manners with adults outside the family? If parents can answer, "Yes, most of the time," for an eight- or nine-year-old, or, "Yes, often," for a six- or seven-year-old, their child is on the right track.

When they're worried, they can talk to their child's teacher. A child who seems self-centered at home, where she feels most comfortable, may be quite considerate with teachers and peers at school. If that's the case, parents can relax. Their message is getting through and she's learning to think of others.

Parents can learn more about her behavior by observing other kids of the same age. A particularly good way to do this is by accompanying a class field trip. When parents see how other children act, they gain insight and understanding and can better judge how self-centered their own child is compared with her peers.

When you observe her acting in self-centered ways, let her know what you expect. She learns by listening to you and watching you. Place firm limits on her selfish behavior: "I won't allow you to talk to your friend that way." "If you want to talk to me, you'll have to change your tone."

Have a calm discussion with her (this will be more successful with your seven- to nine- year- old then with a six-year-old). Explain how you'd like her to behave toward others and let her express her positive and negative feelings. When she believes you're listening, she'll be more likely to hear and absorb what you have to say. Role-playing can be effective. You should take her part and let her play the role of another child. When you say, "No, I won't play with you," ask how that makes her feel. Then, still role-playing, try to find solutions: "Is there something we can play together?" "Would you like to play ball with me?"

Remember to be thoughtful and considerate yourself. In interactions with your child, your spouse, and others, be respectful so she'll have appropriate behavior to imitate. Encourage her to help others. She can occasionally contribute part of her allowance to charity, go with you to buy groceries for a bed-ridden neighbor, or help pick out toys and food for the needy.

Praise her when she thinks about other people and let her know how much you love her. A child who fails to live up to her parents expectations feels unsuccessful and may misbehave out of frustration. A child who feels good about herself is comfortable extending herself to others in a caring way.

Is it normal for my child to speak rudely to me when he's angry?

"Be quiet, Dad. You never let me do anything!"

"I wish Seth's mom was my mother. She lets him stay up late."

"You're not fair! Leave me alone!"

When a child is allowed to spontaneously express his anger, he may say rude, hurtful things without considering his parents' feelings. In the heat of the moment, he can forget all they do for him. He also may ignore their attempts to reason with him. While one father was telling his daughter why she couldn't go outside after dinner, she was writing an angry note: "Dear Dad, other kids get to do things they want. I'm so mad at you. I'm never talking to you again."

Anger at parents is a normal part of growing up. Learning how to express negative feelings in socially acceptable ways takes time. It also takes patience on the part of parents. Yet many parents react harshly to their child's rudeness: "Don't you dare talk to me that way!" "I don't want to hear that tone of voice." If parents overreact toward their child for his disrespectful words, he may learn that feeling angry is bad and that angry thoughts shouldn't be spoken. A child who isn't allowed to show his feelings may never learn to express anger appropriately.

While some parents overreact, others feel helpless when faced with outbursts: "Should we allow this behavior?" "Why does he talk this way?" "Am I setting enough limits?" Many parents grew up with strong restrictions on their speech: "Don't ever say that again. It's not nice." They may be reluctant to impose similar controls on their child's expressions of anger, yet they feel uncomfortable listening to him say things they would never have said as children.

Your child needs a chance to speak his angry thoughts, but you also need to put limits on how he expresses himself. If certain words or attitudes are unacceptable to you, tell him: "It's all right for you to be mad at me, but you'll have to change your tone of voice." "When you stop name-calling, I'll be happy to listen to you." "I don't like it when you talk to me that way." "You'll have to find another way to tell me about being angry." Not only do such statements guide him toward better ways of expressing anger, but they demonstrate a respectful way of communicating that you'd eventually like him to adopt.

If, as often happens, you can't respond calmly when he's rude, walk away or get involved in another activity. Save your discussion for later. Eventually his anger will subside, even if he doesn't get what he originally wanted. His angry words will have helped him release his feelings. And since anger doesn't feel good for very long, once he has expressed himself he may quickly become friendly again.

As you help him control the way he speaks to you, consider his age; a six- or seven-year-old lacks the communication skills of an eight- or nine-year-old. Also, remember that he is greatly influenced by your behavior. If you expect him to speak respectfully, offer examples. Don't say, "Get over here this minute!" "Stop acting like a baby." "Don't be stupid." Instead, treat him as you would like him to treat others.

He allows his anger to surface because he trusts you'll love him in spite of his temper and words. Both he and you desire to live in harmony. With patience, limits, and guidance, he should learn to express most of his feelings appropriately. However, if you become concerned that he can't control his anger, consider seeking outside help such as a parenting class. The way you treat this issue now will set the tone for communication with your child later during his teenage years.

Am I spoiling my child?

All children occasionally act in selfish, spoiled ways. They make demands without consideration for people or circumstances: "Why can't I have Barbie with the beach clothes now?" Still, most six- to nine-year-olds, most of the time, have reasonable expectations and are learning to think about other people's feelings and needs. "Spoiled" children are the ones who remain almost totally self-centered and focused on their own desires, possessions, and activities.

A child who's constantly overindulged often will act spoiled. She might be so used to getting her way that she feels entitled to do as she wishes. This can happen if parents fail to set limits on her behavior, or fail to follow through when she acts in unacceptable ways.

She also can be overindulged with material objects. Owning many toys does not necessarily make her spoiled; children with lots of possessions can be loving and considerate. However, if parents constantly give without reinforcing positive values, they may unconsciously encourage their child to behave in socially unacceptable ways. She may come to expect more and more and find that what she already owns has little meaning.

Some parents have a hard time controlling their buying. They may enjoy giving to their child or feel that buying presents is the only way to please her. Some parents give out of guilt—they may not offer their child the attention she needs, so they buy gifts instead. Even when parents know they're overindulging her, they may rationalize their actions: "She's only a kid for a short time." "Why not? We can afford it."

The danger in continually overindulging a child is that she might come to expect it. She may grow up unable to handle disappointment or tolerate situations that don't go her way. Since parents want their child to become a caring, strong person capable of taking care of herself, they should avoid treating her in overindulgent ways.

They should set limits on her negative behavior. They should act as positive role models, showing her how to graciously accept and offer kindness, and how to deal with disappointment. Although it's not always easy, they should teach her to appreciate what she has, respect friends and siblings, find pleasure in learning and physical activity, and consider those more needy than she. If she grows up with basic values, she won't act spoiled no matter how many possessions she has.

If you feel your child is becoming too self-centered, evaluate your relationship with her. Are you spending as much time as you should together? Are you available to hear about her needs, ideas, and worries?

If you believe that you buy her too many things, gradually cut back so both you and she can get used to a new level of giving. Although you may be disappointed with her attitude, avoid labeling her "spoiled." She may act more selfish than you'd like, but she has good traits that may be overshadowed if you concentrate on one negative characteristic. Instead, talk about areas she needs help with: "I want you to take better care of your toys." "I'd like you to stop interrupting your sister." "You need to be more accepting when things don't go your way." If you do this, she may be less defensive and more willing to change.

FAMILY LIFE

How can I enhance my child's self-image?

Parents spend a great deal of time worrying about being consistent ("Should I always enforce family rules? Should I give in after I've said no?"), but there's really only one thing they have to be absolutely consistent about—letting their child know he's loved, valued, and important. A child who grows up hearing that message will develop a healthy self-image. A child who doesn't will have negative feelings about himself.

Parents can't compromise when it comes to giving their child feedback about his basic nature and worth. He needs to hear again and again that his parents accept him as he is, with his strengths and weaknesses, personality, interests, and appearance. Parents should encourage their child to feel good about himself and his capabilities.

That doesn't mean parents shouldn't show anger and disappointment when their child misbehaves. Parents have to set limits and tell their child what they expect. In fact, when they do set limits, they let him know they care a great deal about him and the way he acts.

However, there's a big difference between expressing disapproval of misbehavior and expressing general disapproval of a child. For whatever reasons, some parents have a hard time accepting their child. They may have unrealistically high expectations and, as a result, constantly feel that he is failing. They themselves may have received negative messages as children and may now unconsciously treat their child as they were treated.

Some parents appear to favor one of their children over another. Although it may be easy to say, "I wish you were more like your brother," or, "I wish you did as well in science as your sister," parents should recognize the harm such statements cause. Rather than motivate a child to do better, these comparisons, with their implied put-downs, make him feel bad about himself and angry. He may only be motivated to get back at the sibling who seems to enjoy more parental approval.

To see how important feedback is to self-image, consider the way you were treated as a child. If your parents valued you as a lovable, worthwhile person, you probably entered adulthood feeling good about yourself. If you received negative messages, you've probably struggled at times with a poor self-image.

What your child needs from you is acceptance, praise, and compliments on his strengths. If he never seems to please you, reconsider your expectations. They may be too high, or your parenting style may be too demanding and high-pressured. You may find that, by being more realistic, you're better able to accept him as he is and give consistent, positive messages.

As you think about his self-concept, you may be worried if he's shy. It's a common belief that a shy child has a negative self-image, but that's often not the case. Many children who are reserved by nature are as confident as their more outgoing peers. One teacher told a parent, "You daughter may be quiet, but she's certainly confident when it comes to doing her work and making friends." Let your shy child know that you love him as much as you love his more extroverted siblings, and that he has as much to offer. As a result, he'll develop a healthy self-image.

A child with low self-esteem will exhibit a number of symptoms. Rather than say he feels bad about himself, he might struggle with friendships, compete excessively with peers and siblings, misbehave, and not work up to his ability in school.

If you're concerned about his self-image or have questions about the impact your attitudes have on him, talk to a school counselor or therapist. It's much easier to resolve a child's negative feelings when he's young than it is to wait until the adolescent years.

Why are my children so different from each other?

Children in the same family can be strikingly different. Parents may believe they're raising their children in similar ways, yet the children have very different personalities, abilities, and interests. Why?

Naturally, heredity plays a major role in determining temperament and abilities. One child in a family may be easygoing by nature, another more sensitive. One may have athletic ability, while another is intellectually inclined.

Gender affects personality differences as well. Boys and girls frequently have different interests and activity levels although each may become strongly involved in activities stereotypically associated with the opposite sex. In addition, kids often imitate what they see, and if parents have very different interests and personalities, one child may imitate her mother while the other follows her father.

The way parents treat their children has a major impact on the development of personality, interests, and abilities. Parents shape and steer their child in many ways, both consciously and unconsciously. They may encourage musical talent while ignoring mechanical ability; they may inadvertently stifle creativity or individuality while urging their child to "be good." They may offer her nurturing role models or help her become a leader.

Within a family, each child's experience is unique. For instance, a first-born receives a lot of attention during her years as the only child. However, because her parents are inexperienced, they may be cautious, demanding, and nervous at the same time that they're loving and proud. Parents are usually more relaxed and lenient with their younger children.

There are other circumstances that lead parents to treat their children differently, often with negative results. One child may have a temperamental characteristic that unhappily reminds her parents of something in themselves or another relative. Parents don't like seeing familiar negative characteristics reflected in their child and may wish—or pressure—her to be different.

The resemblance can be something specific. A parent with a strong temper may single out a child with a similar personality: "Your loud mouth will get you in trouble." The parent who has negative feelings about himself may treat the child who is like him more harshly than he treats his other children.

The resemblance also can be general. A child might simply be a reminder to her parents that they (and she) are not as aggressive, talented, or intelligent as they would like to be. One parent, talking to his spouse about their child, said, "She's stubborn, just like you."

If one child physically resembles a parent or other relative in a way that makes parents uncomfortable, they may voice their displeasure:

"Your hair is so thin, just like my sister's." "You have ears like your mother." "You're chunky like me." More often parents don't mention their feelings aloud, yet still may be bothered by aspects of their child's appearance.

The child who is the unfortunate target of such comments will feel unhappy and singled out among her siblings. If she hears these messages often enough, she'll internalize them: "I'm not smart." "I'm not pretty." "I'm not good at sports." She may behave as though what she's heard is true. Her siblings, who have escaped their parents' criticism, will not have such negative self-images.

Siblings also may develop strong differences if one seems to be favored by her parents. For example, if parents believe one child is prettier than the other and express that belief to both, one will grow up feeling worthwhile while the other will feel less valued and less attractive.

Sometimes parents focus too much attention, time, or money on one child; this can have a negative impact on the other children in the family. If a child sees her brother receive attention and praise for his athletic ability, she will look for a way to get attention for herself. She may try to compete with him, but that's unlikely if she feels she can't match him. Rather than risk having her parents compare her performance to his, she may give up on sports altogether.

Instead, she'll try to find another way to distinguish herself. She may try art or dancing or develop a charming or funny manner. However, if she can't get enough positive attention from her parents, she might seek negative attention, perhaps developing a behavioral problem at home and school. The unhappier she becomes, the more likely she is to become careless with her schoolwork, family, and peers, and the less likely she'll be to get positive feedback from her parents. Her experience will be very different from her sibling's.

Parents sometimes deliberately steer their kids in different directions, often to avoid possible conflicts and competition. If an older child enrolls in dance class, her parents may discourage her younger sibling from doing the same for fear one will outshine the other. Some parents were raised in competitive households and want to spare their children the experience of failing to match a sibling. However, when parents keep one child from pursuing her interest, they rob her of a chance for enjoyment and accomplishment.

Siblings can successfully participate in the same activities as long as their parents don't focus on competition between them or praise one and not the other. Even if one is better, there will always be something good to say about each. Both should be encouraged.

Although it's intriguing and important to consider the differences between your children, it's also important to deal with the differences carefully. Accept each as she is, nurture her, and encourage her to pursue activities that she enjoys and is good at. Don't push and pull her in directions she can't or doesn't want to go. Remember not to compare your children out loud. They'll hear your comparisons as judgments, and one will end up feeling superior or inferior to the other.

It's natural to feel disappointed in your children at times: "He's not the ball player I'd hoped he'd be." "I wish she'd been a boy." "I wish she were more sociable." Try to accept what disappoints you. It's emotionally unhealthy for your children to hear your negative evaluations. They'll wonder, "What's wrong with me?" "Why couldn't I be like my sister?"

The best way to treat differences is matter-of-factly and with respect: "Sam enjoys reading." "Julie likes gymnastics." Your kids will be affected throughout their lives by the way you view them. If you set the right tone, they'll follow your lead and learn to appreciate and accept differences as a natural part of life. As a result, they'll grow up feeling good about their siblings and themselves.

What should I do about sibling rivalry?

Parents are far too accepting of sibling rivalry; many excuse it: "That's just how kids are. All brothers and sisters fight." Many stop trying to deal with it because they don't know what to do. They hear the endless bickering, whining, and arguing, and just give up, only interfering when one child gets physically hurt. Yet, parents are not helpless. There are steps they can take to eliminate most of the day-to-day struggles between siblings.

The key is getting involved. Parents shouldn't ignore their children's rivalry. When kids sense that a parent won't step in, they often escalate their battles. One boy, who was rarely reprimanded for the way he treated his sister, continually picked on her as a way of releasing his frustrations. Some people believe that paying attention to sibling rivalry only encourages it because kids argue in order to get attention. However, kids generally put their efforts into seeking positive, rather than negative attention.

The real root of sibling rivalry is a child's angry belief that he isn't being treated fairly, that his sibling is enjoying more parental affection or privileges. He directs his anger toward his sibling rather than his parents because he needs his parents for love and care. He doesn't want to risk losing their approval. It's much safer to attack a brother or sister.

A child will feel unfairly treated if his parents say, "Your sister is older so she gets to stay up later." During this sensitive period from six to nine years, a child can easily feel inferior and insecure if his parents say, "You need to practice more than your brother does," or, "I wish you could handle things as well as Jake." The child being praised will feel entitled to gloat and may even repeat his parents' words, "You never do anything right." The one being put down will resent his sibling.

This presents a dilemma for parents who believe older children should have more privileges. One mother thought her nine-year-old should stay up later than her seven-year-old. This caused great conflicts. The older child teased the younger, and the younger yelled, "You think you're so great!" and complained constantly, "Why does she get to stay up later and I don't?" Eventually, the seven-year-old fussed so long at bedtime that he was awake as long as his sister anyway.

If an older child is treated as bigger and better than a younger sibling, the younger will fight for the privileges his sibling enjoys. He'll feel helpless, unequal, and powerless to change what he sees as an unfair situation, and he'll take those feelings out on his sibling.

Many parents can remember their own feelings of resentment toward a brother or sister, yet they continue to treat children as they had once hated being treated. A better alternative to granting privileges by age is to treat kids equally, and make allowances for differences in size, maturity, and physical development. While siblings four or more years apart usually go to bed at different times, those closer in age can be sent to bed at the same time. If one needs less sleep, he can read or play in his room before falling asleep. No matter how parents arrange bedtime, they should treat the issue matter-of-factly so their younger child doesn't feel angry.

It's not just younger children who feel unfairly treated. Older children often resent being made overly responsible for their younger siblings: "Take him outside with you when you go to play." "Let Chris stay in your room while I make dinner." "Walk Josie to her friend's house." Older children may also get more than their share of the blame." You should know better, you're older." "It's your fault. You're supposed to be the responsible one." An older child hearing such words feels angry while a younger child feels that his parents will come to his defense. The older child's anger results in increased sibling rivalry.

Sibling rivalry may escalate or develop if a new baby is born. A former "only child" will face the shock of sharing his parents for the first time. A pair of siblings will find their positions in the family altered by the baby's arrival. The middle child, in particular, may feel left out.

Parents can ease their older children's adjustment by giving them extra attention and acknowledging their feelings: "It's hard getting used to a new baby, isn't it?"

Whenever you face sibling rivalry in your family, you should talk to your children, clearly stating your expectations. Let them know what the limits are and discuss ways they can control their fighting: "When you think things are unfair, tell your brother." "Let Joanne know you're mad without teasing her or hitting." "If you're mad enough to push the baby, come tell me and we'll work it out together." "Sometimes you have to include your sister when you play." If you don't set limits on rivalry, your children will believe you accept their negative behavior.

If you catch them in the middle of an argument, make them sit down and discuss the situation with each other or with you. If necessary, act as a mediator and listen to each child's side, even if that means putting up with, "You played with it longer!" "No, I had it first!"

After you've listened, ask them to come up with a solution, offer one yourself, or direct them toward another activity.

Sometimes they will have trouble talking about their fights. They know they're angry but they don't know why, or they're uncomfortable sharing their feelings. Suggest possible reasons for your child's dissatisfaction: "Maybe you think Nicole got a better toy than you did." "You might be mad because Corey got to watch more TV."

Let your children know that if they persist in arguing, there will be consequences. You already know what will work best: taking away (or threatening to take away) privileges, sending your child to his room, warning about an earlier bedtime. Make sure the consequences for misbehavior are appropriate and not too harsh, or you will just stir up more resentment. Instead of thinking, "I'll try harder to be good," your child may be so angry at his punishment that he'll think, "I'm really going to get my brother for this one!"

You may have success by offering your children rewards for getting along. Give the rewards often and be prepared to monitor your children closely. While you might see improved behavior, you also might see an increase in tattling or threats: "Ooh, I'm telling on you and you won't get a treat from Mom." You might also find that the novelty wears off and the rewards gradually become less effective.

Above all, to eliminate rivalry, treat your children fairly. There may be truth to their complaints. If you tend to reward one child and blame the other, reevaluate your attitudes. When you're fair and generous with your praise—"Thank you for sharing with your sister." "I'm glad you let Billy play with you."—your children will feel better about themselves and be less likely to argue.

Of course, you can never stop all the bickering. "Shut up!" "Stupid!" and "I hate you!" are standard sibling exchanges. They're upsetting, but they're the quick, angry expressions of a sibling relationship. Friends rarely relate in the disagreeable terms that brothers and sisters do. If the bickering is brief, infrequent, and quickly resolved, just accept it. But whenever sibling rivalry moves beyond a few words spoken in haste, step in, set limits, and help your children resolve their differences.

Why does my child keep saying, "It's not fair"?

"Billy got to sleep at his friend's house and I didn't."

"You let Courtney stay up and watch TV. It's not fair!"

Kids these ages have a heightened awareness of what is or what isn't fair, but they often make judgments based on how they feel at the moment, not on what makes sense or seems reasonable. A child who got two new shirts last week may yell "unfair" when her sister gets one new one this week.

One child was invited by a friend's family to a baseball game that wouldn't end until late in the evening. The child's mother, knowing her family had to get up early the next morning, declined the invitation. The child was devastated. "You're unfair! I never get to do anything!" Nothing her parents said made any difference.

Parents face a dilemma in such situations. They want to explain their actions and they want their child to know that life often is unfair. Yet, in emotional moments, kids don't listen. All they know is what they feel.

Parents also want to please their child. But when she's very upset about alleged unfairness, nothing will make her happy except getting her way. This is difficult for parents to understand. They may feel hurt and wonder if their child is the only one who acts this way. Actually, such outbursts are so common that parents of early elementary-aged children should simply expect them to happen.

When a child is very angry about unfairness, parents can try to soothe her feelings, offer distractions, or leave her to calm down on her own. In some cases, she may need to spend time alone in her room until she can control herself. Some kids recover quickly while others remain angry and unhappy for an afternoon or evening. Eventually, time heals these temporary wounds.

What parents should avoid doing is lecturing their child when she's caught up in her feelings of unfairness. At such times, no one, child or adults, wants to hear about the unfairness of the world. It's especially difficult for a six- to nine-year-old to pay attention to other people's misfortunes when she's feeling personally mistreated.

Talk to your child about her feelings at a calm time: "I know you were disappointed about not seeing the movie. Sometimes we have to accept when things don't go our way." Gradually introduce the larger issues of unfairness. Tell her about others who are less fortunate than she is, about people who learn to live with difficult problems. You can also talk about your own experiences. When she is angry, she'll roll her eyes and complain if you say, "When I was your age..." At a calmer time, however, she may enjoy hearing about your early years and may understand that she has much to be thankful for.

If your child is saying, "You're not fair!" over and over, you should pay close attention. You may find truth in her complaints. Perhaps she does have more chores than her brother; perhaps she doesn't get to do as much as her sister does; perhaps you've been working long hours and are unavailable when she needs you. If you're willing to look at her situation and make some modifications, she may start feeling better.

Often, small changes make a big difference. If you can't change your work schedule, you can still plan a special weekend with your children. And you can alter the way you treat them so that one sibling doesn't always feel short-changed.

Unfortunately, it's true that life is unfair, and you'll hear occasional complaints about this from your child. She may be unhappy about incidents at home, school, or with friends. One child worked for a week on his science project, only to lose the class prize to a child who put together a display at the last minute: "It's not fair. Kira's wasn't even good!" Disappointment is inevitable. Encourage her to find worth in doing her best, regardless of the judgment of others. Help her to change unfair situations that can be remedied, and trust that, with your love, support, and positive example, she'll learn to accept some unfairness that can't be changed.

What if we argue in front of our child?

All children are exposed to parental arguments. Some parents quarrel frequently and openly without considering their children's reactions and other parents argue in private. Yet parents can't hide the fact that they disagree. Kids are aware of yelling and arguments going on even behind closed bedroom doors.

When parents argue in front of their child, they may frighten him: "Are you and Dad still in a fight?" "Are you getting a divorce?" He may go to sleep scared and go to school worried. He also may take sides and yell at the parent he believes is at fault: "Stop telling Dad what to do all the time. Then he won't be so mad!" "Just leave Mom alone. Don't keep fighting!"

He may blame himself for his parents' quarrels: "If only I'd listened to them more, they wouldn't fight as much." "Maybe if I were nicer to my sister, Mom and Dad would get along better." Such wishful, magical ideas are very real and powerful.

While problems arise when parents expose their child to frequent arguing, there are problems when parents try to hide their arguments. They may do this because they believe disagreements will frighten their child or they feel he shouldn't know about their difficulties. They may hide their quarrels because they had been frightened as children by their parents' fights. They want to spare their child the uneasiness they once felt.

Pretending that all is peaceful, however, can have negative effects. Their child may not understand that disagreement is a natural part of any close relationship. Instead, he may believe that angry feelings aren't appropriate and he may not allow his own anger to surface.

Children at times need to hear their parents express and then resolve their differences. If a child grows up witnessing occasional arguments, he learns that anger is inevitable and that adults can handle it. The best thing parents can do is strike a balance, exposing him to some arguments and keeping others private.

If you argue in front of your child, consider his feelings. He will become quite upset if you and your spouse yell and insult each other. Control your accusations and unkind words. If you can't do this consistently, at least give some thought to the impact your arguments have on him.

He may need reassurance after hearing you fight: "Even though Dad and I argue, we still love each other very much." If you're uncomfortable saying this, offer some other words of comfort: "I know it's hard for you to hear Dad and me fight. We're trying not to disagree so much. It takes a lot of hard work." Listen to his questions and let him express his concerns.

Remember that he considers you a model. Every day, you show him how adults and couples behave. If you and your spouse don't treat each other with respect, if you yell, insult each other, and argue constantly, your child may eventually have trouble with his own intimate relationships.

You may find that he imitates your behavior now. If he's been exposed to frequent blaming and discord he might treat his siblings in ways you find unacceptable. You may find yourself demanding, "Don't treat your brother that way. That's not nice." "Don't talk to your sister like that."

If you and your spouse argue frequently, consider seeking professional counseling. When you are able to get along more harmoniously, your entire family will benefit.

How do we hold family meetings?

Consistent communication is an important part of successful family life. Families feel connected when they know members are free to talk and are willing to listen. Since children become more private as they grow older, families should establish a habit of open communication when kids are young. One way to do this is by holding formal family meetings.

These are discussions held regularly or spontaneously to talk about family issues. Meetings offer each member a chance to speak in a respectful atmosphere and allow parents and children to be together without distractions.

At a meeting, families can make mutual decisions or take votes on specific questions—where to go for dinner, what to do on vacation, how to spend a weekend. They can decide on new household rules or the division of chores.

Family meetings can be used to discuss problems. Parents and children frequently argue about watching TV and playing video games, how allowance is spent, when homework should be done, how family members treat each other, and how much help each member contributes. Instead of yelling, "Turn off that show and do something useful!" parents can say, "Let's have a family meeting tonight to talk about TV." They'll have a chance to cool down, discuss the problem, and come up with solutions or compromises.

Sometimes kids have complaints about parents: "You work too much." "You never play games with me." A child should feel free to air such issues at a family meeting, with the understanding that her parents will listen, offer their opinions, and consider appropriate changes.

Sometimes families meet just to talk about interesting events and affirm their love for each other. They may take turns discussing recent activities or talk about such specific topics as friendship or school. Although family members certainly talk outside of meetings, they often do so only while involved in something else: making dinner, getting ready to go out, cleaning up, reading the newspaper, watching TV. It's difficult to listen carefully while engaged in another activity. That's why undivided attention at family meeting time can be so valuable.

If family meetings are to work successfully, parents must establish rules and a tone of respect and equality. Each member must be allowed to speak without fear of being put down, each should listen to the others, and each should accept majority decisions. In a non-threatening atmosphere, children look forward to sharing: "Can we have a family meeting tonight?"

It's important that family meetings not focus only on discipline or complaints about one child. Discussions about persistent misbehavior should be handled in private. Otherwise, a child will become angry and defensive during meetings ("No, I don't do that!") and will eventually resist participating: "I hate these meetings." She'll make excuses: "I'm too tired." "I don't feel like talking." If forced to participate, she may frequently interrupt: "Can I go play now?"

If parents must use part of the meeting to talk about misbehavior, they should counter that with a discussion of the child's accomplishments. And parents should balance what they say if they have several children. Praising one child and not the other will lead to competition and resentment, just as blaming only one will. Kids will participate in family meetings only if they feel they're being treated equally.

It may take time for your family to get used to coming together formally for meetings. At times you may be frustrated because you can't accomplish what you'd hoped to: "I wish she'd understand that, even if she doesn't make a mess, we all have to chip in and clean up." You may be disappointed if your child doesn't cooperate during meetings. Rather than give up on family meetings, adjust the format to your family's needs. Even if you can't resolve difficulties, you can use meeting time to share happy experiences: "Your soccer team did so well on Saturday." "I'm glad you showed us your school journal." Short, positive meetings will increase communication and help create a climate of acceptance in your family.

How do I know if my child needs therapy?

Dealing with a child's emotional and behavioral problems can be difficult. It's hard for parents to judge how serious their child's problems are or to decide how to handle them. Some upsetting behavior may be temporary, due to circumstances such as a move or the birth of a sibling. Some problems, particularly ones affecting schoolwork, can be resolved after an evaluation by a school psychologist. Other troubling behavior patterns indicate deeper, ongoing problems that require therapy.

Complicating the issue of treating emotional problems are parents' questions and fears. Although parents wouldn't hesitate to contact a pediatrician about their child's physical illnesses, they're often quite reluctant to talk to a therapist about emotional difficulties. Many parents don't know what's involved in child therapy and fear the unknown. They may worry that their child will be stigmatized or labeled. They find his problems too complex to deal with, and they avoid therapy out of a sense of frustration or helplessness. There are parents who can't look at their child's behavior objectively and miss problems that are obvious to others.

The tendency for parents to resist child therapy is natural. They usually blame themselves for their child's problems: "Maybe I should have spent more time with her." "I should have set firmer limits." They feel guilty and may avoid seeking help rather than face their uncomfortable feelings.

Although parents sometimes decide on their own to seek a child therapist, the initiative often comes from a pediatrician, teacher, or school counselor who's noticed troubling symptoms in the child. His schoolwork may be poor, he may be disrupting the class, or he may show physical signs of stress. Parents who are initially upset by a recommendation to seek therapy sometimes feel relief at the prospect of finding answers and help.

It's hard to generalize about the severity and nature of emotional problems, but there are signs parents can look for when evaluating their child. Does he have a difficult time expressing his anger? Does he seem especially angry? Is his home situation stressful? Has there been recent family trauma? Are his behavior patterns significantly different from his peers'? Does he get into fights at school? Do neighborhood parents report that he's too aggressive? Does he work below his potential at school? Does his teacher report negative behavior? Is he withdrawn? Does he have a poor self-image? Has anyone suggested he take medication for behavioral reasons?

Parents should remember that all children display some of these behavioral problems at times, particularly when they are adjusting to changes in their lives, such as school pressures, parents' new work schedules, or tensions in the home. Parents need to worry only when consistent patterns of troubling behavior affect their child's social life and schoolwork.

Most eight- and nine-year-old children begin "talk" therapy while most six- and seven-year-olds begin with "play therapy." Since these younger children usually have a hard time verbalizing their feelings, therapists have them communicate through play sessions. Kids literally play out their feelings. While a child pretends with toys or uses clay or drawing materials, his therapist observes and talks with him. If he sets up a mock battle with two figures, the therapist may say,

"They must be really angry with each other. Does that kind of fighting remind you of other fights you've seen?" A good therapist knows how to interpret play and how to help a child work through difficult issues in the one-on-one setting of a therapy session. One eight-year-old said that his "feelings" doctor helped him stop thinking about robbers and monsters at night.

If you feel your child needs professional help, seek recommendations from your pediatrician or a school counselor. You could consult a clinical social worker, psychologist, or child psychiatrist. Just be sure whoever you select has expertise and experience working with children. You can call your local AMA or American Psychological Association chapter to verify a therapist's credentials.

Consider interviewing at least two therapists, either by phone or in person, to find out about their practices, fees, personalities, and approaches. Ask about the therapist's training and about what goes on during a session. Ask how therapy will help your child and how the therapist will keep you informed. Will she observe your child at school? Will she do testing? Does she have a sliding payment scale and does she submit statements to insurance companies? Ask how she suggests you talk to your child about therapy.

When you've chosen a therapist, tell your child what the initial visit will be like and explain that the therapist is someone who helps children feel happier and more comfortable with their family, school, and friends. You child may develop a strong attachment to his therapist. The therapist is someone he can trust and someone who accepts his feelings—good and bad—without passing judgment.

Throughout the course of treatment, keep in close contact with the therapist. If you don't see the progress you expected, talk to her. She should be willing to answer all your questions.

Although it may be difficult for you to accept that your child needs therapy, you're doing the right thing if you seek help when he's young. It will be easier for him to alter his behavior and work through problems now than it will be when he's a teenager. And even at his young age, change may be slow and gradual. Focus on the progress he makes. It's never easy to alter a child's behavior or self-image, but with time and patience, you and he should find therapy a remarkably positive experience.

"How do I explain the difference between Hanukkah and Christmas?"

Jewish children often feel a sense of alienation during the Christmas/Hanukkah season. Stores and houses are filled with decorations for a holiday Jewish children don't celebrate. Well-meaning strangers ask, "What are you getting for Christmas?" "Have you put up your tree yet?" and Jewish children feel awkward answering. Schools often center art projects and assemblies on Christmas, and some children and adults who know little about Judaism say in amazement, "You mean you don't celebrate Christmas?"

Young Jewish children may feel they're missing something. A holiday when parents are off from work and presents are placed beneath a decorated tree can seem enticing: "Can't we get a Christmas tree too and still celebrate Hanukkah?" "Do we get as many presents at Hanukkah as kids who celebrate Christmas?"

Jewish children can also feel resentment and anger that their holiday, Hanukkah, is not treated as Christmas is: "Why are there Christmas decorations everywhere? Why not Hanukkah decorations?" "Not everybody celebrates Christmas. They should care about other people's religions." These feelings stem from a child's desire to be treated equally and fairly. A six- to nine-year-old wants to be like her friends and classmates. At Christmas, Jewish children become acutely aware of the differences between themselves and their Christian friends.

Jewish parents should let their child express her feelings and they should try to understand her anger. They should then use the holiday season to talk about the differences between religions, the feelings of minorities, and the meaning of various holidays in our diverse culture. Although Hanukkah is not as religiously significant to Jews as Christmas is to Christians, the two often are linked because of their closeness on the calendar and because gifts are given for both. Jewish children should be taught the importance of their own holiday and should be helped to enjoy it for the cultural, historical, and religious occasion that it is.

To help your child focus on the positive side of the holiday season, try recreating Hanukkah activities you remember from your childhood. Ask your child how she'd like to mark the holiday: baking and cooking, playing games, making cards and gifts. Encourage a sense of community by inviting friends and relatives over to light the Hanukkah candles during the holiday's eight nights. Ask your child's teacher if she'd like you to make a class presentation on Hanukkah.

Many Jewish families help their Christian friends decorate a tree. This is one way to share the enjoyment of the holiday season. Also be sure your child has an opportunity during the holidays to perform community service with you or otherwise help you give to people in need.

During this season, as at other times, show the behavior you'd like your child to adopt. Let her see your enthusiasm for Hanukkah and understanding and respect for the religious beliefs of others. Eventually she will be able to enjoy her own holiday and observe the celebration of Christmas without feeling left out.

"Can Grandma and Grandpa come over?"

Grandparents can be very special to a child. In a good relationship, they offer unconditional love and acceptance. They often pay undivided attention and listen with interest to all their grandchild has to tell. Many grandparents are flexible—they have free time and their own lives are fairly settled. Since they don't have day-to-day responsibility for their grandchild, they can get involved without worrying about such tough issues as discipline and education.

Good grandparent-grandchild relationships usually revolve around the child's interests, although children sometimes will listen carefully to their grandparents' stories ("We didn't have computers and videos when I was your age,") and may enjoy participating in a grandparent's hobby. Still, the focus is on the child. During the preschool years, most children are happy to stay near their grandparents during a visit. By the early elementary years, kids are involved in many activities and are often busy when grandparents are around. The relationship changes. Grandparents of a six- to nine-year-old may spend less time directly involved with their grandchild and more time watching his soccer games, class plays, or recitals.

Parents find themselves in the middle of the grandparent-grandchild relationship. In the best situations, parents love to share their child's accomplishments with grandparents and hear them say wonderful things back. It's especially gratifying when grandparents compliment parents for successful child-rearing. But the relationship can be complex and uncomfortable, especially for the generation in the middle.

When grandparents criticize the way their grandchild is being raised, parents resent the intrusion. If grandparents are especially loving towards their grandchild, a parent may angrily or jealously wonder why she didn't experience such acceptance when she was young: "Why are they so nice now? They were never like that when I was growing up." At the other extreme, if grandparents aren't loving enough, parents mourn the loss of a relationship they wanted for their child.

By the time a child is in elementary school, he knows a great deal about his grandparents. He knows how they react to him, how likely they are to pay attention and play with him, and what their personalities are like. A grandchild sometimes sees the same characteristics that his parents once saw. And he, like his parents, may be bothered: "Grandpa thinks he knows everything." Parents can commiserate: "You know, when I was growing up I sometimes felt the same way about Grandpa. I think it's his way of giving advice and helping out." Parents usually find that their child is more tolerant of a grandparent's idiosyncrasies than they are.

If your child's grandparents are intent on seeing and enjoying him, the relationship will flourish. If they are emotionally or geographically distant, there are some things you can do to encourage the relationship.

When grandparents live far away, remain in contact via telephone or email. Exchange audio tapes describing recent activities or send videotapes of your child playing, singing, showing off his room, or telling a story. You can help your child write to his grandparents by giving him several addressed, stamped envelopes ready to send off with a letter, photo, or drawing.

If you've kept grandparents at a distance because of their attitudes or actions, reconsider now that your child is older. One parent who thought her mother overindulged the grandchildren as preschoolers saw that the leniency and generosity didn't harm them or make them greedy. She began to invite her mother over more often.

If you sense that your child is bothered or worried about his grandparents, let him talk about his feelings. If his grandmother is sick or if there's a sudden change in her health or living situation, he will ask lots of questions and seek reassurance: "Will Grandma be all right?" "Will she always be sad now?" "Will we still get to see her?"

The relationship between grandparents and grandchildren can enrich both generations. When it works, it's wonderful. When it doesn't develop as you would wish, there still will be benefits. As the parent in-between, try to accept whatever disappointment you feel and nurture the good parts of the relationship.

GETTING ALONG

Why does my child brag so much?

Every child at times talks proudly about his possessions, his activities, and his family. Usually he just wants to share his excitement with friends. Sometimes, however, he boasts, exaggerates, or lies about his possessions and accomplishments. He may try to show off or to impress his friends. This is bragging, and it's difficult for most parents to listen to. They wonder, "How did this child become so materialistic?" "Why doesn't he think about other people's feelings?"

Elementary school-aged children brag because they have competitive feelings about each other. They sometimes judge themselves and their peers by abilities—"Can you do a cartwheel?"—and by possessions—"She's lucky. She's got a lot of toys." Friendships at this age are based on shared interests, and a child may feel threatened if he doesn't have what his friends have. This in turn may lead him to lie, brag, and put down others just to feel accepted by his peers. One boy exaggerated the size of his baseball card collection because he felt left out when his friends talked about their cards. Bragging made him feel like he belonged.

Some kids brag because their self-esteem is low. If a child feels inadequate, he may seek attention by lying about what he owns or by making up elaborate stories about family activities. Boasting makes him feel important. Siblings may brag because they feel jealous of each other. One will chant, "I got to go outside twice today for recess and you didn't!" and the other will respond, "I can sleep at Julie's and you can't!"

Bragging often has a negative effect on young listeners. Children between six and nine usually believe what friends tell them, so they may end up feeling hurt and angry about seemingly far-fetched claims. One girl said she had a new necklace and her friend responded, "So? I got five new bracelets." Some children just listen, feeling uncomfortable. Still others are so impressed by their friends' bragging that they start boasting for them: "My friend has a huge train set!"

Parents, overhearing their own or another child brag, wonder what to do. If you're concerned about your six- to nine-year-old's boasts, remember that he may not realize he's bragging. In the early elementary years, kids are just leaving the stage of egocentric, self-centered thinking and only beginning to consider other people's needs. His feelings of respect for others will come and go in this stage before he fully understands the impact bragging has.

Still, it's important to talk with him about boastful behavior. Let him know that his innocent exuberance may be thought of as bragging by those who have less than he does. One boy who liked to talk about his comic book collection was upset by a friend who lied about having a similar collection. The boy's mother used the incident to talk about friendship and jealousy. You can speak to your own child about bragging, using real or hypothetical situations. You may be frustrated during your discussion if he shows a lack of concern for others, but keep talking and listening. If he feels heard, he'll eventually be more willing to listen to you.

When you overhear him and his friends bragging excessively, let them try to handle the situation themselves. If one seems to be getting upset, step in and either distract them all or set limits for them. If your child is bothered by bragging at school, remind him that he can set limits, too. He can say, "I don't want to talk about that anymore," or, "That's all I want to hear about your bike."

If your child boasts excessively to his siblings, try to find out what the underlying issues are. Your children may need more attention or may be bothered by problems at school or in the family. Once you discover the reasons, you can help your children build better sibling relationships.

Finally, you can help by demonstrating the right behavior for your child. If you boast about your home, cars, vacations, and even his accomplishments, you're teaching him to act similarly. However, when you're respectful of others' feelings, you help him learn to control his bragging and become a more thoughtful and considerate person.

Why is my child so competitive?

"I'm in a higher reading group than Sara!"
"I won! I beat everybody!"

"Emily still needs training wheels on her bike and I don't."
All children have competitive feelings and all run into competitive situations during the early elementary years. There's competition in games, sports, the classroom, social life, and family life. When properly handled, competition can motivate children to do their best. Some need the "jolt" of competition to put energy into studying, practicing, or performing.

For a number of reasons, some kids are more competitive than others. A younger sibling tries to keep up with, or even surpass, his older brothers and sisters. He'll compete in anything from schoolwork, sports, and music to crafts, skate boarding, and game playing. The younger child tries harder, earlier than his older siblings did, and often he fails because he's not developmentally ready to compete on an equal basis.

Schools often encourage kids to become competitive. Grades are given and sometimes announced: "I'm better than Monique in math. She got a C again." Teachers give stickers to the child who has the right answers, the best picture, the neatest handwriting, or the nicest behavior. Only the top homework projects go on display and only the best book reports get read out loud. In gym class, teachers may single out the most athletic children: "Everybody watch how fast Mark runs." "Look how Susie jumps!"

Recreation class leaders and team coaches also encourage competition: "Let me tell you the other team's weaknesses. Then we'll go get 'em." "Play better and we'll win." Children compete with other teams and also with their own teammates to be the best or the first or the one who spends the most time on the field.

By far the greatest influence on a child's competitive sense is his parents. Some parents, ignoring their child's strengths, weaknesses and interest, put intense pressure on him: "You can do it." "Go out there and beat them." "Andy stinks. You're a lot better than he is." They may do this because of their own unresolved competitive feelings. They may have been similarly pressured as children and now repeat old patterns. They may feel insecure about their skills and push their child in order to compensate for their own feelings of inadequacy.

They might pressure him to compete because they feel he's lazy and unmotivated. By reinforcing competition, they hope to spur him to greater accomplishments: "If you'd just tried harder you could've won that match. Next time pay attention to what you're doing." "I know you can get the highest grade on the test. Just study more."

When parents invest time and energy urging their child to compete, he may feel humiliated when he doesn't perform as they wish. One parent berated his child for dropping the baseball during a game. Another was angry because her child got fewer points than a neighboring child in a classroom competition. Parents may justify such pressure by saying, "It's tough out there, and if he doesn't learn how to compete now, he's never going to make it in the real world."

The unenthusiastic child who competes does so because his parents want him to. He may simply fail for lack of skill or desire, or he may put on a swaggering front. Even after swinging at the baseball and missing, he may say to a teammate, "I'm better than you are. At least I swing harder." Some unwilling kids compete angrily, becoming extremely frustrated if they lose. They know how much their failure disappoints their parents.

In moderation, competitive feelings are acceptable, especially if a child has confidence in himself and his abilities. A child with a good self-image will not think badly of himself if he loses or exaggerate his importance if he wins. An insecure child may only compete when he's sure to win, or will compete and have his self-image fluctuate, depending on his performance. One girl who was not competitive by nature became so to please her father. Her teacher reported that the girl hesitated to try something unless she was sure she'd do well.

Some kids are excessively competitive. They're consumed with being bigger and better, and they want to win at everything. Even if they are highly skilled, their attitude is disturbing and unattractive. Many parents of highly competitive children worry about their intense drive. They know that the fun of participating is lost when their child is obsessed with being the best. One girl became upset with her score while bowling. When her request to take her turn over was denied, she got angry and demanding, eventually ruining the game for her family.

If you're concerned about your child's excessive competitive feelings, there are several approaches you can try. Work on his attitude, and talk to him about competition from the opponent's point of view. Explain that part of competing is learning to lose gracefully and congratulating the winning opponent. He will adopt your point of view if you model the behavior you'd like to see in him. Be a good winner—and loser—and, after trying your best, minimize the importance of competition and move on to another activity.

If you don't understand your child's competitive drive or can't affect it, take a look at his overall situation. Does he need more of your time and attention at home? Do his siblings consistently out-perform him? Do they include him in their activities? Does he have enough success at school and at home? Is he involved in too many competitive activities? Should another interest be encouraged? Are his activities appropriate for his age level or does he struggle to keep up?

Once you've stopped placing pressure on him, help him put less pressure on himself. Although he may continue to be highly competitive, stress the enjoyment and fulfillment of participating in activities and let him know what he's missing by focusing so strongly on winning.

What about shyness?

Shyness is often viewed as a problem. Many people believe it is an undesirable trait, one that reflects a poor self-image. Actually, it's only a problem when people perceive it as one. A reserved child who is not taught that something is wrong with her will be just as confident, happy, and involved as her more outgoing peers.

One woman who was shy as a child had parents who never made her feel bad about her quiet nature. As a result, she's a reserved adult who moves confidently through life. Another woman remembers being chastised for her shyness. Her parents constantly tried to change her: "Why don't you act like the other kids?" "Why are you so anti-social?" She still feels self-conscious and uncomfortable and imagines her mother saying, "Talk! Just go ahead and talk to them!"

The way a child perceives her shyness depends mostly on her parents. If they accept her personality and don't focus on shyness as a problem, she also will be matter-of-fact about her shyness. She will see herself as able to do and enjoy the same things other children do. But if her parents try to change her or focus too much on her shyness, she'll become self-conscious. It's a fine line between acceptance and feeling bad about having this trait. The more parents concentrate on shyness as a problem, the worse their child will feel about herself.

Shyness is a personality characteristic and should be accepted as one, not as a flaw. Reserved children are often nice, well-behaved, and generous. They are usually good listeners and enjoy and respect privacy. They also can enjoy watching other children participate in activities. Although they are shy in some circumstances, they may handle other situations well. They're often fine in small groups of two or three children or in one-on-one conversations with an adult. A shy child who is involved in an interesting project won't appear shy. It's only when she becomes the focus that her shyness becomes apparent.

While shyness should not be seen as a problem for a child, it can be frustrating for parents. They may feel uncomfortable or embarrassed when she doesn't respond as other children do. They may feel judged and they may see her ignored by adults who engage with other, more talkative children.

Parents can help themselves and their child by avoiding uncomfortable situations and protecting her when necessary. For instance, many shy children don't like to be put on the spot to say hello or otherwise talk on demand. If she appears unlikely to respond to an adult's questions, her parents should matter-of-factly respond for her and then quickly steer the discussion away from her. The alternative, trying to force her to talk, will only make her feel worse and will probably be ineffective.

Parents can sometimes help their child by role-playing uncomfortable situations with her: "Let's pretend you meet Jackie in the hall at Sunday School. How could you say hello to her?" "Imagine Aunt Karen asking you, 'How's school?'" Practicing may be useful. However, when she is actually confronted with an uncomfortable situation, she may not respond as she had rehearsed.

If parents expect guests at their home, they can prepare their child or make special arrangements for her. She might feel more comfortable if she has a friend of her own over. She might prefer helping before the guests arrive rather than when the visitors are in the house. If parents generally arrange situations so she doesn't feel focused on, everyone will feel better.

Parents often wonder how to approach the subject of shyness in school. If that's a concern of yours, wait and see how comfortable your child is in class. Don't begin the school year by telling the teacher your child is shy; the teacher may treat her differently or anticipate problems. If your child feels self-conscious about being made to speak in class, schedule a conference at school. Let the teacher know you don't want your child to receive negative messages about shyness. You have to correct any adult who believes she can change your child's personality.

Many teachers prefer quiet students. Your reserved child may be rewarded for her behavior, perhaps more than you would wish. One shy first-grader received stickers at school for being so "good" and quiet. Then, during a school conference, the teacher told the parents the girl was very shy. "But you reward her for being quiet!" her parents replied. They asked the teacher to stop reinforcing her shy behavior and instead reward her for finishing her work or participating in class.

Sometimes your child will come home from school or play feeling frustrated because she couldn't participate comfortably. She may become whiny or demanding. Accept that she needs understanding and an outlet for her feelings. If she feels comfortable enough, she may talk to you about shyness and how it sometimes interferes with activities. Certainly as she gets older, an accepting atmosphere at home will make it easier for her to share her thoughts.

You may be convinced that she will always be shy, but it's hard to predict the paths she'll take. Some kids who are extremely shy during the elementary years may gradually become more outgoing. In any case, your job is to accept her as she is and help her find activities and situations that make her feel good.

Why does my child want to be with friends all the time?

The early elementary years are a time of increased socializing. As kids become less egocentric they're better able to consider other children's feelings and viewpoints. Six- to nine-year-olds not only tolerate each other's differences, but actually enjoy learning about friends' interests. They generally play cooperatively, work together, and follow the rules of games. Although there are still arguments, they now have an easier time letting go and accepting others' opinions.

Kids may have many friends in school or in the neighborhood, but usually find one or two they most enjoy being with. It sometimes seems to parents that their child is more interested in friends than family, and increasingly this may be the case. While six- and seven-year-olds look almost exclusively to their parents for love and acceptance, an eight- to nine-year-old also looks to friends for approval. He wants to be like his peers and may argue with his parents: "I don't want to go to Aunt Jan's. I want to go skating with Joey." "Why can't Judy come over today?" "Can't we bring Bailey to the circus with us?"

When a child forms a strong friendship, his entire family is affected. There are phone calls back and forth and weekend and after-school plans to make. He may badger his parents to buy him what his friend has or to let him do what his friend does. Friends may want to play the same sports, join the same activities, dress similarly, be in the same class, and go to the same camp.

You may find yourself in the middle of arrangements between your child and his friends. Although it can be frustrating to plan around kids' requests, you'll also see the value of friendships to your child. He'll share some ideas with his friends that he'd hesitate to share with you. They'll laugh at the same jokes, enjoy the same activities, accept new friends and talk about those they don't like, listen to each other's stories, and show concern and compassion.

At times, include his friend in your family's plans. This is easy if the friend lives nearby. But if he lives some distance away, as often happens when children attend private school away from the neighborhood, you'll have to make an extra effort.

Invite the friend to dinner, to sleep over, or to go with you on an outing. Even if you're busy with errands, you can take him along to the grocery store or shopping center.

Elementary-aged visitors are often easier to have around than preschoolers. They occupy themselves independently, make less noise, need less supervision, and make less of a mess. You'll still have to deal with cleanups, of course, and there will be disagreements, although bickering between good friends is usually brief.

You should monitor your child and his friend to be sure they're playing safely. You also should make sure they don't constantly exclude your other children. While friends need some privacy, they also need to know that siblings shouldn't be shut out: "Your brother would like to help you build a snowman."

If a close friend moves away, your child will go through a difficult period. Although distant friends can stay in touch, the loss may be very hard. It will be difficult for you as you witness your child's sadness and help him get through the separation. Let him know about the move ahead of time, suggest he give his friend a good-bye gift or card, and take a last picture of the friends together. Support him and listen as he talks about his unhappy feelings. You can encourage him to write or email his friend, and you can arrange periodic visits. However, he will gradually focus less and less on the friend who moved away. As he builds new friendships, he'll remember his old friend primarily when reminded of the things they did together.

How can we have fewer problems with our carpool?

Carpools can be helpful and frustrating at the same time. Parents welcome the driving assistance, yet struggle with the personality, style, and scheduling conflicts involved. Carpools are created for convenience. Most kids would just as soon have their parents drive them everywhere. However, parents need carpools to make their hectic lives run more smoothly.

When children (and parents) are not compatible, carpooling can become a problem. This is especially true when the drive is long and frequent, as is often the case with private-school carpools. Children who don't get along whine and complain that the radio's too loud, the other kids talk too much, the car's too hot or too cold. One child may start arguments or brag so much about her possessions that she makes the others miserable.

Children's ages sometimes affect the success of a carpool. Some mixed-age groups work well, but others fail. One mother listened to her seven-year-old daughter complain that the eight-year-old in the carpool always wanted to listen to rock music on the radio. The next year, the daughter herself wanted rock music, to the dismay of the younger children in the carpool.

Some kids complain bitterly about carpools, hoping their parents will let them drop out: "I hate Emily and Robert! Do I have to ride to school with them?" Parents should listen to their children's opinions; they may even share them: "You're right. Emily does talk too much on the way to school." Yet, parents have to explain that carpooling is not an option but a necessity. The arrangements are unlikely to change, so parents and children have to try and make the best of them.

There are a number of things you can do to help make carpooling more successful. First, reach an agreement with the other drivers on matters of car safety, schedules, and acceptable carpool behavior. Keep communicating with these parents when there are problems, but also let your child know that when she's the passenger, she has to follow the driver's rules.

Be sure your child has plenty of time to get ready so the carpool won't have to wait while she hunts for her gloves, homework folder, ballet shoes, or change for a drink.

When it's your turn to drive, set limits on unacceptable behavior and let your riders know how you want them to act. You may not like dealing with the tension, but you have to step in to ensure a safe and relatively peaceful ride. You can say, "When you act so silly, I have trouble concentrating on driving." If children won't stop arguing, tell them to take out a book and read quietly. When you're the driver, it's up to you to set the rules: "You can't bring a toy in the car unless you let the others have a turn with it." "You can't insult each other." "I won't let you yell like that."

You can try to prevent tension by providing distractions such as food, pocket video games, audio tapes, CDs, small pads with pens and pencils, books, miniature cars, dolls, action figures, even gum. One parent kept her carpool busy singing. Another mother kept a conversation going involving all the kids. Often, children can come up with their own ideas for activities.

If the kids you drive complain about seating arrangements, try assigning seats on a rotating basis. That may stop arguments over who sits in a window seat. As an alternative, you may want your own child to sit up front when you drive so you can talk.

You may have a child in your carpool who gets upset or cries when you drop her off. After an apparently happy ride, she'll start crying at her destination because she wants her parents with her. She may be nervous about a new activity or just generally uneasy. When you're the driver, you have to decide how to deal with the situation. If she goes off with the other children, you can drive away without worrying. But if she regularly stands and cries, ask her parents how they'd like you to handle the situation. Sometimes she actually cries longer when her parents drive than when another adult does.

Crying children, arguments, worries about being on time—all are frustrating parts of carpooling. After trying to make your carpool as successful as possible, just accept the remaining frustrations in exchange for the convenience.

SCHOOL

My child is having trouble getting used to first grade. What can I do to help?

First grade is very different from kindergarten and preschool, with new demands, expectations, and experiences. Parents and children look forward to first grade because it's the beginning of "real school" and a sign of growing up. They also feel anxious and uncertain, however, and in the case of parents, nostalgic about the passing of the preschool years.

Some children are better prepared than others for the increased demands of first grade. Age is an important factor, since children sometimes aren't developmentally ready for first grade until they've almost turned seven. Children just turning six at the beginning of first grade may not adjust as well as those with earlier birthdays.

A child's adjustment is also affected by his home situation. If he has a new sibling, if his family has just moved, or if there's tension between his parents, he may enter first grade feeling insecure or fearful. Any negative experience outside of school—including a bad time at summer camp—can interfere with his school performance.

On the positive side, he will have an easier time adjusting to first grade if he has friends in his class and if he has a warm and attentive teacher. A caring teacher knows that first graders arrive with varying academic skills, social skills, and experiences. She will patiently help her students get over their fears and hesitations and offer them support and encouragement.

Most kids feel better about first grade if they're familiar with the school and the classroom. Ideally, kindergartners should be invited to their future first-grade classrooms to meet the teachers. If this doesn't happen, parents can prepare their child by talking about first grade and encouraging him to ask questions.

Once first grade starts, some kids say, "I love school!" and go off happily each day. Others have a hard time getting along. They may be unhappy and hesitant, or they may resist going. They may feel insecure if other students seem able to read and write. They'll feel inferior if they've been placed in the low reading group. Although parents want to be sympathetic, many get angry and frustrated with their child's complaints about going to school: "Why can't he just be like the other kids?"

You may find yourself intolerant of your child's attitude if you feel guilty or embarrassed. But if you lose patience and pressure your child to do well in school, such pressure puts him in a bind. He wants to please you, yet he can't fully control his feelings and actions. Often, if you are understanding and supportive for the first few weeks of school, your first grader will get over his initial anxiety.

If your child is having trouble adjusting to first grade, there are many ways to help. First, stay in close contact with the teacher. She may give you a fuller picture of his behavior. While you see him go off hesitantly, she may see him joining in class activities and getting along with other children. Even the most reluctant first-graders have good periods during the day. They feel sad or lonely sometimes, but at other times they're fine.

Help him connect with another child who rides the same school bus. Consider telling the bus driver or the parents you carpool with about your child's reluctance to go to school. If you usually drive him yourself, consider asking another parent to give him a ride in the morning. Some kids have an easier time separating if they aren't with their parents during the moments before school starts. Your child may be entertained or distracted if he goes to school with another family.

Try giving him a "love note" to carry in his pocket or offer a reward at the end of the day. It can be a small toy or sweet treat for entering school with a smile and not crying during the day.

If he's having trouble making friends, encourage him to invite classmates to your house and talk about other ways of getting to know kids. Having him join a club or after-school activity will help him meet others and feel more connected to the school.

You may have success with role-playing games. Suggest that you and he play school—you'll be the student and he'll be the parent. Use real situations that come up in first grade. Have the "student" cry in class and ask the "parent" what to do. You may be surprised at the good suggestions your child comes up with. He may say, "Call your friend and ask him to go to school with you." Role playing can be therapeutic for him, and it can offer you insights into his difficulties. If you're having success with this approach, try it once a day for a week or so. For your story themes, choose adjustment to school, sadness about leaving home, schoolwork, and other topics that seem to bother him.

If, after several weeks, you see no improvement in his attitude toward first grade, talk to the school counselor or principal and ask her to observe him in the classroom. Perhaps she can suggest some solutions. In addition, consider his readiness for first grade. Does his social and emotional development seem slower than that of his classmates? Does he seem too young for first grade? Is the classroom atmosphere appropriate for him? Are the teachers' expectations realistic? Even if he's not quite ready for the demands of first grade, it's likely that he'll adjust as long as you continue to be patient, offer help with his work, and seek support from the school.

How can I get my child to complete her homework?

As children enter elementary school, they have their first experience with homework. Kindergartners and first graders usually have minimal assignments, while older children are gradually given more. Some teachers assign work every night and some give homework every Monday to be completed by Friday. Many kids resist doing their homework, causing family struggles and frustration.

"Why won't she finish her reading and be done with it?" "Why do I have to yell before he'll get started?" "Why does she wait until the last minute?" Parents want their child to be responsible and do her work carefully and on time. They don't like resorting to arguments, bribes, and threats.

There are many reasons why children struggle with homework. Assignments may be confusing: "Did she say finish page thirty-three or thirty-six?" "I don't remember what to do with these math problems." A child who has difficulty in school or who lacks the skills to complete her work may become angry and refuse to do—or even acknowledge—assignments: "I hate homework!" "I don't have any homework."

Many kids are bored with their assignments and are therefore reluctant to do them: "I already know how to spell these science words." Common weekly tasks have students copying spelling words over and over or coloring in mimeographed pictures. Even to parents, assignments can seem time-consuming and pointless.

Some children have problems with homework because of their schedules. They go from school to after-school activities or child care and may not arrive home until early evening. With limited time to eat dinner, be with family and friends, and relax, a child may put off homework.

Parents may find that struggles intensify in the evening. If a child is too tired or too distracted to do homework at night, her parents should encourage her to get some or all of it done after school. Most child care centers provide a quiet workspace. If she comes home in the afternoon, her parents can arrange a flexible schedule of play and homework. This is usually better than a rigid requirement to finish homework first.

To help your child become more responsible about homework, try some of these suggestions. Have her write down assignments in a special notebook. When she comes home from school, find out what her homework instructions are. That way you'll learn what she's doing in school and when she has long assignments. This will help you avoid late-night surprises: "I just remembered. My book report and poster are due tomorrow." One father found himself at the drugstore at 9:00 at night buying supplies for his son's school project.

Sit with your child while she does homework. Since the kitchen is often the center of family activity, have her work at the table while you prepare food, read, or pay bills. Take short breaks together. Offer your help, but be prepared for possible arguments about assignments. Kids often take their anger out on parents since they can't yell at a teacher. Your child might resist your suggestions: "It doesn't matter if it's neat." "That's not the way my teacher said to do it." "I know my vocabulary words. I don't need to go over them." Be gentle when pointing out mistakes, and, if necessary, set limits on your child's way of expressing herself: "When you can explain what you need in a calmer way, I'll be happy to help you." Occasionally, if she's bogged down with repetitive work you know she understands, it's all right to help her out with answers.

If she has trouble with a particular subject, consider offering more intensive help yourself or hiring a tutor. If your child consistently struggles to complete assignments, speak to the teacher. The work may be inappropriate or too difficult. You should work with the teacher to improve your child's academic experiences, including homework.

Your child will probably continue to need reminders about homework. At times you'll have to be firm: "You have to start your homework right now." By third or fourth grade, although she'll still need some help, she will be more responsible about getting her work done independently.

What if I disagree with my child's teacher?

Parents feel dissatisfaction at times with their child's teachers; the teachers may not be meeting the child's needs or may be cold or inattentive. Parents become aware of problems through their child's complaints: "The teacher wouldn't let me go outside today because I laughed at Matt's joke." "Every time anybody talks she says 'shhh.'" "My teacher wouldn't let me finish my math problems because she said I was taking too long."

Parents get to observe the teacher themselves during field trips and classroom visits. The teacher sets the tone in a class; her personality and teaching style determine how the standard curriculum will be taught. When parents are unhappy with her manner or approach, they often feel helpless. Yet they have more power to initiate classroom changes than they realize.

If they suspect a problem, they should listen carefully to their child's description of what goes on in the classroom. Are her complaints consistent? Is her work or self-esteem hampered by the teacher? What seems awful to a child one day may be insignificant the next, or may have no lasting negative effects. Also, kids sometimes exaggerate, especially as a way of avoiding a reprimand. For example, a child who did not complete an assignment may blame the teacher: "It's not my fault. She never gives us enough time."

If a child's complaints seem to have merit, parents should call or email the teacher: "My son says you've been dissatisfied with his social studies work and he doesn't understand why." Parents also can plan to meet with the teacher. Either option can be difficult for parents who dislike confrontation or who fear that an angry teacher will retaliate against their child. While some teachers may do this, most will listen to parents and try to work out solutions to classroom problems. As long as parents present their concerns in a respectful way, they have little to fear. However, regardless of the teacher's response, it's the parents' right and responsibility to set up a conference and try to improve their child's classroom experience.

If you request a meeting with the teacher, prepare ahead of time. Gather facts and notes and have suggestions and solutions in mind. Begin the meeting on a positive note: "You and I have Lisa's best interest in mind. What can we do together to improve her schoolwork and make her feel better about herself?"

Make reasonable requests: "If you give Andrew a little more notice about his assignments, he'll have an easier time finishing them." "I think Mia would feel more interested and challenged if you moved her to another reading group." Tell the teacher about approaches that work at home: "John generally does better when he gets some positive feedback." Ask for her ideas and suggestions. She should be willing to make the changes you request or to explain why such changes are impossible.

Throughout the conference, remember to speak mildly and respectfully. Many teachers feel vulnerable talking to parents and become defensive if they perceive parents to be hostile or aggressive. Let the teacher know you sympathize with her workload and the difficulty of teaching so many students at once. You aren't there to attack her teaching methods, but rather to come up with solutions and compromises. Give careful thought to her opinions and recommendations since she may offer valuable insights. You should leave the conference with a clear understanding of how you and she will work together to make changes.

Let your child know ahead of time about the conference. She too may be afraid the teacher will "take out" her anger in the classroom. Assure her that it's fine for teachers and parents to meet. Ask if there are some things she'd rather you not mention during the conference, and as much as possible, respect her wishes. If she's very worried, tell the teacher during the conference: "Kara is afraid you'll be angry with her after this meeting." When the conference is over, let your child know something of what went on: "Your teacher was glad to meet me." "She answered my questions and is going to give you more time to finish your reading." You should also pass on the teacher's suggestions.

After the conference, you'll have to wait and see if the teacher makes the changes she promised. You'll also have to see if she does, after all, react negatively to your child. If you aren't satisfied, contact the principal to discuss your concerns. Gently but firmly pursue your child's interests. If you're unhappy with the principal's response, you might want to contact her supervisor.

You can resolve many school problems if you're persistent. However, in spite of your best efforts, you may eventually fail to improve your child's situation. Many teachers, administrators, and school systems are inflexible. If you can't get improvements, you have several choices: you can accept the facts and offer more home enrichment and encouragement, you can hope that next year will be better, or you can consider enrolling your child in another public or private school. Let your decisions be guided, as always, by what's best for your child.

What should I do when my child says he's bored at school?

Learning should be an exciting part of a young child's life. Children these ages are striving to be competent and successful in school. Yet, they often say, "I hate school. It's so boring!" They drag their heels when it's time to go in the morning, and they come home with nothing to report.

There are many reasons why a child might find school boring. The work may be too easy and presented too slowly, too much time may be spent preparing for standardized testing, or there may be too much paperwork and not enough hands-on experiences: "The teacher does all the science projects and we just get to watch." A child with an active mind needs a challenge, and a curriculum geared toward a child with average intelligence will not meet the needs of brighter students. Since many school programs are inflexible, teachers often give faster students "busy work"—coloring, additional workbook pages, cleaning chores—while the rest of the class catches up. Naturally, someone in this situation will be frustrated and bored.

A slow learner also may claim to be bored. The work may move too quickly for him to understand or so slowly that he loses all interest. After a few tries, he may give up and daydream. School seems boring, and he may easily view himself as a failure.

Children may feel distracted and disinterested if they're unhappy with themselves. A child feeling parental pressure to succeed may dislike school and say it's boring. Likewise, a child experiencing problems at home may be too preoccupied to focus on learning. And, if at any point during the day he's hungry or tired, he may complain of boredom.

Since "school's boring" can mean so many things, parents have to find the cause of their child's complaints. Occasional dissatisfaction is normal, but repeated claims should be taken seriously.

Talk to your child about the problem: "Can you tell me why you're bored?" Try to assess the situation from his response. Is class work too easy? Too hard? Is something bothering him socially or at home? Does he have school friends? Do children tease him? When you've isolated the probable causes of his boredom, ask what changes he'd like to see: "How could your teacher make reading more interesting?" "Would you feel better about going to school if Dad and I were calmer in the mornings?"

If you discover that problems at home are the root of your child's unhappiness, you can try to remedy the situation yourself or seek professional guidance. Often, a few changes—spending more time with him, easing up on parental pressure—will make it easier for him to concentrate on schoolwork.

If the school curriculum is causing boredom, talk to the teacher. If the material is too difficult, ask how she can accommodate your child's needs. Perhaps he requires more concrete examples or more time to complete classwork. Ask if the teacher can involve you with teaching certain material at home.

If your child is bored because the work moves too slowly, let the teacher know that busy work is not acceptable. Ask if he can go to the library, use the computer, read a book, write a story, help another student, or go on to the next lesson when he's done his work early. If you don't push for such changes, the teacher won't see the need to stimulate him and he may finish the year with a sense of loss and frustration.

If you're dissatisfied with the teacher's response to the problem of boredom, discuss the matter with the principal. Ask for suggestions and seek ways you and the school can work together to have your child's needs met.

Ultimately, you may not be able to make your child's school experience less boring. Yet, you still have choices. You can talk to school district officials, you can work with an advocacy group that pushes for improvements in education, you can investigate transferring your child to another public school, or you can enroll him in a private school. The expense of a private school has to be weighed against the dramatic improvement you may see in his educational development.

School boredom is a major problem. Kids spend their formative years in school—precious time that should not be wasted. Parents have the responsibility to monitor their child's education and do all they can to ensure quality in the classroom.

How can I tell if my child is doing well in school?

Parents often don't know how their child is doing in school. While they certainly hope her work is average or above average, they have only a vague notion of what the school expects. Curricula vary from school to school, even from class to class. One school system may introduce multiplication tables in second grade while another waits until third or fourth grade. Schools offer only minimal information about coursework and expectations. This makes it difficult for parents to judge how well their child is mastering the material.

If you're having trouble evaluating your child's progress, first check the work she's bringing home. (You may have to search the bottom of her backpack for crumpled papers.) What kinds of assignments is the teacher giving? Are directions clear? Does the level of work seem appropriate?

See what kinds of comments and grades the teacher is putting on the papers. You may be dismayed to find red "X"s and negative comments. Such markings don't necessarily mean your child is doing poorly. Many teachers single out mistakes, ignoring the many correct answers on a page. Sometimes make your own evaluation of your child's written work.

Talk to your child about her classwork. Does she feel she's doing well? Keeping up? Kids usually know where they stand in the class. You may hear, "I keep getting bad grades on my spelling papers," or, "I finish reading before anyone else does."

You can learn about the school's curriculum and standards by talking to your child's friends—those in her class and those in other classes. Ask what they're doing in school. Be specific: "Are you on subtraction? Have you studied the planets? Do you write reports?"

Whenever you have questions, talk to your child's teacher. Find out specifically what material is covered in class. Ask for suggestions to improve your child's performance and offer any suggestions you may have.

Report cards are the standard means of teacher-to-parents communication. Yet, a series of check marks or letter grades without written comments is often not enough. Does a "B" in social studies mean your child is truly mastering the subject, or does it mean she's a cooperative student who hands in her worksheets on time?

You want your child to get good marks and you also want to know that she's learning. Unfortunately, grades don't always reflect mastery. One second-grader, for instance, had neat, legible handwriting. Her teacher wanted her to write on paper with oversized lines. The girl had trouble making exaggerated letters and therefore was given a low grade even though her writing looked like that of an older student. Another child was good at math, but balked at doing repetitive, easy drill work. He got a low grade that did not reflect his high mathematical ability.

At times you may feel your child is receiving a mark that's too high. You know she doesn't understand her science book, yet the teacher gives her a high grade for being neat and paying attention. Since grades may or may not accurately reflect progress, rely on your instincts as well as on graded papers and report cards when judging your child's achievements.

You can sometimes learn more about how she's doing by examining the results of standardized tests. After she's been tested at school, ask if you can see the results, including a comparison of her scores with those of her peers. If the school isn't required to disclose results, consider having your child tested by an educational specialist. If the testing shows she's learning well, you'll feel reassured. If it shows less favorable results, the specialist may be able to discover the reasons your child is not doing as well as you'd like.

How can I encourage learning at home?

Learning is not just something that happens at school, and learning is not dependent on textbooks and formal lessons. A family that is involved, interested, and curious can learn all the time.

The best way parents can encourage learning at home is to be learners themselves. When they read, their kids read. When parents have many interests, kids develop interests and hobbies too. Parents show positive attitudes toward learning whenever they try to master a skill, research a new topic, or spend time at a museum or concert.

An important way parents can enrich their child's education is to follow up on his interests by providing materials, books, and experiences. With imagination and a creative use of available resources, even parents on the most limited budgets can offer active encouragement.

For example, if a child is interested in rock collecting, here are some of the activities his parents can help with or suggest: he can look for colorful picture guides in the library or on the Internet, go on nature walks to locate specimens, visit collections in local museums and nature centers, and write away for catalogs and free educational materials put out by many corporations and nonprofit organizations. He can join a rock collectors' club, talk to teenage and adult collectors, trade specimens with his friends, and go to local gem and mineral shows. In addition, he can collect and organize pictures of rocks and minerals from magazines and advertisements. He can subscribe to a specialized magazine, watch educational programs and videos related to geology, keep his own "scientist's journal," or arrange his collection in a home-made display case. There's no limit to the ways parents can follow up on his interest. They should help him find activities that meet his needs and allow him to explore a hobby or skill as fully as he desires.

If he wants to pursue an academic subject, they can encourage him to go beyond the school's lessons. A child who likes the challenge of math can be introduced to puzzles, brain teasers, chess, new computer software, or topics in logic. There are many math games, puzzles, and curiosities for children available in libraries, book stores, and on the Internet. All will stimulate a child more than the "educational work-books" often marketed to parents.

Parents can help by talking regularly to their child about his school-work, their own interests and work, and current events. Discussions can revolve around sports, the environment, history, popular entertainment, space exploration, fashion, music, or animals. As long as the subject is interesting to the child, the talk will be valuable. Parents should listen carefully to his opinions and questions. That way, he'll come to see himself as an important participant in family talks.

Sometimes learning at home supplements inadequate learning in school. If a child finds a school subject boring, his parents should try to show that the subject has another side. A child who dislikes creative writing may enjoy hearing about the early experiences of well-known writers, or may enjoy seeing his parents' own attempts at creative writing.

If he's having difficulty mastering a school subject, parents can help at home. Sometimes it takes only a few minutes to answer a question; sometimes parents have to do research of their own before they can assist their child. Either way, parents' involvement will help him do better in school and may spark a new interest for him.

Learning doesn't have to be parent-initiated. A child can teach his parents and siblings a new skill or share a new fact, and he can learn from his siblings. One child wanted to try cursive writing, a subject not taught in her grade. Her older sister showed her how, using an old workbook for practice.

To enrich your child's education at home, follow some of these suggestions. Have your child keep a diary or journal, writing in it as often as he likes. Make regular trips to the library and find books your child can read as well as ones you can read to him. Encourage him to read whatever and whenever he can. Have him go online (to sites you approve of). Scan newspapers and magazines together, or get your child his own subscription to a children's magazine. Collect reference books, dictionaries, an encyclopedia, and educational software for your home library. Periodically post a new vocabulary word on the refrigerator and challenge your child to use it during the week. Go to museums, nature centers, concerts, and plays together. Watch educational programs, particularly ones on nature.

Make learning a pleasurable, shared experience and your child will join in. Don't give negative judgments about his progress or compare his achievements to his siblings'. He'll do better without pressure.

If you sense that he's losing interest in a particular subject or hobby, try a new approach, wait awhile, or look for alternative ways to involve him. There are so many possibilities for learning at home that you're sure to continue finding interesting and challenging activities.

What are the alternatives to public school?

Many parents are dissatisfied with their child's public school education. They know her potential and they've seen her enthusiasm and capacity for learning. Yet, in public school she may be consistently unhappy, bored, or unchallenged. Parents who feel that their local public school is failing their child can consider transferring her to a better public school or a public magnet or charter school. If these choices are unavailable or unsatisfactory, parents can look at other alternatives.

The most common are private schools. Many parents don't consider private education because of the costs. Yet, some private schools are less expensive than others, many offer scholarships, some are co-ops accepting volunteer work in place of tuition, some help arrange loans, and some offer free or reduced tuition for parents who are employed by the school. When considering costs, parents should evaluate their priorities. Some people decide to invest in their child's education and accept a simpler and less costly lifestyle in exchange.

Some parents are wary of private school for another reason. They fear their child will lose the social benefits of attending a neighborhood school. While most private schools encourage a strong sense of community and plan many social activities for their students, it is true that a child who does not attend his neighborhood school will probably have a smaller social circle. However, private school students can still play with their neighborhood friends after school and on weekends in organized activities and on sports teams.

Parents who choose private education do so because they want a social, moral, academic, or religious atmosphere they can't find in public schools. Some parents have always known—either because of their own backgrounds or because they have firm preferences for a particular type of education—that they would send their child to private school. More often, they choose private school because they're unhappy with their child's public school. They may want their child to experience smaller classes, less emphasis on preparing for standardized tests, and a more challenging curriculum. While some parents plan on a full thirteen years of private education, some only want private school for the early elementary years. However, many parents find it hard to put a child back into public school, since they often find private school more effective and individualized.

There are many kinds of private schools: religious, Montessori, Waldorf, college preparatory (strict or liberal), academically accelerated, and schools for children with learning disabilities or emotional problems. In large urban areas there are many choices, while small cities or rural areas have fewer options.

Parents who don't know what they want should begin by visiting private schools. They can talk to each school's principal or admissions counselor, attend an open house, and sit in on a class. How structured is the work? What are kids expected to achieve? How does the teacher present material? How does she relate to the class? Do the students seem happy and interested?

Parents should ask other families for advice about private schools and, if necessary, consult an educational specialist who can test and observe a child, interview parents, and then recommend likely schools.

For parents who choose not to look at private schools but who are unhappy with the public ones, there's another alternative—home schooling. A growing number of families have children who learn at home, taught by their parents. Many local school districts allow home education, and some districts cooperate with home-schoolers, letting them use school resources.

People are often shocked when they first hear of home schooling: "How can parents teach their child?" "How will she learn to get along with other kids?"

The fact is, most parents who are able to make the significant time commitment can teach their child successfully. Kids in school spend part of each day marking time. They wait in line, wait for their turn to read, wait to have their questions answered. They do "busy work" while the teacher works with other students. They sit while she disciplines others. In some schools, little of the typical school day is actually spent learning. In contrast to this type of situation, when a child is schooled at home, she can master material quickly and efficiently.

Home-schooled children usually get along fine socially. Like private-school children, they still play with neighborhood friends and join them in organized activities such as classes, teams, and scouts. They don't miss out on much socializing at school because socializing is generally discouraged at school. Students are rewarded for being quiet, and reprimanded for talking to friends during class. During recess, interaction may be competitive, fueled by students' need to be smarter, better, faster than classmates. A child learning at home doesn't get caught up in that competition and for that reason may get along better with other children.

If you're considering home schooling, explore the many resources available. There are supportive national and local home schooling organizations. There are also curriculum guides available from school systems, local libraries, the Internet, and educational bookstores. You might decide to follow the plan offered by a correspondence school, or get together with other home-schoolers to share material.

Since you're familiar with your child's learning style and interests, you can individualize her work. Sometimes you can use books; other times you can do hands-on projects with her. Her schooling can include frequent trips to museums, libraries, performances, and nature centers.

Most home-schoolers give their children standardized tests once a year to be sure they're making good progress. Find out what tests your school district gives and either ask to have your child tested with other students or ask for a copy of the test to administer at home.

One of the hardest parts of picking an alternative to public school, whether private or home schooling, is dealing with the criticism of other adults. Families who are satisfied with public school may be intolerant of your choices: "I think it's crazy to keep your child out of school!" "Why spend all that money for private school? I'd never do that!" They also may feel threatened because you've chosen a path different from their own.

It's unpleasant to be judged. But the unpleasantness is more than made up for by the satisfaction of seeing your child blossom in a new school environment. Because of the choices you've made, your child may flourish in ways she never would have otherwise.

WHEN PARENTS AREN'T HOME

How can I evaluate before- and after-school care?

Since early elementary-aged children are not fully ready to take care of themselves, working parents have to arrange before- and afterschool care. The alternative—having a child spend mornings and afternoons alone—is neither safe nor appropriate. Most parents recognize that six- or seven-year-olds should not be left on their own, but many parents consistently leave eight- and nine-year-olds to care for themselves. Some of these children even supervise younger siblings.

Parents who leave young children alone spend much of their working time worrying, and with good cause. Eight- and nine-year-olds have trouble remembering and following rules. They may open the door to strangers, go outside, use the stove, look at inappropriate TV shows or websites, or have a friend over against their parents' wishes. Kids this age are not equipped to handle emergencies, including ones involving younger siblings.

In addition to physical supervision, children need emotional support, which they can't get when they're alone. Before school, a child needs a caregiver to offer a good breakfast and a cheerful, "Have a good day at school. Hope your science project is a success." After school, he needs to talk, have a snack, hear someone say, "How was your day? Did you work things out with your friend? Do you need help with your homework?"

The caregiver can be a relative, neighbor, teenage sitter, or day care center worker. Many public schools lease space for independent day care operations. Since the programs are convenient and presumably screened by the school administration, parents often sign their children up for this before- and after-school care.

Private schools also may provide care, operated according to the school's standards and values. The school's administrator usually has responsibility for the program. Since the quality of the day care reflects upon the school, private schools sometimes show a particularly strong commitment to providing good programs.

A problem with all day care, whether in an institutional setting or a private home, is finding educated staff to work with early elementary-aged children from 7:00 to 9:00 in the morning and 3:00 to 6:00 in the evening. Child care workers are notoriously underpaid and receive few benefits. Qualified caretakers are hard to find and day care administrators must spend considerable time training inexperienced staff and coping with frequent turnover.

Before settling on any type of arrangement, get recommendations from people you trust. If you hire a sitter for your home, check her references carefully. Determine how responsible a neighborhood teenager is before allowing her to stay regularly with your child.

Whether your child is being cared for in a day care program, a private home, or your own home, pay attention to the kind of care he's receiving. Don't feel complacent if he's enrolled in a public or private school program. Although all such programs should be carefully screened and supervised, they often aren't.

To reassure yourself and help your child, evaluate the quality of his day care. For a morning program outside your home, find out what kinds of activities are offered. Can your child bring his own toys or projects? Can he finish his homework before school? Is breakfast or a snack served? Is the atmosphere friendly? If a sitter comes to your home in the morning, is she pleasant while helping your child get ready? Your child's school day will be influenced by the start he gets each morning.

Learn about the after-school program. Is a snack provided? Are there active and quiet activities? Indoors and out? Can he go to an organized sport or activity in the school building or elsewhere? Is there a quiet place to do homework? What is the staff/child ratio? Is the staff warm and helpful? Can you use the center on a drop-in basis? If he spends the afternoon with a sitter, is he well supervised? Does he watch too much TV or spend too much time on the computer?

You can tell a lot about the quality of care by talking to and observing your child. He may complain about his baby-sitter or his day care program, especially if he sees other children going home from school each day. Yet, he may be happy when you see him in the evening, and he may talk excitedly about the activities and kids he's been involved with. If you're pleased with the sitter or program and your child seems content, you can feel confident he is well taken care of. If you aren't pleased, talk to your caregiver and ask for and offer solutions. Eventually you may consider seeking alternative arrangements, rearranging your own schedule, or cutting back on your work hours to better meet your child's needs.

How can I feel less distant from my child's caregiver?

Even though the relationship between parents and caregivers is less intense during the early elementary years, it often remains strained. Ideally, both sides should extend themselves, and parents and caregivers should relate in a cordial, informative way. However, many parents and caregivers are uncomfortable with each other and try to avoid contact. This leaves all parties feeling dissatisfied.

To some parents, a caregiver may be an intimidating figure. She has influence and power over a child, and parents may hesitate to alienate her with questions or complaints. They may feel that inquiries about their child will bother her, and they fear that she'll take out anger and frustration on their child or threaten to drop the child from the program.

Some parents stay distant from a caregiver because of guilt. They feel bad about leaving their child with another adult and avoid any contact that will make them feel worse. They drop her off and pick her up as quickly as possible ("I'm so busy!") and never extend themselves to the adult in charge.

There's another reason parents remain detached from their child's caregiver. They may not take her job seriously, viewing her as a babysitter and treating her as they might a neighborhood teenager. They come and go from the day care center, the caregiver's home, or their own home with barely a nod. Since many caregivers are younger than the parents they work for, it may seem natural for parents to act this way. Yet, regular caregivers do much more than occasional sitters do. They plan activities and programs, help with homework, and offer comfort and advice.

Sometimes it's the caregiver who's reluctant to form a friendly relationship. She may feel uncomfortable with parents because she's younger and less experienced than they. She may feel awkward telling them about their child's behavior, giving them advice, or discussing the differences between their standards and her own. She may be generally unsure of herself around adults. Many child care workers enjoy being with children but are not as positive and confident with adults. In addition, caregivers who see parents rush in and out may hesitate to talk to them for fear of holding them up.

Here are some things you can do to improve your relationship with your child's caregiver. Take the first step and offer a friendly hello and good-bye each day. Smile and wave if the caregiver is busy when you arrive. If she has a few minutes to chat, have a brief conversation. Talk about the weather, an upcoming weekend, children's artwork on the wall. Try to leave a few minutes at the end of the day to stay and watch your child finish a project or to talk to the other children. If you seem unhurried, the caregiver will consider you more approachable.

Most importantly, let your caregiver know you appreciate her services. She'll find it easy to talk to you about your child if she believes you take her seriously. Listen carefully to her observations and suggestions, respect her standards, and work cooperatively with her. It takes time to build trust, but effort and consistent friendliness will enhance your relationship.

Am I over-scheduling my child?

Six- to nine-year-olds are developmentally industrious and hardworking. At these ages, they have plenty of energy to keep busy. They're happy to play in unstructured ways—building forts, climbing tree houses, playing house or school, building with Legos, and participating in spontaneous neighborhood games. They also enjoy the many organized activities and lessons available: sports, arts and crafts, collecting, dance, music, hands-on science, scouting, clubs, and more.

Parents, educators, and childcare professionals often worry that children are enrolled in too many classes and activities. But during the elementary years, kids really can't be over-scheduled as long as they're doing what interests them and aren't feeling pressured to succeed at everything. These are the times when they develop new skills and discover what interests them, sometimes taking part in four or more activities a week. Both active play and organized programs offer kids a chance to try out different experiences, find out what works, and be with friends.

Classes, activities, and lessons (some with low or no fees required) are offered through schools, city and county recreation centers, religious organizations, individuals, profit and non-profit groups. Many kids go to these programs directly from school. Parents who work outside the home still can make activities available to their child by carpooling, rearranging their schedules, enrolling him in evening or weekend classes, or choosing an afterschool day care program that includes extra activities.

As parents choose from the wealth of recreational possibilities, they have to consider their child's interests (spontaneous or otherwise), their own ability to pay for classes and arrange transportation, and the quality of individual programs. They should ask some of these questions: will their child have friends in the class? Is practice required? Are parents signing him up for their own convenience? Will the class be too rigid or too unstructured? Will a sports activity reinforce competition or teach sportsmanship? Will an art class enhance or stifle creativity? How often will the class meet? Will the program interfere with schoolwork, a reasonable bedtime, or a sibling's schedule? And finally, will participating in the activity allow him time to relax and play at home?

Be sure the activities your child participates in are not just ones you think he should try. You'll know when the initiative is his because he'll ask again and again if you've signed him up for a special program. One mother, after talking to a basketball coach, decided her son should play, so she pressured him to try. He lasted through only a few practices before saying he wanted to quit.

If your child does lose interest in a program, evaluate the situation. Is the instructor or coach too harsh? The class too demanding? Are you putting too much pressure on your child? Is he having problems with another child in the class? At times, an activity may just not be right. One girl started with gymnastics, lost interest, and switched to soccer. While playing on the team, she also went to a tennis clinic with a friend and ended up loving and seriously playing the game for years.

It's possible that your child wants to quit an activity because he feels inferior as he compares his skills to those of other kids. The coach or leader may be able to help him feel more competent, or your child simply may decide to drop out and try another activity. This is fine as long as he won't let his team down—if they are counting on him, urge him to finish out the season before moving on. Quitting activities and starting new ones are very common during the elementary school years as children discover lots of inviting opportunities. Your child's intense interest in trying new things will disappear by the time he's an adolescent, so help him take the time now to start building his identity and learning about his interests, abilities, and strengths.

What should I tell my child's baby-sitters?

Early elementary-aged children are usually happy to spend an evening with a "nice" baby-sitter. Kids this age no longer worry about being separated from their parents and can enjoy time with a teenager or adult who's interested in having fun. Parents, too, have an easier time with a baby-sitter once their child is older. They're less worried about his physical safety and needs, and are more confident about his ability to follow rules and report problems.

Parents of children this age still need to carefully prepare their sitter. They should leave emergency phone numbers and written instructions about medications. They should remind their child and the sitter of family rules, writing down important ones if the sitter is new. If there are special circumstances—a child's friend sleeping over, a special TV show, outdoor play—parents should leave specific instructions. In addition, they can let the sitter know if she can use the phone or invite a friend over.

Some sitters get involved in play and easily keep children occupied. Others are more distant, watching the children but not interacting. If parents know their children will have to amuse themselves, they should leave activities to occupy the entire evening, including video and computer games, board games, crafts, and videos.

Many six- to nine-year-olds test their sitters, behaving in ways they know their parents wouldn't accept. Even the most involved sitter won't know all the family's rules and may inadvertently find herself letting kids "get away with" inappropriate behavior. If parents anticipate problems or if they worry that siblings will fight with each other, they should give the sitter ideas for distracting the children and defusing arguments. They can leave special snacks, small surprises, or a good book for the sitter to use if the children get out of control.

Parents who don't mind some of the rules being broken should let the sitter know. They may not care if the child leaves his meal unfinished, skips his bath, sleeps with his clothes on, or sleeps in his parents' bed until they come home.

Sometimes a child is invited to spend time at a friend's house, supervised by a sitter. Parents should use their judgment in such situations. One mother wouldn't allow her child to go because she considered the sitter unreliable.

Occasionally, parents leave their child with a sitter for extended periods. Children will be most comfortable with a familiar sitter, but they can warm up to a friendly new one. Recommendations from trusted sources are essential when choosing a sitter to spend several days with a child.

Parents should leave daily plans, including notes about sleep-overs, outside play, homework, after-school activities, and special events. They can fill the refrigerator with treats and leave a "thinking of you" present to be given to the child half-way through their absence. They should call home and ask their child about the sitter: "Is she nice?" They also should ask an adult relative or friend to check in to be sure things are going well.

As kids grow, the "sitter" is often an older sibling. Twelve-year-olds can baby-sit successfully for their six- to nine-year-old brothers and sisters, especially if parents provide lengthy, distracting activities.

Video games and rented movies are especially effective. Some young children are comfortable being alone with an older brother or sister as long as the older sibling pays attention to them. But if there is much rivalry, a young child may fear or resent his older sibling. Parents should be flexible when an older child is in charge. Rather than have the older sibling enforce many rules, they can let both children stay up, share the same snacks, do the same activities.

Parents should stress to both children the importance of getting along. You can talk about ways to work out differences and let both children know how to reach you if they need help. Call home as frequently as you like to see how the evening is going. If there are problems, you should intervene, and if there aren't, you can feel reassured. Always be careful not to take advantage of the older child; he should not be forced to baby-sit if he has conflicting activities of his own.

If your child complains about a sitter, even one you've used for years, listen carefully. Teenagers change their behavior as they get older. One child said, "Jennifer used to play with us, but now she just watches TV and talks on the phone." Tell an uninvolved sitter specific activities she can try, then see if she follows through. If things don't work out, stop using an unsatisfactory sitter and search for one you feel more comfortable with.

CREATIVITY AND PLAY

What do six- to nine-year-olds play?

During these industrious years, play is very important to children. They need unstructured time for exciting, challenging activities—sports, games, hobbies, toys, and pretending. Play can be anything a child does that's interesting and enjoyable.

Six- to nine-year-olds spend time riding bikes and scooters, playing with action figures or dolls, sledding, skating, playing ball, making crafts, using the computer, playing video games or board games, and getting together in groups. They incorporate their friends' thoughts and ideas into play and are much more cooperative than they once were. Because kids this age are less egocentric, they have an easier time getting along and sharing. However, they still need reminders about treating each other fairly and including others in their play.

Young elementary-aged children enjoy exploring and becoming more independent. They may discover new paths or secret places near home, or ride their bikes to friends' homes. They enjoy describing what they've seen and may exaggerate their adventures. They also like spending time at playgrounds with large, imaginative pieces of equipment, and going to children's museums with hands-on exhibits.

Many kids continue to play with their old toys, but in new ways. Games are more elaborate and often planned in advance. Children may expand on favorite themes like house, war, good-guy/bad-guy, school. They also make up spontaneous games.

They often play out real experiences or feelings. In pretend "school," a child can be the teacher and fantasize about having control: "Now class, you didn't turn in your work, so no recess today!" When they play house, they take roles that make them feel comfortable. One might choose to be a decision-making parent while another wants to be a baby who cries and needs nurturing. War games let children feel temporarily strong and powerful. Some parents object to imaginary violence. One parent was upset to hear her eight-year-old tell a friend, "Let's play that terrorists are attacking." Pretend fighting games are a normal part of play. If parents are watchful, such games won't get out of control.

Many kids get involved in big, dramatic projects—building a fort or a treehouse, designing a haunted house or a house out of blankets, putting on a puppet show, or creating a garden. They thrive on these activities and proudly show off the results.

If your child has an interest in such projects, offer him support. If, for example, he wants to build, help him find materials. He'll make good use of large boxes, scraps of wood, tires, rope, sheets, and blankets. Once he's carried out a large project on his own, he'll feel successful and competent.

In one neighborhood, kids wanted to put on a play. Parents provided dress-up clothes and paper and paints, and the children spent a week preparing and rehearsing. In another neighborhood, several children used scraps of wood to build a clubhouse. The project lasted much of the summer and parents were involved only as supervisors making sure the building was safe. When the kids finished their project, they not only had a clubhouse, but a strong sense of satisfaction and accomplishment.

My child doesn't like to lose. How can I help?

Parents of a preschooler know that games are not always fun. A young child often insists on playing by her own rules and gets upset if she loses. However, by the time children turn six, most begin to genuinely enjoy games. Young school-aged children have better control over their feelings and may no longer focus entirely on the need to win. They're starting to understand other people's points of view.

Six- to nine-year-olds enjoy all kinds of games. They like organized sports and spontaneous games of tennis, badminton, volleyball, and basketball. They're interested in board games, card games, and strategy games like chess, checkers, and Chinese checkers. Table games and videogames are popular, and so are traditional outdoor games of hopscotch, red light-green light, and four square.

Kids enjoy the planning and maneuvering involved in games of skill and strategy. Once past the pre-school years, a child can think carefully about her moves. She can anticipate other players' actions and prepare for a possible loss or a quick recovery. She may also like keeping score and evaluating her progress: "I can jump rope fifty times without missing."

Game-playing is essentially a social activity. Children who've learned to cooperate with each other have fun with games. Others have trouble playing by the group's accepted rules. Six- to nine-year-olds keep a close eye on each other, watching for cheaters: "Hey, you already had your turn!" Children often spontaneously change the rules of their games: "From now on let's say you can bounce the ball twice." But if all participants don't agree to the changes, there will be arguments.

Some kids are intent on winning. For them, game-playing can be a source of conflict: "That's not fair. You can't take my man!" Games, of course, are competitive. While many children easily accept the fact that there are winners and losers, others become "sore losers" who end each unsuccessful game feeling angry.

Children who need to win may feel general pressure from a number of sources—school, siblings, and parents who may themselves hate losing: "Dad will be in a bad mood all day if he loses his golf game."

As your child gets older, she'll be better able to handle the competition in games, although she may retain her strong desire to win. Be patient, encourage her to have fun playing, and continue to stress good sportsmanship. And consider the positive side of "not wanting to lose." Your child may be a determined, disciplined, well-behaved hard worker who strives to do well in many areas, including school.

Is it natural for my child to want my attention constantly?

"Look! I'm going to jump off the diving board."
"Dad, watch me ride my bike."
"Mom, see how I fix my hair."
"Watch. I'm going to do a cartwheel."
Children constantly ask their parents to pay attention. Even in the car, a child will ask a parent who's driving to look at a picture in his

notebook or watch him make faces in the mirror. He doesn't think about what his parents are doing, only about his immediate desire to be watched. Sometimes these calls for attention are delightful. Sometimes they're annoying.

A child does a lot of things he considers exciting, and he wants to share them with his parents. As he perfects a skill or does something new, he wants to be acknowledged and praised. Kids thrive on attention and positive feedback from parents. They want to hear, "Terrific," "Great job," "Nice throw," "Good try." Since parents don't always pay attention spontaneously, children say, "Watch me!" again and again.

Parents often underestimate the importance of watching. Those who do pay attention, especially without being asked, send a strong message of acceptance and love. A child who believes he's interesting and important enough to capture his parents' attention will develop a healthy self-image. A child who has trouble attracting their attention will feel that what he does isn't valuable enough.

Parents can learn a great deal about their child's interests and abilities by watching him participate in activities. However, they should be careful about offering unasked for advice. A child who says, "Watch me," wants approval, not coaching. One boy who used to say, "Watch me play baseball!" gradually lost interest because of his father's constant instructions: "Hold your glove like this. Lift your arm higher when you throw. Let me show you how to hit the ball." The boy's enjoyment faded because—whatever his father's real intentions—the boy heard only criticism.

You may find that you are, as most adults, engrossed in your own activities. There are phone calls to make, bills to pay, laundry to do, repairs to make. When you're occupied, you may not want to take time and watch your child perform some seemingly trivial activity. Yet, childhood years go by quickly and children's requests are reasonable and increasingly infrequent. A few minutes of acknowledgment and interest (solicited or unsolicited) can enhance his view of himself and give you something to think about and remember. Once it's too late, many parents wish they'd spent more time "watching" when their children were young.

Why does my child enjoy collecting?

Kids are natural collectors. They collect action figures, dolls, baseball cards, seashells, stamps, coins, comic books, stickers, model horses, fossils, rocks, and anything else that captures their interest. They trade collectibles with friends, learn the value of favorite items, and work on displays. While some children are causal collectors, others are intensely involved. One boy who collected baseball cards spent hours each week organizing his collection and studying the players' game statistics.

Children become interested in collectibles in a number of ways. A teacher might spark involvement with lessons on dinosaurs or national flags. A child's friend might talk him into becoming a co-collector so the two can trade items. A book, a TV show, a trip to an exciting place, or a gift can start a child's hobby.

Some kids collect because their parents or siblings do or used to. When a child sees how excited his parents are about a special piece of pottery or a political button, he may be inspired to state his own collection. Even parents who don't collect now can inspire their child with stories of their old childhood collections: the pleasure of trading stickers with friends, working on a train layout, or gathering action figures or Legos. Most parents now regret having thrown out those collections.

If your child is starting a collection, there are lots of ways to help and encourage him. The most important is to take an interest. Ask him to tell about parts of his collection and listen to his stories about special finds. You may be astounded by how much he knows.

You can help him find books, articles, shops, or exhibitions that specialize in his hobby. One girl bought rocks and gems inexpensively at collector's shows and museum stores. A mother and child searched flea markets and garage sales together, looking for old magic tricks.

You can find or buy your child pieces for his collection, or tell inquiring relatives which items he would enjoy receiving. You also can help him store and display his items. Depending on his hobby, he could use scrap books, picture frames, a bulletin board, cases, or shelves. He might decide to make his own custom display. One child hung his key chain collection on a heavy piece of cardboard cut in the shape of a key. Other kids arrange their animal or doll collections in scenes using homemade props. Whether your child makes an elaborate display or just piles his collection up, he'll enjoy showing it off and sharing it with others.

He's likely to eventually lose interest in his hobby as he enters the teenage years, but don't get rid of his old treasures. Keep them as souvenirs or as items to pass on to a younger sibling, or simply for your child to enjoy again once he's grown.

Should I limit TV-watching, video games, and computer time?

Kids enjoy watching TV, playing video and computer games, and going on the Internet. Parents often are ambivalent and worried about these occupations. They want their child to be happy, they welcome the peace that comes when he's occupied, and yet they consider many of his programs, games, and websites a waste of time or even dangerous. How can they balance their feelings and their child's desires?

They can begin by considering the appeal of TV, games, and the computer. Children relax in front of TV, just as many adults do. Appropriate programs are entertaining or at least diverting. Even commercials are interesting to a child. The toys look inviting, although six- to nine-year-olds may no longer be convinced by a sales pitch: "That truck doesn't really climb mountains."

Video and computer games are popular for a number of reasons. They're exciting, challenging, and action-filled. A child works on the skills that help him win, such as visual-motor and small muscle coordination. Games offer immediate feedback in the form of points and new action, and a child always has the option to start over if he loses or doesn't like the way a game's going.

Game-playing is also appealing because it leads to social contacts. Children share games, and playing tips, developing an information network that excludes adults. Six- to nine-year-olds enjoy playing video and computer games together, taking turns, watching and encouraging each other.

When a child plays these games, he feels powerful. He's controlling characters that fight and capture each other, win sports contests, or go on mysterious quests. It's easy to see how attractive this is to a child who spends most of his day being controlled by others. In the classroom the teacher tells him when he can talk, how long he has to eat lunch, when to go outside, and what to do. At home, parents are in charge. But while playing a video or computer game, a child has power over a made-up world.

The appeal of the computer is obvious to adults. Kids, especially eight- and nine-year-olds, can visit interesting sites, do research and homework, enter chat rooms, send emails and instant messages, use word processing and arts software, do puzzles, and otherwise be exposed to new and intriguing things.

But there are problems with TV, video games, and computers. Their content is often violent, sexual, or otherwise inappropriate for elementary-aged children. Parents have to put strong limits on the kinds of shows, video games, and computer sites their child is exposed to. Parental controls, ratings, reviews, and mechanical devices can help parents protect their child from questionable material. And while parents can't necessarily control what he watches at friends' houses, they can discuss their wishes with other parents.

Even without content problems, video and computer games can be very frustrating for children these ages. A child may work on a game for hours or days, only to lose and have to start all over. Parents sometimes hear screams of anger from a child who can't take the pressure or frustration. When he has trouble dealing with this aspect of game-playing, he may take his feelings out on whoever's closest: "Get out of my room!" "Leave me alone!" When kids are upset about their games they don't often get sympathy from their parents: "If you're this upset, why do you play?"

Watching TV has its own negative effects. Children may be confused and upset because they're not always sure what's real or made up, and they accept as fact much of what they hear about disasters, sickness, violence, drug abuse, war, and crime, as well as what they see about relationships and how people treat each other. The evening news can frighten a child.

After a disturbing program or misleading show, a child needs explanations, reassurance, and answers to his questions. Unfortunately, parents are often not watching with him and may not be available to help. Even when they are there, he may still may be exposed to disturbing or uncomfortable sights that remain with him. One child worried continuously after seeing news clips of an earthquake. An eight-year-old saw passionate kissing on TV and said, "Is that their real lips touching? Oooh. That's so gross." And certainly all children and their parents are upset after seeing clips of terrorists, school violence, and shootings.

There's another problem related to this issue: children who spend too much time watching TV, playing video games, and being on the computer have less time for reading, playing outside, sports, crafts, homework, socializing, and being with the family. Some kids spend time watching and playing video games because they can't think of anything else to do. In such cases, parents should offer alternatives such as a parent-child board game, time with a friend, reading aloud, or going to a playground. Also, they should consider enrolling him in organized activities, lessons, or sports.

Parents take many different approaches to controlling TV, time spent on the computer, and video games. Some forbid their use on weekdays, some allow them after homework is done, and some set a precise time limit: "You can have the TV on for an hour a day." "I'll only let you play video games for half an hour when you come home from school."

Some parents set no limits, instead using TV, video games, and the computer to occupy their child. As long as he's quiet and out of the way, they don't regulate this time at all. While all parents occasionally resort to these activities to keep kids busy, it's harmful to give children total control over how they occupy their time.

When deciding how best to manage your child's watching and playing, evaluate the impact TV and the computer are having on him. Is he falling behind in his schoolwork? Is he getting his homework done? Does he play outside? read? get involved with hobbies, crafts, and extracurricular activities? Is he tense or preoccupied with thoughts about TV programs? Is he playing too aggressively? Does he focus too much on playing and winning video games? Are his fears increasing?

You can limit your child's viewing and playing time without setting up a strict schedule. Take a flexible approach, letting him spend more time on video games when friends are over since he's socializing as he plays. Allow longer playing time when he has a new game or is almost finished solving an old one. Extend TV viewing hours during weekends and holidays or when a special show is on. Cut back when you want him involved in other activities. If he has trouble tearing himself away, give him fair warning: "You have fifteen more minutes on the Internet, and then you'll have to find something else to do."

Factors such as the weather and sickness will help determine how much viewing, computer time, and game playing you'll allow. Your goal is to strike a balance between his wish to spend time on games and shows (ones you've OK'd), and your desire to see him use his time more productively.

How can I encourage art at home?

The art projects kids do in school are not particularly creative. Some teachers distribute pre-cut figures to be decorated, or tell the whole class to make identical orange pumpkins or Mayflower ships. Students are given coloring book-type sheets and told to color them in neatly. Such work leaves little room for expression and creativity. If parents want their child to have fun doing original artwork, they usually have to encourage it at home.

They can begin by providing a variety of appealing art materials: clay, sculpting compounds, candle wax and beeswax, an assortment of pens, pencils, paints and markers, good quality paper, glue, scissors, popsicle sticks, small pieces of fabric and felt, wood chips, buttons, or glitter. These materials can be found at variety stores, hobby and art supply shops, and office supply stores.

If a child already has a preference for one medium, parents can provide appropriate materials. A child who enjoys painting can be offered a table easel and paints of different sorts, including watercolors, acrylics, oil, and tempera. Parents can try giving different sized brushes, paper, and canvas. The materials they buy should allow open-ended artwork. Coloring books, paint by number pictures, and pre-cut projects limits a child's creativity. Parents who want to encourage their child's free expression should avoid them.

A child will be tempted to try new art materials if they're stored in a accessible place or set out in an appealing way. Parents can leave markers and paper on the kitchen table where she will see them and be tempted to start drawing. They can reserve an accessible shelf, box, or drawer for art materials. They can set aside space in the basement or elsewhere for large art projects and materials such as easels. She will feel she has a special place for her big cardboard sculptures and creations made out of straws, papier mâché, or clay.

One of the best places for working on smaller projects is the kitchen, since it's often the center of the home. While a child works, her parents can be nearby, ready to look at a new project or listen to her talk about her creation.

Some parents hesitate to encourage artwork at home because they fear a mess. However, table surfaces can be protected easily with newspaper or vinyl covers. A child can wear old clothes when she works, or cover her clothes with a smock. Also, parents can avoid presenting messy supplies such as paste and glue, instead offering an interesting selection of colored pencils, pens, and markers.

Parents shouldn't make clean-up a major issue. A child may avoid artwork altogether if she knows she has to do a big clean-up when she's done. Parents who aren't willing to help their child with the job should provide materials that are easy to put away.

When your child is finished with an art project, compliment her work and avoid passing negative judgments. Since children's art is often assigned and judged in school, let her work at home be enjoyable and free from criticism. She will be upset and discouraged to hear you say, "Straighter lines," "Less paint," "More trees." Even if she asks for your advice, be gentle: "Do you want to add some flowers to the garden?" or, "Can you think of a way to add more color?"

Comment positively on her use of shape, design, and color. If you're sure of the subject of a drawing, say, "What a beautiful bird," or, "That looks like a very fast car." If you're not sure, simply say, "Very nice. You spent a lot of time on that." You also can ask her to tell you about the project: "Where did you get your idea?" "How did you swirl the colors together?" "Do you want to describe this picture for me?"

She may be very concerned about the success of her artwork. If a project doesn't turn out as she'd planned, she may feel frustrated and disappointed. Try to encourage her and suggest ways her "mess up" can be turned into something else.

Sometimes a younger sibling will give up on art if she decides her older brother or sister is better than she. Don't let this happen. Continue to provide materials, praise your child's attempts, and don't compare her to her siblings. Since most kids enjoy the sense of accomplishment finished artwork can bring, she will most likely continue creating as long as you provide materials and let her know you appreciate her work.

Finally, encourage her to do as much artwork as she likes. The more she draws, paints, and sculpts, the better she'll become and the better she'll feel about her creations.

My child is starting to participate in organized sports. How can I help him?

Parents are usually pleased when their child begins an organized sport. Not only is there the excitement of games, meets, and exhibitions, but there's the knowledge that sports provide many benefits. Kids who participate can learn valuable lessons about skills, perseverance, self-discipline, meeting challenges, responsibility, sportsmanship, teamwork, wining and losing, and doing their best.

A child chooses a sport based on his interests and his desire to participate with friends. Parents usually help make the selection, occasionally vetoing a sport. One father wanted his son to play pee-wee football and excitedly took him to the first practice. However, the other kids were much larger than the boy, and the father quickly changed his mind.

As parents help their child pick a sport, they should keep his abilities, interests, maturity, and age in mind. Some six- and seven-year-olds are not ready for organized sports. Parents should consider practical issues. A sport requiring a great deal of practice may not leave enough time for homework, play, and relaxation. Above all, parents should help him pick a sport he'll enjoy and feel good about, since a successful experience with organized sports can enhance his self-image. As his skills improve and he learns to get along with teammates and coaches, he'll feel proud of his abilities. This, in turn, will reinforce his desire to keep playing and getting better.

Of course, some children are more serious about sports than others. While one child may view baseball as just activity, another child may be intensely interested. He might practice on his own, have his gear ready, and keep careful track of his game schedule.

A vital part of a successful sports experience for any child is parental involvement. Kids like their parents to come to games and exhibitions. When parents offer support—cheering the team on, watching occasional practices, practicing with their child, talking about games—a child is likely to maintain a high level of interest.

Another important aspect of organized sports is a child's relationship with his coach. Coaches are generally friendly, inspiring, and fair. An effective one will bring out the best in his players or students while setting a tone of good sportsmanship and respect. Some coaches may mean well but lack the interpersonal or athletic skills to do a good job. Then there are coaches so focused on winning that they bully their players and offer a poor role model. Parents should discuss any concerns with a coach, offering suggestions if necessary: "I have a sensitive child who's afraid you'll yell at her if she misses the ball." "Would you let my child compete in the backstroke? He'd really like to give it a try."

Kids playing organized sports can face considerable pressure, not just from aggressive coaches. Some parents are overpowering, forcing their child to play a particular sport or speaking critically of his abilities. At many games, they can be heard shouting harsh comments from the sidelines: "Next time kick the ball harder!" "What's wrong with you? You shouldn't have missed that."

Of course, it can be difficult for parents to watch their child compete. If he doesn't do well, they may feel embarrassed: "Why can't he play better?" "I wish she'd remember her moves." They may feel unhappy if he seems nervous, distracted, or tired. It's common for young children to forget the rules, yell, miss the ball, throw things in frustration, and cry.

Before criticizing, parents should consider the frustrations their child may feel. He has to abide by rules that sometimes seem arbitrary or unfair, and he has to get along with children who are more or less skilled than he. He may be disappointed if he's not a starter or doesn't play the whole game, and at times he has to accept losing. A child involved in sports needs parental support and guidelines.

At some point, if your child is particularly good at a sport, he may be encouraged to compete at a more advanced level. Various sports have select or tournament teams or classes for children with outstanding athletic ability. Such groups offer new challenges and a chance to demonstrate and improve skills in a highly competitive atmosphere. While you and he may be very pleased with his acceptance into an elite group, you may be unsure about pursuing the opportunity.

Ask yourself these questions: Does he want to participate? Can he accept the pressure he's likely to feel from coaches and teammates? Can he handle the competition? Does he have time for added practice? Are you able to do the necessary driving? pay the additional fees? give the time required?

If he does join a select team, you may see a difference in his attitude. His emphasis may shift from having fun with a sport to perfecting his skills, getting better, and winning. Select coaches are often inflexible about their standards and demands, and your child may have some trouble adjusting at first. He may complain about his coach: "Just because I didn't do a perfect handstand, he made me start over." "I missed a couple of shots in practice and now I can't do the corner kicks in the game." Stay in touch with the coach so you can evaluate and discuss your child's concerns.

Whether your child is involved with a highly competitive team or a regular one, at some point he may want to quit. Don't let him make an impulsive decision—many children never go back to a sport once they've quit. Talk to him about the pressures and his feelings. If he's upset over one incident, speak with his coach and try to resolve the situation.

In most cases, have your child finish out the season, especially if his teammates are counting on him. However, if pressures of his sport seem to have a consistently negative effect on his family life or schoolwork, allow him to stop a team sport mid-season or mid-class. Even then, present his quitting as taking a break from sports rather than ending his involvement altogether. Your child might welcome the suggestion that next season, you and he can look for another team so he can try again.

My child complains about piano lessons. What should I do?

The most common musical instrument for six- to nine-year-olds to play is the piano. Sometimes children eagerly ask to begin lessons. More often, parents arrange lessons because they want to introduce their child to music. It makes sense for her to start piano lessons at these ages. Young children often catch on easily, quickly learning to read music and play.

However, many kids grow tired of piano lessons because of practice, written work, or an unsympathetic teacher. A child who's still getting used to homework will balk at having to practice piano each day. She also won't want to do written theory work. And if her teacher is demanding, the child will dread lessons and ask to quit.

This leads to a dilemma. Parents don't want endless struggles over lessons, but they also don't want their child to give up. Many parents took lessons as children, quit after a few years, and regret not having continued their musical education. They don't want their child to repeat that mistake.

In most cases, a child is too young to make the decision to quit. Parents should decide for her, and only after they've done everything they can to make lessons succeed.

First, parents should choose a teacher wisely and look for a new teacher if the current one is not effective. They should consider the personality, philosophy, and expectations of a teacher. The teacher should enjoy working with children and display patience with them at various skill and interest levels. Tolerance is important because skills and interests constantly change as kids grow and develop.

Most parent-child battles about piano lessons are about practicing. Many children who enjoy the weekly lesson dislike playing alone each day. If parents find that forcing or pressuring their child to practice is causing her to hate playing, they should reevaluate the need for daily practice.

She can slowly learn to play the piano just by playing half an hour per week during her lesson. Rather than have her quit lessons, some parents decide to let their child cut back or give up practicing altogether for a while. Once the pressure to practice is off, many kids begin to enjoy the piano again. They may later resume practicing on their own or according to a modified schedule put together by parents or the teacher. If a teacher isn't willing to work with a student who practices sporadically or not at all, parents should look for a new, more flexible instructor.

Some parents deal with the problem of practicing by getting more involved. They sit with their child as she plays, praising and encouraging her or just listening. Many children practice willingly when their parents take an interest. Parents also can stress the importance and joy of music, making it part of their everyday life. They can play an instrument (if they have the skill) or sing, and they can listen to recorded music or attend concerts with their child.

Most kids enjoy lessons and practice more if they have some say in selecting the music. It's more fun for a child to play an occasional piece that's familiar than to play straight through a beginning piano book. Parents, teacher, and child can talk together about pieces she might enjoy. In addition, parents can take her to a music store and let her select some easy sheet music.

Finally, they can try a system of rewards to motivate her to practice. The promise of a treat at the end of the week or month can keep her playing until the natural enjoyment of music takes over.

If your child is complaining, resist the temptation to give in and let her quit immediately. Once she stops piano, she will most likely never begin again. You may find it's better in the long run to ease up on all pressure than to let her stop completely. Even if she's only playing for her weekly lesson, if you're patient, she may discover the pleasures of making music. It's better for her to learn slowly, without stress, than to quit altogether.

SUMMER PLANS

How do I choose a day camp?

Parents have a lot to consider before selecting a day camp for their child—cost, location, hours, transportation, the program's activities, the quality of the program, their child's interests, his friends, and the availability of after-camp day care. Since some camps fill up rapidly, parents may have to make camp decisions long before they feel ready to think about summer.

Urban and suburban areas offer many choices. There are private daycamps run for profit and ones run by non-profit organizations such as the YMCA. There are municipal camps. Many private schools have summer camp programs and some public schools are leased during the summer by private or public camps.

If parents want to keep costs down, they'll find that municipal camps are the least expensive. If transportation is a problem, they should look for camps close to home or work, or ones offering bus transportation. If parents need after-camp day care for their child, they should inquire about extended day programs.

After considering the practical side of summer arrangements, parents will still be faced with choices. Since there are general as well as specialized day camps, you should carefully consider your child's hobbies, interests, and personality. Would he enjoy a sports camp? arts or music camp? computer camp? Would he prefer an indoor camp? Would he be happier in a camp offering a mix of activities? Will he be unhappy without a friend along?

Some kids are reluctant to go to camp without knowing someone, since the two- to eight-week sessions may not be enough time to form friendships. Parents sometimes make decisions based only on where their child's friends are going. Also, some parents send all of their own children to the same camp regardless of the children's interests, because they want the siblings to be together.

As you look for camps, ask other parents for suggestions, write for information, and check with local government recreation departments for recommendations.

If your child's school is the site of a summer camp, he may be anxious to go there because it's familiar. This may be a good idea, but he may be upset if he's expecting the summer to be like the school year. He may be troubled, especially if he's only six years old, to see different furniture in the classrooms, different adults in charge, and different kids. If you enroll him in a local school camp, prepare him for the changes he'll see.

If he has special health needs, look for a camp that will make the summer pleasant and successful. For instance, one child with asthma triggered by allergens did best in an air-conditioned environment. He attended an indoor camp offering arts and crafts, sports, and computer instruction.

Your child may tell you he doesn't want to go to camp although he will still need to be busy and productive. A summer at home may be fine if your schedule can accommodate it. However, you may be put in a bind if you work or if you feel he should be enrolled in an organized program for the summer. One solution is to look for a camp with reduced hours. You also can find out why he's reluctant to go to camp. If he doesn't want to take swimming lessons, is uncomfortable changing his clothes in a locker room, doesn't want to take part in some of the activities, is generally hesitant about new situations, or has another problem, talk to him about his feelings and offer ideas and reassurance. If necessary, seek suggestions from camp counselors or directors. You should be able to find a flexible program that will accommodate his needs.

Is my child ready for overnight camp?

Going to sleepover camp for the first time is an important event in a child's life. It's often the first long separation for parents and child and it signals an increasing independence. Parents of early elementary-aged children wonder when and if their child should take this big step.

Many factors determine her readiness to be away from home for an extended period. Age is a major consideration. A six-year-old is too young for even a one-week program, but some seven- and eight-year-olds and many nine-year-olds can handle being away for one to four weeks. Sometimes the maturity of a child, rather than her age, will determine how successful her camp experience will be.

A child who wants to go to overnight camp will have an easier time than one whose parents have convinced her to go. Some kids, especially those with older siblings, are anxious to start sleepover camp. They may have felt a great sense of loss seeing a brother or sister go off: "My life will be ruined when Marissa goes away!" "It's not fair, Mom. You let Stephen go away to camp. I want to go too!" A young child who's heard camp stories from siblings, friends, parents, and other relatives may have exciting visions of overnight camp: "Molly says you have so much fun, you forget you have parents."

A young child who's not interested in overnight camp shouldn't be sent. If parents, anxious for time alone, push her into a program before she's ready, they may pay for the mistake later. She may be angry and resentful or feel insecure about leaving home before she's comfortable doing so. One eight-year-old told her friend, "You cry a lot at camp because you miss your parents."

If a child does want to go to overnight camp, how can her parents tell if she's ready? They should ask themselves these questions: Does she enjoy overnights with friends or relatives? Is she asking to go to camp? Does she like lots of activity? Does she make friends easily? Can they imagine her recovering quickly from the inevitable homesickness she'll feel at camp? How does she deal with small hurts and frustrations? Can she handle a lack of family contact for one to four weeks? Many camps have done away with visiting days and allow no personal phone calls.

Parents should ask if their child has any real idea of the time involved. She may want to go away for two weeks without realizing how long that is, since most six- to nine-year-olds have a changing view of time. A birthday four months away is coming "soon." A TV show that she's anxious to see the next week may not be on for a "long time."

Once parents have decided she's ready for camp, their decisions about the summer will hinge on finding a camp that meets their needs.

They should seek recommendations from other families and send away for information. Some camps offer videos for home viewing. Some set up slide shows for prospective campers or put families in touch with former campers.

If parents think ahead, they can visit a camp the summer before sending their child. Both parents and child may be surprised at what they see. One young girl was dismayed to find that campers sleep on cots in a bunkhouse rather than in beds in bedrooms. She lost her interest. Another child was delighted with the craft and drama projects she saw: "I love it. This is the camp I'm going to."

Parents should gather as much information about a prospective camp as they can. What is the counselor/child ratio? What is the camp director like? How many kids attend the camp? What activities are offered? How structured and full is the day? Does each camper pick a specialty? Are there field trips and special events? How is discipline handled? Are a doctor and nurse on duty at all times? Can a child receive allergy shots? How are dietary restrictions accommodated? What strategies are used when campers get homesick?

As you make your decision, don't be swayed by pressure from others. Some parents may try to convince you to send your child: "What are you waiting for? Don't be so overprotective." Others may try to persuade you to keep her home. Do what seems best for your family. Many kids never go to overnight camp, and many who do, wait until they're ten, twelve, or even fourteen years old. The right time to send your child is when she wants to go and is mature enough to have a good time.

How can my child maintain academic skills over the summer?

Most kids view summer as a welcome reprieve from the classroom and aren't anxious to work on academic subjects at home. This causes many parents to worry that their child will lose ground over the summer. They believe that after two and one-half to three months without math, reading, and spelling, he'll forget a great deal and may fall behind.

Some parents decide to enroll their child in summer school, either for remedial work or enrichment. Most school systems offer a summer program, usually aimed at students with academic difficulties. Some parents hire a tutor to maintain or enhance their child's academic skills. However, most families don't pursue such structured learning during the summer.

Instead, they design their own plans (or plans suggested by their child's teacher) to keep the summer months from being all play and no work. Parents may have him read for a certain period each day, or she may set goals for the summer such as learning multiplication tables, studying vocabulary words, researching a topic, or working through a book of science experiments.

The most important thing you can do to help your child maintain his skills is encourage him to read. You can get reading lists from the school, libraries, on-line sites, and books about literacy. Encourage your child to join the local library summer reading club. Let him choose materials that interest him—novels, biographies, sports stories, magazines. If he has a hobby, urge him to read about his subject and study it in-depth.

You should also encourage him to write. He may like keeping a journal or computer file of his daily activities, thoughts, and feelings. He can write stories and poems or a play that he and his friends or siblings can act out. He can also write letters and emails to friends, relatives, or a pen pal.

You can set aside time to read out loud to him or to work on specific areas with which he needs help. But keep the lessons short and light and consider offering occasional rewards to keep him going. If he does math or spelling periodically, he may accomplish quite a bit before school begins. Academic learning can certainly continue during the summer, but you should present it in a relaxed way, remembering that your child sees summer primarily as a time for fun.

How can I handle long car trips with my child?

"Are we almost there?"
"How long 'til we get there?"

"I'm tired of riding!"

Traveling by car with children can be a challenge. They get bored and restless when confined to a small space for hours, and siblings forced to sit with each other often end up arguing and whining. It takes advance planning and patience if parents want travel to go relatively smoothly.

Before the trip, tell your child some of the travel details, including where you'll be driving, when you'll be stopping each day, and how long the trip will take. Talk about points of interest along the way, perhaps consulting guide books for information about an area's history and special sites. Also talk to her about behaving in the car. Let her know ahead of time how you want her to act.

Try to make the drive as physically comfortable as possible. Have her bring a pillow and blanket, and be sure she's wearing comfortable clothes. Have her wear shoes she can take off during the ride and quickly get into for short stops.

As much as possible, time your travels to coincide with your child's schedule. Early morning and late evening are usually calm times for six- to nine-year-olds, and she may sleep if your drive includes those hours. Plan plenty of stops for snacks or exercise. Look for rest stops with playgrounds or safe areas for jogging or jumping jacks. A ten-minute break can help her feel less restless. Changing seats periodically may help, too. Let her have a turn in the front seat where she'll have a good view as you drive.

Listen to the radio, a tape, or CD together, or let her bring a Walkman with headphones. Sing together or play car games such as Twenty Questions, I Spy, or Road Bingo. If you're able to read while riding, pick a story to read aloud to the family. You can buy or rent audio recorded stories or poems or bring a tape recorder so she can make her own cassette.

Pack several small bags for her to have in the car—one with food, one with things to do. The food bag can contain drinks and a variety of snacks that can be easily handled. The "fun" bag can include a deck of cards, paper, pens, stickers, a book, a magazine, a comic book, pipe cleaners, a small jewelry making kit, a pocket video game, or a simple map you've drawn showing where you're going and what's interesting along the way. Also encourage her to bring her own bag of amusements from home.

Periodically during the trip you may want to give her small surprises geared to her interests. One child spent an hour making bracelets out of colored string and beads. Another worked on a book of mazes.

Any new toy, game, or interesting object will hold your child's attention for a while, but if the trip is long, you'll eventually hear, "Are we almost there?" (Be prepared to answer that several times.) But at least with patience and planning, you can avoid major conflicts and keep her reasonably content for most of your drive.

Is it OK if I just want my child to take it easy?

A child's summer doesn't have to be filled with camp and organized activities. Some parents decide not to send their children to camp at all, opting instead for a relaxed, unstructured few months. This works best for parents who can tolerate a loose schedule and follow their child's lead, and who don't mind a day without plans. Parents who prefer more structure or who can't let their child stay home because of work schedules can still set aside some free summer time for the family to take it easy together.

For a child, "taking it easy" can mean finding enjoyable things to do at home or in the neighborhood. Kids can play in backyard pools and sprinklers, plant a garden, fly kites, play with sand, play hopscotch, draw a chalk design on the sidewalk, play tennis and baseball, skate, have a yard sale, play board games, build a fort, go to playgrounds, ride a bike, sell lemonade, learn to knit or draw, read, or write a story. Kids can play with friends, by themselves, or with the family. They can continue many of the recreational classes and lessons they took during the school year.

Summer is an important time for families. Schedules are often less hectic and there are more opportunities to be together. Even if both parents work, longer daylight hours leave evenings open for such activities as soccer, badminton, swimming, hide and seek, acting, hiking, baking, and reading together. If parents have errands, they can take their child along and include time for an ice cream stop. If they have to work over the weekend, they can take him with them and let him work at something too.

If you decide not to send your child to camp, try to strike a balance between freedom and structure. Whatever he does, he'll still need supervision. A six- to nine-year-old lacks the judgment to play without being frequently checked on by an adult. On the other hand, free time should remain relatively open. Don't fill all his hours with prearranged activities or pressure him to accomplish many goals. Leave him time to explore and play on his own.

While he is home, his friends may be off at camp; this won't be a problem if he can occupy himself. But if he gets bored or lonely, you should help him find activities to get involved in. You may decide to compromise and send him to camp for part of the summer, letting him have the rest of the summer free.

Part Three

The Ten- to Thirteen-Year-Old

"How can I get my kids to be more respectful?"

"Why is my child so moody?"

"What can I do about peer pressure?"

"How open should I be about my own personal problems?"

Pre- and early adolescence is a time of transition and great change. There is the rapid physical growth experienced by many kids these ages. In addition, children approaching puberty develop a heightened awareness of themselves and the world and begin to seek an identity. Their thoughts are more organized and logical. They think about the future and about hypothetical and abstract ideas.

As they develop a set of values and sense of morality, they often say what's on their minds. In a positive way, your child may share her feelings more openly with you. However, she may also complain and criticize: "Why won't you listen to me?" "You just don't understand!"

Kids increasingly seek independence and acceptance as they approach thirteen. They often want to spend more time with peers and less with family, they may want privacy, and they have a desire to make some of their own decisions. As your child pushes the limits, you may frequently ask yourself, "When do I let go? When should I hold on?"

Ten- to thirteen-year-olds benefit from guidance, support, and supervision. To effectively steer your child away from impulsiveness and toward a responsible, confident adolescence, you truly need to know where he is, what he's doing, and with whom. And he has to know what is and isn't acceptable and what the consequences of misbehavior are.

The best way to help your child is to take every opportunity to strengthen your relationship with him. Talk more with him, listen to him, consider his point of view, do things together, and encourage him to pursue his own interests and talents. These basic tasks of parenting will help set the tone for pre- and early adolescence.

TALKING AND LISTENING

Why is it so hard for my child to listen to my side?

Parents usually have good reasons for offering advice and guidance. From an adult perspective, they can see behavior in context and understand consequences. They give advice in order to help their child.

Yet kids often reject their parents' lessons. What seems like good advice to an adult may sound like nagging to a child: "You'd get a better grade if your paper were neater." "Homework before TV." "Try to get along with your sister." Many ten- to thirteen-year-olds react negatively to such words, especially if they don't like the ideas or suggestions presented: "Leave me alone!" "Okay, okay, I hear you!"

What a child reacts to sometimes is the way advice is presented. Anything that sounds like a lecture is rejected: "When I was your age…" "You really should…" "You must stop…" "I know what's best…" After hearing his child's karate instructor speak about discipline, one father tried adding his own thoughts on the subject. "Dad, I already heard all this," his son said.

Most often, kids don't pay attention because they themselves feel unheard. In the rush to give advice, parents don't always listen to what their child has to say. Instead, they interrupt him, ignore his words, or dismiss his arguments. Once he believes that they aren't listening, he stops being receptive when they speak. Instead, he shows anger and frustration. He rolls his eyes, looks exasperated, stomps off, or slams his door, shutting out whatever advice they offer.

This, of course, leaves parents feeling upset and confused. Parents want to get their opinions across, but they don't know how. Many parents become harsh and demanding because they fear losing control over their child. They listen less and become more rigid in an attempt to make a point. Everyone is unhappy, and good advice goes unheard.

Communication doesn't have to be this antagonistic—families can learn to speak and listen in friendlier, more respectful ways. A first step is letting your child express his opinions, even when they differ from yours. If he makes a seemingly unreasonable request, don't respond with an automatic "No!" Instead, let him explain his side. He'll feel heard, even if you turn down his request, and the fact that you listened will make it easier for him to pay attention to your ideas and advice.

Consider the words and tone you use when speaking to him. One parent lost his temper when his son asked for ten dollars: "What is it now? All I hear from you is 'I need money.' You've gotten enough!" Angry words or put-downs can make your child feel too defensive to listen. Instead, he'll focus on defending himself when he finally has a chance to speak. If you use a patient, friendlier tone ("I know you'd like fifteen dollars for a T-shirt, but your blue shirt is still practically new,") your child may not come around to your point of view, but at least he'll feel less threatened. He'll have an easier time listening to you and he'll have an example of respectful communication to imitate.

To increase give-and-take in family communication, try asking him questions before offering your opinions: "What do you think you should do about your room?" "Why do you think Joey's parents let him stay outside so late?" When you disagree on an issue, ask, "Why do you think Dad and I don't want to say yes?" By this age, he should be able to predict your reasoning.

Take your time when responding to his requests, especially ones that make you angry. A moment spent considering your answer will give you time to calm down and will give your child a chance to rethink what he's said. If you want to bring up a troublesome issue, try to choose a calm time and then take a few minutes to plan your advice or instructions: "We need to talk about how your short temper is affecting the rest of the family." He will listen more readily to your reasonable statements than to a sudden outburst.

On some important or immediate issues, you will want him to listen to you without discussion: "It's not safe to play around that way." "You must change your tone of voice." As long as he doesn't always feel backed into a corner, unable to have his opinions heard, he'll listen and respond when your words are urgent.

You may worry that you'll lose parental control if you allow him to express his thoughts. However, letting him speak won't interfere with your ability to set limits. Instead, it will create an atmosphere of mutual respect, making it easier for him to listen to you.

Throughout his life, your child will encounter people with different points of view and different ideas. The positive communication skills you model for him now will help him get along with his family and others in the future.

How can I teach my child to be more respectful?

Getting kids to be respectful seems a never-ending struggle. Parents start working on this issue when their child is a preschooler. They continue through the early elementary years and still are giving reminders when she is in middle school. Despite increasing maturity, most ten- to thirteen-year-olds have to be told how to treat siblings, parents, teacher, coaches, and peers. Kids these ages do understand why they should treat people kindly. They can imagine themselves in another person's place, they know what it's like to be teased and have hurt feelings, and they think about the impact of their behavior. Yet, for a number of reasons, they can't consistently translate their understanding into respectful action.

Some children are disrespectful because of the way they've been treated at home. If they don't feel listened to or understood, they may react angrily. Kids also imitate their parents, and if a child's thoughts, feelings, and ideas have been ridiculed, she will criticize and be inconsiderate of others. One mother told her child to stop being rude, then said, "Just shut up and leave me alone." Another parent constantly found fault: "Why are you so lazy and disorganized?" Kids copy such words and attitudes.

Unfortunately, school is another place they learn disrespect. Most teachers have rules about acceptable classroom behavior: "Listen when others are talking." "Don't make fun of someone else's mistakes." However, some teachers are not kind when they talk to students. One thirteen-year-old told his mother, "The teachers are so mean. They tell us to show respect, but they yell at us and put kids down and order us around all day."

Some kids are disrespectful because their parents don't place sufficient limits on inappropriate behavior. Parents may believe that rudeness at these ages is inevitable and they may excuse their child when she picks on unpopular classmates or calls them names: "Kids are cruel. They attack each other all the time."

Consciously or unconsciously, parents may encourage their child's disrespectful behavior. One boy loudly questioned a referee's call during a Little League game. The boy's father said, "Good. Somebody had to tell that guy off." That parental attitude can be seen almost anywhere there's competition: tennis matches, soccer fields, classrooms, neighborhood games.

Kids who are rude to parents may be quite polite when they're away from home and talking to teachers, coaches, and their friends' parents. Like adults, children tend to take their daily frustrations out on the ones they love and are most comfortable with. As long as a child is courteous away from home, her parents can be assured that she's learned important lessons about getting along.

If you want your child to show more respect, set limits, and give frequent reminders. Let her know in a firm, clear way how she should behave: "I expect you to tell your sister what you feel without calling her names." "You may not speak to Dad and me so rudely. We'll listen if you change your tone." Show her the difference between thoughtless and respectful language: "Instead of calling Sara a pig, say, 'I'm angry at you for eating the candy. I wanted some.'"

When you see your child acting rudely in public, avoid giving an immediate lecture. She won't listen, but will only defend herself ("It wasn't my fault!") or talk back to you ("Leave me alone!"). Instead, give her a quiet suggestion or instruction: "You're being too harsh." "You need to be a better sport." "You shouldn't pick on a friend."

Later, when the incident has passed and you and she are calmer, talk about what happened. The discussion may stir up feelings, so handle the subject delicately. First, listen to her defense and thoughts, then tell her what you've observed: "When you ask for something, you sound very demanding." Let her know how important her tone and choice of words are. Tell her to imagine herself in another person's position.

Teaching your child to be respectful takes time, patience, and a lot of involvement; you also need to be a good role model. Eventually your words will get through and your child will learn to be respectful on her own.

How can I encourage discussion with my child?

Good communication is a basic part of successful family life. Parents and children should talk to each other often about a whole range of subjects—school, friends, news events, hobbies, sports, politics, art, humor, science, music, religion, nature. The more children discuss at home, the more they learn about themselves and their world and prepare for adult life. Home is the best place for wide-ranging discussions, since schools often emphasize silence and order, and young peers have only limited information and perspectives. At home, a child can test out his ideas and start to think critically, analytically, and abstractly.

Discussions come more easily for some families than others. Some parents never think of tossing ideas back and forth with their child. Others feel they don't have time to sit and talk. Children who aren't used to regular discussions rarely initiate conversations.

Most parents are greatly influenced by their own early experiences. If they grew up in families that valued talking, they speak often with their own children. One father remembers frequent discussions that turned into loud political debates. Although keeping up with his family was a constant challenge, he believes he learned a great deal from those early talks. Another parent has very different memories. Throughout her childhood she had to listen silently to her parents' opinions. When she entered college, she froze if asked to speak in class. She'd had little experience sharing her ideas.

If you'd like your family to do more talking, set aside time for discussions. In the car, turn off the radio and start a conversation. Watch a little less TV, wake up twenty minutes early for a family breakfast, take an evening walk together, chat during dinner or over a late-night snack. If there are enough opportunities, you and your child will start talking.

Show your interest by asking him questions: "What did you think of that movie?" "What's the best thing that happened today?" "What changes would you make at your school?" "If you were given money to help others, what would you do?" Share anecdotes about your day, describe articles from the newspaper, offer stories about your past or your child's early years, tell jokes. If he's not used to discussions, let him do a lot of the talking. This will show you value his ideas and will enhance his self-esteem.

Don't overwhelm him. In your eagerness to share information or insight, you may speak too long or too forcefully. Like most parents, you want to express your beliefs and shape your child's views. But if he believes you will lecture him, dismiss his words, or start arguing, he'll avoid family discussions. He's most likely to listen and respond if conversations are low-key.

It's important that you make the effort to talk with him. At times it may be difficult to listen to his opinions or focus on his interests. Still, by talking together, you show the value of sharing ideas. From simple family conversations, he'll discover how to present himself, how to learn from others, and how to see the world from different viewpoints.

How much should I share about my personal problems?

Every parent has problems. There are the relatively minor ones of daily life—hectic schedules, errands, stressful commutes. There are chronic problems—job dissatisfaction, financial worries, conflicts in the extended family. And there are crises—impending divorce, job loss, serious illness, substance abuse. A difficult issue for all parents is deciding how much to tell their children about these problems.

Many parents want to shelter their child, thinking she has enough pressures of her own from school, peers, sports, and chores. They don't want to further burden her with parental problems she can't solve or fully understand. Besides, parents are often embarrassed by their own problems or worried that their child will spread personal information outside the family.

However, parents may remember their own early feelings about family problems and secrets. One woman recalls having little information about her parents' arguments, but feeling worried and responsible: "They would yell and I would hide my head under the pillow, hoping the noise would go away." Some adults remember sneaking to overhear conversation and wishing their parents would reassure them: "I was scared when my father got so sick. I thought it was my fault."

It's difficult to keep serious problems from kids. When something is wrong, they sense their parents' uneasy moods. They hear snatches of private phone calls and discussions. One ten-year-old whispered to a family friend who called, "My Mom can't talk now. Her mother is very sick, but she doesn't think I know." Some kids hear angry outbursts: "I wish he'd stop drinking!" "Her whole family is crazy!"

During stressful times, they also experience differences in their parents' behavior, since a parent may be distracted or less patient about common annoyances: "Go do your homework in the other room!" "Turn your music down!" In the face of difficulties, some parents have a hard time controlling their emotions and actions. One mother, dealing with her husband's job loss, took her frustrations out on her nine- and eleven-year-olds. She found fault with them and sometimes hit them, only to feel guilty about her lack of control: "My problems were so big, I couldn't even handle a question like, 'Who's taking me to baseball practice?'"

The most common and upsetting problem children witness is marital stress. When a child overhears arguments between her parents, she feels frightened, powerless, and worried. If she's not supposed to know about their conflict because they haven't told her, she can't ask questions or talk about her feelings. The problem may seem worse because she doesn't have information. Like most kids, she may be quick to draw dreadful conclusions, blame herself, and fantasize about solutions. What she wants most is reassurance, but she can't get it if her parents are secretive.

When deciding how much to tell your child, you have to consider many factors, including your need for privacy, your level of comfort, her emotional makeup, and her desire—or lack of desire—for information. If you're an open person, you may not want to keep problems to yourself. If you're private, you may be too uncomfortable to share. If your child is mature and empathetic, it may be fine to talk about some of your difficulties. A mother decided to tell her thirteen-year-old son about her nephew's drug use. The boy was worried about his cousin but also relieved to know what had been bothering his mother.

However, if your child is not able to handle family problems, respect her wishes. One child, hearing of her parents' conflicts with relatives, said, "Don't tell me any more bad stories about Uncle Alex. They keep me from having fun when we go there." She wanted to believe her family was happy and secure, and she felt overwhelmed by their conflicts.

It can take considerable energy to keep kids from knowing about your personal problems. You will have to hold on to your thoughts and hide your feelings. Yet, at times, the effort may help you put your difficulties in perspective: "I only stopped worrying about our finances when I concentrated on my son and his activities."

Inevitably, there will be issues you want to or have to share with your child: "I may lose my job." "I'm worried about Grandma's health." Tell her as much as she needs to know—not all the details, but enough to open communication and give her a chance to ask questions. If you are having marital conflicts, let her know about the general problem and make an effort to keep actual arguments private, behind closed doors.

When you tell her about your difficulties, apologize when appropriate for losing your temper or not being available. She may understand, but don't expect her to feel as you do about your concerns or to offer solutions.

If communication is open without being overwhelming, she will feel included. Just knowing she can talk will lessen her anxiety, keep her from blaming herself for your problems, and make it easier for her to concentrate on school and her other activities. As you go through difficult times, she'll see you handling hardships. She'll understand that problems don't have to be hidden and that it's all right to ask for help. Even though there are few easy answers, you want her to learn that talking about hard times is helpful and healing. Later, when she needs your advice about her own difficulties, she won't keep them to herself or worry that you can't handle them emotionally. She'll have learned from your example that problems don't have to be secret.

Why is my child's view of adults negative?

"The principal is so strict."
"Grown-ups think they know everything."
"My coach doesn't put me in the game enough."
"Adults always get in front of kids."
Many kids complain about adults. They speak disparagingly of them, show them little respect, and shut them out. For some kids, this negative view is an inevitable result of being young and dependent. For others, it's an adopted attitude, influenced by peers, TV, and movies. But for some, it's a sign of troubling relationships with the adults around them.

At its simplest level, a negative view of adults comes from a child's sense of powerlessness. Parents, teachers, grandparents, coaches, and counselors have high expectations and often make harsh-sounding demands: "Clean your room." "Stop talking during class." "Get over here." "Don't fight with your brother." "Be on time." Children, especially sensitive ones, are easily affected by an unkind tone or manner. They feel hurt, angry, or defensive, and react with skepticism and a broad generalization: "Adults are mean."

Negative attitudes are reinforced by peers and the media. It may be "cool" to look down on adults. Since ten- to thirteen-year-olds are increasingly influenced by their friends, the attitude of one child may be copied by others. Many cartoons, sitcoms, and movies portray adults, especially parents, as bumbling, wrong-headed, or even evil. The more exposure kids have to TV, the more they hear about incompetent, uncaring adults.

Of course, there are some uncaring adults, and the negative attitudes of some kids are justified by the harsh treatment they've received. A child who feels threatened by the adults in his life will be angry and frustrated and he may act in a belligerent way. Any child who lives in an atmosphere of mistrust and inflexibility will have a hard time being open and cooperative. Misbehaving may be the only way he has to release his hostility and give back what he receives.

If your child shows a superficial dislike for adults, explain how you feel about his attitude and set limits on his behavior: "I don't talk to you in a rude way, and I don't want you to be rude to me." "I want you to sound more respectful when you speak to your grandmother." To lessen the impact of negative influences, limit TV time and talk to your child about his friends' attitudes.

If he has a strong negative feeling toward adults, find out why. The cause may lie in the way he's treated at home. Ask yourself, "Am I too controlling? Do I offer him choices or let him make decisions? Do I yell too much? Is my tone too angry? Do I compromise or listen enough? Am I a good role model?"

Let him express his feelings. This may be hard for you and for him if he hasn't had much chance to speak out. Because of pent-up emotions, he may say very negative things about adults in general and you specifically: "You treat Jeffrey better than you treat me." "You're never home." "You always make me do what I don't want to do." "You're never happy with my report card." "You get too mad." "You never say I do a good job." As difficult as it is to listen to such words, it's important to take your child seriously. If necessary, use a timer so each of you can speak for five or ten uninterrupted minutes.

Once you know the causes of his negative attitude, both you and he will have to make changes. As a first step, give up unrealistic expectations for each other—there are no perfect children or parents. Show that you're willing to compromise and cooperate. This may include treating him with more respect and changing some of the ways you act. Then set limits, letting him know how you expect him to behave. As he makes changes, offer frequent encouragement: "I'm enjoying our relationship much more now." "Your attitude seems less negative." "I appreciate the way you've been acting." With patience and continuing effort, you and he can establish a more trusting and harmonious family life.

FAMILY LIFE

Why is my daughter jealous of her siblings?

Every child feels some jealousy toward her siblings. A younger child resents an older one's abilities, privileges, and experience. A quiet child resents the attention her more outgoing or accomplished sibling receives. All kids feel at least temporarily jealous of siblings who have higher grades, newer shoes, more praise.

While some jealousy is inevitable, consistent jealousy comes from a child's belief that she's being treated unfairly, especially by her parents. Parents' attitudes and actions shape the relationships between siblings. A child may be right about her treatment, or she may be misreading her situation. But as long as she thinks she's being slighted, she'll be jealous.

Kids are very sensitive to their parents' words: "My dad always says my brother's real smart." "They don't yell at her like they yell at me." "What's so great about Ben?" Parents at times give more positive attention to one child. Perhaps they feel that he needs encouragement or is temporarily vulnerable: "You did a terrific job on your math test!" They may feel proud of one child's accomplishments: "Show Grandma and Grandpa what you learned in ballet."

Sometimes, without realizing it, parents favor one child. They may believe they're fair, but in subtle and powerful ways, they give great cause for jealousy: "Becky's very organized, but Stacey is so messy." "Matt is so much slower at homework than his brother." "Thank goodness Katie's such an easy child."

When kids feel jealousy, whether justified or not, they may want to talk about it: "You always let her sit up front!" However, many parents get angry or won't listen: "That's nonsense!" "You have just as many things as your brother." If a child gets in trouble for protesting, she'll stop speaking up. If she believes she's hurt her parents, she'll also feel guilty for her negative thoughts about them. Complaining is too risky if it means making parents angry or losing their love. A child who can't express the truth or who doesn't fully understand her feelings will direct all her anger toward a safer person—her sibling—thereby reinforcing their rivalry.

Although family relationships are well established by the time a child is ten, there are constructive changes you can make if you want to lessen sibling rivalry. The most important is to listen, especially if jealousy between your children is significant. Have them explain how they feel about your words and actions. Let them say what disappoints them. You may find this difficult, but when problems are out in the open, change is more likely to happen. If they don't raise the issue of jealousy but you believe it's a problem, initiate the discussion yourself.

Let them know that you've heard them: "You're saying that things don't seem fair in this family." Listen to their suggestions: "I want you to tell me my work is good." "You and Dad should come to my games more." "Don't always talk about Ian."

Put limits on their rivalry: "While Mom and I are working on changes, we expect you to work on getting along better." Tell them you won't tolerate constant bickering. Sometimes kids struggle with each other because they haven't been firmly told not to.

Honesty and openness will gradually enhance your children's relationship. When your jealous child feels heard and sees that changes are being made, she'll start to feel better about her siblings. During this time of change, you may want assistance from a third party such as a therapist or counselor. Even positive differences can be hard to accept or get used to.

While one of your children may be enjoying the attention you begin to give her, a previously "favored" child may have to adjust to a new situation. That child may have to learn to share your time and attention. Tell her, "We never realized your brother felt left out. We love you as much as always, but we're trying to be more fair now to both of you." You may find that your "favored" child is relieved to be out of the spotlight, just as a teacher's pet may be glad to give up that title. It's often awkward for a child who receives better treatment than others.

Think about the ways your children's lives affect each other. As one child succeeds in school, another may need more attention. As one goes off with friends, the other may need support. Don't expect the same behavior from each of your children. Try to create a balance so that, despite differences in age, interests, personality, and skills, each of your children feels special and important.

Finally, encourage them to be nice to each other. Praise their kind gestures, recognize the times they accept each other, and show them, by your words and actions, the benefits of an improved family relationship.

How should I handle our changing family celebrations?

Celebrations and rituals are essential—they're part of the glue that keeps families together. Many holiday rituals, such as trick-or-treating or a visit to Santa, are aimed at young children. Other family traditions involve all the generations: Thanksgiving, the Fourth of July, Kwanzaa, the Passover Seder. In spite of the work involved, parents look forward to these annual celebrations as a time for family togetherness. But as kids reach ten to thirteen years old, they may no longer want to participate in the same ways, if at all. Instead of being excited about an upcoming event, a twelve-year-old may shock and disappoint his parents by asking, "Do I have to go?"

By these ages, some kids reject family traditions because they're beginning to be self-conscious or don't see the purpose anymore. A child may feel awkward about dressing up, playing games, and being in the spotlight. He wonders what others think of him: "Do I look stupid in this costume?" He may feel he's outgrown a celebration: "I'm too old for parades!" Because twelve- and thirteen-year-olds are easily embarrassed, they may not want to be seen with their parents, especially if friends are around: "I don't want to go to the fireworks with you. I'd rather go with Gwen."

It's sad for parents when certain rituals end. Adults who've enjoyed decorating Easter eggs and hosting cake-and-ice-cream birthday parties don't want to give up the close times they've had with their child. His reluctance to participate in holidays reminds them of his growing independence and inevitable separation.

Still, people of all ages need family traditions. If your child is beginning to reject your rituals, you can make some accommodations while still reinforcing the importance of celebrating together.

For example, try changing the way you mark a holiday. One mother who always decorated for Halloween didn't want to give up the tradition when her children became teenagers. Now she decorates only the hallway for trick-or-treaters to see, and her children, though perhaps "too old" for the holiday, like seeing the ritual continued.

Your child may feel better about family celebrations if you modify the circumstances a bit. Let him bring a friend along. Suggest that he take a Walkman or a book to a gathering; however, let him know he should spend most of his time socializing. Occasionally, you might limit the amount of time you spend at family get-togethers. You'll have fewer struggles if you bend a little.

Create new celebrations to mark the changes in your child's life. On the last day of school, go out to dinner. Finish the sport's season with a special lunch. One ten-year-old prompted her family to start an annual Kids' Day.

There are some holidays you won't want to change. If certain celebrations are very important, let your child know he has to take part: "We always go to midnight mass on Christmas eve." "You have to spend Passover with us at Aunt Lil's." In busy times these events bring your family together and give it an identity. As your child grows, these annual celebrations will become the traditions he remembers and carries on.

We're spending less time together. What's happening?

Families always seem to be busy. Parents' weekdays are filled with work, appointments, car pools, chores, errands, and volunteer projects. Weekends, rather than being relaxing, are times for shopping, driving to children's activities, laundry, household repairs, and paying bills.

Kids' schedules are full too. In addition to school, homework, and chores, a ten- to thirteen-year-old may have lessons, classes, sports, or religious school. She may spend time talking on the phone, getting together with her friends, working on hobbies, reading, listening to music, working on the computer, watching TV, or playing video games. Between her activities and her parents', there's little time for the family to be together.

Eventually, this lack of closeness can lead to problems. Everyone knows older parents who say, "I wish I'd spent more time with the kids when they were young." The parent-child relationship is built during childhood and adolescence, and once the time to be together on a daily basis passes—usually by age eighteen—parents can be left with many regrets.

You should make a special effort to be with your child, even if you seem to have little opportunity or energy. By rearranging your schedule or giving up some of the things you now spend time on—socializing, volunteering, working long hours, keeping the house in perfect order—you can make yourself more available.

If your child wants to tell you a story, put down the paper or the mail and give her your undivided attention. When she practices piano, occasionally sit with her and listen. When you're both in the car, use the time for discussion. Start having breakfast together or stay off the phone or computer in the evenings so you and she can talk.

The initiative has to come from you because she may be too busy or self-absorbed to think about your lack of time together. While it's natural for her to want to be with friends much of the day, make it clear that family time—whether regularly planned or spontaneous—is important, too. One way around conflicts is to include her friends in some of your family activities.

When you focus on her interests, she'll welcome your increased attention. You can sit in her room while she talks about her day or you can listen to her music together. You may be surprised to find that you and she like some of the same kinds of songs. Try playing a board game or video game together, making dessert, reading out loud, or sitting at the kitchen table with a cup of hot chocolate.

Try not to use your limited time together to reprimand her. In some families, the only time parents and children talk is to argue. While it's important to settle disagreements, the calm and enjoyable hours you spend together are valuable. They help create an atmosphere that makes it easier for her to be cooperative and open.

This is a period of rapid changes for her. One father realized with a shock that in only five years his thirteen-year-old would be off to college: "I don't have much time left with him." The everyday events that fill your calendar should not keep you from spending time with your child as she grows and matures. Being together is an important of strengthening the bond between you.

Why does my child care so much about privacy?

"Leave me alone!"

"I want to be by myself."

As kids get older, their desire for privacy increases. Ten- and eleven-year-olds like occasional time alone, but many twelve- and thirteen-year-olds spend considerable time by themselves. This is a natural consequence of their growing independence; however, some parents find it troubling: "It doesn't seem right when my daughter goes off to her room. It feels like she's rejecting the whole family." Parents remember how their young child used to follow them and how he felt most comfortable and secure when they were close by. They may wonder why he now wants to spend so much time on his own.

Kids often go into their bedrooms and shut the door because they want to relax in a quiet atmosphere. Some read, listen to music, draw, or organize baseball cards. Some enjoy private time in a room playing a video game, watching TV, using a computer, or talking on the telephone. Going off by themselves, kids are able to get away from the stresses and noise of younger siblings and household activities.

Kids also seek privacy to get away from adult demands. After a day spent with teachers and coaches, parents' questions and expectations can seem overwhelming. And in some families, when a child is in sight, he's given spontaneous chores: "As long as you're in the kitchen, please set the table." "Take Katie out to play." "Help me straighten the family room." A child learns that if he goes right to his room he's less likely to receive added responsibilities.

In some cases, he may isolate himself in an attempt to escape from problems. He may be having trouble making friends or keeping up with schoolwork. He also may be retreating from family conflicts. Time alone can offer a short reprieve from difficulties, but parents should be concerned if he shows signs of depression, such as eating less, sleeping more, losing interest in friends and activities, moping, or appearing sad or angry.

If you're worried about your child's excessive desire for privacy, talk to him about your concerns. You may discover that he goes to his room out of habit, and your reminders may be enough to change his behavior. You may learn that he's upset about school and homework or that he feels pressured by responsibilities or arguments at home. Try to decrease his stress—offer help with assignments, time with a tutor, fewer demands. Provide encouragement and positive attention.

As long as his time alone is not excessive, respect his wish for privacy and, if necessary, help him out. Ask younger siblings to keep their distance for short while. Allow him free time during the day. If your children share a bedroom, have them work out a schedule for time alone, or let each spend periods by himself in another room. If you allow your child adequate privacy, he'll probably balance that by spending time with family and friends.

My child thinks I'm an embarrassment. When will this end?

"Don't come in when you pick me up at school."
"Please don't be a chaperone."
"We can't go to the mall together—my friends might be there."
Twelve- and thirteen-year-olds are easily embarrassed by their parents. They may feel humiliated by anything their parents do in public, such as laugh out loud, cheer at a game, sneeze, wave, or simply stand around. Parents may put up with their child's embarrassment and

even be amused by it for a while. But sometimes they find it annoying to be warned off, criticized, and ignored.

A child this age is self-conscious and uncertain about her own behavior. She can easily extend her self-consciousness to include her parents' behavior, feeling that what they do reflects on her. If her parents "make a mistake," she worries that her friends will think less of her. One father, out with his son, said, "Hi Andy," to a child whose name was really Annie. Annie didn't mind, but the son was extremely embarrassed: "When you said the wrong name it made me feel dumb."

Being part of the group is very important to twelve- and thirteen-year-olds. They are becoming increasingly independent of their parents and want to spend more time with their peers. A child wants to act the way her friends do, which is different from the way she acts at home. When her friends and her parents are together, even briefly, she feels embarrassed and awkward. She doesn't want her parents to see her joke around and relate to her peers, especially those of the opposite sex. And she doesn't want her friends to see how she behaves with her family. One child was invited to a Bar Mitzvah along with her parents. She told them, "I'm not going to like this. I can't dance if you're there looking at me."

A child cares a great deal about her friends' opinions, including their opinion of her parents. It's hard to convince her that her peers are emotionally removed from all parents but their own—she still feels that her parents are the focus of attention. And even if her parents are young in spirit, have a good relationship with her, and are comfortable with her friends, she'll continue to worry.

You may think your child's embarrassment is silly. But she's showing common early adolescent thinking and behavior. You probably can remember similar feelings about your own parents. One mother told her grown daughter, "You used to be just like Erica is. You always wanted me to walk three feet in front of you." If you and your child discuss the issue honestly, you will probably hear that she likes being with you at home or at activities where parents are usually involved, such as watching a game or eating out. She just doesn't want to be with you in front of her friends.

You can try modifying some of your behavior to show respect for her feelings. If she doesn't want you to tell jokes when her friends are present, go along with her. However, if her embarrassment is consistently excessive, let her know you will have to be together in public at times. You should continue to talk to her friends when you see them.

Don't try to lessen her embarrassment by becoming "friends" with her and her peers. Dressing, talking, or behaving like an adolescent is not appropriate. She needs to feel separate from you. Work on building a positive relationship with her by talking, showing an interest, guiding her, and respecting her.

While the majority of children feel embarrassment over minor incidents, some have to deal with seriously embarrassing situations involving irresponsible parents. If your family is experiencing complex problems, your child—and the rest of the family—can benefit from professional help.

In most cases, however, embarrassment is short-lived and nothing to worry about. Once your child gains more independence and experience socializing, her comfort with you will increase.

How can I help my child deal with divorce?

Parents don't want the breakup of their marriage to harm their child. Before divorce, many parents seek advice from a family therapist about minimizing their child's suffering. During and after the divorce, most parents' love and concern for their child remain unchanged. Yet, the stress of divorce can be so intense that parents eventually find it hard to keep concentrating on their child's needs.

Divorce is almost always devastating for kids. Many parents want to believe their child will bounce back: "Kids are so resilient." "He'll get over it after a little while." But children don't recover easily. Some may seem unaffected simply because they have busy schedules and many distractions. Others keep their feelings to themselves for fear of further upsetting or angering their parents. A child who is confused, ashamed, or embarrassed may hide or deny his feelings rather than talk about this tough issue. And many emotions are repressed.

What a child of divorce feels is sadness, anger, hurt, and sometimes a sense of abandonment. Even if he was exposed to frequent turmoil when his parents were together, he usually won't greet the divorce with relief. Almost all kids want their family to stay together, and they feel powerless when they can't make their wish come true. One twelve-year-old whose parents had been separated for a year told her friend, "For my birthday I don't want any presents. I just want my family to have dinner together again." A ten-year-old wrote a note to a classmate: "You're always happy. Is that because your parents aren't divorced?"

After divorce, a child is often expected to behave more maturely than before, take care of himself, assume some of the absent parent's responsibilities, or provide emotional support to the parent at home. These are impossible burdens for any child who finds the condition of his family life and the state of his childhood dramatically changed.

Even the most comfortable parts of a child's life may suddenly become stressful after divorce. Dinner and bedtime may be awkward. Family celebrations may be uncomfortable, and relationships with grandparents, aunts, uncles, and cousins may be strained or even cut off.

If parents are very angry about the divorce, all aspects of a child's everyday life will be affected. Some parents may coerce their child into taking sides, leaving him feeling guilty, disloyal, and resentful. If he does blame one parent for the breakup, he may idealize the other one, praising him or her in the presence of the "bad" parent.

All these potentially negative experiences, if not dealt with carefully by parents, can cause great emotional harm. A child may develop a poor self-image, distrust, a pessimistic outlook, or depression. He also may have trouble in school or with peers and siblings.

During and following a divorce, parents have to commit themselves to putting their child's needs first—to consistently giving love and attention and being deeply involved in his life. He needs extra affection and understanding during and after a breakup, and he needs both of his parents to be nurturers and role models.

Parents have to refrain from speaking ill of each other in their child's presence. The parent who does not live with the child has to have frequent contact, drive carpools, go to his special events, and help with homework. If a parent does not stay involved, the child will feel rejected and unworthy of love.

To help your child through divorce, encourage him to talk. Let him know he can share his worries, anger, and questions. You'll find out what he's thinking and you can clear up confusion: "No, we aren't going to move. We're staying right here in our house."

Offer information and answer his questions. He'll want to know about changes. Will he still go on vacations and visit relatives? Where will the other parent live? What should he tell his friends? Who will he celebrate holidays with? You should raise these issues if he doesn't bring them up. He'll feel less worried knowing you and he can talk openly.

Don't expect too much from him. He won't be any better at making decisions or being responsible than he was before your divorce. He's still a child and his needs should come before yours or your ex-spouse's. If the practical side of parenting seems overwhelming, simplify your life to make more time for your child. Have easy meals, let some housekeeping chores go, cut back on outside commitments.

Encourage him to stay in touch with your ex-spouse's relatives. Continuing his relationship with grandparents and cousins will help him feel part of an extended family.

Over time your child may begin to understand and accept his situation, although it will be difficult for years, perhaps for the rest of his life. He'll probably continue to wish there had never been a divorce. As a parent, you have to understand that your divorce will inevitably cause your child hurt and pain. Your attention and consistent understanding are needed to help your child with his emotions.

I'm a single parent. How do I talk to my child about my dating?

It's common for kids to have a hard time if their single parent begins to date. They may complain, sulk, or otherwise act out their discomfort and unhappiness. One girl told her mother, "When you go out with a man, it's worse than the divorce!" Another child cried whenever she saw either of her parents with a new companion.

Parents who are looking forward to resuming their social lives may resent this display of anger and sadness: "Don't ruin things. I need a life too. It's not my fault your father left me." While parents can understand some of their child's unhappiness, they're often surprised by the depth of her negative feelings.

Most children resent their parents' dating because they believe it makes a family reconciliation less likely. Ten- to thirteen-year-olds may still think that they can bring their parents back together, or that their parents will re-unite on their own. A child may act rudely to her parents' dates in hopes of discouraging relationships outside the original family.

She also may worry about receiving less attention once her parent begins dating. In a sense, she feels abandoned as her single parent focuses time and energy on a new companion. A date is an intruder and a threat.

Sometimes a child remains distant toward her parents' dates because she fears involvement: "I think this guy will walk out on us like my dad did." The child doesn't want her parent to get hurt, and she doesn't want to get hurt herself. Depending on the circumstances of the divorce, she may fear that her parent won't be loyal to the new companion.

Finally, she may be uncomfortable with her parents' social life because she herself is becoming interested in dating. Twelve- and thirteen-year-olds who are discovering their own sexual and romantic feelings dislike imagining that their parents might have similar thoughts.

To deal with your child's worries, keep the lines of communication open if you start dating. Find out what she thinks, even if you'd rather not know. She'll feel better talking openly about her concerns. Acknowledge your difficulties: "This is awkward, isn't it?" "How can I help you feel better about my dating?" Imagine yourself in her place—it might help you understand and be more patient.

When you begin to date someone, meet him or her at a location other than your home. There's no point in upsetting your child by having her greet the people you go out with.

Before bringing dates home, tell them about your child and offer advice on dealing with her. If they seem overly friendly, she may withdraw. Brief, casual contact is best. If dates show a genuine interest in her, she may respond favorably, although she may not want to spend much time with them. If they compliment you or act affectionate in her presence, she may feel threatened and worry about losing you.

Don't have a date spend the night at your house. Your child will feel embarrassed and awkward knowing that you're sleeping with someone in the family's home. In addition, she'll be negatively influenced by what goes on. She's looking to you as a model, and eventually she'll copy you. If you want her to have good values as she enters adolescence, don't expose her to sleepovers.

As you continue to date, you may be tempted to ask your child for acceptance or even advice. But don't expect too much. She won't be able to understand or validate your social life. She's more likely to be uncooperative since she'd prefer that you didn't go out. If your expectations are unrealistic, you'll only become frustrated and angry.

You'll have to work hard at helping her adjust. The more time you spend talking with her, being with her, and building a positive relationship, the easier that adjustment may be. If your dating takes time and attention away from her, you and she will be in conflict. If she has unusual difficulty with your dating, she may need extra support, including a therapy group.

Once you understand the problems your dating can cause, you may want to consider an option some parents have chosen: not dating until your children are older or even grown. Certainly this involves a sacrifice and may seem an unusual alternative. But the years of active parenting go quickly and you may find that putting your energy into family life, especially after a divorce, will have lasting benefits while still leaving you time for personal intimacy later.

How can we adjust to our blended family?

All families have to work at living in harmony. Blended families, especially ones with ten- to thirteen-year-olds, have to try particularly hard. Kids these ages go through tremendous physical and emotional changes as they form their adolescent identities. In the midst of their internal upheavals, they often react quite negatively to a new stepfamily. And new stepparents may have negative feelings of their own. They rarely feel the same bond with a stepchild that they do with their natural children. Adjusting to life in a blended family requires much commitment, patience, and understanding from all members.

Parents may have an easier time if they understand the child's point of view. Because he may still be sad about his parents' divorce, he may fear attachment to another adult who might leave. He also may worry about losing the love and attention of his newly married parent, seeing the stepparent as an intruder and rival.

The stepparent is another authority figure, and a pre- or early adolescent will resent new or different rules and restrictions. He doesn't want his natural parent to give up control: "If he didn't live with us, you wouldn't make me clean my room so much!" "Why do I have to go to bed early just because Margaret said so?"

When a stepparent joins a family, many rituals and routines change, and a ten- to thirteen-year-old finds that upsetting. He doesn't want his natural parent to act differently, and he doesn't want to alter the patterns of everyday life.

A child who resents a stepparent may act on his feelings in a number of ways. He may try to sabotage the new marriage by being intentionally uncooperative and belligerent. He may fantasize that his actions will bring his natural parents together again.

He may use his stepparent as a target for all his frustration and anger: "It's Jim's fault I didn't do well on the test. I can't study when he's around." "It's never fun going to dinner anymore because of Ellen and her dumb kids." He feels safe doing this because he has little to lose—he doesn't necessarily care what his stepparent thinks of him.

One reason a child may focus so much blame on the stepparent is because he wants his natural parent to be the "good" one. If he gets upset at him or her, he risks feeling guilty, losing his parent's love, and facing his mother or father's anger.

Another complication in blended families is the presence of

stepsiblings. At these ages, kids don't want to be told whom to like. Yet, in a blended family they're thrown together with new siblings and forced to socialize, have their weekends interrupted by visits from each other, share possessions and perhaps even a bedroom, and compete for attention from parents. It's natural that stepsiblings feel resentment about perceived unfairness. And if the parents in a remarriage have different discipline standards, stepsiblings will argue about who has to listen to which adult.

In spite of the difficulties, blended families can succeed. To help your family during its adjustment, look for stepfamily social or support groups in your area. They offer an opportunity to talk about concerns, hear tips on getting along, and listen to other families' experiences. You also might consider using a therapist to help improve your family's relationships.

Talk often at home. Hold family meetings, allowing each member to speak without interruption about troubling issues. To avoid angry outbursts, set ground rules—no put-downs or criticism and no yelling. Such meetings can create a positive atmosphere and clear up misunderstandings.

If you are a stepparent, be patient as you get to know your stepchild. Ask him about his activities and interests, go to his games, and help him with his hobbies. Don't create or enforce rules unless you have a good relationship with him, and don't try to replace his absent natural parent. If he rejects you, look for possible openings. Will he let you help with homework? Can you play tennis, cook, bike, garden, sing, or read together?

If you're the natural parent, spend time alone with your child, reinforcing your relationship. Praise him when he tries to get along with his stepfamily: "I know it's hard sometimes. Thanks for trying." Be realistic in your expectations for the relationship between him and your child. Tell him how you'd like him to act and remind him, if necessary, that disrespectful behavior is not acceptable: "We don't treat you that way and we don't want you treating us that way." Take on the role of disciplinarian for him, rather than leaving that responsibility to your new spouse.

Be sensitive to the difficulty stepsiblings have with their arrangements. It takes time for kids to adjust to each other. Sometimes ask them for suggestions about getting along and dealing with conflicts.

As you adjust to your blended family, it's important that your marriage remain loving and stable. Remarriages are often difficult, and stepfamily tension coupled with everyday stress can be very disruptive. If you put time and effort into your relationship with your spouse, you will not only strengthen the bonds of your marriage, but your bonds with your child as well. When he sees that you love and enjoy each other, he may try harder to accept his situation. And he may realize that his anger and stubbornness are causing him to miss out on a satisfying family life.

CHANGES

Why is my child so moody?

"All I did was ask about the party and my daughter started crying."

"Every day my son comes home from school in a bad mood."

"Why does my child get so angry when plans change?"

Emotions during the pre- and early adolescent years are intense and unpredictable. One moment a child feels rage and the next she seems calm and delightful. Mood changes and bursts of temper often take parents by surprise. A simple question asked of a thirteen-year-old ("Do you think that sweater will keep you warm?") can solicit a furious response: "Mom, you just don't understand anything. I hate talking to you!" One eleven-year-old instantly went from happy to belligerent when his mother ran a brief errand on the way to baseball practice: "Why do you always have to stop at stores?" A twelve-year-old left for school in a bad mood because she was out of hair gel.

Everyone feels moody at times; emotional ups and downs are a normal part of life, but they're exaggerated at this time, especially for twelve- and thirteen-year-olds. During these years, kids go through great physical, intellectual, and psychological changes, all of which affect their emotions. A child begins to think about her beliefs and values. She is capable of considering other people's thoughts and opinions. Unfortunately, she often assumes people are thinking about her, especially in critical ways. She may act very self-consciously: "Will my freckles go away?" "Why is everyone staring at me?" "I wanted to die when I tripped on the steps at school." She may feel inferior to her peers: "Why am I the one with horrible hair?" Such insecurity causes frequent mood swings.

As part of the normal drive for independence, a child distances herself from her parents, and in the process becomes more critical of their actions and choices. She can imagine an ideal self and family. When she or her parents fall short, she can easily become unhappy or angry.

In addition, thoughts and emotions that were suppressed or not easily verbalized during earlier years might surface now. She may become very upset about unfair treatment in the past: "You're always so critical. I can't be perfect!" Through bad moods and angry outbursts, she releases her frustration with her parents.

There is another reason for mood swings: life gets more complex and stressful for kids at these ages. Competitive sports, adjusting to middle school, an expanding social life, busy schedules, family conflicts, and worries about the world outside the home all affect a child's emotions. Parents' expectations also increase as kids get older. One thirteen-year-old said, "My parents make me so mad. They order me to clean up, go somewhere, do something, and they ground me if I don't listen."

These are some of the underlying causes of mood swings. And almost any event can trigger a short temper or bad mood—a low grade on a test, a teasing remark, a disagreement with a friend or sibling, any embarrassment. If a child isn't invited to join her classmates after school, she may come home and shout at her brother. A boy who's criticized during gym class may in turn criticize his parents' choice of conversation at dinner.

Because many of the changes in a child's life are not experienced on a conscious level or are subtle, a pre- or early adolescent may be puzzled or upset by her own shifting moods: "I don't know why, but I'm depressed." "What's wrong with me?" "I'm sorry I get mad all the time." There's so much to sort through and understand that kids sometimes feel out of control.

You can help your child feel less confused by telling him what you think is causing his anger: "You didn't expect to do poorly on the math test, did you?" "That was a tough game." "Brooke should have invited you, too." Share experiences from your youth: "I remember how awful it felt not having someone to talk to at the bus stop." "I used to be mean to Aunt Joan a lot when I was in a bad mood."

Resist asking frequently, "What's wrong?" or, "Are you all right?" because your child will eventually react defensively. One twelve-year-old told her mother, "I hate when you ask me if I'm in a bad mood."

While you should allow your child the occasional harmless outburst—everyone needs to let out some frustration—in general, don't accept rude or disrespectful behavior. Tell her when her words are inappropriate—"I'm really bothered by your tone." "You need to control your temper."

—she might not view her moodiness or short temper in negative ways. Let her know that her negative behavior will have consequences.

Examine and, if necessary, change your own behavior. If you have a short temper or frequently act moody, your child may be copying you. Think about circumstances that might be exaggerating her moodiness, such as difficulty with schoolwork, tension at home, or excessive pressure to excel. If you can ease some of these problems and bolster her self-confidence in any way, you'll see an improvement in her temperament. One child began to feel calmer when his parents let him drop out of competitive swimming.

When your child is pleasant or cooperative, compliment her. In general, tell her she's a "good kid." And try to have a sense of humor in the face of normal pre-teen and early adolescent behavior. One parent told his thirteen-year-old, "Stop acting like a thirteen-year-old!"

Your child, like most, probably saved her short temper and moodiness for home, where she feels relatively safe and secure. At school, with friends, and with adults other than her parents, she's most likely polite and controlled. Moodiness at home is a normal part of development. Although it may be difficult for you, try to be supportive and patient.

I'm tired of reminding my child to use deodorant. What should I do?

One of the earliest signs of puberty is increased body odor. In the beginning, it may only be detectable after a child finishes playing a sport or participating in gym class. As he gets older, the need for deodorant becomes more obvious.

Kids sometimes hear about body odor from teachers who discuss general hygiene in class. Sometimes they hear about it from classmates: "You have b.o." "Jeremy stinks!" More often, however, they won't mention body odor to a friend for fear of hurting his feelings. Instead, it's a parent who first tells a child to start using deodorant.

His reaction will vary, depending on his maturity and his ability to practice good hygiene. Some kids are quite practical. They're independent about getting ready for school and activities, and they easily incorporate deodorant use into their daily routine with only an occasional reminder.

Many other ten- to thirteen-year-olds need frequent reminders. They have much on their minds, especially in the morning: "Where's my lunch money? Did I study enough for the math test? What pants should I wear? I wish I could go back to sleep." They have trouble remembering about teeth, cleanliness, and nails, and deodorant is just one more thing that's easily forgotten.

Finally, some kids these ages may not be ready—or willing—to think about bodily changes, especially increased odor. They don't yet have an adolescent's concern about image, and they can't easily detect the odor themselves. They would just as soon ignore the issue.

This is frustrating for parents who want to spare their child and themselves embarrassment. They don't want him to be teased and they don't want other adults to say, "He shouldn't let his kid smell like that." One teacher announced to her class, "Somebody in here has body odor."

To get your child to use deodorant, make it easy for him. Put the container in clear sight along with his toothbrush, soap, and hair-brush. If deodorant is kept in a cabinet, he may never think about it. Post a friendly or humorous note on the bathroom mirror. Remind him every morning. Put deodorant in his overnight bag when he sleeps out.

New routines always take time to learn, and soon enough your child will take over responsibility for this and the other aspects of grooming. The closer he gets to adolescence, the more he will focus on his body and his appearance.

For now, he's not being neglectful or lazy. He's either genuinely forgetting about deodorant or he's uncomfortable about this new part of his life. Let him know that his feelings are common, and keep talking to him about the importance of good hygiene.

How can I help my child during puberty?

Puberty is a time of growth and change for children, and it's also a time of stress. They have worries and questions about their bodies.

They become increasingly private. They're concerned about their social lives and they're starting to distance themselves from their families. Parents are often unsure of how to deal with all the issues raised during this period.

One cause of concern for many kids is the difference in rates of development. The desire to be like their peers is so strong that pre- and early adolescents who are maturing slowly may become upset and jealous: "When am I ever going to grow?" "Everybody treats me like I'm so young." A child who matures quickly may feel awkward and embarrassed: "People act like I'm already a teenager."

Girls are often self-conscious about their developing breasts: "I'm wearing a T-shirt over my bathing suit." Because this aspect of puberty is so obvious, friends or classmates may tease her about her breast size. Some younger girls who develop early don't want to wear bras. The process of shopping in a lingerie department may be too intimidating for a child who feels modest.

Another issue of puberty is when to shave body hair. Girls—usually by age twelve—are shaving their legs and underarms, and many boys are shaving off a mustache by thirteen. But some girls want to shave at an earlier age, and some twelve- and thirteen-year-old boys don't seem ready to shave, even if they have dark facial hair: "Why do I have to shave and my friends don't?" Parents and kids may end up arguing about this aspect of personal hygiene.

Just as many families are uncomfortable discussing sex, they're also reluctant to talk about puberty. A child may mention worries about height, but a girl may be embarrassed to share her fear of being flat-chested, and a boy may not talk about changes in his voice.

Parents may sense this self-consciousness; they also may feel reluctant to open a discussion about their child's body. They are often startled by the "sudden" changes they see, and they're curious about the changes they don't see. Yet, it rarely feels appropriate to ask a child personal questions about her body.

Even if conversations about puberty seem awkward, let your child know she can ask you anything. Offer her a book or articles on puberty and treat her concerns and questions with respect.

If you think she's focusing on her body too much, try to involve her in more activities and talk about her interests and accomplishments: "I love to hear you practice guitar." "Why don't you try the cartooning class at the youth center?" Give your child frequent compliments: "You're a great kid!" "You look great all dressed up." "It was really nice of you to help Grandpa."

Give her practical help. If she's embarrassed about buying bras, bring some home from the store for her or let her go into the dressing room alone. When she develops pimples, find appropriate soaps or creams and, if necessary, take her to a dermatologist.

Talk to your daughter about menstruation to be sure she knows what to expect. (She'll certainly feel more comfortable talking with her mother than her father.) As long as she understands the basic facts, you can wait until she gets her period to discuss details such as pads, tampons, cramps, and irregular cycles. When she does begin menstruating, talk about her feelings and such practical issues as changing pads or tampons at school and handling accidents. You might choose to discreetly let her siblings know, depending on their ages, that their sister has started menstruating. Be careful when you do this. You don't want your other children to become alarmed if they see a used pad, but you also don't want to violate your daughter's sense of privacy.

If she's maturing more quickly or slowly than average, keep treating her in a way that's appropriate for her chronological age. An eleven-year-old who looks quite mature is still eleven. Some parents make the mistake of letting their older-looking pre-teen wear makeup, dress more maturely, and go places without supervision. Similarly, parents of a more slowly developing child may tease her or treat her like a much younger person.

Throughout puberty, she will be especially vulnerable. Try to be patient and understanding. In the face of changes, she needs to know you love and accept her. The more support and encouragement you give, the better she'll feel about herself and her body.

What do I say about sex?

During a school meeting on pre-adolescent behavior, parents were asked to write down the one subject that was most difficult to discuss with their child. One mother was too embarrassed to write "sex," so she put down "homework." She later found out her friends had done the same thing. They wrote "chores," "talking back," "sibling rivalry"—anything but "sex."

Most parents and kids have a hard time talking to each other about sex. Parents find it difficult to imagine their child as a sexual being, and they're ambivalent about giving detailed information. Discussions often become embarrassing as parents blush and kids try to change the subject: "Okay! I know about that. Let's not talk about it anymore."

Pre- and early adolescents are definitely interested in sex. They just don't want to discuss it with a parent: "I'm not going to tell my father what I'm thinking about some girl." Kids are much more comfortable and uninhibited talking with friends about sex. They also look for information from older siblings, books, TV, movies, and magazines. Some of what they find out is accurate, some isn't. They rarely hear a discussion of values from these nonparental sources.

Most parents believe they should talk more about sex to their child than they do. They remember their own lack of knowledge as pre-teens and want him to grow up in a more communicative home.

When kids are young, parents have a relatively easy time telling them the basics of intercourse and childbirth. Yet as they approach adolescence, parents avoid discussions about the details: wet dreams, sexual arousal, masturbation, etc.: "I'll wait a little while." "They talk about that in health class." "He's probably heard a lot already." Avoidance is not surprising. Adults rarely speak seriously about sex with anyone, even close friends.

As uncomfortable as you may be, try to find a workable way to communicate information and strong values to your child. If you want to discuss an aspect of sexuality, acknowledge your discomfort: "I feel really awkward, but there's something I want to tell you about." "I was too embarrassed to talk about this before, but I want to try now."

Briefly share your information. If your child wants to learn more, continue. If he doesn't, don't force a longer discussion. He may be more open if you talk about your own lack of information as a child: "When I was a kid, I pretended I knew all about sex, but I didn't." Don't be surprised by blunt responses and questions: "Was Dad the first man you had sex with?" If discussing sex is too difficult for you, give your child one of the many good books on the subject, written for his age and maturity level. Urge him to read it, and offer to answer questions he has.

At these ages, it's important to share your thoughts on relationships and intimacy. Some parents clearly believe their child should abstain from intercourse until marriage, while other parents, looking ahead, are not quite that absolute. Whatever your position, make it clear that sexual intimacy is not appropriate until the people involved are grown and mature. Talk to your child about responsibility to himself and others and about loving relationships. Discussions about contraceptives and safe sex can generally wait until your child is older.

Learning about sex is a gradual process, and each person's feelings and knowledge about the subject will evolve through a lifetime of changes. When you raise your child in a caring and loving home, he'll feel good about himself, acquire strong values, and have a positive model for all his later relationships.

APPEARANCE

My child and I have different tastes in clothes and hairstyles. What should I accept?

As kids get older, they want more control over clothing purchases and haircuts. Depending on age and interest, they may ask for a little more say or they may ask to make all decision themselves. As long as parents and kids share the same taste, there's usually little conflict. But when tastes differ, as they often do, there can be frequent struggles. Some parents first deal with this issue when their child is ten to twelve years old; other parents have been arguing about clothes since their child was in preschool.

Most kids decide how they want to look based on how their friends look. Dressing like a friend gives a child a sense of belonging. Specific styles are less important than "fitting in." Some groups of kids like clothes and hairstyles that draw attention. They want to wear outrageous shirts, cut their jeans, or color or shave part of their hair. Some groups dress for comfort or prefer a conservative look. Still others are label-conscious and like the latest fashions.

Under the influence of peers, a child may quickly change her mind about what she likes. One eleven-year-old refused to wear the jacket her mother handed her. But when the girl's friend said, "I like that coat," the girl put it on. Another child pleaded with his mother to buy a pair of decorated jeans. After wearing them to school one day, he said he'd never wear them again because everybody teased him: "I was so embarrassed I didn't want to stand up the whole day."

Even without peer influence, a child's taste can change suddenly. She may get dressed for an occasion, look in the mirror, and say, "This dress is too big." "I like the pants but I don't like the shirt it came with." "I look terrible." She may think everything looks better on someone else. She may like her friends' clothes better than her own, even when the items are almost identical. Some kids even exchange clothes with friends in school bathrooms.

All of this can be very frustrating for parents. Their suggestions are often ignored and their purchases rejected: "Mom, nobody wears that." Their advice is met with defensiveness. One parent told her twelve-year-old daughter she dressed too much like a boy. The girl said, "But all my friends have these shirts!" One boy who got a stylish haircut over the objections of his parents said, "Now I look like a normal thirteen-year-old."

A child's desire for faddish or inappropriate clothes and hairstyles can easily lead to tension. Some families struggle constantly over makeup, shaved heads, pierced ears, ripped jeans, and long bangs.

If you're unhappy about your child's taste, set firm limits. The standards you reinforce now will set a precedent for what you'll accept in her later adolescent years. Tell her which styles you won't allow: "You can't wear that tight shirt." "You're too young to wear make-up to school." "That's an offensive picture on that T-shirt."

Try compromising on items that are acceptable but make you uncomfortable: "You can buy baggy jeans, but those are too large." "We can look for that shoe in another color." Let your child know when she can wear certain clothes: "Those shorts are fine if you're with your friends, but I want you to wear something neater to Uncle Alan's." If a major family event such as Thanksgiving is approaching, tell her she'll have to wait until afterward to change her hairstyle.

While it's appropriate to set limits on extreme styles, try to accept many of your child's choices and compliment her as often as you can. She still wants your approval, and constant criticism from you can harm her self-image. Remember your own feelings about clothes, appearance, and independence while growing up. Your frustrations then are similar to hers now.

You may find tensions decrease if you give her a clothing allowance, as many parents of thirteen-year-olds do. Go over spending guidelines: "Use this money to buy one shirt and one pair of pants." "You can get one shirt for thirty dollars or two for thirty dollars, depending on which store you go to."

Whatever your differences in taste, try to keep the issue in perspective. As long as your child does well in school, has friends, and is involved in activities, the style of haircut and clothing she prefers may be relatively unimportant. The only need for concern is if she generally isn't doing well or if she consistently chooses styles to antagonize you and others. This may be the sign of a deeper problem you need to pay attention to.

How should I handle fads?

All kids are attracted by fads and want at least some of the latest, short-lived styles in music, haircuts, clothes, gadgets, or games. At the beginning of the school year, they may be wearing their pants a certain way. Two months later, a sixth-grader says, "Nobody wears that anymore." A rock group that a girl has idolized may be quickly forgotten. A sports hat that a boy wants may soon end up in the back of his closet.

Fads are popular because kids want to be like their peers. If enough kids have a particular object, others want it too, since no one wants to feel left out. In the same way, younger siblings desire what their older brothers and sisters have. Kids are also heavily influenced by television commercials and magazine ads. Just as young children want the toys they see on TV, ten- to thirteen-year-olds think that much of what is advertised for them looks wonderful.

Of course, adults can be attracted to fads of their own. But most adults know which styles will last awhile and which will quickly vanish. Children don't distinguish in the same ways. A child wants a gadget because it's appealing now, and he's not thinking about its value or looking ahead.

That difference in perspective causes tension when parents discuss fads with their child. They may feel that a particular fad is too expensive or a waste of money: "I'm not paying that much for cheap-looking jewelry." They may disapprove of a fad or be completely against it: "That band sounds terrible—how can you listen to such junk?" "You're too young. You can't wear that lipstick." "You may not pierce your ear."

Many parents try a rational approach with their child: "You shouldn't believe what you see on TV." "It's better to think for yourself." "You don't have to have something just because other kids do." But what appears silly or wasteful to a parent may be important and fashionable to a child. That's why kids react defensively when their parents dismiss their requests: "You don't understand!" A child feels frustrated because, unlike an adult, he can't buy something simply because it attracts him. He needs approval, permission, and money, and he often has to listen to a lecture.

When your child wants something badly, hear him out. Don't label his request "just a fad." He'll feel better knowing he can talk without being put down or dismissed.

It's all right to let him follow a fad that's harmless and inexpensive. If you recall your own pre- and early adolescence, you'll remember longing to be like others. If a fad seems acceptable but you don't want to pay for it, let him know he'll have to spend his own money.

When you have some negative feelings about a fad, explain your point of view and then, when appropriate, compromise: "You can listen to that music, but only with your door closed or your headphones on." If you feel a fad isn't right, set firm limits: "You can't wear clothes with rips and holes in them." "You may not style your hair that way."

While an interest in fads is normal, your child shouldn't become too involved with them. If he cares excessively about clothes and possessions, help him to broaden his interests. If he follows fads in an attempt to attract friends, encourage him to find other ways to connect with peers. Finally, model the kind of common-sense approach that you want him to follow. If you communicate your sense of values, he shouldn't get overly caught up in a quest for whatever is new.

My daughter thinks she's fat. Should I be concerned?

Children learn at an early age to be aware of their weight. They see thin celebrities on TV and in the movies, and they look at ads for weight loss programs. They hear their gymnastics or wrestling coach urge them to slim down. They hear their parents talk about dieting or say, "Don't eat too much or you'll get fat," and it becomes clear that thinness matters.

Many girls describe themselves as overweight: "I look so fat in this outfit." "There's so much flab on my legs!" "I hate the way I look!" Often a child with a good self-image says such things to receive a compliment or be reassured: "What are you worried about? You're so skinny." "I wish I were as thin as you are. You look great!"

Sometimes she truly believes she's overweight even though her parents are convinced that she isn't. Parents have to evaluate her statements about weight, especially once she reaches twelve or thirteen. Some kids these ages become so obsessed with "being fat" that their self-image suffers and they risk developing an eating disorder.

While it's natural for your child to pay attention to her changing body, try to keep her from dwelling on weight and appearance. Also keep her from dramatically altering her diet. Talking will help: "You seem to believe you're overweight and I'm trying to figure out why. Do your friends feel the same way about themselves?" Discuss physical development and body shapes as well as healthy eating, but don't lecture or she'll stop listening.

Focus on her interests and strengths. She may be less concerned about her body if her time is spent on enjoyable or challenging activities. Encourage her to pursue hobbies or sports. Help her get involved in volunteer work, art classes, a school club, rearranging her room, caring for a pet, or learning a new skill.

Examine your own eating habits and attempts to lose weight. If there's too much emphasis on dieting at home, your child may be influenced in a negative way. Be less open when discussing your weight, put out fewer magazines with dieting articles, and show her, by your example, how to eat and exercise in a healthy way.

She may be concentrating on weight as a way of dealing with stress. She might find it easier to worry about being fat than to think about other problems. Try to find out if something is bothering her. Does she do well in school? Does she get enough attention at home? Does she get along reasonably well with her siblings? Does she have conflicts with friends? Can she occupy herself when she's alone? If you can help eliminate some pressures in her life, her self-image will improve. This, in turn, should lessen her preoccupation with weight.

Make it clear that you love her as she is and offer reassurance if she seems to need it. She may feel comforted to hear, "No, you're not fat." However, it's possible your words of praise and love will have little effect. If she genuinely believes she's overweight, she'll continue to see herself that way.

If your child is ten or eleven and talks about being too heavy, keep a watchful eye on her. If she's older, take her repeated complaints or changes in eating habits seriously. It's better to start dealing with the issue now because weight will continue to matter to her throughout adolescence (and adulthood). The older your child gets, the harder it may be to help her accept herself. If you're really worried, you might want to talk to a counselor or take your child to a nutritionist. A professional can often prevent serious eating problems and help your child view herself more realistically.

What should I do about my child's weight problem?

Parents who believe their child is overweight may feel a mix of emotions. They might be disappointed and embarrassed because he doesn't fit some "ideal" or because his situation reminds them of their own struggles with weight. They may be worried about his health and self-image and feel very protective if he's teased by his peers. Concerned parents may not know how to talk to him or help him lose weight. And frustrated parents may sometimes explode in anger, belittling or blaming him for something that may be beyond his control.

There are various reasons some kids become overweight. Heredity and metabolism are contributing factors for most children. Some kids have only a temporary weight problem that a growth spurt will eliminate. Some, who are not involved in activities outside the home, may spend too much of their time eating. Also, when a child is sedentary, he tends to gain weight.

If a child's emotional needs are not met, he may try to satisfy himself by eating, and naturally, eating habits, especially over-eating, can have an effect. In rare cases, an underlying medical condition may cause him to be overweight.

If you think your child has a weight problem, check with your pediatrician. You may find his weight is actually within normal bounds, and if it's not, the doctor can explain why. She also can help plan a safe weight-loss program, offer advice on talking to him about the issue, and refer you to a nutritionist.

Before discussing weight with your child, see if there are changes you can make that might help him. Alter your cooking methods (less frying, more grilling), your buying habits (fewer chips, more pretzels), and the portion sizes you serve. Encourage him to be active; rearrange your schedule so you can drive him to practices, watch his games, take him to friends' houses, and generally make it easier for him to spend time outdoors.

It's important to plan what you want to say before talking to your child about being overweight. Ten- to thirteen-year-olds are very sensitive. Use a respectful tone and begin by speaking in general terms about appearances: "Lots of kids your age are concerned about how they look. How do you feel about your appearance?"

He may welcome a chance to talk. Find out how other kids have been treating him. Ask if he would like to try losing weight. If he says yes, work together on a plan to change his—and perhaps the whole family's—eating and exercise habits. The more cooperative he is, the easier it will be to deal with his problem.

You may find, however, that he becomes defensive when you bring up his weight. He may act distant or angry or speak negatively about himself. This is especially true if you are rigid or harsh or dwell on his appearance. He may overeat as a way of rebelling.

If you encourage him to diet, he may resist your efforts, partly out of fear of drastic change: "Forget it! I just won't eat as much. I can plan my own diet. Let's not talk about it anymore!" Instead of arguing back, ask him for suggestions. An idea of his ("I just won't drink soda and eat dessert") may work. Offer encouragement: "You've got some good plans." "We'll try it your way first." "It may be hard, but I think we can do it."

Losing weight is very difficult, as most adults have learned, and your child may or may not be successful. Even if he loses weight now, he may regain it later. Be patient and supportive. His self-esteem depends on your unconditional love and acceptance, not your evaluation of his appearance.

INDEPENDENCE

Does my pre-teen need much supervision?

Pre- and early adolescents often behave responsibly, showing that they understand safety rules and know right from wrong. However, they also can act irresponsibly, and for that reason they need consistent parental supervision.

When kids are away from home, they're almost always supervised. They're watched at school, at camp, in organized sports, at social gatherings, and on field trips. Only at home are kids these ages left without an adult for significant periods. And when they are unsupervised, especially if they're with friends, they take more risks and are likelier to end up in trouble.

In a spontaneous moment, they forget rules, perhaps because of peer pressure or the desire for excitement. One thirteen-year-old walked to a pizza parlor at night, although she was told to stay indoors when her parents weren't home. An eleven-year-old teased a five-year-old neighbor until she cried. Two unsupervised twelve-year-olds poured squeezable cheese on each other "for fun." A ten-year-old and her friends made a mess in the basement, leaving spilled soda, chips, and candy. Physical fights broke out at an unchaperoned party for thirteen-year-olds.

Although your child is becoming more independent, she needs your supervision. Your degree of watchfulness depends on her age and the circumstances. A ten-year-old obviously needs closer supervision than a twelve-year-old. But whatever her age, you should know what she's doing and where she is, and you should set limits and offer guidelines. Your responsibility remains the same whether you're at home, working, socializing, or vacationing.

If she has any kind of party, even one involving just a few friends, be home. If she's going to a party elsewhere, make certain parents will be present. Supervise sleepovers. Tell the kids when they're making too much noise or staying up too late. If you're keeping an eye on things, you can end a troublesome situation or suggest alternative activities for your child, whether she's with friends or alone: "Why don't you play out front?" "I'll take you to the tennis courts." "Come get some pizza."

As part of supervision, give frequent reminders about safety and manners. It's important that your child clearly understands your rules. She may still forget, bend, or break some, but as long as you're supervising her, she's more likely to act responsibly.

"Why can't I go by myself?"

Most parents had more freedom as ten- to thirteen-year-olds than they allow their own child. Their parents didn't have the same worries about crime that contemporary parents do. The media constantly expose families to frightening stories of rape, abuse, kidnapping, and murder. Even schools can be places to fear as more children are found carrying weapons, acting in extremely aggressive ways, or becoming the victims of violence there.

Parents have mixed feelings about allowing their child independence. They want him to do things on his own, yet they're afraid for him. Kids feelings are more straightforward. Most don't share adult concerns; they think their parents are overly protective: "No one's going to hurt me." "I can take care of myself." "Nothing will happen. Why do you treat me like a baby?"

Since contemporary life has many uncertainties, it makes sense to err on the side of caution. Ten- and eleven-year-olds naturally need to be watched more closely than twelve- and thirteen-year-olds. But all children in this age group are vulnerable and need supervision and restrictions.

In general, insist that your child be with someone when he's away from home. Kids are more at risk and likelier to get into trouble when they're alone: "You can't go to the park by yourself, but I'll let you go with Brett." If you drop him at a movie, make it clear you expect him to stay with his companions: "If you have to use the bathroom, go together."

When he's with friends, check on him periodically or have him check in by phone or in person. If you allow your twelve-year-old and a friend to separate from you at a shopping center, meet them at regular intervals. And if you let him walk alone to a friend's house several blocks away, have him call you when he arrives and before he leaves.

He may be upset with the limits you impose, especially if you don't allow him to go places because he would be alone or because a location seems unsafe for someone his age. When he asks, "Why can't I go by myself?" you don't need to describe your fears. Instead say, "I'm not comfortable letting you go there. It would be fine if you were with someone or if you were older, but not now."

He may not like hearing this, but he won't be surprised. He's heard enough news and observed you long enough to know your concerns. He sees you lock your house and car doors. He's heard you and others voice your concerns: "Someone broke into a place near here." "I'm worried about my daughter's safety now that she's going off to college." "I don't like parking garages." "I hate to carry cash around." The world can be a frightening place. You don't want to scare or restrict your child unnecessarily, but you do want to supervise him enough—and limit his independence enough—to keep him safe.

Can my twelve-year-old baby-sit?

Baby-sitting is an excellent activity for early adolescents who are mature enough to care for young children. Baby-sitters learn to be responsible, creative caregivers, and in return for their efforts, they earn money and feel the reward of doing a good job. With parental support, children as young as twelve can be successful sitters.

A twelve-year-old generally does best with toddlers or older children. She may be overwhelmed by the tasks associated with a baby: changing diapers, warming a bottle, and dealing with crying. If a sitter is going to watch an infant, she should first spend time with the baby when his parents are home so she can practice caring for him.

Twelve-year-old sitters often want to work in pairs. Although they have to split their earnings, they like the security of having a companion. Unfortunately, sitters are sometimes less responsible when friends are with them and may need extra guidance and supervision.

Before your child baby-sits, talk to her about how young kids behave. She should know that they often act silly, enjoy attention, resist going to sleep, are fearful, have a hard time listening, cheat at board games, and can quickly get into trouble if left alone.

Give her strategies for dealing with difficult behavior. She can try to distract a youngster, offer a snack, read a story, or pat the back of a child who can't sleep. To keep young children busy, she can draw with them, watch a video, read a book to them, listen to music, build with blocks, dance, or make up a story.

Safety is an important issue, both for your child and for the children she watches. To ensure her safety, check out any casual acquaintances or strangers who want to hire her. You can call them and chat, ask how they got your child's name, and set up a time when you and she can meet them. When you do meet, try to evaluate their children's behavior—you may not want your child to sit for difficult youngsters. Tell the parents what time you want her home and work out transportation arrangements. If you're uncomfortable, don't let her take the job.

Talk to her about keeping babies and young children safe. Since many parents don't give enough information to their sitters, you need to prepare her. Discuss possible emergencies and tell her which questions to ask. She should find out how to get in touch with the parents and with you. She should also know what to do if someone knocks at the door or calls for the family.

Encourage her to ask her employers practical questions too. How late does the child stay up? Can he play outside? Does he go to the bathroom alone? Will he climb out of his crib? What can he eat? What can your child eat when she baby-sits? Can she use the phone? Does she have to clean up?

As you may recall from your own days as a baby-sitter, any twelve-year-old can be irresponsible at times. Even if your child is well prepared and mature, she may finish all the brownies, break something, or fail to pay enough attention to a youngster. Keep giving her tips, talking to her about each job, and stressing the importance of quality care. If you want to check on her while she works or simply reassure her, give her a call. She'll feel more secure knowing you're home and easily available.

Should my child stay alone after school?

Many ten- to thirteen-year-olds spend considerable time on their own every day. While twelve- and thirteen-year-olds may be mature enough to stay alone, ten- and eleven-year-olds are too young to be by themselves regularly or for long periods. Some local governments, through their social service agencies, set recommended limits on the amount of time kids these ages can be left unsupervised.

Nevertheless, many parents feel they have no choice but to leave their children alone. Parents are working, there are few sitters available, after-school care for this age group is hard to find, and alternatives are too expensive. Parents either convince themselves that their child will be all right, or they go off to work each day feeling guilty and worried.

Few kids, even thirteen-year-olds, would choose to stay alone regularly. They'd rather be greeted after school and have the comfort of an adult or teenage siblings nearby. A child left on his own can become bored, lonely, or scared. He may hear strange noises or worry about frightening events he's seen on the news. Even his parents' warnings can be alarming: "Don't go outside." "Don't answer the door." "Never tell a caller I'm not home."

One child told her mother, "I hate being alone, but there's nothing I can do about it so I never complain." Many kids don't speak up. They feel they have no control over the situation and fear upsetting their parents. A child may sense that his parents don't want to know what he really thinks.

Many parents never ask their child what it's like to stay alone every day. They avoid discussion rather than risk hearing something that would make them feel guilty. When he does voice opposition to staying by himself, his parents may say he's selfish or silly: "We do a lot for you. The least you can do is take care of yourself after school." Some parents rationalize: "It's a good time to get homework done." "You like to watch TV." "You can get your chores out of the way."

It's best not to leave your child home regularly, but if you do, minimize his time alone. Arrange for him to go home with a friend. See if a neighbor or a high school student can help out, if only to check on him for a few minutes each day. Find out about organized afternoon activities and transportation home, such as a late school bus or a carpool. A classmate's parent may be willing to drive your child in exchange for a service you can provide, such as weekend baby-sitting. See if he can stay after school to help his teacher, work in the library, or volunteer in the school office.

Consider letting him invite a friend over as long as both kids are mature and responsible, and the parents of the other child know you won't be home. However, if you have many doubts ("What if they do something unsafe?" "They might get silly or destructive") wait until your child is older. Too often, kids these ages do what they want, assuming their parents won't find out: "We can go skateboarding for a while." "Let's make some macaroni."

If you don't arrange supervision or companionship for your child, you still can provide home activities such as art projects, magazines and books, music, and puzzles. Leave a snack and a friendly note. Call shortly after you expect him home and give him time on the phone to tell you about his day in school. Let him know he can call you or a relative or friend if he wants to talk or has a problem. Keep a list of his friends' phone numbers with you so you can call if you have to. You may be tempted to keep him busy with chores, but after a day of classwork, he may resent this. He needs a chance to relax and pursue his interests.

Even if you continue to have him stay alone, keep the lines of communication open. Listen to his thoughts about staying by himself and avoid lecturing. If you say, "I have to go to work to pay for the things you need," he may stop sharing his feelings and instead feel guilty about being a burden. Let him express himself openly. Simply talking about being home alone may help both of you feel less stressed about the situation.

Should I let my child decorate her own room?

Kids' bedrooms are the closest they have to "personal space." It makes sense that they want to individualize their rooms as much as possible. Yet, many parents are reluctant to let their child do much, if any, customizing: "Your walls have to be white to match the rest of the upstairs." "Those posters are ugly—you can't hang them." "You can't have a beanbag chair. They collect dust."

Kids with creative ideas become frustrated if they can't try them out. One boy wanted to hang his baseball hats on the wall. Another asked to string Christmas tree lights around her window. A ten-year-old wanted to put her mattress in a tent made of sheets.

If a child sees something appealing in a friend's room, she may want to copy it: "Shannon has a neat lamp in her room. Can I get one?" "Alex's wall is covered with posters and it looks great."

A child who feels she has little control over many aspects of her life may fight to make decisions about her room: "Why can't I pick the color? Why do I have to have the pictures you like? It's my bedroom."

Although you may have firm opinions about how your house should look, at least consider some of her ideas. Whenever possible, allow some flexibility. You may not want her to draw murals on her walls, as some kids are allowed to do, but you can let her pick out pictures or make nonpermanent changes. If she wants to rearrange the furniture or put the mattress on the floor, let her try for a while and then switch back if you like.

If your children share a bedroom, have them compromise on temporary decorating changes, divide the space so each has room to individualize, or take turns making changes.

If your child seems overly focused on redoing her room, think about her motivation. She may see decorating as an escape from other problems. If she's troubled, a new room arrangement won't help her feel better. However, if her social life, family life, and schoolwork are going reasonably well, you can assume her desire to redecorate is motivated by curiosity, creative ideas, and a desire to express herself.

There are some real benefits to letting her try her ideas. She may pick up some artistic or practical skills. She'll feel more independent. And she may become more cooperative as she sees that you're willing to give her choices and some control.

Don't make her promise to keep her newly arranged room neat. If she's already an orderly child, she'll automatically straighten up, whatever the arrangement. And if she isn't orderly, your insistence on being neat will only dampen her excitement. Instead of enjoying the new look, the two of you will end up arguing about her broken promise and your unrealistic expectations. It's better to treat cleaning up as a separate issue, not tied to her desire to personalize her own space.

Should my child decide how to spend his money?

Parents want their child to handle his own money responsibly. They want him to plan ahead, spend wisely, and save for the future. Most ten- to thirteen-year-olds, however, are less interested in being responsible than in buying what they want. This causes a dilemma for many parents. They know he should make decisions and learn from his own mistakes, yet they want to keep him from wasting his money. These conflicting aims make it hard for them to be consistent.

Sometimes the child's point makes sense: "It's my money. Why can't I get what I like?" "If I'm saving up for a video game, why do you care if it's expensive?" Parents' points are also sound: "You shouldn't spend your money on junk food." "Wait until it goes on sale." "Get two sweaters instead of one expensive one." "Don't throw your allowance away on something that won't last."

In general, it's best to let your child decide how to spend his own money. But if you feel his spending is out of control, set limits. At a time when you're both feeling calm, talk about money. Listen to his side, even if he complains that you aren't being fair. You need to understand him in order to know what will work. Tell him why you think saving and planning are important. Let him know you realize how difficult managing money can be and how easy it is to buy impulsively.

Together, come up with a management plan that allows him flexibility. Within reasonable guidelines, you want him to make money decisions on his own: "You can spend some of your chore money as long as you save some every week." "When I give you your allowance, I want you to put some aside to donate." If he receives a significant sum as a gift for a birthday, Christmas, or a Bar Mitzvah, give him a portion to use as he wishes and have him save the rest. You also could have him use this money for his first investment. This is a good time to start a discussion of stocks, bonds, and other financial alternatives. Perhaps you and your child could meet once with a financial planner who's willing to work with a child.

To help your child make spending decisions, work out a budget: "How much money do you think you need for snacks and movies?" Offer specific compromises: "Instead of spending all your money now, buy the video game this month and the sweatshirt later." Encourage him to save by taking him to the bank to open or make deposits in his own account.

Don't be too restrictive or he may feel resentful and start lying about money and purchases. But be firm about spending you don't approve of: "You can get a different CD with your money, but not that one." "You're too young to wear eye shadow, even if you plan to buy it with your own money." At these ages, you still need to set clear limits.

Your child may want to use his money for an expensive purchase. One girl saved for a tennis racket; another planned to buy a CD player. A thirteen-year-old paid for a lawn mower so he could earn more money cutting grass. As long as the item is one you would allow him to have, let him make the decision. You might question his judgment, but he will learn from the experience whether he's ultimately happy with his purchase or not.

Dealing with money is challenging, and you and he will continue to discuss this issue. Keep stressing your values, and show your child, by your actions as well as your words, how spending and saving can be responsibly managed. You want him to take money seriously, but you don't want it to become a source of guilt and tension. Show him that money also can be a source of enjoyment and that it's all right to splurge or make impulse buys at times and to use money to pursue his interests and hobbies.

What can my child do over the summer?

Kids look forward to summer as a reprieve from school, a time to relax and have fun. Many ten- to thirteen-year-olds, tired of homework and busy schedules, want to hang around and "do nothing." At these ages, however, they still need supervision and planned activities during the summer, especially if both parents work outside the home.

Without a schedule of activities and an adult nearby, kids may spend the summer watching TV, using the computer, playing video games, eating junk food, and hanging out with other children whose parents aren't home. Leaving a child alone for a short time may be all right, depending on her age and maturity. But leaving her alone or even in the company of a young teenage sibling every day for several months is a mistake. At best, the summer will be boring and aimless. At worst, she will get into trouble.

There are many alternatives to staying home all day, some inexpensive or even free. Some kids spend time at a pool, join swim teams, or play in various competitive leagues. Many park districts run supervised playground programs, and there are public and private daycamps, specialty camps, sleepover camps, lessons, classes, and summer school programs. Many of these activities offer bus service or help parents arrange carpools.

If you aren't available to drive during the day, your child's choices will, of course, be determined by location, starting and ending times, and availability of transportation. As much as possible try to enroll her in programs of interest to her or ones her friends will be attending. Kids these ages are usually happiest doing whatever their peers do.

If your child is going to sleepover camp for the first time, the separation may be emotional for both of you. One mother said, "I'm a little nervous. Actually, I'm a lot nervous." To prepare her, try to visit the camp ahead of time, look at pictures, or talk to someone who's been there. Talk to the camp director about concerns you or your child have. Let your child know that homesickness is natural, but that she'll soon get involved in camp activities.

Some ten- to thirteen-year-olds want to work during the summer. Under supervision—yours, a neighbor's, or a friend's—your child can care for pets, weed, mow lawns, or baby-sit. You or a relative also may have odd jobs she can do for pay.

Summer is a good time to visit out-of-town relatives, catch up academically, or pursue interests in learning and the arts. Encourage your child to read every day, keep a journal, write stories, draw, start a collection, make animated flip books, learn to type, create a web page, play an instrument, build, invent, make up plays, sing, act, sculpt, play chess, or learn a new craft. All of these activities can be entertaining, but too often they're associated with school or lessons. If you take a relaxed approach—and if you pursue such activities yourself—your child will find that learning on her own can be enjoyable and satisfying.

Finally, make time to be with her, even if you work all day. On weekends, evenings, and days off, get involved in her activities and interests. Make plans together—go biking, camping, shopping, or swimming. Go to a museum, a baseball game, a historical site, the library, or a park. Get ice cream together or go on a picnic. She needs your attention, involvement, and watchfulness. She'll be spending less and less time with the family as she gets older, so enjoy her company now, especially during the summer when schedules and people are more relaxed.

RESPONSIBILITY

Should my child need reminders about manners?

"Shake hands with Uncle Jack."

"Remember to thank Mrs. McDonald for the ride."

"Please hold the door."

"Offer your friend a soda."

Most parents don't understand why their ten- to thirteen-year-old still needs to be told these simple things: "I've been teaching my son manners since he was two years old and he still doesn't know how to act!"

The truth is, most kids these ages continue to need reminders. This is true in part because they tend to be self-absorbed and frequently moody. In addition, it's hard for them to keep track of all the polite behavior they're responsible for—how to greet guests, what to say to relatives, how to answer the phone, and how to treat friends and adults.

Kids also may be unsure about politeness because they receive conflicting messages. Parents and teachers stress manners, but they sometimes demand good behavior in unpleasant ways: "I've told you a hundred times not to start eating 'til everyone's served. What's wrong with you?" A teacher admonished her students for interrupting: "I want you dumb kids to keep quiet." Kids often imitate adults' behavior.

Most children display their worst manners at home, where they want to relax without worrying about politeness. Parents often despair when they imagine how their child acts with other people. But even the most forgetful kids are better behaved when they're away from home. With company, they become more careful about manners and usually remember to say "please" and "thank you" and generally to speak more politely.

One twelve-year-old demonstrated how she had folded her towel when she slept at a friend's house. Her mother was delighted because at home the girl usually dropped her towels on the floor. Another parent, who was upset by her son's lack of table manners, was relieved when his dinner with relatives went well.

When you correct your child's manners, try not to be too judgmental. It's better to say, "Next time please sound friendlier when you answer the phone," than to say, "You're so rude on the phone!" His forgetfulness is normal and condemning him may only harm his self-esteem, since he still depends heavily on your good opinion.

If you anticipate a problem, prepare him. Tell him firmly and consistently how you expect him to act when his grandparents visit, when he goes off in the carpool, when an important call comes, or when he sleeps at a friend's house.

The most important way to reinforce manners is to model polite behavior for him. If you treat him and others with respect, he'll eventually take on your attitude as his own.

My child forgets to give me phone messages. Should I be more patient?

A mother found a stray piece of paper with a week-old phone message, "Mom, call Carol." Two days after taking a message, an eleven-year-old asked his father, "Did I tell you Uncle Mike called?" One woman's phone conversations often begin with her caller asking, "Did Jennie tell you I called?"

Many kids forget to relay messages. Parents hope that their ten- to thirteen-year-old will be thoughtful and responsible enough to tell them about calls. But for a number of reasons, kids often don't remember. A child who's distracted by TV or homework when the phone rings may not listen carefully. She may become absorbed in an activity after taking the call and quickly forget the message. She may not write the message down immediately, which usually means she won't write it at all. Or, if the call doesn't pertain to her, she may soon stop thinking about it.

She doesn't forget on purpose. She usually feels bad when she lets her parents down, and she doesn't intentionally disappoint or frustrate them. When confronted, however, she'll defend herself because she also doesn't want them to be angry with her: "I was going to tell you later." "I started to write it down, but there wasn't any paper." "I thought I put her name somewhere." "I forgot. I can't help it. I'm not perfect."

Try to be patient—this behavior is very common. Keep telling your child how important message-taking is. Then, to make it easier for her and likelier that you'll get your messages, put pen and paper next to every phone. Create a central spot to leave messages. Tape a reminder note to the phone. Every time you come home, ask right away, "Any calls for me?" If you're expecting an important call, consider leaving your answering machine on so you'll be sure to get your message. If you don't already have caller ID, think about adding this service.

You may be tempted to teach your child a lesson by ignoring phone messages for her, but don't do this. When you say, "See how it feels?" or, "If you don't give me my messages, I won't give you yours," you teach her to be spiteful. She'll be upset by your intentional act and feel that you've deceived her. Your tactic won't motivate her to remember messages. Instead it will show her that when she's disappointed in people's behavior, she can act without considering their feelings.

Focus on the times she does remember to give you a message: "Thanks for letting me know about Mr. Johnson's call. I was waiting to hear from him." And remember that most people who want to get in touch with you will call back—especially if they left their message with a child.

"Who cares if my room's a mess?"

"You're not going out until you clean your room!"
"I'm tired of telling you to straighten up."
"Pick up your clothes and make your bed!"
Most parents and children argue about messy rooms because parents care about keeping things neat and kids don't. Most don't mind waking up, going to sleep, playing, and doing homework amid a jumble of clothes, toys, books, and papers. They're unembarrassed for their friends to see a messy room, and they don't think their parents should get upset.

A child may appreciate a clean room if someone else cleans it, but he won't straighten it on his own because to him it's an unpleasant and unimportant task: "I hate putting clothes away." "All my friends have messy rooms." "Why make my bed if I'm going to sleep in it again?"

Parents have little success getting their child to think as an adult does about this issue, although they may be able to persuade or force him to clean up, using a variety of strategies—paying him, bribing him, punishing him, or listing consequences: "If you don't keep your room clean, you can't have friends over." None of these techniques is particularly successful. A child may straighten up once or twice and then not again. Or he may clean his room in a half-hearted way, leaving much undone. Many kids are punished over and over and still don't keep their rooms neat.

One of the most common parental threats—"If you don't clean your room, I won't do your laundry!"—often backfires. Parent and child stay mad, the room and laundry stay dirty, and the child picks up an I'll-get-back-at-you attitude from his parents.

Most kids want to please, but they have trouble focusing on their rooms when their interests and energy are directed elsewhere. If parents continually attack their child for his messiness ("You're a slob!"), he'll internalize their criticism. He'll feel upset and frustrated because he can't live up to their expectations.

The most successful and realistic way to handle cleaning up is to compromise, even though it means lowering your standards. If your child isn't keeping a neat room at this age, more punishment and harsh words won't help. Use a calm tone. If you're feeling tense after a frustrating day, wait a while before discussing clean-up.

Offer to help him with his room: "I'll do this half of the floor while you work on the closet." He'll appreciate your assistance, since straightening up alone can seem overwhelming. Suggest a timed cleanup: "See how much you can get done in fifteen minutes."

Don't worry about being consistent. Some days you'll care a lot about how his room looks and other days you'll shut his door and walk away. You might decide to ignore the mess unless company is expected, or you might decide to wait until an every-other-week "family clean-up day."

Recognize that this is a common problem. You probably kept a messy room yourself when you were young. One mother, thinking her daughter was more disorganized than most kids, was amazed to see the girls' bunkhouse at sleepover camp. Possessions were strewn everywhere and all the campers seemed happily unaware of the chaos: "We just push the clothes to the bottom of the beds when we sleep."

The years from ten to thirteen are filled with turmoil, and you and your child may face some difficult issues. As long as he generally does well in other areas of his life, try to put the problem of a messy room in perspective. As he grows older, he'll eventually care more about neatness and order.

How can I get my child to do chores?

Parents feel frustrated telling their child over and over to help around the house. They know that what they're asking—take out the trash, set the table, rake the leaves—is minimal compared to the full adult responsibility of running a household. They also know how much time they spend meeting their child's needs, driving her to special activities, shopping for her clothes, and preparing for her friends' visits.

Most parents believe that everyone in the family should routinely help out. They think that doing chores will teach their child responsibility, help her mature, and let her make a contribution. But in reality, most kids don't do regular chores without constant reminders, threats, bribes, and arguments. This was true when they were younger, it's true of ten- to thirteen-year-olds, and it usually remains true of kids until they leave home. It doesn't seem to matter whether they are paid for their efforts or not. The problems involved in getting them to do routine chores often outweigh the benefits.

Kids don't do their chores because the work is not a priority for them. They don't care about order and cleanliness the way their parents do. Dirty dishes, an overflowing trash can, toothpaste in the sink, roller blades left out, and a backpack on the floor don't bother them. A child never complains to her parents, "The kitchen's a mess!"

Kids often resent chores because their busy schedules leave little free time. A child who spends a full day in school, then goes to afterschool care or an activity followed by an evening of homework, will not willingly wash the dishes. In addition, if stresses have built up during the day, chores can become a target of frustration: "Everybody always tells me what to do!" It's easier for a child to argue with her parents than with a teacher who may have been especially demanding earlier in the day.

When she isn't interested in a routine chore, she avoids it. She'll procrastinate, move slowly, or be easily distracted. Many parents label this behavior laziness, but it's really a normal response to something a child doesn't like.

If she actually does do her chores, her parents may still be frustrated because of the quality of the work. The table won't really be cleared, crumbs will be left on the floor, the top will be off the toothpaste, and clothes will still be in a pile. When parents express their displeasure, she becomes defensive.

If you want her to do regular chores, you'll probably have to continually remind her. Try to stay calm. If you use a harsh tone, she will be less cooperative: "I hate cleaning up!" You'll get a better response if your begin your reminders with, "Before you leave, please…," or, "Don't forget to…," or, "I'd like your help with…."

Offer her choices or vary her assignments. Some families have success with a job wheel of rotating responsibilities. Teach her the most efficient way to do a task. She may resist an assignment because she's never learned how to do it. One boy told his mother, "I don't fold the laundry right because you never showed me how." Surprise your child by taking over one of her routine tasks: "I know you've been busy with schoolwork, so I'll vacuum for you this week."

If regular chores are causing too much conflict in your family, reconsider your expectations. A neat, well-managed home may not be worth the unhappiness and pressure your child feels. You might decide not to give her routine chores at all and instead have her focus her time on schoolwork, hobbies, and extracurricular activities. You can still reinforce responsibility around the house by asking her to do specific jobs as the need comes up: "You take care of the basement while I straighten the living room." "Please clean your room before your friend gets here." "I want you to set the table tonight." "Give me a hand with these groceries." You will find your child more willing to help if the need is apparent and if she isn't overburdened by routine household tasks.

Of course, asking for help when you need it means the initiative is yours, not hers. However, that's probably the case even if she has regular tasks assigned, since she'll need reminders.

Everyone, including you and your child, grows up hearing adults stress the importance of cleaning up and doing household chores. Most people don't fully integrate and act on these messages until they're grown and on their own. The summer before freshman year at college, many parents are still trying to teach their child the best way to do laundry, mend clothes, and cook.

It's right to expect your child to be generally helpful and responsible at home, in school, and with others. However, it's realistic to assume that her help around the house will be neither as frequent nor as efficient as you'd like. Try to be patient, and reinforce the jobs she does, letting her know that you do appreciate her efforts.

Should the dog be my child's responsibility?

Taking care of the family dog is a big job, one many parents want their ten- to thirteen-year-old to handle alone. They hope that caring for the dog will teach their child to be responsible and to consistently meet another creature's needs. They also hope that the tasks involved—nurturing, feeding, cleaning, and exercising—will help their child mature and pick up valuable life skills.

In theory, that makes sense. But it's usually a parent who ends up walking the dog on wet nights, cleaning up after it on cold mornings, putting out food, and changing the water. No matter how hard parents push, most kids don't take full responsibility for a dog.

Some of the tasks, such as buying food and visiting the vet, are usually impossible for a child to do alone. Others, including all the walking and grooming, can seem overwhelming to kids who have a lot to think about and keep track of. A child may promise to care for his dog, but he's only saying what his parents want to hear. He'd like to be helpful and he loves and cares about his pet, but the job is too big.

Knowing that it's typical for ten- to thirteen-year-olds to neglect some pet-care chores may help you be more understanding of your child. Although you may be disappointed, don't be too demanding. Harshness and threats won't make him more responsible. Instead, he'll feel more stressed and angry and may take out his frustrations on others.

Offer to share responsibilities. He will appreciate your help if you don't make him feel guilty or neglectful: "Why don't I take over the morning walk for a while, since you're having trouble getting ready for school on time." Ask him to do specific, short tasks: "Would you please feed the dog this morning?" Give frequent reminders: "Don't forget to brush Spike this afternoon." Show your appreciation: "I'm glad you played with Missy. She really needed to run around."

Although you may be disappointed that your child doesn't care for the dog on his own, he'll still have the experience of chipping in and helping in a practical, necessary way. The real value of your pet is the chance it offers your family to share enjoyable times and feel more connected.

How do I get my child to go to bed and wake up on her own?

Parents want their ten- to thirteen-year-old to act responsibly at night and in the morning. They expect her to go to bed at a reasonable time so she can be healthy and alert, and so they can have time alone at the end of the evening. They also expect their child to get up and get ready on her own each morning. But many kids have trouble with daily routines. In some homes, bedtime and mornings are times for threats, frustration, and conflicts.

Kids resist going to sleep because after a day of school, homework, and chores, they don't want their free time to end. They'd rather read, watch TV, talk on the phone, use the computer, or play. Also, as they get older, they want more independence and may argue against a set bedtime. If parents are very rigid about evening routines, kids may procrastinate as a way of rebelling. And some children simply don't require as much sleep as their parents want them to have.

Morning conflicts can be as troublesome as bedtime ones, especially if everyone has to be out the door early. Some kids, perhaps like their parents, don't function well when they first wake up. Others may be tired because they aren't getting enough sleep. If the family's morning is always rushed and stressful, a child may dawdle to avoid confrontations or to show resistance. She also may oversleep because she doesn't want to face problems at school, at home, or with peers.

If you and your child argue frequently about morning and evening routines, try changing your approach. She may be more responsible and cooperative if you're flexible and allow her some choice. As an experiment, push her bedtime back half and hour and see how she gets along, or try letting her stay up later than usual as long as she remains in her room.

You may decide to turn the decision about bedtime over to her. Many kids who are given that freedom go to sleep at a reasonable time. When your child no longer has a rigid bedtime to resist, the evening routine may stop being an issue, and staying up late may stop being so attractive. She'll probably go to bed when she's tired.

Letting her choose when to go to sleep doesn't mean giving up all control. You still have to set limits: "Ten o'clock is just too late for a week night." Give reminders: "It's getting late. You have to get ready for bed." If she consistently stays up too long or is tired in the mornings, she's not ready to take responsibility for bedtime. Decide on an earlier time for her, but give her another chance to change in a few months.

Once she feels she has some say in decisions about bedtime, she may be more willing to compromise in other areas of her life, including how she acts toward you and her siblings and how she reacts in the mornings. If mornings continue to be a problem even after you've eased up on bedtime, talk to her about it: "It seems to take you so long to get ready." If you want her to get herself up, firmly remind her about setting her alarm. Don't turn this into a struggle over personal responsibility, however. It's also fine if you just get her up yourself each morning.

She may always wake up feeling grumpy. Try being patient, but set limits on her behavior and attitude: "You have to stop snapping at me when you get up." Change parts of your family's routine until you find a morning arrangement that works. For instance, let your child shower last so she can have a few minutes more sleep, make breakfast for her so she doesn't have to do that task, or have everyone get up ten minutes earlier so there's less hurry.

If nothing helps, try to find out why your child is reluctant to start her day. Is she having trouble at school? With peers? Is there too much tension at home? Are there too many rules and chores? Talk these issues over with her and let her know you're concerned and determined to help. You'll send a message of love and care, which might motivate her to take more responsibility for her mornings and evenings.

How can I help my child get ready for his Bar Mitzvah?

Bar and Bat Mitzvahs are the traditional coming-of-age ceremonies for thirteen-year-old Jewish boys and girls. The ceremony is the culmination of years of general study plus an intensive six months of tutoring and preparation. The Bar Mitzvah itself is a moving and spiritually fulfilling event. As the child reads and interprets his Torah portion, he offers wisdom and insight to his listeners. The periods before and after the Bar Mitzvah are exciting, but they can sometimes be hectic or stressful.

As family members look forward to the ceremony, they may have ambivalent feelings. Twelve-year-olds wonder how they'll do: "What if I make a mistake?" "Will my speech be all right?" The hours spent on Hebrew and Bar Mitzvah preparation can cause considerable pressure: "I'll never be ready!" "All I do is homework and my Torah portion!"

Parents feel proud and sentimental as their child prepares to take on the responsibilities of a Jewish adult; however, preparations for the coming ceremony can put a strain on family life. Parents have to support their child as he learns and practices, and help him focus on the spiritual meaning of the event. They also have to take care of the practical arrangements, including scheduling lessons, driving, discussing the service, working with the rabbi and cantor, and reserving the sanctuary. If a party is planned, they have to handle other details, too: invitations, food, entertainment, decorations, and clothes. These responsibilities, added to everyday routines, leave many parents feeling stressed.

Siblings, too, can be affected by the Bar Mitzvah. A younger child may be jealous: "It's not fair! I want my Bat Mitzvah when Jessie has hers." An older child who's already had a Bar Mitzvah may feel neglected as attention shifts to his sibling.

As you and your child approach the Bar Mitzvah, you can decrease stress by concentrating on the religious nature of the occasion, rather than the preparations or the party. Talk about Judaism and your child's connection to past generations. Discuss Jewish history, holidays, and customs, the Holocaust, and the beliefs and history of other religions. Also emphasize the need to help others. Many families make community service and charitable donations an important part of the Bar Mitzvah period.

Get involved with your child's studies. Your interest, help, and support will make it easier for him to learn his Torah portion and prayers and write his speech. Involve him in planning the service if the rabbi allows some flexibility. Your child may be able to choose prayers, recite a poem, or pick out appropriate music.

As you plan your party, let your choices reflect your family's style, budget, and values. You may have to resist pressure from relatives who want you to celebrate as they would, and you may also have to resist internal pressure to "keep up" with friends and acquaintances.

Your child will be feeling social pressures of his own: "I want kids to like my party." "Why can't we have the same things Aaron had?" If he feels in competition with others, help him focus on the meaning of the occasion and the honor of having friends and family with him. Whatever your celebration is like, he, as the center of attention, will enjoy it.

It's appropriate to expect your other children to be happy for the Bar Mitzvah child. However, you may have to help them cope with jealousy. Encourage them to share their thoughts: "Brian's been getting a lot of attention because his Bar Mitzvah's coming up. What do you think of all this?" Spend extra time with them and involve them, if they wish, in some of the preparations.

Since Bar Mitzvahs are planned far in advance, there's always a chance of unexpected events, even disappointments. Illness, bad weather, or family conflicts may interfere with plans. A relative may not come. One of your child's classmates may have a Bar Mitzvah on the same day as your child's. If you remain calm in the face of changes or disappointments, he will follow your lead.

After the Bar Mitzvah, you'll feel happy and proud but also somewhat let down after so much anticipation. Your child's feelings may be similar to yours, but he'll quickly be distracted by school, social life, sports, and other interests.

Your final responsibility is to have him write thank-you notes. Make up a schedule: "I want you to write five cards every night." Give him a set of sample notes to follow. Sit with him and offer suggestions on personalizing his cards.

If he received money as a gift, give him guidelines for handling it—have him save a large portion and keep a small amount at home to spend as he wishes. Some parents ask their child to give one of his presents to each of his siblings. Many parents ask their child to donate some gift money to charity. Being generous to those in need is a value that is particularly appropriate at the time of a Bar Mitzvah.

PEERS

Should I be nervous about peer influence?

Parents worry about the effect of peer pressure on their child, especially once she turns thirteen. They hope she'll be strong enough to reject what she knows is wrong. But they understand from their own childhoods that resisting peer pressure is difficult. They also remember how they were turned off by standard warnings and lectures: "If your friend jumped off a bridge, would you?"

Peer influence is an inevitable part of pre- and early adolescence. Kids look to each other when choosing clothes, hairstyles, or music. They behave the way friends do because that makes them feel part of a group. Peer influence often can be positive. Kids suggest good books, introduce friends to new interests, and encourage each other to study, take on neighborhood jobs, or be more polite. One twelve-year-old told his friend, "You could be nicer when you ask your mom to do things for you."

Of course, there's also a negative side to peer influence. A susceptible child may be swayed to join a rough crowd or do something dangerous, thoughtless, or illegal: intimidate younger children, shoplift, get into fights, drink, smoke, or try drugs.

Kids who are most vulnerable to peer pressure are those who don't feel close to their parents or who don't receive firm, positive direction from them. A child may be largely ignored at home or forced to follow overly strict rules. As a result, she may look to friends for the attention and guidance she lacks at home. She also may be insecure. She follows her peers' bad suggestions to gain a sense of identity and feel accepted.

Most kids these ages, however, aren't led into deep trouble by peers. A child chooses friends who are like her. And ten- to thirteen-year-olds usually can't be persuaded to violate their basic family values. They can be talked into mischief, though, so parents have to stay alert. One twelve-year-old snuck out of a school dance, violating the rules. He told his parents, "Scott and John told me to." He wasn't thinking about the rules, the worry he caused, or the potential danger. He only considered the thrill of the moment and the fun of being with his friends.

Your child will be less affected by negative peer pressure if she has a good self-image and a strong connection to family. The more involved you are with her, the more she'll want to please you. And if her identity is relatively secure, she won't be so dependent on the approval of her friends.

Set limits on her behavior so she'll know what you expect and what the consequences will be if she doesn't follow the rules. If you find out after the fact that she did something you disapprove of, discipline her. Then keep a closer eye on her and her friends.

Discuss peer pressure with her. Let her know you expect her to stand up to the group at times, even though you realize how difficult that can be. Try role-playing: "What would you do if a friend stole a necklace while you were shopping together?" "If everyone was picking on someone at school how would you act?" Let her know that being independent won't mean the end of her social life.

Encourage her to share her worries and talk about her relationships with friends. Peer pressure and risky behavior will be increasing concerns as your child gets older, and you need to anticipate the inevitable problems. As she moves through adolescence, she'll need your guidance, watchfulness, and support if she's going to resist the pressure to "go along."

"My friends get to do more than I do!" How do I react?

When kids complain "I never get to do anything good," parents sometimes react with anger and frustration: "So we're horrible parents." "Maybe you should go live with Ray if you think his parents treat him so much better." "Why don't you stop feeling sorry for yourself? You do a whole lot more than I did when I was a kid."

Kids these ages want permission to do what their friends are doing, whether it's staying out later, wearing makeup, seeing certain movies, or going to an unchaperoned party. They aren't thinking about safety, arrangements, costs, or their parents' values. And when they complain, they're not deliberately trying to hurt their parent's feelings or act in inconsiderate ways. They're simply focusing on their need to be part of the group.

When a child repeatedly makes requests that his parents consider unreasonable, they may feel upset not only with him but with his friends. Parents wonder if their child is too dependent on his peers, and they worry that particular friends may be bad influences: "I don't trust Jose's judgment. I don't want you playing inside his house."

Parents also become frustrated with other parents, especially those they believe are too lenient. One mother refused to let her eleven-year-old walk around a mall with a classmate who was allowed to spend hours at the shopping center unsupervised: "I don't care if Angela's mother lets her go by herself. I'm not comfortable letting you wander in the mall without an adult."

If your child complains about the restrictions you impose, try to listen patiently without responding immediately. He may just need to vent his feelings: "It's not fair! I'm always the first one who has to go home." "You're too protective. You worry all the time." He may not argue as much with your decisions if he feels heard.

Avoid angry defensive statements, even if you feel unfairly attacked. When he says, "You never let me do anything," explain why you're refusing permission for a particular activity; if your refusal is non-negotiable, let him know that there's no point in trying to persuade you: "Every family is different. These are our family's rules."

Offer acceptable alternative activities: "Call Jay and ask if he can come over." "See if you can find a friend who'd like to go to the pool." "Let's stop at the video store so you can get something to watch."

Periodically re-evaluate your rules, and gradually allow him more freedom as he gets older. But as you ease some restrictions, continue to give firm direction: "Stay with your friends." "Check in with me." And continue to say no to things that seem unsafe or inappropriate. Throughout these pre- and early adolescent years, your child needs clear limits, guidelines, and supervision.

Should I limit phone use?

As pre-teens become increasingly involved with friends, they spend more time on the phone. Some make short calls for practical reasons: "When's the game?" "Do you want to come over?" "What's the homework?" Others spend long periods on the phone every day. They call each other to talk about school, tests, social activities, who likes whom, clothes, weather, sports, music, movies, and families. They even call to "watch" television together: "We've both got *The Simpsons* on."

Parents wonder why their child wants to make and receive so many calls. Adults try to minimize their own time on the phone, especially in the evenings. Yet some kids want to talk constantly, even to people they've just seen. A girl leaving a friend after a sleepover may yell, "Call me!" as she gets in the car. One parent described her thirteen-year-old's visit to her grandparents: "Hi, Grandma and Grandpa. Can I use your phone?"

There are many reasons children like to call each other. Talking on the phone is an activity—something enjoyable to do, especially during the long afternoons if parents aren't home. It's a way to stay busy.

Phoning also gives kids a chance to talk about their feelings. Twelve- and thirteen-year-olds share less and less of their personal lives with their parents. They'd rather discuss family and social problems with friends who won't criticize or lecture them. As friendships become increasingly intense at these ages, kids stay in touch out of a sense of loyalty and concern: "Did you get in trouble with your dad?"

Another reason friends call each other is to finish conversations they've started in school. Although classmates are together all day, they rarely have time to socialize. Since talking in class can get them in trouble, they call each other at home to talk in detail about the day's events.

Most parents don't want their child to spend a lot of time on the phone. They worry about the hours away from homework, chores, and physical activity. They dislike the frequent interruptions caused by phone calls and get angry when the line is busy. "I'm expecting an important business call," sometimes gets the response, "But I have to tell Jen just one more thing." In addition, parents don't like siblings arguing about phone use: "You always let Michelle talk longer." "John's on the phone all the time. It's not fair!"

Some parents try to control phone calls with rigid rules, but this rarely works. Tracking calls and strictly allotting phone time takes considerable effort, and there are always special circumstances. If parents forbid all weeknight social calls, their child may end up sneaking calls or lying: "I wasn't on the phone." "I just had to ask a question about our math assignment."

One solution to arguments about phone calls is flexible scheduling: "You can use the phone from 7:30 to 8:00 and then it's Tim's turn." If you try this, make sure all family members know there will be exceptions to the schedule. An important call might come in, someone may have to return a call, or an extra few minutes may be needed to finish a conversation.

You also can try a flexible approach without specific scheduling. If you remind your children to be patient and considerate of each others' needs, they may be able to juggle phone time according to daily circumstances. You and your spouse also should try to follow the guidelines you set up. Your child will feel angry and uncooperative if all of your calls, even unimportant ones, take precedence over hers.

If you find your child is not spending enough time on homework or other responsibilities, limit her use of the phone: "You can only make a call when your assignments are done." "You have a big project due in two days. No calls until it's finished." You also should limit your child's calls if you want to spend more time with her: "I just got home and I'd like to hear about your day. You can call Carmen later."

If she spends too much of her free time on the phone, suggest alternatives. You don't want phone use to be a substitute for other activities. Try interesting her in drawing, playing a game, writing, reading, going outside, having a friend over, or taking part in after-school activities or sports.

When she uses the phone (even if it's her own phone line), be sure she knows how to act responsibly—no late-night calls received or made, no trick calls, no calls with silent friends eavesdropping, no rudeness to adults who answer the phone. Be aware of the ways she uses, or misuses, services such as conference calling.

Telephone technology changes constantly, offering options that may help (but also may complicate) home phone use: answering machines, additional phone lines, call-waiting, call-forwarding, computer-dedicated phone lines, cell phones, caller ID, and other services and devices. You and your child may be using email and computerized instant messaging as phone alternatives. Whatever options you try, continually encourage your child to share, to be reasonable and responsible, and to show respect for others.

My child feels unpopular. How can I help?

Being part of a group is very important to pre- and early adolescents. They spend a great deal of time thinking about their popularity and the main factors that affect it—personality, athletic skills, talents, and looks: "Will Scott invite me to his party?" "Am I as pretty as Lisa?" "Is Ian going to make the team instead of me?" "Who will I walk to school with?" "Will Samir like me if he knows I'm friends with Joey?"

Kids constantly weigh their relative positions in a group. Since friendships can shift at these ages, a child may feel liked one week and rejected the next. Sometimes children who have been best friends through much of elementary school drift apart because of differing interests and developmental changes. If one joins a new group, the other may feel temporarily alone. A pair of friends may be broken up by a third child who bonds with only one of the original two. In some cases, a child may be deliberately targeted by school or neighborhood bullies.

Most kids, however, don't intend to be cruel. They simply aren't thinking about the consequences of ending friendships, but instead concentrating on their own interests and desires to be liked.

Parents have mixed reactions to their child's worries about popularity. At times they're impatient with concerns about trivial incidents: "I'm sure Beth still likes you. It doesn't matter if she says hi to Anne first." They know that these kinds of issues come and go.

However, parents suffer along with their child when he feels truly rejected. They're upset by his hurt feelings, anger, and confusion. Yet, they can't make the situation better, as they could during earlier years, with a phone call to another parent or an invitation to a new friend. Parents can say, "Call someone else from your class," but they can't force others to accept their child and they can't create friendships for him.

What they can and should do is listen and offer reassurance and help. A child who's vulnerable needs a great deal of support, and if he doesn't get it from his parents, he won't get it at all. They must remind him that he's worthy of friendship and love and that he'll get through these tough times.

When your child talks about feeling unpopular, be a sympathetic, understanding listener. If he expresses inevitable doubts about his place in the group, help him put his experience in perspective: "Everybody has an occasional bad day when they play baseball. I'm sure your friends didn't mean to insult you."

If he describes deeper hurt, first offer comfort and remind him of his strengths: "This is a hard time for you. But you're a great kid and I know you'll make new friends." Pay enough attention to his friendships so that you know when things aren't going well. If he doesn't talk about social problems, raise the subject yourself: "I notice Nick doesn't call here anymore. Are you two still friends?" "It's hard to talk about feelings, but I'd like to help you." Share stories about your experiences while growing up: "I know how you feel about Josh. There was a really popular cheerleader named Sandy in my class and I was jealous of her and wanted to be friends at the same time."

If you think he's losing friends because of negative behavior, let him know that he has to be less aggressive and self-centered, and generally nicer to people: "You need to listen to other kids' suggestions more often." "Don't be so tough on your friends."

If shyness is keeping him from joining a group, have him invite friends over individually. You also can help him focus on hobbies and organized activities he enjoys. That way he can meet people with similar interests and start new friendships with kids who are more like him.

Talk to him about why kids exclude each other and why friendships change. He should understand that former friends probably didn't mean to hurt his feelings—they just developed new interests.

Likewise, if your child has given up some of his own friendships, help him see what the consequences may have been. If you think that he's mistreating others because they're unpopular, demand that he change his behavior. Explain how it feels to be ostracized, and don't accept excuses for his actions. If you find him consistently acting out and bullying, you probably need professional guidance.

You also may need help if your child is the one being deliberately excluded or picked on. Try to find out what's going on and why he's a target (since some kids "invite" bullying). Contact his teachers if you think that will make a difference, consistently give him help and encouragement, and get professional advice if you believe that emotional problems are either causing or resulting from his lack of popularity.

It's become impossible to discuss even the most ordinary issues of unpopularity without at least mentioning the tragic cases of school violence associated with a pre-teen or teenager's sense of isolation and anger. While news about these frightening incidents receives a great deal of attention, the events are extremely rare. The real lesson for everyone is that parents—and not schools—play the most important day-to-day role in how kids act, feel about themselves, and treat others. It's appropriate to expect teachers to set and enforce limits on all students and to encourage inclusiveness. But realistically, parents are the ones who have to stay on top of what's going on, teach responsible behavior, and be active advocates for their child.

EVERYDAY CONFLICTS

How should I discipline my child?

Parents wish their pre- and early adolescent had more self-control and better judgment. They want to spend less time supervising and disciplining their child. Yet, kids these ages continue to be irresponsible at times. They may make bad decisions, spend too much money, stay out too long, show disrespect, curse, skip a class, or neglect chores.

In some families, discipline becomes a major issue. Kids misbehave frequently or in serious ways and parents struggle for control. In other families, misbehavior is minor, and discipline is not a source of stress. The difference often lies in the nature of the parent-child relationship.

Parents who show continual love and respect for their child, spend time with her, and communicate their values give her a strong incentive to behave well. She values her relationship with them and wants to please, not disappoint them. In addition, the guilt she feels if she lets them down helps keep her from doing something wrong, even when they aren't there to supervise.

To improve your child's behavior, begin by strengthening your relationship with her. The closer you are, the more effectively you can influence her conscience and help her become self-disciplined. Take an interest in her activities and include her in yours. Let her know that you care about her opinions and feelings, and that your love—although not necessarily your approval—is unconditional.

If she does something wrong, show your anger and disappointment, but don't yell insults or use put-downs and sarcasm: "I told you that you couldn't watch TV until you finished your homework, and I expect you to listen to me." It can be useful to stir up some feelings of guilt or shame to help her remember how to act: "When you didn't call, I was worried that something happened to you." You want her to think about the consequences of her behavior. She may act more responsibly next time in order to avoid feeling bad. One twelve-year-old said, "Feeling guilty is worse than getting grounded."

Talk to your child about her misbehavior: "Why did you go home with Jeremy when I told you not to?" Listen to her side, then explain what was wrong with her actions and what the consequences will be. A discussion is more effective than a lecture, especially because at these ages she feels that her good intentions should count as much as her actions: "I went home with Jeremy because he needed my help with homework." She will tune you out or react angrily if you do all the talking and she's forced to listen to long, negative comments about herself.

Don't slap or hit her. Her behavior will become worse rather than better. She'll be so angry that she'll continue to misbehave or she'll aim her resentment at siblings and peers, becoming aggressive, rebellious, and selfish.

Although physical punishment is not effective, let her know her misbehavior will have consequences. Use whatever seems to work best: grounding; taking away allowance or privileges; refusing permission to use the phone, computer, or TV.

Be sure the consequences you pick will have the desired effect—to get your child thinking about and improving her behavior. If you always ground her for a day or two, she may continue to misbehave, knowing the punishment is short-lived and not severe.

On the other hand, don't be too harsh or strict. If she's grounded for weeks or months or constantly loses her allowance, she'll focus on her unfair treatment. She'll be unwilling to change her behavior, and if she's forced to, she'll misbehave in other ways. She may become sneaky, resentful, or withdrawn.

In general, be flexible about consequences. If one technique doesn't work, try another. You may need to talk more and punish less. Or, if you depend too heavily on reasoning with your child, you may need to set firmer limits with heavier consequences. If you're having trouble finding an effective punishment, ask her what she thinks a fair consequence for her misbehavior would be. While her suggestions may be too mild or too harsh, you may get some useful ideas.

Remember that setting limits alone won't solve ongoing behavior problems. Continually work on establishing better communication and understanding. Look for the causes of inappropriate behavior. Are there frequent family conflicts? Is she dealing with your divorce? School difficulties? Does she feel neglected or less favored than a sibling? You may need a therapist's help to find the roots of discipline problems.

Finally, set a good example. Show her, through your actions, how you expect her to behave and treat people. Try to be thoughtful, concerned, and courteous with others as well as with her.

How can I be more patient?

Parents' impatience takes several forms. One is situational—they lose their tempers and snap at their child for his misbehavior. A second form is more general. They lack the patience to listen to him, get involved in his interests, accompany him to activities, watch him play sports, or help him with schoolwork. Both kinds of impatience can have a negative impact on children and make parents feel guilty.

All parents lose patience at times, especially when they're rushed or busy or feeling badgered by their children's demands: "I've got to get to work." "I'm trying to pay bills. Don't make so much noise." "I can't drive you to Glen's again." Parents experiencing stress at work or at home are especially likely to snap at their child.

Such impatience due to circumstances is often mild and temporary. More harmful is constant criticism and rudeness. Parents with a low tolerance for frustration may routinely yell at their children, ridicule them, and call them names: "Don't be so stupid! I've told you a hundred times not to leave the front door open." "All you do is whine." "I'm not a servant. Make your own lunch."

Parents with high expectations and a strong desire to be in control can become intolerant when things don't go their way. They expect perfection. If their child can't meet their standards, they react with harsh impatience. In the process, they may hurt his self-confidence, harm family relationships, and cause him to become less, rather than more, cooperative as he copies the treatment he's received.

In less dramatic ways, parents also show impatience when they neglect to make time for their child. It takes a reordering of priorities to put aside adult concerns and answer a child's question, look at his model rocket, walk him to the basketball court, listen to his music, go to his school assembly, or read a book to him. Even the busiest parents can stop what they're doing several times a day to concentrate on their child. But some parents, even ones with time to spare—don't make their child's needs and interests a priority.

Becoming a more patient parent takes purposeful effort and may require a change in attitude, priorities, or behavior. If you're easily frustrated, try to make your life less stressful by easing up on your expectations. It's more important to spend time with your child than to have a clean house. It's better to stay calm during the early evening than to prepare a complex dish for dinner. If work or family problems are difficult to cope with, you may find stress-reduction techniques useful. You can learn about them from books, magazines, or classes.

Think about your tone of voice when you talk to your child—try using the same tone you'd like him to use. Instead of shouting, "Hurry up!" or, "Get going!" say, "Please hurry or we'll be late." The more you take your child's feelings into consideration, the better his behavior is likely to be. In the long run, he'll respond more positively to your calm words than to rude orders.

Make a decision to spend more time with him. Put your book or work down periodically, stay off the phone at night, forgo some evening plans, and get involved with him. This is not always easy, since it means giving of yourself without necessarily receiving an immediate return. But there are definite benefits. He will have you as a model of more tolerant, patient behavior. He'll feel better about himself because you're interested in him. And the relationship between the two of you will improve, making it easier for you to react to his behavior in a mature way.

I want my child to be more honest. What can I do?

"It wasn't me who left food in the basement."

"There wasn't any change from the money you gave me for the movies."

"You never told me I was supposed to feed the cat."

Kids lie for many reasons. The main one is to avoid getting into trouble. A child who fears punishment may lie, hoping she'll avoid the consequences of misbehaving. The harsher the possible punishment and the stricter and more inflexible her parents are, the more likely she is to bend the truth.

Kids also lie to get out of chores or schoolwork ("Can I stay home today? I have a really bad stomachache") or to feel part of a group ("Yeah, I saw that video too"). Kids may use lies to impress others and prop up a poor self-image: "I got an A on that test." "I go to Florida all the time." "The coach said I was the best on the team."

Some kids lie because they're able to get away with it. Their parents fail to set adequate limits and don't teach the value of honesty. And finally, twelve- and thirteen-year-olds sometimes lie to protect their friends. At these ages they become more secretive and show great loyalty to friends, even ones who smoke, drink, cut classes, or do other things parents don't approve of.

To get your child to become more honest, be unambiguous about your expectations: "I won't accept lying." "People in a family have to trust each other. If I can't trust you, I can't let you do the things you ask and I can't count on you to be responsible." "I always expect you to tell me the truth."

Be a good role model to your child. Since your child will know when you're lying to her, be honest about everyday events as well as important issues such as illness, separation, and unemployment. Show your distaste for acquaintances, celebrities, politicians, and publications that exaggerate or distort the truth. Don't make excuses for people who lie.

Make a clear distinction between acceptable white lies told outside the family and the need for honesty within the family. She can understand that white lies are sometimes necessary for safety or to keep from hurting someone's feelings: "I had to tell her I liked her hair. She just had it cut." "If someone calls when I'm not home, just say I'm in the shower."

Set firm limits and let her know there will be consequences if she doesn't tell you the truth. Punishment can include grounding, or loss of allowance or privileges. Use a firm, calm tone to discuss the seriousness of lying.

You may find that punishment isn't needed at all. If you emphasize your disappointment and hurt, she may decide that the consequences of lying—including feeling ashamed and guilty—are worse than the consequences of confessing to the original misbehavior. Appealing to her conscience this way will work best if you have a good relationship and if she values your approval. An important way to get her to become more honest is to strengthen the ties between you.

When she does tell the truth about misbehaving, praise her honesty. If she lies but later offers a genuine apology for doing so, accept the apology. You will still have to decide if the original misbehavior requires punishment. Being honest shouldn't wipe out the consequence of negative actions, but you may decide to be a little more lenient to encourage her honesty.

Don't put yourself in a bind by offering to forgo punishment in exchange for the truth. You'll lose no matter what your child says. Either you'll give up the option of punishment even if you find out it's necessary, or you'll change your mind once you hear the truth and come down harshly, in which case she will see you as dishonest yourself. Instead of being lenient or manipulative, simply demand the information you want, make guesses until you arrive at the truth, or punish your child if she won't tell you want you want to know.

If your child regularly lies and exaggerates, try to find out why. Are you too accommodating? Too inflexible? Does your child feel jealous of a sibling? Do you spend enough time with her? Do you give her enough positive feedback and encouragement? Is family discord causing stress? Does she have low self-esteem? If lying is a symptom of deeper problems, limits and punishment won't improve her behavior, you'll need to change the circumstances that keep her from being truthful.

How can I help my child be a better sport?

Most parents want their child to be a good winner and loser. They want him to try his best in every situation and accept any outcome with grace. They have a strong stake in his sense of sportsmanship. They believe his behavior reflects on them, and if he's a poor sport, they're not only disappointed and angry, but embarrassed.

Kids like to win games, have the highest grades, get the starring roles, be first in line, win elections, and get prizes. Most of the time, though, a child is not number one. Defeat and mistakes are inevitable. Occasionally a coach or teacher will give a good sportsmanship award or credit a child with trying. But there are few rewards for those who lose.

A child who is a poor sport loses control easily. He may be moody or angry. He may have outbursts and throw a tennis racket, tear up a paper with a poor grade, kick a chair, or curse at an opponent. He also may be disrespectful to a teacher, counselor, umpire, coach, or parent as he vents his frustration. On a team he may belittle his peers: "Why can't you hit the ball?" "What kind of throw was that?" "It's your fault we're losing the game."

Sometimes a child will get down on himself and question his abilities: "I'm never entering another stupid art show again." "I always lose the camper contests. I must be the worst kid here." "I'll never get on a select soccer team."

While no one likes to lose, there are several reasons why some kids become poor sports. A child may have unreasonable expectations and become upset when he fails to live up to them. His parents may encourage his high standards by overemphasizing winning: "I hope you beat this kid because I hate the way he plays and I can't stand his father."

Parents may be impossible to please: "You're not trying hard enough." "I know you could have won the science fair if you had put more time into it." "Too bad you came in second." Some parents don't set firm enough limits on their child's displays of bad sportsmanship. They encourage his misbehavior by not trying to stop it. Poor sportsmanship is sometimes a sign of low self-esteem. A child who lacks confidence may get easily upset when he doesn't do well. Lack of sportsmanship may also indicate that he's in over his head, frustrated because he's competing in situations where he doesn't stand a fair chance. A child who doesn't enjoy competition may not react well no matter how much support he receives.

Most poor sports are aware of being out of control and would like to change their behavior. However, they don't know how to handle difficult situations. They need help and guidance when they make a mistake or lose a competition.

Tell your child about how important good sportsmanship is. Talk about how other people—friends, acquaintances, famous competitors—react to success and adversity: "She lost the election, but she still promised to support her opponent." "When that tennis player threw his racket and cursed, everybody booed." Let him know that it's also important to be a good winner, one who is gracious rather than cocky.

Before he enters a competition, remind him about his behavior: "You look better when you show control." "Have fun." "I don't want to hear you yell or complain." Set limits on his negative actions and discuss consequences: "If you keep throwing your helmet, I won't let you play." "If you can't control your emotions, you'll have to quit the swim team." Praise signs of good sportsmanship. If he handles himself well reward him with a hug, a pack of baseball cards, a note, or a treat.

Evaluate the competitions he participates in. Perhaps they're too stressful. Some kids are spurred on by competition, while others are upset by too much of it. Your child's sportsmanship may improve in a less intense atmosphere.

If you suspect that his attitude is rooted in a poor self-image, think of ways to increase his confidence. Spend more time with him, have fun together, encourage him in all his activities.

Don't let winning or losing affect your love and acceptance of him in any way.

Try to be a good sport yourself. Do you react angrily when things don't go your way at work, at home, on the road, or during leisure time? Do you congratulate others on their successes? Are you gracious when you succeed? Do you put too much pressure on your child? If you change your attitude, you are likely to see a difference in his behavior.

Talk to coaches or teachers about helping your child become a better sport. Suggest they hold a team or class meeting on the values and characteristics of good sportsmanship. Look for books or articles on the subject to share with your child.

At times, he may have a legitimate reason for feeling "things aren't fair—I shouldn't have lost." An umpire may make a bad call. A teacher may make a mistake. Another player may cheat. One girl became upset in gym class as the teacher continually called on the most skilled girls to demonstrate volleyball techniques. When she asked why, the teacher said, "I don't want the other girls to be embarrassed if they miss the ball." Your child may have a right to complain, but he should learn, with your help and guidance, how to handle situations without acting like a bad sport.

How can I encourage self-confidence?

One of the most important tasks parents have is to consistently let their child know she's capable, loved, and worthy of attention. Her self-esteem is based largely on feedback from her parents. If they show they value her, she'll generally feel good about herself. If they concentrate on her faults, she may develop a poor self-image.

It's normal for ten- to thirteen-year-olds to have changing opinions and fleeting self-doubts during this self-conscious stage. One moment they boast about their skills and the next moment put themselves down: "I'm a good hockey player." "I can't sing." "I'm too tall." "I'm smart and do really well in school." "I can make people laugh." "I stink at lacrosse." "I'm so fat and ugly." "I do everything wrong."

Because kid's feelings about themselves fluctuate, it's important for parents to emphasize strengths rather than weaknesses. The attitude a child develops about herself during pre-adolescence, whether positive or negative, helps determine the direction she'll go in when she enters adolescence, a period of even greater uncertainty.

Some parents are not supportive. In an effort to improve their child's behavior or to express frustration and disappointment, they speak harshly: "You're such a slob." "Why can't you be like your sister?" "What's wrong with you? Why don't you speak up?" "You run too slow." "You'll never get to college at this rate." A child who hears these messages feels she can never please her parents or live up to their standards. Her grades, her appearance, her abilities, or her personality will never be good enough. In such circumstances, it's hard for her to develop confidence.

Some parents who speak negatively were themselves criticized as children and may have grown up with a lack of confidence. Even though they once struggled against harsh words and treatment, they repeat the pattern with their own children.

Other adults, particularly teachers, can influence a child's self-image. Schools rarely work hard enough at building confidence or offering praise. More often, students are reprimanded for turning in work late, making mistakes, or talking. One child may get a poor grade on a project even though she put in hours of hard work. Another who is forgetful may be embarrassed in front of the class: "You're always turning your work in late."

Coaches, too, can affect a child's sense of confidence. An encouraging coach can make a child feel good, regardless of her athletic ability. A demanding coach can make even a skilled young athlete doubt herself: "One more bad pitch and you're out." "What's wrong with you? Go after the ball."

You probably know if your child lacks confidence, since a poor self-image is hard to hide. She may frequently put herself down or say, "I can't," "I'm no good," or, "I'm the worst on the team." You can tell a lot from her body language, especially if she slouches, doesn't make eye contact, or carries herself in an overly self-conscious way. If you detect a consistent pattern of negative thinking, you need to help her feel better about herself.

Start by evaluating the messages you give her. Do you encourage her self-doubt? Are your expectations too high? Do you respect her feelings? Are you too demanding? Do you say things that make her feel inferior? Do you tell her you love her? Are you hard to please? Do you dwell on her weaknesses but take her strengths for granted?

Give her more verbal rewards. Praise her accomplishments and point out her talents and endearing traits. Talk often about her successes and ignore or minimize her faults. Encourage her and offer support when she takes risks such as trying out for a school play.

Talk, as a family, about what you like in yourselves and each other, and what you have to offer: "Your smile makes other people feel happy." "Why do you think Alison and Megan like you so much?" Discuss issues that contribute to your child's lack of confidence: "Would being taller really make you a better person?" "What's wrong with being shy?"

Help your child find activities in which she can succeed. If she's not good at team sports, have her try an individual sport such as swimming, tennis, karate, or gymnastics. Encourage her to pursue special interests in computers, music, art, or dance. Involve her in community service—she'll feel good about helping others.

If she's discouraged about her schoolwork, help her with difficult lessons and assignments, consider hiring a tutor, and investigate special programs that might make her feel better about her abilities as a student.

Once you start treating your child in a more positive way, you should see changes in her behavior and attitudes. She may seem more confident and begin to smile more. She also may start to treat friends and family members in nicer ways as she begins feeling better about herself. In all areas of her life, improved self-esteem will help her feel happier, more satisfied, and more successful.

Why is my child a show-off?

"Hey, watch me!"
"Look what I've got!"
"I'm buying a better one!"
"See what I can do!"
All kids, particularly at ten and eleven, show off. They demonstrate their skills or show possessions they're proud of. Bragging can be a way to get peer approval or to feel equal to others. It's also done in fun. As long as a child is generally caring and responsible, occasional showing off is not a problem.

Some parents actually encourage their child to be a show-off. A parent who repeatedly says, "You're the only skilled one on the team," or,

"You're much prettier than the other girls around here," will reinforce self-centered ways. A child who's not taught to consider others' feelings won't realize that most adults and children find showing off offensive.

While some kids are encouraged in their negative behavior, most who constantly boast and act silly do so because they're insecure or unhappy. A child who behaves this way may feel unpopular with his peers or may lack sufficient support or guidance from his parents. He may show off in order to hide disturbing feelings.

Such a child often creates problems. At school he may be the "class clown," and at home he may argue frequently with his siblings. With friends, he may be silly and disruptive. Such acting out is a way for him to release frustration and seek attention.

If your child consistently shows off, try to find out why. Begin by asking him what he thinks, although you may find him confused and unable to explain his feelings. Ask yourself these questions: Do I spend enough time with him? Do I encourage and compliment him? Does he feel overshadowed by his siblings? Is he jealous of them? Does he have friends? Does he do well in school? Is he compensating for what he sees as a defect, such as being overweight or small for his age?

Also ask yourself if you are somehow encouraging your child to show off. Do you talk about respecting other people? Do you make it clear that bragging is unacceptable? Do you set a good example for him? If you haven't been setting firm enough limits, let him know what your expectations are. Talk to him about the importance of being considerate, modest, and patient.

If you have been setting limits on showing off, becoming stricter won't necessarily change your child's behavior. He may feel angry, pressured, and upset at not being able to please you. He may continue to show off and become louder and more boisterous to rebel and express his frustration.

Instead, help him deal with the problems that cause him to show off. If he's doing poorly in school, work with him on lessons and assignments and talk to his teachers. If he has few friends, make it easier for him to join a team or have classmates over.

If the problem is his relationship with the family, work on changing the way you treat him and his siblings. Concentrate on his strong points rather than his weak ones. Don't compare him to his siblings. Try to give him enough positive attention so that he feels good about himself and has less need to brag.

Will we always argue about movies, music, video games, the computer, and TV shows?

"Your music's too loud!"

"Turn the TV off!"

"That movie is way too violent."

"Get off the Internet."

As kids get older, they struggle with parents over control of leisure activities. Kids want to relax with TV, satisfy their curiosity by watching R-rated movies, listen to popular music, explore the Internet, and play video games until they win. To a child, these are enjoyable—and at times fascinating—activities. She gets to do what her friends do, stay busy, find things out, and avoid stressful situations. She doesn't always think about the value of these pursuits. She just wants to pass the time, get involved in something interesting, and have fun.

Parents do think about the consequences. They know that time spent in front of the TV or playing video or computer games is time taken away from schoolwork, physical activity, socializing, reading, and creative hobbies. And they worry that exposure through the computer and the media to violence, sex, profanity, alcohol, drugs, and questionable morality will have a harmful effect on their child.

The main issue for parents is deciding what to let their child see and do, and for how long. They must set limits, but they also have to compromise, allowing her enough freedom so that she won't pursue forbidden activities behind their backs.

If you have rules about TV-watching, make exceptions for special programs, nights when homework is done early, rainy days, and other circumstances. Allow her to spend more time on a video game when a friend is over or when the game is new. If she's begging to watch a rented video that you consider marginal, watch it with her and then talk about it. And let her play her music loudly at times when no one will be greatly disturbed.

Provide alternative activities for your child based on her interests. Enroll her in classes; encourage increased involvement in extracurricular activities; have books, magazines, art materials, and games available. Suggest she read the paper. (She can find movie, music, TV, and concert reviews there.) Spend time doing things as a family. Plan trips to museums, stores, or parks, and have your child bring a friend along.

Follow your instincts. You know what's appropriate for your child and approximately how much time she needs for homework, physical activity, socializing, and relaxing. Decide what you're comfortable allowing her to do, and decide on your "absolute no's." Then don't be swayed by what other children are permitted to do. Families rarely have identical values.

If you and your child argue about movies, try to read as much as you can about the ones she's interested in. Talk to people who've seen them. If a movie seems acceptable, let her go. But if you believe it will frighten her too much, be too intense, or expose her to sights and ideas you disapprove of, say no. Don't rigidly depend on the ratings. Some R-rated movies may be acceptable if you don't mind your child hearing profanity, while some PG movies may glorify immoral acts and characters.

Choose home videos as you would theater features. If a movie's not right for your child, don't let her see it. Restrict access to cable movies, using the control feature on the cable box if necessary, and let your child know what kinds of movies she should and shouldn't watch when she's at friends' homes.

Handle TV-viewing in a similar way. Let your child watch programs that are good or at least harmless. Preview an episode of a questionable series or read about made-for-TV movies ahead of time to see if they're acceptable. Let your child watch some music videos if she's interested, and at times discuss the contents with her. Use electronic parental control mechanisms when appropriate. If you have a job outside the home, keep a copy of a TV schedule at work so you and your child can talk by phone about afternoon shows. Monitor how much time she spends watching. TV should be a minor entertainment, not a major occupation that takes up a disproportionate amount of time. Your child should save TV-watching for the short breaks between the truly important activities in her life.

Video and computer games, by their nature, require a lot of playing time. It's OK to let your child occasionally spend several hours at a time at a video game, as long as she doesn't do it regularly and she's devoting enough time to schoolwork, socializing, and outdoor activity. Since you won't approve of many games, question your child closely and read reviews before making buying or renting decisions. One mother told her ten-year-old son, "You can get a game, but not one that shows any torture or killing."

You probably view your child's computer use as a mixed blessing— you're glad for the time she spends on homework, research, and exploring her interests. The Internet offers amazing learning opportunities. You also may accept time spent on instant messaging as a good alternative to phone use. But you may be concerned about extended Web-surfing and on-line chatting, and justifiably worried about the harmful or dangerous content she may encounter. Again, use whatever electronic parental controls you find appropriate and limit computer use in the same common sense way you limit TV and video game time.

Finally, like many parents, you may argue with your child about her choice of music. Try to be patient. Occasionally listen with her and let her play her music in the car. She'll appreciate your interest, and you'll learn something about her taste and thinking. You may be surprised to discover positive messages in music you'd previously considered harsh or even harmful. In general, let her listen to the music she likes, but keep her from buying CDs you strongly object to. Educate yourself by looking for reviews and questioning other children and adult listeners. It's hard to control what your child hears, especially on the radio, but you can express your displeasure with certain lyrics and ideas.

As long as your relationship with your child is strong and she's doing well in school and with peers, you don't have to worry about lyrics having a negative influence on her. If she's having trouble at home and elsewhere, she may be more susceptible to the negative messages in her favorite songs. Rather than censor the music, try to make positive changes in her life. Strict limits alone may only encourage her to lie about what she's doing.

When you set limits on any of your child's leisure activities, be calm and don't make fun of her choices. You want to criticize a program or product, not your child. Instead of shouting, "Only a stupid person would waste time on such trash," say, "Don't you think this program makes girls and women seem unintelligent? I don't like our family watching shows with that message." She might be more willing to follow your suggestions and rules if you explain your objections and treat her with respect.

How should I handle profanity?

All ten- to thirteen-year-olds use profanity at times. They may curse, as adults do, out of frustration, anger, or sudden pain. They may use profanity when they're with friends as a way to feel part of the group or to act older. It's easy for kids to learn profanity—they hear it on TV and CDs, in movies, and from peers and parents.

Most adults don't like to hear kids swear. They may tolerate their own child's occasional outburst but otherwise feel that cursing at these ages is rude and disrespectful. Many parents set firm limits: "You're not allowed to use that language here." "I don't talk that way and I don't want you to." "Don't ever use those words around adults."

Children who are generally secure and know their parents' expectations are not likely to use excessive profanity. One twelve-year-old said she wouldn't curse a lot, even if her parents said she could: "I know you don't like it." Some ten- to thirteen-year-olds ask permission before using profanity: "I have to tell your what this kid said in school. Can I say the 'b' word?" After a losing soccer game, a frustrated player asked, "Is it all right to cuss now?"

Parents can usually limit profanity at home, but they have less control when their child is with peers. Experimenting is common, and he wants to be like his friends. If they use profanity, he will also.

One eleven-year-old told his mother, "Kids cuss all the time at camp. Everyone does it when they aren't around their parents." After school vacation, another child said, "I'll be back with my friends, so I'll probably start cursing again." It's common for kids to tell each other dirty jokes and to use profanity, especially with friends of the same sex. However, most children of these ages know it's unacceptable to speak the same way in front of adults.

Some kids, though, don't get clear messages about cursing. Their parents might use a lot of profanity themselves or may not communicate values. Children who don't learn limits at home are likely to be reprimanded by other adults, including teachers, coaches, and their friends' parents, "Please watch your language."

If you generally feel good about your child's behavior, try to accept occasional profanity. Continue to set limits and discuss standards of behavior. Remind him that cursing is not appropriate social behavior. Modify your own language. If you frequently curse, he will follow your example. Also, limit his exposure to movies, TV shows, and music that contain bad language.

If he continues to use profanity, ask yourself if underlying problems are causing him anger and stress. He may be cursing in order to express his frustration. If he's having trouble with schoolwork, peers, family members, or self-esteem, setting limits on profanity will not improve his situation. You'll have to identify and begin to resolve his basic problems in order to see an improvement in his language.

BIGGER PROBLEMS

What should I do when my child complains about school?

Many kids don't like school. They complain about the work, the rules, the teachers, the bus ride, their classmates, or homework. Sometimes the problem centers on the child. Her unhappiness may be a symptom of stress at home, low self-esteem, or problems with peers. At times a child may "hate" school because she isn't doing well. The work may be too hard. The class may be too large or the setting too distracting for her to concentrate. A child starting middle school may need time to adjust.

Often, however, the problem is school itself. Kids may have valid complaints: "Workbooks are a waste of time." "Field trips are no fun because you spend your time taking notes and doing what the teacher says to do." "The book reports we turn in are stupid. You don't even have to read the book." "I worked so hard on this paper and she marked it all up and said to do it again. Next time I'm only writing a little." "All we do is prepare for the standardized test."

Schools have a responsibility to teach subject matter, help students become independent and responsible learners, and encourage them to think critically and analytically. Children and teachers should respect each other, and teachers should be tolerant of mistakes. Schools also should help parents understand how the education system works and what they can do to help their child. Unfortunately, schools fail at these tasks.

Classroom rules and teaching methods may bore children and discourage learning: "I don't like science because we never do experiments." "We have to do the same work as everyone else, even if we already know it." "You're never allowed to talk." "She always calls on the same kids." There is often not enough flexibility, spontaneity, or creativity in schools. Kids don't understand or take into consideration all the constraints a teacher faces, dealing with administrative rules, a rigid curriculum, overcrowded classrooms, and difficult students and parents.

"Gifted and talented" classes can be especially disappointing. In some schools, the accelerated and regular curriculums are the same. A gifted child is simply expected to do more of what everyone else is doing—four similar worksheets, for example, instead of two. One mother took her child out of his middle school gifted program: "The only extra thing the G-T classes had was more busy work!"

Since children don't have the power to change what happens in the classroom, they complain, hoping adults will help. Some parents listen sympathetically. Like their child, they're frustrated. They want her to be an active, involved learner, but they fear she won't be motivated by daily, uninspired lessons.

Other parents don't want to hear complaints: "I got through the system and so can you." These parents may defend the status quo and blame their child for not going along with teachers' demands: "If Mrs. Cooper won't give you extra credit, she must have a good reason."

If your child is unhappy in school, she needs your help. Try to find out what's wrong. If family problems are interfering with schoolwork, make an effort to relieve your child's stress. If the work seems too hard, find a peer who can coach your child, hire a tutor, do tutoring yourself, or talk to the teacher. If she has continuing difficulty with schoolwork or with a particular teacher, ask if she can switch to another class. If you can't resolve issues at your child's school, consider changing to another public school or to a private school that addresses her needs.

Get involved in your child's education. Encourage her efforts, help with homework, talk about what she's learning, and be supportive, even when she gets a low grade. Provide the stimulation that may be lacking in school; this will increase her interest and skills. Go to museums, special exhibits, libraries, bookstores, nature centers, and the zoo. Talk about articles from newspapers and magazines. Do research together. Stop in educational stores to pick up interesting materials. And make reading—individually or aloud—a priority.

Talk to your child about her dissatisfaction with school. She may be very perceptive about the problem or she may have only a vague idea of what's wrong. Many ten- to thirteen-year-olds lack the experience and understanding to analyze their situation. But most can offer some ideas for improvement: "Why can't we work in groups?"

"Why can't we make suggestions about subjects to study?" "I wish the teacher would stop putting kids down." "If she were nicer, I'd ask more questions."

To help change your child's school situation, become an active member of the PTA and get to know the teachers and principal. Talk to them about her problems, offer your suggestions, and ask for theirs. If you're calm and respectful, they should be willing to listen. Contrary to parents' fears, most teachers won't react negatively to a child whose parents have a complaint. If you're not happy with your local school's response, take your issues to the school district administration. However, be realistic about the improvements you can bring about. School systems change slowly, if at all. Rather than wait, do all you can to keep your child interested in learning.

What if my child experiments with alcohol or drugs?

Parents want to believe that their kids won't try drugs or alcohol. After all, preteens have been constantly exposed to anti-drug messages in school, at home, and in the media. They hear about celebrities' drug addictions and overdoses, about drunk-driving fatalities, alcoholism, and drug- and alcohol-related violence. Parents hope all this information, plus the values stressed at home, will keep their child from trouble.

However, kids are curious, and drugs and alcohol are easily available. The same media that broadcast the "bad news" about drugs also glamorize drug and alcohol use. Many teen heroes are drug users, and many rock songs, videos, movies, and TV shows make drugs and alcohol seem acceptable and even desirable.

Seventh- and eighth-graders usually can point out the "drug group" at school. One thirteen-year-old frequently tells his parents about kids who buy drugs at his suburban school: "They stand at their lockers and pass little bags to each other." Children are fascinated by the subject of drug use. They want to know who does it, why, and how it feels.

The most vulnerable kids are those who are left unsupervised, who feel consistently left out socially, who have too much stress in their lives, or whose parents abuse alcohol or drugs. If such children don't experiment at these ages, they are likely to in high school, where exposure, access, and peer pressure are greater.

Peer pressure plays a big part in early drug use. Children are easily influenced by their friends and fear rejection for not "going along." A child needs a strong counter influence at home, giving him the reasons and the inner resources to resist. Otherwise, as he goes through adolescence, he may create a negative identity for himself as a drinker or drug user.

The best way to keep your child away from these temptations is to let him know that drug use and underage alcohol use is absolutely wrong. Give a clear, strong message that will become part of his conscience. He'll need to remember your words and values when friends urge him to experiment, especially as he hits the mid- and late-adolescent years. Then, he'll see many more of his peers becoming involved, and not understanding the bigger picture, he may rationalize, "Everyone does it and nothing bad happens." Don't waffle now, even if you think (in the abstract) that a little drink or occasional marijuana is not so bad. What starts out as fun can easily lead to a pattern of abuse and permanent damage.

If you suspect that your child is already experimenting, act quickly. Question him about drug use, keep a close eye on his behavior, friends, and activities, and search his room and belongings. If he's drinking or using drugs, don't try to deal with the problem entirely on your own. Get advice right away from books or a counselor experienced in treating adolescent drug use.

While you're getting help, try to learn why your child turned to drugs. Is he escaping from his problems? Who are his friends? How does he spend his free time? Are you home enough? Is school too stressful? What family values do you stress? Are you dealing with substance abuse by adult family members?

Stopping drug use early is essential, but it takes strength and perseverance. You'll not only have to work on the immediate problem, but establish an involved and positive relationship with your child so he can move more safely through adolescence, with its increased temptations, peer pressure, and opportunities.

I think my thirteen-year-old smokes cigarettes. What should I do?

Parents become quite upset if they suspect their child has been smoking. Kids constantly hear that smoking is unhealthy. Many have urged their parents to quit: "I'll never smoke! It's ugly and bad for you!" "People who smoke cigarettes are stupid!"

But some kids change their minds when they hit early adolescence. Peer pressure, curiosity, and the media can make smoking seem attractive. Kids who smoke at these ages are often just experimenting. They force themselves to inhale, then cough, feel nauseous, and stop. That's usually the end of it.

However, some thirteen-year-olds begin to habitually smoke. They may be children with difficult home lives, little interest in school or activities, and a weak identity. Or there may be less obvious reasons why they're attracted to smoking.

Sometimes a child will talk at home about classmates who smoke: "Just don't tell their parents." A child who speaks often about smokers may be testing her parents' reaction. She doesn't realize that, while her parents may be only mildly interested in another youngster's smoking, they would be furious if their child started.

Aside from a desire to experiment, kids these ages may smoke because they think it makes them seem "cooler" and older. Slick advertising campaigns tend to further this myth. A child may know about the health risks associated with tobacco, but she'll smoke anyway because she doesn't believe bad things will happen to her.

Young adolescents are focused on the here and now. They think, "Teenagers don't get lung cancer." The more support a young smoker has from her peers, the less likely she is to think about future problems.

If you find out your child has experimented with tobacco, express your firm disapproval, talk about the harmful effects, and then—if she's stopped smoking—let the matter drop, although you need to keep a watchful eye on her.

However, if you suspect that your child is becoming a regular smoker, treat her habit as a serious problem. Verify her smoking by searching her room for cigarettes and matches. Most children don't hide things very well. Confront her: "I smell smoke when you come in the house." "I found a cigarette lighter in your jacket pocket." If she lies, don't accept what she says, even though you might prefer to avoid the issue.

Set firm limits and consequences: "I'm very angry and disappointed." "You made a bad choice and I won't accept it." "Smoking at your age is terrible." Take privileges and allowance away if you think that will be effective. Talk about the major risks of smoking, and about the other problems smoking causes, such as stained teeth, an unpleasant odor, and lack of wind for sports. These immediate effects might impress her more than long-range threats to her health.

If necessary, change some of your own behavior. Give up smoking. Spend more time with your child and work on creating a strong, positive relationship with her. Monitor her activities and friendships, and consider telling her friends' parents about the problem. Be persistent—the temptation to smoke will only increase as your child moves through adolescence.

Does my child need therapy?

Because ten- to thirteen-year-olds change so rapidly, it can be hard for parents to distinguish between emotional problems and the normal upheavals of pre- and early adolescence. Is a child depressed or just moody? Seriously unmotivated or merely preoccupied? Deeply angry or beginning the inevitable separation from the family?

Parents won't necessarily find answers to such questions in discussions with their child. Kids these ages often avoid sharing their thoughts with adults, whom they may see as sources of criticism, lectures, and unwanted advice. Parents may be left to evaluate their child's situation based on their own observations.

Identifying serious, persistent problems is usually not difficult. Most parents know to seek help if their child shows clear signs of drug or alcohol abuse, an eating disorder, depression, or dangerous or illegal behavior.

Beyond such clear-cut cases, many parents are confused. They don't know if their child needs help ("It's just a phase. Everybody gets depressed sometimes.") and they don't know if they "believe" in counseling for any but the most critical problems. Some parents associate therapy with shame and embarrassment. They fear the implication that something is wrong with their child, and they worry that counselors will blame them for their child's problems. They also may worry that he will speak badly of them or reveal family secrets. Such fears keep many families from getting the help they need.

If you are unsure about your child's situation, ask yourself these questions: Has the troubling behavior been going on for a long time, despite your attempts to help? Do teachers, coaches, or other parents complain about him? Is he frequently angry? Does he regularly put himself down and act discouraged? Does he do poorly in school? Does he have trouble making friends? Is he consistently jealous of his siblings? If he has continuing difficulties in several areas of his life, he can benefit from professional help and possibly from medication.

He also can benefit if his problem is an unreasonable fear or phobia. A counselor experienced in treating phobias can desensitize your child. One boy who greatly feared elevators was able to ride them alone after six counseling sessions. A child who feared airplanes flew off on vacation with her family after only a few weeks of counseling.

You might turn to therapy to help your child deal with recent or continuing trauma, such as the death of an immediate family member or close friend, divorce, or a frustrating stepparenting situation. During counseling, he can express his pent-up anger, fear, and doubt to a sympathetic, experienced listener.

If you decide to try therapy, ask your pediatrician, family doctor, or local medical bureau for referrals. Set up an appointment with the therapist for a consultation without your child present. Describe your concerns and ask for advice. You may hear that therapy is not necessary and you may get helpful suggestions for improving your situation at home.

If the therapist does recommend counseling, talk to your child about it. Explain what therapists do: "There are some problems we can't solve on our own." Let him know there's nothing wrong with seeking therapy. In fact, he may already know of friends who are in counseling, and some of the celebrities he admires may be quite open about seeing someone. Tell your child about the benefits of therapy: "Dr. Graham will help you feel happier and better about yourself." "Susan is used to talking to children about their fears." If your child resists, don't give up on counseling. Ask the therapist for the best approach.

Therapy can take a number of forms: individual, group, or family counseling. Any one, or a combination, can be effective. If he is seen individually, schedule occasional consultations with the therapist so you can learn more about your child's situation. You also may want to join a parents' discussion or support group in which your questions and concerns can be addressed.

Therapy in any form can be prohibitively expensive. Most health insurance companies and HMOs cover a percentage of the cost. Local and state government agencies as well as some nonprofit organizations offer therapy at reduced or sliding scale fees. In addition, many private therapists are willing to lower their fees when patients are unable to pay the full rate.

Although it can be difficult to start therapy, it's wise to work on emotional problems while your child is ten- to thirteen-years-old. As he gets older, his situation and behavior only will become more complex. If you get help for him now, your family will have a much easier time as he moves through adolescence.

INDEX

nature, young children's understanding of, 86–87

negative view of adults, 336–39

nursery school, 153–56, 156–57; preparing young children for, 157

O

over-scheduling, 291–93

overnight camp, 317–19; 387

P

pacifiers, 10–11

parental approval, 236

parents, adjusting to day care, 160; comparison to others, 405–6; divorce, 214–19, 348–50; effects on sexual intimacy, 25–28; embarrassment, 346–48; internal arguing, 245–47; responding to "I hate you," 135–36; sharing problems 333–36

paternal rejection, infants, 16–17

patience with kids, 416–17

pediatricians, 150–51

peer influence, 404–5; early drug use, 435; on clothes and style, 368; popularity, 409; positive and negative, 404

personal problems, sharing with your child, 333–36

pets, 146–49, 396–97

phone messages, 391–92

Piaget, Jean, 91

piano lessons, 311–15

play, 298–99; big projects, 299; pretend games, 298; video games, 303–6

playgroups, 122–23

playmates, 120–21

playpens, 46–47

popularity, 409–13

praise, excessive, 77–78

pregnancy and birth, explanation of, 93–95

privacy, 345–46

private schools, 283–84; before- and after-school care, 288

procrastination, 199–200

profanity, 142–43; 227–28, 429–31

puberty, 360, 361–63; discussing with your child, 362

public school, alternatives to, 282–87. *See also* school

punishment. *See* discipline

putting objects in mouth, toddlers, 39–40, 48; exploration through taste, 39–40

Q

questioning, 87

quitting, desire to, 310–311

R

reading, 320

reality, young children's understanding of, 88

recreation classes, 165–67

rejection by peers, 410–11

rejection of advice, 328–30

respect for others, 136–37

responsibility, 6–9 years, 190–92; chores, 191; reminding your child of, 191–92

About the Authors

Robin Goldstein, Ph.D., is a specialist in child and adolescent development and a faculty member at Johns Hopkins University. She frequently leads seminars on parenting for corporations, and has been a guest on radio and television programs on NPR, Fox News, CNN, CBS, and others. As a private consultant, she advises educators on improving schools and helps parents with the everyday challenges of raising children. Dr. Goldstein has also contributed to parenting articles in magazines including *Redbook*, *Working Mother*, *Good Housekeeping*, and *Child*. She and her husband have two children and live in Maryland.

Janet Gallant is a writer specializing in family issues and education. She is the author of several books, including most recently *Simple Courtesies: How to Be a Kind Person in a Rude World*. She is a faculty member at Montgomery College in Rockville, Maryland. Ms. Gallant and her husband have two sons.